CHRIST, PROVIDENCE AND HISTORY

Christ, Providence and History

Hans W. Frei's Public Theology

MIKE HIGTON

T&T CLARK INTERNATIONAL
A Continuum imprint
LONDON • NEW YORK

T&T CLARK INTERNATIONAL
A Continuum imprint

The Tower Building   15 East 26th Street
11 York Road   New York 10010
London SE1 7NX   USA
UK

www.tandtclark.com

First published 2004

British Library Cataloguing-in-Publication Data
A catalogue record for this book is available from the British Library

ISBN 0 567 08052 8 (Paperback)
ISBN 0 567 08062 5 (Hardback)

Typeset by Waverley Typesetters, Galashiels
Printed and bound in Great Britain by Antony Rowe, Chippenham, Wiltshire

One step at a time, no more than that for the task of public theology ... It is a slim line, but a goodly cause (Hans W. Frei, 'H. Richard Neibuhr on History, Church and Nation' (1988d), pp. 232–33).

Contents

Abbreviations

1956a   We know quite precisely when Frei wrote many items. Such items have dates in roman type.

1957a   For some items, we know only the date of publication. In the latter case I give the date in italics.

?1960a   Some items are not easily datable. Where I have been able to give a pretty good guess at the date, I have put them in the relevant location in the bibliography, but listed them with a question mark before the date.

U1   Where I have not been able to get further than a vague hunch as to date, I have listed items at the end of the bibliography, with U (for undated) and an identifying number.

YDS   I have listed below many items that can be found in the Hans Wilhelm Frei Papers, Manuscript Group No. 76, Special Collections, Yale Divinity School Library. I indicate these items with 'YDS' followed by the item's box and folder numbers. So YDS 13–199 is box 13, folder 199.

TCT   Hans W. Frei, *Types of Christian Theology*, ed. George Hunsinger and William C. Placher (New Haven: Yale University Press, 1992).

TN   Hans W. Frei, *Theology and Narrative*, ed. George Hunsinger and William C. Placher (New York and Oxford: Oxford University Press, 1993).

GF   From the collection of Geraldine Frei.

CD   Karl Barth, *Church Dogmatics*, 14 volumes (Edinburgh: T&T Clark, 1956–75).

Acknowledgments

I am very grateful for all the support and encouragement I have received while writing this book. In particular, I am thankful to the Master and Fellows of St John's College, Cambridge for appointing me to the Naden Studentship for Research in Divinity between 1997 and 1999 and therefore providing me with time to do the bulk of the research for this book; to Graham Howes, John Milbank, Timothy Jenkins and, above all, David Ford for helping me through the doctoral thesis which was its precursor; to Geraldine Frei, Garrett Green, George Hunsinger, David Kelsey, George Lindbeck and John Woolverton for conversations, insights and clarifications; to Charles Campbell, Gordon Davies, Terry Foreman, Katherine Grieb, Brooks Holifield, William Mallard, William Peck, William Placher and Ruel Tyson for plugging some of the gaps in my knowledge; to Mark Alan Bowald for his transcript of Frei's 1974 address to the Karl Barth Society in Toronto; to Martha Smalley at Yale Divinity School library, Angela Morris at Louisville Seminary Library, and staff in the libraries of Oregon State University, Fuller Theological Seminary, Concordia Publishing House, Concordia Seminary and Yale Alumni Magazine for helping me chase some of Frei's unpublished writings; to John C. McDowell and Jon Cooley, two good friends whose theological conversation has been a lifeline; and, more than to anyone else, to my wife Hester, who has seen this through from beginning to end, and to whom I dedicate this book.

Introduction: A Public Theology

Christian theology is most at home in public. At its source it has narratives of public circumstance, of action and interaction in public spaces; it lives by ongoing engagement with communities whose lives are never lived entirely in private; and it issues in descriptions and counsels which are applicable in the public world of politics and history. My aim in writing this book is to argue that this is a fair, if unexpected, description of the work of Hans W. Frei: to argue that, far from leading Christian theology (intentionally or accidentally) in a retreat from public discourse to the private enclaves of a sectarian faith, he painstakingly calls Christian theologians to a public task, providing us with tools which make that task easier and exposing confusions which have too often prevented us from carrying it out with conviction.

Certainly Frei accepts that theology must speak from convictions and commitments that are not shared by all. Nevertheless, he insists that it will always speak using languages that *are* shared, and that, even if beyond public proof, it will always make public sense. We need make no sharp distinction between avowedly public discourses (those, say, of religious studies or of academic historians) and the language of Christian theology; Christian theology speaks in a public register, and makes its claims in the realm of public history.

For Frei, theology as an intellectual discipline never stands far from history. It understands that history is the arena in which God works – or, better, the idiom in which God speaks.[1] It serves a community that is utterly historical, fully ingredient in the complex ebb and flow, the contingent causes and effects of history. It allows all its concepts and formal instruments to be immersed in history, recognizing both that they must be responsive to the character of history, and that they are themselves historical. It is constantly on its guard against any retreat from history, any attempt to shore up some reservation of the spirit against history's encroachment. It recognizes that it is constantly tempted to futile flights from history: tempted to claim for itself some immunity from creatureliness; tempted to relocate its heart in some ontological, psychological, spiritual or sectarian realm above or below or apart from history. And it combats that temptation only by a fierce ascesis: the determination again and again to acknowledge its finitude, again and again to allow itself to be regulated and determined by history, because history is God's history, history providentially ordered in Jesus Christ.[2]

1

For Frei, theology can only have the flexibility to do justice to history if it lessens its stake in methodological sophistication. We are, he is convinced, better able to speak about history than to explain how to do so; our skill in paying attention to the messiness of history quickly outstrips all but the most informal of our theoretical accounts of that skill. Modern theology has been cursed by the domination of one esoteric methodology after another, the dry yields of which have been consistently thin, and a discussion of method can serve our attempts to grapple with history only when it removes to a secondary and subordinate location within theology, only when it serves not as an attempt to push solid foundations beneath history's shifting sands, but as partial clarification and temporary guidance for lives lived within history.

And whether we can account for it or not, it turns out, Frei says, that Christian believers have been able to hold together in their lives and in their theology the reading of the Gospel narratives about Jesus of Nazareth in which the focus of God's history is displayed, the reading of their newspapers in which the bewildering scope of God's history is opened up, and theological commentary which seeks to clarify something of what it means to find both to be God's history. That these things *can be* held together is not the result of any esoteric technology that lies only in the hands of experts, but is a gift of God's Spirit distributed more widely than we might think; that they *have been* held together is demonstrated by the fact of Christian lives lived fallibly but well in the public world; that they *will be* held together is a hope and a task to which Frei dedicated all his theological and historical work.

1 A Public Theologian

The argument that this is a productive and plausible way of understanding Frei's work will take us into a good deal of detailed conceptual discussion of his various writings, and at times the prospect of a 'public theology' will seem a long way off. An initial impression of Frei's commitments can, however, be gained more quickly by glancing at the qualities he described and praised in his teachers and colleagues. We will be exploring Frei's appreciation of Karl Barth in detail before long, but that was a largely book-based appreciation, and should be set alongside the appreciation which Frei expressed towards various of his own teachers and colleagues, in particular H. Richard Niebuhr, Robert L. Calhoun, Julian Hartt and George Lindbeck.

Of Calhoun, he said:

> He taught us to use the time-honored orthodox term 'doctrine' once again, and not even to be afraid of the word 'dogma' ... [O]rthodoxy was a matter of a broad consensus within a growing and living tradition with wide and inclusive perimeters. His theological teaching was above all else *generous*, confident that divine grace and human reflection belonged together and that the revelation of God in Christ was no stranger to this world, for the universe was providentially

led, and human history was never, even in the instances of the greatest follies, completely devoid of the reflection of the divine light ... What he did ... was to hand on to his students in the pulpit as well as the classroom the vision of a living, integral and open-ended Christian tradition, a strong tradition.[3]

In H. Richard Niebuhr, Frei found

the boldest yet at the same time most self-limiting of post-critical theologies, [in which] there is the admission of a realistic vision of God, an element not so much of the innermost secrets of the Godhead but of that parabola by which God reaches low into the time-filled curvature, so that a partial, mysterious and imperfect sense of a pattern of human history is fragmentarily unveiled, [and the recognition that] we create the very concepts by which we apprehend those very patterns of God's incline into this fragmentary, non-eternal, historical world. This grasp of realistic vision and self-critical limitation – each of these moves haunts, limits and supplants the other.[4]

Alongside Niebuhr the 'phenomenological analyst of faith', whose philosophy Frei found uncongenial, stood 'Niebuhr, interpreter of history and theologian who stands very much in the Reformed and Puritan tradition'.[5] This Niebuhr gave 'testimony to the experience of the sheer contingency of one's own life and of life among contingent creatures, and at the same time ... effective witness to the sheer grace of God's glory', and pursued a 'quest to understand contingent existence as the manifestation of divine glory as sheer grace'.[6]

In his colleague Lindbeck, Frei appreciated something not many commentators have seen – the vision of 'the orthodox Christian as liberal humanist':

the paradigmatic Christian person whose experience is authorized by the reconciliation enacted in our world through Jesus of Nazareth, whose community is the community founded on that reconciliation. Under this impetus and authorization, such a person becomes a reconciling presence wherever bitter enmity threatens to pit human individuals and groups against each other ... All appearances to the contrary, (s)he is not a contradiction in terms but *fits naturally into our world.*[7]

And, lastly, Frei spoke fondly of Julian Hartt:

Julian is a *political* person in the best sense of the word ... His respect for history forbids his turning it into a platform upon which to strike dramatic moral postures and upstage the principals in the cast. He has no morbid appetite for martyrdom. Not even 'the honor of the thing' would tempt him to court being ridden out of town on a rail. He understands the nature and uses of courage too well to make it a substitute for careful attention to responsible strategy. He has a patient and amused affection for the democratic process, something that is available only to those who have a sound doctrine of human nature. And if he exhibits an a-typical charity for politicians, it is because he knows that their jobs are as complex as their constituents are fickle and that a decent respect for public office is a foundation stone in the structure of our freedom.[8]

In other words, Frei praised in his teachers and colleagues that generous orthodoxy which is unafraid of dogma yet sees Christianity as an hospitable and 'open-ended' stream; which is bold in its realism about God's involvement in history and yet realistic about the finitude and frailty of history, and therefore about its own finitude and frailty; which finds itself drawn by concentration upon Jesus of Nazareth into patient, reconciling work in the world, including political work, and yet pursues that work carefully, by way of careful strategic attention and political realism. And my own claim about the man who said each of these things of others can, perhaps, be put no better than this: that he was a theologian who found a way to hold all these things together.

2 Christ, Providence and History

How Frei held those things together is not so quickly stated. We will begin with the various forms of the question of faith and history which Frei posed to himself. He did not simply ask how faith fosters the discernment we need for Christian life in the public, historical world, but also asked how contemporary faith is related to the history of Jesus of Nazareth, and how we might understand faith as true faith in God without claiming it as an aspect of our lives somehow immunized against history's fallibility.

In one or other of these forms the question of faith and history has dominated Western theology from the Enlightenment onwards, and it is deeply involved in two theological debates, both involving Friedrich Schleiermacher, the analysis of which proved decisive for Frei's own posing of the question. On the one hand, it was the question that David Friedrich Strauss posed to Schleiermacher in the nineteenth century (we shall discuss this in chapter 1); on the other hand, it was involved in the questions that Karl Barth posed to Schleiermacher in the twentieth century (these are discussed in chapter 2).

Faced with Schleiermacher's concentration on the indissoluble presence of God given within all human consciousness, Frei found Barth concerned above all to proclaim the freedom and sovereignty of a God who cannot be tied to any such relation. This concern with God's freedom, however, included within it a concern with human freedom – not, in this case, a concern with indeterminacy or freedom of choice, but rather a concern to allow human beings to be fully human. Barth was concerned to overcome any confusion about the distinction between Creator and creature, and so insisted that we must allow creatures to be finite, contingent, particular and fallible – and must reject Schleiermacher's insistence that an introspective gaze will discover a window onto infinity within humanity, somehow preserved intact in the midst of history's turmoil. Let God be God, said Barth – and let history be history.

In a strange alliance, this insistence gives Barth a resemblance to Strauss, who also considered that Schleiermacher's relational theology did not allow history its proper integrity. Schleiermacher sneaks the absolute in under the folds of the conditioned, said Strauss; he isolates a portion of human historical being from the vicissitudes of history, and claims that God can be found in that portion; this is the undeclared hand that must eventually wreck every negotiation between Christianity and historical consciousness. But whereas Strauss declares that there can be no room for Christian faith, no room for any manifestation of divine life in a history that is truly history, Frei, by following Barth in developing an understanding of 'faith' which refuses Schleiermacher's path, insists that if Christian faith is truly Christian, truly faith in God, it already acknowledges its own creatureliness, and thus in some sense already acknowledges itself to be thoroughly historical. Frei, in other words, both joins Strauss in rejecting Schleiermacher's preservation of faith from historical consciousness, yet also turns Strauss's question on its head. Instead of asking, 'Where in history can we fit faith?' he asks, 'Where in faith should we fit history?' That is: how does Christian faith proclaim that, on faith's own grounds, it is fully historical and creaturely? What is the historical consciousness proper to faith?

The alliance between Barth and Strauss can, of course, only go so far. Barth's insistence upon history's creatureliness is thoroughly theological, being based on claims about what God has done in Jesus Christ, and in following Barth Frei is certainly not looking for a form of Christian faith that can fit unobtrusively within the realm of history defined by Strauss. As we shall see, Frei's account continues to have at its centre claims that Strauss would have regarded as impossible, even nonsensical – claims that apparently betray a casual disregard for the due process of historical-critical judgment. Nevertheless, although Frei will continue to begin his arguments from a point which does not appear on any of Strauss's maps, he does end up making on that foreign ground an affirmation of the nature and limits and possibilities of history that puts him into an *ad hoc* alliance with Strauss. Historical consciousness is not faith's inevitable antagonist, nor the triumph of a long-imprisoned secularity now released from faith's weakening restraint, but is properly an implication of faith.

There are two sides to the question of faith's historical consciousness for Frei. On the one hand, he wants to understand the character of the creatureliness, the historical existence, professed by Christian faith, and wants to know how far it resembles the secular historical vision of a Strauss. On the other hand, he wants to know how Christian faith proclaims that such creatureliness is caught up by God and made, precisely as creaturely, to relate or conform to God.

When in his doctoral thesis he first posed these questions to Barth (at a time when he was familiar with Barth's work only as far as the earliest volumes of the *Church Dogmatics*) Frei was left with a nagging doubt. He felt in general that Barth had only allowed historical existence to be defined in negative terms, and had not provided a positive theological account of its nature. Barth had rightly, in Frei's view, asserted that it is first of all the historical humanity of Jesus Christ that God has assumed, and that any claims we make in general about the catching up of history into relationship with God must be governed by the recognition that Jesus Christ is the paradigm of creaturely existence conformed to God. Frei considered, however, that although the technical machinery of this assertion was all in place and running like clockwork, and although the assertion rang out loudly and regularly, just as it should, there was nevertheless a hollow at its centre. Barth had somehow managed, Frei thought, to make this incarnational assertion without paying detailed attention to Jesus Christ's actual historical humanity – the events, encounters, actions and interactions that make up his historical life.

If we follow this effectively monophysite approach we make the catching up of Christ's history into God an abstract marker, intelligible without reference to the content that is caught up, which could in principle have been placed beside any historical content whatsoever. And in turn we end up with a doctrine of the providential ordering of history as primarily an abstract doctrine of God's bare power, which is only accidentally shaped by the particular content that God happens to have given to his providential will. Such a theology is made attentive to history – to Christ's history and to the history that is providentially ordered in him – only as a secondary move, and such a theology will therefore always generate the suspicion that a theological bed has been laid without real reference to the history of Jesus of Nazareth, or to history more widely, and that Jesus and wider history have subsequently been chopped or stretched to fit it.

The question of an historical faith, of faith's own historical consciousness, turns out therefore to be a dual question. On the one hand, it is a question about the incarnation. How may we speak of the catching up of Jesus' humanity into unity with God in such a way that we do not bring in the content of that particular humanity as an afterthought? On the other hand, it is a question about the providential ordering of history in Jesus. How, once we have confessed belief in the incarnation, might we go on to speak of history more widely as providentially ordered in Jesus Christ, precisely in its historical contingency and complexity and particularity?

Another way of putting the incarnational question is to ask whether we can allow our claims about Jesus' significance, about his power to save, about the cosmic scope of what is enacted in him, about his relationship to the Father, to be inherently shaped by the details of his humanity. Can we let our claims about Jesus' conformity to God be *constituted* by reference to the particular content of his life? In chapter 3 we will see that the breakthrough which initiated Frei's own positive theological project was his recognition that this question is not simply one posed by the wranglings of modern theologians, or by the failures of Barth's early work, but is one also posed for us by the Gospels themselves. The Gospels insist, Frei claimed, that Jesus' significance, his power, and the nature of his relationship to God, are so caught up with and reshaped by the particularities of his unsubstitutable identity and fate that we cannot understand them in the abstract but only as they are decisively constituted by his particular identity. He argues that this insistence is made dynamically in the Gospels, and traces the way in which, although Jesus is initially claimed to be significant in a way that is separable from his concrete identity (i.e., by means of claims that could, equally well, have been attributed to someone else), those claims are nevertheless progressively reshaped and owned by him as the Gospels progress, until they would not make sense attributed to anyone who did not have this same peculiar story. Even apparently abstract virtues that are attributed to Jesus, such as 'obedience', are eventually given a distinctive twist and subordinated to the patterns of his particular story.

This dynamic reshaping reaches its climax in the cross and resurrection sequence. Leading up to the cross, the Gospels have already asked how familiar assertions of messianic power can possibly be true of one who lives and acts in such an unexpected way. On the cross, however, the connection between Jesus and those generalized descriptions of salvation is called even more deeply into question. How can they be true of one so utterly powerless? How can they be true of one who dies? The resurrection is the point, in the logic of the narratives, where those questions are decisively answered, not by some explanation of how salvation works, but by God's effective declaration that the divine will for human salvation is identical with Jesus' historical humanity. At the resurrection, as it were, the Gospels portray God changing the question, from 'How can this man own our claims about salvation?' to 'How can we now understand our salvation in the light of this man's identity?' From one who was the recipient of the generalized hopes and expectations of the people, Jesus has become the one who completely recasts those hopes, and gives them back to the people in a new shape now inseparable from his identity, and so gives the people a new identity related to his.

If we follow the guidance given by Gospels, Frei says, we *must* allow our account of Jesus' significance, of his relationship to God's salvific will, and so our account of the incarnation, to be shaped in its entirety by the particular story of Jesus. And if we travel to our assertions of Christ's significance by that route, then we will be able to laugh at the claim that those assertions have involved us pushing an historical content into an ahistorical box: the box itself will have been shaped by and for that historical content, and be inseparable from it. We will have found that a properly Christian account of the incarnation is at the same time a properly historical one: not in that it involves nothing which would upset a Strauss (Frei has no qualms in asserting that the resurrection trespasses far beyond the limits of our historical imaginations, for instance), but in the sense that our claims about Jesus' significance are claims precisely about the winding, particular, public course which his portrayed life takes, rather than claims about some ahistorical codicil – messianic consciousness, perhaps – secreted within that public life.

In the resurrection accounts it is true both that Jesus is portrayed as entirely his unsubstitutable, particular self and that he is portrayed as the action of God on behalf of humanity. God acts, but Jesus appears; Jesus is displayed as the enactment of God's saving will. There is, therefore, no limit to Jesus' significance, as portrayed in the Gospels, because it is united with God's significance: the humanity of Jesus is given truly God-sized scope in these narratives. The Gospels themselves, according to Frei, require us to make the transition from thinking about God's catching up of Jesus' humanity into conformity to God, to thinking about God's ordering of the whole of history in and through Jesus. The Gospels themselves require of us the acknowledgment that the significance of Jesus is unlimited: that the whole of history, the whole of creation, is caught up in the story told here.

However, the Gospels themselves do not *perform* that acknowledgment in the same way that they perform the description of Jesus' significance in complete unity with his particular identity. They make the assertion, and so require our acknowledgment, but the precise form which that acknowledgment must take is left obscure. Frei had answered his first question, about how we may speak of the catching up of Jesus' humanity into unity with God in such a way that we do not cease speaking about his particular humanity in the process, by turning to the Gospels, and finding that they do speak in this way: finding that they present Jesus' relationship to the Father precisely in and through the presentation of his particular, historical identity. (And this was not a speculative *explanation* of the incarnation, nor an identification of some mechanism by which God could unite Jesus' humanity to himself, but a *demonstration* that the Christian Gospels manage to hold two things together which we have too easily assumed cannot mix.) With his second question, however – his question about how, once we have confessed belief in the incarnation, we might go on to speak of history more widely as providentially ordered in Jesus Christ – Frei turns from the Gospels to the Church.

He sketches a description of the Church that sees it as the location on the one hand of a constant re-presentation of the identity of Jesus Christ (a re-presentation in which Christ is present by his power and not by ours), and on the other hand a constant seeking for the illumination which Christ casts more widely upon the world. That these things hold together is again not proved by some speculative explanation, nor achieved by the skill of the Church; it is a gift of the Spirit. The Church, in other words, fallibly and partially *lives* this unity, by the grace of God: it has, Frei claims, been able fallibly and partially to discover again and again the significance of Jesus for history at large without denying the unsubstitutable particularity of Jesus' story (and has found in the process that it is also required to acknowledge the unsubstitutable particularity of history at large).

What does it mean, however, for this unity to be lived? Part of Frei's answer is given in a conceptual discussion of the constraints that must be fulfilled if this unity is to be upheld. He argues, for instance, that if the Church is to discern Christ's significance for history in a way that is faithful to the form and content of the Gospel portrayals, it cannot think that it has in Christ some diagram or grid that can be laid across history to explain every event;

Jesus has a particular, unsubstitutable and still-unfinished historical identity, and such identities are not the stuff of which diagrams are made. Christians are not, in this light, given some instruction manual with which to predict the course of events and propose correct remedies. They are given a key to history which is thoroughly historical, and which requires of them a kind of fallible discernment that continues to allow history's complexity and particularity, its suddenness.

This, however, is simply a negative constraint. What Frei needs in order to make his theological case more fully is not simply an indication of the constraints which will face any attempt to practice this unity, but also a demonstration that this unity has been lived and can continue to be lived. In chapters 6 and 7, therefore, we turn to Frei's attempt to do just that, by describing and championing the practice of figural interpretation which he believed to be the linchpin of a Christian attempt to acknowledge God's providential ordering of history in Jesus of Nazareth.

Before we get to that account, however, chapter 5 clarifies certain aspects of the argument so far. For instance, an unhighlighted shift has taken place from the claim that we must confess the incarnation in a way which is constitutionally connected to *Jesus' historical humanity* to the claim that we must confess it in a way which is constitutionally connected to the *Gospel portrayals of Jesus* – and yet Frei has deliberately if temporarily bracketed questions about how historically accurate these portraits are. At this early stage in his work, Frei barely acknowledged this question, and simply said that we use the Gospel portrayals in this way *because we can* – because they are, precisely, historical in form. They portray a public world of character and circumstance, action and interaction, and that is enough to get our argument started. In quiet moments, later in his argument, he admits that to take this seriously does involve some kind of belief in inspiration – in the sense that it involves *trusting* these accounts, trusting that we are not misled if we rely on their form and their content. In his later work, to which we will turn in chapter 8, he became far more explicit in his acknowledgment that this reliance upon the Gospel is an aspect of Christian faith.

Nevertheless, if we once accept that we should make claims about incarnation sensitive to the form and content of the Gospel portrayals as they stand, Frei argues that we are indeed dealing with an 'historical' reality – not so much in the sense that it is historically accurate (though he will come back to that), but in the sense that the Gospels are written in a form which is appropriate to the messiness and particularity of history. This 'history-likeness' is, as Frei explains it, a matter of hermeneutics, of anthropology and of ontology. In the first place, Frei's claim involves a contrast between two kinds of narrative. On the one hand stands 'mythic' narrative, the true subject-matter of which is not the particular characters and occurrences apparently described, but some deeper, more general truth – a truth that can be seen to apply in all sorts of times and places; a truth that is 'repeatable'. On the other hand stands 'unsubstitutable' narrative, which is that kind the foremost subject-matter of which is precisely the characters and circumstances apparently depicted in it. This is the kind of narrative for which the correct response to the question, 'What is it about?' is a re-telling of the story. He argues that the Gospel narratives stand, to a significant degree, on the 'unsubstitutable' side of this divide – and this is part of what he means by calling them 'history-like'. Frei also distinguishes between anthropologies of alienation and anthropologies of manifestation. On the alienation side stand those accounts of human being that see the public and accessible entanglements of a person as necessarily foreign to, even a distortion of, her true, authentic inwardness. On the manifestation side stand those accounts of human being that do not take this distinction as a primary one, and hold that a person's identity is (or at least can be) given in and through her public manifestations and entanglements. Frei argues that, if we take the Gospels to be apt identity descriptions of Jesus of Nazareth, then we are working (for this purpose at least) with something more like a manifestation anthropology than an alienation anthropology. The Gospels present Jesus as unproblematically and naturally one with his public manifestation, and provide no handhold for the posing of questions in the idiom of alienation anthropology. Lastly, Frei tries to sum up a pervasive idealist ontology which has too often been taken to be the only available way of approaching questions of Jesus' significance: the hunt for ways in which his subjectivity can have an impact in the present upon our subjectivities across the vast gulfs of objective history. Frei argues that if we allow our concept of Christ's 'presence' to be governed instead by what the Gospels have to say about Christ's identity, it will have all the idealist stuffing knocked out of it, and be reduced to the status of a low-key, secondary and dispensable theological concept. Idealist metaphysics, with its separation of history into 'outer' and 'inner', and its tendency to isolate the latter from history, is demoted in favour of less systematic accounts. This is another part of what Frei means by 'history-like'.

In all this, Frei's attempt is not to erect his own hermeneutical, anthropological or ontological theory as a rival to the mythical hermeneutics, alienation anthropology or idealist ontology that he attacks, and then to use his favoured theory as a foundation for his own theology. Rather, his aim is to show that pervasive hermeneutical, anthropological and ontological assumptions in modern theology have stood in the way of sustained attention to the Gospel narratives, because they systematically stand in the way of a recognition of these texts as 'history-like' – and that once we pay serious attention to the history-likeness of these narratives, we inevitably end up sketching in, at least informally, alternative accounts. Those alternative accounts should be kept low-key and secondary, however; they should retain the status of clarifications along the path of careful reading, rather than be allowed to become rigidly defined theoretical positions which may henceforth govern that reading.

Chapter 5 also eventually returns to the other side of the claim that the Gospels are historical: the question of their historical accuracy. Frei acknowledges that, even if we accept that we are to start with the Gospels and to treat them as trustworthy, the question of historical reference is one we cannot avoid. On the one hand, the question of factual reference has become possible in the modern world in distinctive and urgent forms, and on the other hand the Gospels on their own terms make claims that allow us at least a partial alliance with such questions about reference. To isolate ourselves from all such questions, now that they have been raised, would be to run against the grain of the Gospels themselves.

Frei explains this with reference to the resurrection. First of all, he claims that the Gospel narratives focus Jesus' identity precisely in the (cross and) resurrection: Jesus simply *is* the risen (and crucified) one. Second, the Gospel narratives present Jesus' identity (as we have seen) in an historical form – that is, they present Jesus as an actor on the ordinary public stage of history, and continue to do so even when they reach the resurrection – and so the question of the factuality of Jesus' resurrection becomes quite proper. Third, the question of the factuality of the resurrection is forced upon us, because the Gospel accounts insist that the risen Christ is not simply a pleasant fiction but the living Lord of the one true world in which we live. This is not a claim that we can isolate in a history-like fictional world designed to entertain us – the Gospels will not allow us to keep the claim at arm's length in that way. If we operate with the categories of 'factuality' or 'historicity' at all, we will have to say (if we trust the Gospel depictions) that Jesus cannot be thought of as not factually, historically risen – even if we are unable then to go on to explain exactly what a factual, historical resurrection looks like. At least at this point, the Gospels are historical in reference as well as in form.

With chapter 6, we will return to the main argument, and the question of the nature of providence, and of the ways in which the Church has been able to pursue the acknowledgment of Christ's unlimited significance called for by the Gospels. Frei learnt from Erich Auerbach that early Christian figural interpretation is precisely the instrument by which the discernment of significance of Jesus' unsubstitutable identity for the equally unsubstitutable details of public history can be practised. It is not an infallible instrument, nor can the doctrine of providence be reduced to its exercise, but figural interpretation is (according to Auerbach and Frei) the central form that has been taken by the practical acknowledgement of God's providential ordering of history in Jesus Christ.

Figural interpretation provides no explanation of how God manages providentially to order the world, no theory about how the world is susceptible to such ordering; rather, it gives concrete force to the existing conviction that the world is so ordered, and allows that ordering to be displayed in such a way that the unsubstitutable integrity of both figure and figured is preserved. As such, it was an essential element of a pre-critical Christian interpretation that sought to combine a robust belief in the universal significance of what had taken place in Christ with continued attention to the realistic, public narratives both of Christ and of that world which Christ saves.

Auerbach had his own argument about how figural interpretation relates to secular historical consciousness – or at least to secular literary realism, which is historical consciousness's partner. He argued that figural interpretation found its apotheosis in Dante, for whom the characters in the *Comedy* are each displayed in their final place within God's scheme of judgment, but precisely as such are portrayed as more fully themselves, more richly particular, more living and unsubstitutable; he then constructed a narrative in which this achievement by Dante marked both the triumph and the dissolution of the tradition of figural interpretation – the moment when the attention to lifelike history which it fostered burst its theological banks and washed a path for secular realism. And while he gladly accepted Auerbach's exposition of *figura*, and was captivated by Auerbach's Dante, Frei narrated the fate of figural interpretation very differently. He argued that it was still a staple of Christian interpretation for the Reformers, and that in them it provided an apt and mature means for the display of God's historical providence. Frei tells instead the story of the eclipse of biblical narrative – that complex process by which modern interpreters of the Bible came increasingly to turn away from the unsubstitutable identities portrayed in history-like Gospel narratives, and to turn towards the supposed ideal truths, or underlying salvific transactions, or hidden religious inwardness, to which these texts were held to refer. This story of the eclipse of biblical narrative is also precisely the story of the eclipse of *figura*: the eclipse of that Christian skill which, by the grace of God, allowed Christians to see the order in such realistic narratives, and to find them Christianly significant. In other words, the eclipse of biblical narrative is a process in which the providential ordering of history in which we are included with Christ is itself eclipsed – either by a set of saving transactions whose influence affects us, or by a set of ideal truths whose acknowledgment is our salvation, or a form of religious inwardness whose growth within us is Christ's real significance. This loss was, however, not the outworking of some quasi-Hegelian necessity (like the end of Auerbach's tale) nor the result of some inevitable pressure towards modernity, but an accident – a contingent state of affairs that can be at least partially reversed, even if a retrieved, post-critical figural interpretation is bound to look different, now that it has passed through this eclipse.

The last element in this argument, to which we will turn in chapter 7, is another that Frei learnt from Barth, for in the later volumes of Barth's *Church Dogmatics* Frei found the outlines of precisely the post-critical retrieval of figural interpretation for which his diagnosis called. Yet, looking at Barth's figural exegeses of various Old Testament passages, he noticed a strange ascesis on Barth's part: Barth, it appeared, refused to find Jesus *too easily* in the Old Testament texts. This, Frei says, is right and proper, for to find Jesus written inherently into the structure of an Old Testament passage (and still more to find Jesus written inherently into some historical situation beyond the pages of the Bible) is to get dangerously close to making 'Jesus' mean something generalized and abstract: making this name's referent first and foremost a pattern that can be repeated in all sorts of places. If God's word, as the Gospels assert, is spoken not in such generalities but in the specific identity of Jesus of Nazareth, we should not rush to find him in the Old Testament or in any other historical reality. Rather, the figural relationship can only properly be discerned once we have placed specific beside specific: once we have placed the Gospels and the Old Testament side by side, or the newspaper and the Bible side by side. The discernment of figural relationships is a matter of faith, guided by the Spirit, rather than of deduction, and it must also be a matter of a constant return to the specific identity of Jesus Christ, and a constant scanning of the intractable particularity of the history which Christ's identity illuminates.

And with this ascesis, refusing to turn too quickly from the stubborn particularity of either pole of the figural relationship, Frei notes that Barth's figural exegesis, far more explicitly than its pre-critical forebears, contains a positive assertion not just of Jesus' unsubstitutability, but also of the historical nature of the world about which we read in our newspapers – a world which, precisely because the discernment of its place in God's providence emerges (to the extent that we grasp it at all) only in specific relation to Gospel identification of Jesus, is in its own way a secular world: a world where we have no need and no ability to find religious messages or significance outside of that specific relationship. Such figural exegesis, and the belief in providence which it displays, contains within it an affirmation – a strong affirmation – of a kind of historical consciousness. Of course, Barth and Frei believe that Jesus tells us truth about the whole of history – that history really is ordered in Jesus Christ, and that this is not simply an 'interpretation' which Christians happen to place on a history which is itself neutral with regard to such claims. Nevertheless, that truth is given to us in such a way as to confirm and proclaim the true creatureliness, finitude, contingency and particularity of history, and to call us not to the explanation or avoidance of history, but to careful, fallible but resolute political action in the midst of the world's mess.

This, in my reading, is the central achievement of Frei's theology. It is not the identification of a certain kind of narrative, nor the development of a certain kind of hermeneutics, nor the proposal of a new 'cultural-linguistic' mode of theology. It is both grander and more modest than any of these: grander, because it is a call to the Christ-centred reading of the whole of history, a call to dare fallible Christian involvement in the public world; more modest, because it recognizes that, however painstaking they may be, methodological arguments like Frei's are of very little help in the pursuit of figural interpretation, except insofar as they weaken some of the forces which would keep us from throwing ourselves into this engagement, and so help clear a space in which this engagement might flourish. All the technical innovations and achievements which tend to dominate interpretations of Frei's work are in themselves of secondary importance; they matter only insofar as they provide modest support to Frei's central intention: to keep alive, in a context in which it seems fatally weakened, the possibility of a public Christian theology.

It is strictly in this light that we turn, in the final chapter, to various corrections and qualifications that Frei made to his arguments later in his work. On the one hand, he realized that he had placed too much reliance on arguments constructed with concepts that were themselves isolated from history, and that he needed more fully to acknowledge that concepts like 'realistic narrative', for instance, have a history and a place in historical life. Such concepts might well still be appropriate, but only for use in specific historical situations, by the people of God working to be faithful witnesses to the Gospel in a particular time and place, not in some abstract and absolute way. Realizing this, Frei turned in the mid-1970s towards a more obviously social history (or at least an intellectual history more thoroughly grounded in social history), and to a clarification and recasting of the grounds of his various arguments.

It became clear to him that we don't read the Gospels in the way he suggested simply because they fall into a category, 'realistic narrative', that inherently requires to be read in one way and one way only, but rather because this is the use which Christians have, on the whole, made of these texts. He continued to claim that this Christian use is one for which these texts are apt, that it allows them to stand over against Christians as an objective stumbling-block, and that it finally makes sense only on theological terms (a use which is, as it were, given to Christians with their understanding of God's work in Jesus). Nevertheless, the shift of focus from the investigation of literary categories to the investigation of Christian practice is marked and pervasive in Frei's later work.

Frei also turned again to the question: What kind of academic theology can best do justice to this usage, and under what conditions will such academic theology flourish? He investigated this question in large part by means of an (unfinished) history of modern academic theology and of its relation to the churches and to popular Christianity. He affirmed even more clearly than before that a theology which can do justice to this Christian practice, to the Christian ideas that uphold it, and to the content of the Gospels that becomes visible in its light, needs to be a theology which sits loose to methodological sophistication: which pays attention to the practices of Christianity and to the readings of the Gospels that those practices sustain, and which makes plentiful and piecemeal use of any philosophical concepts and procedures that will help in this, and of any partner disciplines that are also good at paying attention to public practices, but which refuses to be governed by any one of them, and is convinced that our ability to pay such attention, and to learn from it, quickly outstrips our capacity for methodology.

The net effect of these changes in Frei's later work, however, is simply a clarification of the kind of academic theology that will be best able to assist the Christian practice of figural reading, and so best able to acknowledge the providential ordering of history in Jesus Christ which that practice confesses. His later work is a clarification of the ways in which the historical consciousness proper to that faith also includes theology itself, such that we must recognize that theological concepts and practices are themselves thoroughly historical: partial, contingent, finite and fallible. Neither his earlier work nor his later work, however, takes us further than the threshold of a renewed figural theology. Devoted to undermining the barriers which would keep us from that theology, Frei is a theologian who stands at the gateway into new possibilities, holding the gate open, but he does not himself take more than tentative and exploratory steps in the land beyond the gate. To follow Frei's lead, to explore more fully the historical and faithful territory to which he points, will be to go beyond him.

3 Life and Work

There is, then, a final poignancy to Frei's work, for much of his systematic theological achievement is, quite explicitly, an exercise in ground-clearing, designed to show us that we do not need to be afraid of robust affirmations of resurrection and providence. It calls us to read the newspaper and the Gospels alongside one another unapologetically, to work to find connections, to pray that by the grace of the Spirit we will not be drawn away into Christian platitudes but delve ever deeper into the thick of history and of the Gospels, convinced that we do not need methodological or theological sophistication to pursue this task, even if we might need theological sophistication to fight against those forces which would declare the practice impossible or nonsensical. As a theologian, Frei is best thought of not as a major dogmatician, nor as the builder of a major systematic position, but as a teacher – not one who says, 'You need my theory!', nor even one who says, 'Go away and build on the assured foundation that I have provided', but one who clarifies our task, and shows us that apparent blockages in our way are no such thing. Frei is the kind of teacher who frees us to be theologians.

Indeed, Frei has been one of the most influential of late-twentieth-century theologians, certainly in America, but also in Britain – not as the founder of a school (despite claims about a 'Yale school') but precisely as a teacher, one who has indeed freed many others to be theologians. In part, then, this book must share something of the modest ambition of Frei himself: an analysis of Frei's writings, it will necessarily fail to do justice to the influence of a man whose writings were not the heart of his influence. A very different book, one which perhaps cannot yet be written, would be needed to overcome this failure: a combined biography of Frei and history of academic theology in America and Britain in the last few decades of the twentieth century, focused on but not limited to Yale. It would ask about the flourishing of the kinds of theology which Frei championed, and look for the quiet influence he had on family and close friends, on his many colleagues, on hundreds of correspondents, and on thousands of students. In other words, it would explore the ways in which, informally and quietly, Frei helped others through the gate which he held open. This is not that book, even though I have made some attempt to convey the character of Frei's developing sensibility as a theologian and an historian. I have pursued a much more modest ambition: to show how it is that Frei's writings point towards richer theological possibilities; how they help to keep those possibilities open and make them visible; but I have not, in any detail or with any depth, attempted to exploit those possibilities themselves.

Nevertheless, although this book is not the fuller theological biography which might one day be written, it is important, if we are to register sensitively the *sensibility* which animates Frei's work, to understand a little of the life from which his writings emerged.

Frei once described his early years as involving a series of 'worlds left behind'.[9] The first such world was Germany: Frei was born in Breslau, Germany on 29 April 1922 to Jewish parents (Magda Frankfurther Frei, a paediatrician, and Wilhelm Siegmund Frei, a venereologist on the medical faculty of the University of Berlin). Baptized into the Lutheran church along with most other members of his class, and forbidden from using Yiddish phrases at home, his family's Judaism was thoroughly secularized (although his father was to return to religious Judaism as a protest, once Nazi anti-Semitism began to grow more powerful); they were a respectable and well-to-do family with memories of a distinguished past, who gave young Hans a solid German education, and familiarized him with German literature. However, as the atmosphere in Germany soured, he was sent for his safety from that world – away from his family and away from Nazi Germany to the Quaker school in Saffron Walden, England, in January 1935.[10]

Despite an initially daunting language barrier and bouts of loneliness, Frei found England a welcoming and courteous place, and despite his own isolation and anxiety he was struck by the absence in England of the pervasive fear that had been a feature of life in 1930s' Germany. However lonely he may have been, he (already a politically alert observer) believed that war was on the way for his homeland, and was relieved to be in the safety of exile. It was while at the Friend's school that Frei saw a picture of Jesus and suddenly 'knew that it was true' – an experience that led him to a form of Christianity which at this stage had nothing to do with attendance at church. Quite what effect the Quaker setting had on this conversion is difficult to judge, but later in his life, even when it ran against the grain of his theology, he reported finding that Quaker meetings were still more deeply satisfying than his adopted Anglicanism.

Three years after he arrived in England, Frei's parents too left Germany, and Frei moved with them to the United States in August 1938 – another world was left behind. America was bewildering, and after the initial, terrifying arrival in New York, Frei found it very difficult to feel that he belonged. His family, living in Washington Heights, found themselves now very short of money and were unsure what to do about Frei's further education until an advertisement in a paper led him to a scholarship to study textile engineering at North Carolina State, and eventually to graduation with a BS in 1942. The world of textile engineering was soon to be left behind as well, however – although perhaps with fewer backwards glances than the others.

Frei may have begun his American life as a bewildered stranger, but slowly and definitely he took to his adopted country and made it thoroughly his own. When he went back to Germany for a visit in the 1950s he felt very much more like a visiting American Professor than a returning German exile. Part of this process, no doubt, was his marriage to Geraldine Frost Nye, and the birth of his three children; part of it, however, was also the finding of an academic home, in Yale, as a theologian and historian.

While at North Carolina State, Frei had heard a lecture by the prominent theologian H. Richard Niebuhr. Fascinated, he began corresponding with Niebuhr, and eventually enrolled for a BD degree at Yale Divinity School, Niebuhr's base. Despite some wanderings in the years between 1945 and 1947, and 1950 and 1956, Frei was later to describe Yale as the 'world not left behind' – as home. He was taught at Yale Divinity School by Niebuhr and by R.L. Calhoun and Julian Hartt, and there some of his deepest theological attitudes were shaped, some of his deepest friendships formed, and all his most important work done. He read widely, and was captivated by Luther, John Donne, Kierkegaard, Dostoevsky, 'Augustine, and particularly the anti-Pelagian Augustine',[11] Calvin, the New England Puritans, Karl Barth and Albert Schweitzer.

He graduated in 1945, and, having been a member of a Baptist young people's fellowship, became Baptist minister at the First Baptist Church, North Stratford, New Hampshire – although he also briefly considered becoming a monk at about this time. Despite the work involved in parish life, in being a local preacher, and in taking some teaching work, Frei found time to read a great deal in solitude. In particular, he read *Essays Catholic and Critical*, *Lux Mundi*, and William Temple's *Nature, Man and God*, and found himself drawn towards the more obviously 'generous' orthodoxy of Anglicanism, to such an extent that in later life he was to say that Baptist ministry had always felt like a staging post on the way to somewhere else.

At the same time, his reading helped feed a yearning for more academic work, and Frei returned to the graduate school at Yale Divinity School in 1947 to begin a lengthy doctoral dissertation under Niebuhr, on Karl Barth's early doctrine of Revelation. This was to take until 1956 to complete – but at least some of that delay is explained by the other things happening in Frei's life: his marriage, on 9 October 1948; his landing two years later of a job as Assistant Professor of Religion at Wabash College, Indiana; the birth of his son Thomas in 1952; his appointment in 1953 as Associate Professor of Theology at the Episcopal Seminary of the Southwest (with some time as Visiting Lecturer in the Southern Methodist University in 1954); his involvement with St John's Episcopal Church in Crawfordsville; and the birth in 1955 of a second son, Jonathan.

Frei completed his thesis in 1956 and was promoted to Professor of Theology at the Seminary. A year later, the same year in which his daughter Emily was born, he returned to Yale as Assistant Professor of Religious Studies, where between 1958 and 1966 he worked away more or less in obscurity. As can be seen from the annotated bibliography at the back of this book, very few writings remain from this period: after the publication of two essays for a festschrift for Niebuhr in 1957 (including extracts from his thesis), and a short article on 'Religion, Natural and Revealed' in a handbook of Christian theology published the following year, there is a great gap. All the indications are that he threw himself into teaching, and into the slow, painstaking research that would eventually emerge as *The Eclipse of Biblical Narrative*. In many ways he felt that the stands he had taken in his thesis against prevailing modes of apologetic and anthropocentric theology isolated him (again), making his work a struggle against the tide – even against his mentor Niebuhr. He did not have the temperament for the kind of sweeping statements and rabble-rousing clarion calls which might have pulled supporters to his side, and he produced his careful and complex writings only after taking great and solitary pains.

It was during this period of obscurity that Frei received a Morse Fellowship and a Fulbright Award for research at the University of Göttingen (1959–60). A little later, with the help of an American Association of Theological Schools Fellowship and a Yale Senior Faculty Fellowship, he spent some enjoyable time in England, at Cambridge (1966–67). His trip back to Germany confirmed his sense that he belonged in America: he was oppressed by the sense that the recent past had been brushed under an inadequate rug, and that Germany had re-invented itself rather than dealing with what had taken place. A meeting with the great theological historian E.D. Hirsch, which was only granted when Frei agreed not to raise the question of Nazism, confirmed his impressions.

Frei was appointed Associate Professor in 1963, about the same time that he began avidly reading Wittgenstein (1962) and Erich Auerbach (1964). Then, between 1966 and 1968, almost as an interruption to the work which was proceeding towards *The Eclipse of Biblical Narrative*, Frei produced a 'theological proposal' in Christology – a lengthy article, expanded a little later into an adult education course, commented on in his 1967 lecture at Harvard, and accompanied by a contribution to a seminar on the work of Karl Barth, after the latter's death. This 'proposal' emerged to wider scrutiny only some years later, when (in 1975) the adult education course was republished as *The Identity of Jesus Christ*. This strange project, an exercise in the rethinking of the structure and bases of dogmatic theology, particularly Christology, is one of the most interesting theological works to be produced in America since the war, and even though Frei soon developed doubts about various important aspects of the work, it set the tone and themes for most of what he went on to say concerning theology.

After that brief flurry of activity, Frei returned to honing his work on *The Eclipse of Biblical Narrative*, which was eventually published (to much wider recognition than *The Identity of Jesus Christ*) in 1974. By that time, much of his energy was being absorbed by administrative duties: he had been Acting Master of Silliman College, Yale (1970–1), and Master of Ezra Stiles (from 1972), going on to hold the latter post until 1980, chairing the Council of Masters in 1975. The publication of *Eclipse* coincided with his appointment to a full Professorship. Frei then entered another period of comparative silence, at least in terms of publications, although it was not this time the silence of complete obscurity: his name was out, rattling around in theological and historical circles attached to the massive and ground-breaking *Eclipse*, with *Identity* as its strange accompaniment. His silence was not so much due to the pressures of teaching or to isolated and exhaustive research, but to his commitment to his job as Master of Ezra Stiles – and, in any case, his silence was far from total. He delivered the Rockwell Lectures at Rice University in 1974, the 10th Annual Greenhoe Lectures at Louisville Seminary in 1976, and the Michalson Lecture at Claremont together with the George F. Thomas Memorial Lecture at Princeton in 1978.

Frei's work in the 1970s is a strange mixture of confidence and anxiety. On the one hand, he felt that he had 'found his voice' – not so much in the dogmatic arguments of *Identity*, but in the historical material in *Eclipse* – and he turned with gusto to the analysis of one modern religious thinker after another, Lessing, Kant, Herder, Strauss and Schleiermacher prominent among them. On the other hand, he found himself increasingly troubled about his links to the Church. Firmly convinced theologically that he should have some kind of ecclesial grounding and location for work as a theologian, he nevertheless felt emotionally distanced from his adopted Anglican home, while theologically uneasy about the places where he felt less isolated – Quaker meetings in particular. Without strong ecclesial connection, he found himself unable easily to call himself a theologian, particularly not a systematic theologian, and so concentrated his energies instead on his historical investigations – yet without feeling able to call himself a professional historian either: the questions he asked, the issues which interested him, the way he pursued that historical work, all were thoroughly theological. The ambivalence seems not exactly to have haunted him, but at least never to have been far from his working mind.

In the late 1970s, Frei's outlook began to shift. He found himself increasingly drawn away from purely intellectual history and towards social history; in tandem he found his doubts about aspects of the *Identity* and *Eclipse* phase of his work crystallizing in a shift away from more theoretical hermeneutical solutions towards more social, 'cultural-linguistic' – and, we might also say, more ecclesiological and pneumatological – solutions. In the 1978 George F. Thomas Lecture, he issued what can in retrospect be seen as something of a personal manifesto, using the word 'sensibility' to denote the object of a kind of historical study which would look for the shape and development of religious styles, attitudes and doctrines firmly embedded in the development and interaction of social institutions of various overlapping kinds. In 1981, he spent some time in England during which he looked, on advice from Owen Chadwick, at visitation returns and sermons from the eighteenth-century life of a couple of English parishes, hoping to find a way to combine the more social and cultural historical insights which these gave him into the Christianity of the time with the insights he had hitherto gained through a more traditional study of well-known high-culture theologians and philosophers.

From 1981 until 1988, his time as Master over, Frei returned to publishing and writing with renewed energy. Although still not prolific by the standards of many of his contemporaries, by his own standards his output was vast. In 1982 he delivered a paper on the interpretation of narrative at Haverford College, in 1983 the Shaffer Lectures at Yale (in which he began to develop what has subsequently become a famous five-place typology for understanding modern theology), and a long paper on hermeneutics at the University of California. His work did not even flag when he became chair of the Department of Religious Studies from 1983 to 1986. He spoke in 1985 in response to an assessment of his work by the evangelical theologian Carl Henry; in 1986 he spoke at a conference in honour of Jürgen Moltmann, delivered a lecture at Princeton, and another, on Barth and Schleiermacher, at a conference at Stony Point, New York. In 1987 he delivered the Cadbury Lectures in Birmingham, England, and the Humanities Council Lectures at Princeton. He prepared a contribution to Bruce Marshall's festschrift for George Lindbeck, and another for a conference on H. Richard Niebuhr to be held in September 1988.

Most of these papers and lectures were indirectly or directly directed towards one end: a history of the figure of Jesus in popular and high culture in England and Germany since 1750 – a history which would at the same time have been a clarification and republication of his own Christological proposals. One moment Frei can be talking about the rise of the professions in Germany and the impact that had on theology in the universities. The next moment he can be making systematic theological proposals about the *sensus literalis* of Scripture, and theology as Christian self-description. The next moment again he can be talking about providence and pilgrimage. It is hard now to gauge exactly what shape the final project would have taken in which all this rich material would have been combined, but it is clear that Frei wished to combine detailed historical work, close attention to the identity of Jesus Christ, and conceptual clarification of the ways in which we recognize that identity and its significance in the world. The project, however, was never completed. Before he could deliver a paper he had written for a conference on H. Richard Niebuhr, he fell ill, the paper being given in his absence. On 12 September 1988, at the peak of his theological and historical career, he died.

4 The Approach of this Book

This premature end to Frei's theological career presents some problems for a commentator, and a brief description of my solution is necessary before we turn to detailed exposition. Although I have chosen to proceed largely chronologically, the bulk of my argument is concerned with Frei's earlier work, leading up to the publication of *The Eclipse of Biblical Narrative* and *The Identity of Jesus Christ*. Only in the final chapter will I consider how that earlier work was qualified by the work Frei undertook from the mid-1970s onwards. This is, I think, appropriate: when he died in 1988, only the barest bones of that later work had been put in place, and in the absence of a mature statement of his qualification and continuation of his earlier work, I have judged it best to treat the later work only as a *commentary* upon the project set out in the 1960s and 70s. Frei was a cautious theologian who might well have been horrified to see the tentative beginnings of his restatement treated as a completed work of theology.[12]

For Frei's earlier work, my approach is only partially and, to some extent, accidentally chronological, for it turns out that this work makes sense as a nearly coherent whole, and that each of the parts welcomes being treated from the vantage point provided by the whole. Frei said of the writing of *Identity*:

> The work grew as it went along. From a basic conviction to which I found it difficult to give precise form, the essay took on complexity, scope, and breadth of implication as I continued writing. At every single point of its development the immediate next step looked tentative, even though the underlying conviction and the essay's final aim remained firm.[13]

It has seemed to me that the most theologically interesting reading of Frei's earlier work emerges when it is read in the light of the clarification which that 'basic conviction' received in the project as a whole – and even (although we have to tread cautiously) in the light of the insights into Frei's original intentions which are provided by their modification in his later work. This is not, then, strictly speaking a genealogical analysis, but an attempt to discover what questions and convictions hold Frei's apparently diverse work together.

On the whole, I have chosen to remove extensive reference to secondary literature, even though Frei's work has been widely and sometimes informatively discussed by many writers both before and since his death, and even though Frei carried out his own work in constant critical conversation with those who approached things differently. I have seen it as my primary task to present a coherent, comprehensive and somewhat unusual picture of Frei's work, and although my interpretation is by no means unprecedented, I have on the whole found that the conversations into which the secondary literature drew me were, though fascinating, too often a distraction from the aspects of Frei's work on which I wished to concentrate.

I owe a great debt, though, to many careful readers of Frei's work, and this Introduction would be incomplete without an acknowledgement of that debt. In particular, I have benefited immensely from Charles Campbell's book, *Preaching Jesus*, especially its discussion of the context of Frei's work; from David Demson's *Hans Frei and Karl Barth*, which seems to me a model of careful critical engagement; from John David Dawson's *Christian Figural Reading and the Fashioning of Identity*, which I think has got closer to the heart of Frei's project than any other study I have read (but which, sadly, arrived after my book was all but finished); from the several fine articles in the festschrift edited by Garret Green, *Scriptural Authority and Narrative Interpretation* (particularly those by Kathryn Tanner and Gene Outka), and all of those in the special edition of *Modern Theology* on 'Hans Frei and the Future of Theology'; and from the various papers or chapters by George Hunsinger, William Placher, John Woolverton, Cornel West, Eugene Klaaren, William Werpehowski, Kenneth Surin and David Ford listed in the bibliography. I have provided at the end of the book a bibliography of such secondary works on Frei, and another, annotated bibliography of the published and unpublished works by Frei, among which I have spent the last several years slowly discovering more of the public theological vision modestly and tentatively set out in their pages.

Notes

1. The phrase is borrowed from John David Dawson, 'Figural Reading and the Fashioning of Christian Identity in Boyarin, Auerbach and Frei', *Modern Theology* 14.2 (1998), p. 187.
2. Cf. Leslie Brisman's review of *Eclipse* and *Identity* in *Comparative Literature* 28.4 (1976), pp. 368–72, which speaks of Frei's 'war against what he would term bad faith – the pretension to "transcend" or evade mundane reality in general and the realistic character of biblical texts in particular' (pp. 368–69).
3. 'In Memory of Robert L. Calhoun' (1984a), pp. 8–9.
4. Notes on H. Richard Niebuhr (?1988a[i]), pp. 17–18.
5. Notes on H. Richard Niebuhr (?1988a[ii]), p. 1.
6. 'H. Richard Niebuhr on History, Church and Nation' (1988d), p. 220.
7. 'George Lindbeck: *The Nature of Doctrine*' (1984d), pp. 281–82, my emphasis.
8. 'Reflections upon the Retirement of Julian Hartt' (U5), pp. 11–12.
9. The following biographical sketch is mostly drawn from John Woolverton's 'Hans W. Frei in Context', *Anglican Theological Review* 79.3 (1997); William Placher's 'Introduction' to *Theology and Narrative*, ed. George Hunsinger and William C. Placher (New York and Oxford: Oxford University Press, 1993); Charles Campbell's 'Hans W. Frei: 1922–1988', in *A New Handbook of Christian Theologians*, ed. Donald W. Mussner and Joseph L. Price (Nashville: Abingdon, 1996); and from some brief and enigmatic autobiographical notes which Frei made in 1983 (1983g). The quote comes from the last of these sources.
10. Frei gives a series of poignant vignettes from his life in Germany under the growing Nazi threat in the video he made for the Fortunoff Video Archive for Holocaust Testimonies (1980a).
11. 'Notes for an Oral History' (1975g), p. 1, quoted in Woolverton, 'Hans W. Frei in Context', p. 380.

12. George Hunsinger and William Placher recognize this in their 'Editorial Introduction' to *Types of Christian Theology* (New Haven: Yale University Press, 1992), p. x.
13. *The Identity of Jesus Christ (1975a)*, p. vii.

1

Laughing at Strauss

Although the bulk of this book will proceed chronologically, I am going to begin my exploration of Hans Frei's theology in the middle, at a point during the 1970s when long simmering had clarified his intentions, and he declared that he had finally 'found his voice'.[1] During that decade, Frei repeatedly suggested that the connection between faith and history was one of the pivots around which his work turned, and in this chapter I aim to distinguish the precise forms of the question of faith and history that Frei found pivotal, before in subsequent chapters examining the component parts of his theology from the mid-1950s onwards, to see how and to what extent they revolve around this centre.

1 Faith and History

In his 1957 article on H. Richard Niebuhr's theological background, Frei concluded with long sections on each of two figures whom Niebuhr had regarded as his foremost teachers: Karl Barth and Ernst Troeltsch. The question of faith and history in Niebuhr is, at least to some extent, raised by the attempt to hold the account of faith which Niebuhr found in Barth together with the account of historical consciousness which he found in Troeltsch, and the difficulty of this enterprise is suggested by the fact that these two teachers in turn correspond to major strands in Niebuhr's own influence. If Frei represents one side of that influence, having apparently left Niebuhr's classroom through the door marked 'Barth', Van Harvey is a good example of those who left through the door marked 'Troeltsch' – i.e., of those for whom a Troeltschian account of historical consciousness was primary.[2] In his 1966 work, *The Historian and the Believer*, Harvey repeated Troeltsch's claim that the historical method 'constituted one of the great advances in human thought; indeed that it presupposed a revolution in the consciousness of Western man'.[3] The assumptions on which historical enquiry proceeds have

> already penetrated to the deepest levels of Western man's consciousness. They are a part of the furniture of his mind. Therefore, one must be willing to see the matter through to its final consequences, to let burn what must burn, hoping that a new synthesis might emerge on the other side, a synthesis all the stronger for having been purged by the fire.[4]

Harvey's book was shot through with the dismay that he felt when confronted with Christian theologian after Christian theologian eager to proclaim the investment of Christianity in historical occurrences, but desperate to insulate those investments from the frosts of historical judgment. The deep-seated assumptions of historical consciousness form, for Harvey, a 'morality' of historical judgment which requires of us certain kinds of attention to particular evidence, certain kinds of responsibility in weighing that evidence, and certain kinds of humility when we draw conclusions from that weighing – and this morality is not one which we can choose or abandon, for it is built in to the kind of world we now inhabit: these requirements are, for us, categorical imperatives. Christian theology must choose between an obscurantist and defensive retreat from participation in a world of historical thinking and practice, or must face the painful task of opening up Christian belief to historical consciousness's stern morality. 'Actually,' wrote Harvey, 'Troeltsch believed the church had no real option, because it is impossible even to think without the new assumptions.'[5]

In choosing the Barthian door from Niebuhr's classroom, Frei might seem to have rejected not just Harvey's particular conclusions, but also the whole ground on which those conclusions are built – and so to have rejected the Troeltschian, historical side of Niebuhr's influence. Barth, after all, is one of the usual suspects in Harvey's line-up: a theologian who wriggles inconsistently and infuriatingly from historical claims to anti-historical methods, and who seems to pay no serious attention to the moral imperatives of modern historical consciousness. Writing in *The Christian Scholar* in the same year in which *The Historian and the Believer* appeared, Frei could have provided Harvey with another easy target: speaking of Jesus' resurrection – the same topic in which Harvey had found Barth's deepest inconsistency – Frei argued that

> both because what is said to have happened here is, if true, beyond possible verification (in this sense unlike other 'facts'), and because the accounts we have and could most likely expect to have in testimony to it are more nearly like novels than like history writing, there is no historical evidence that counts in favor of the claim that Jesus was resurrected. This is a good thing, because faith is not based on factual evidence.[6]

Yet Frei also claimed that the resurrection is 'more nearly fact-like than not', and is subject to the possibility of historical-critical falsification.[7]

It is an unexpected twist in this contrast, then, that one of Frei's rare explicit declarations of his theological intentions is contained in a friendly letter written to Harvey in 1976. In it he says 'I've only gradually found out how much we have in common', and 'I'm tempted to say that my sensibility is a cousin but not a twin brother to yours.' This was not because either theologian had moved greatly in the previous decade, nor was it a fellow-feeling based on aspects of their work far removed from those I have just mentioned. Rather, they had in common, said Frei, a shared commitment to 'the question of the continuity between Jesus and faith (or whatever one calls the issue Strauss put before us)'. This issue

> suddenly and distressingly ceased to be discussed nearly a decade ago. Nothing much had been solved; I personally believe none of us had as yet stated rightly the whole issue, when all of a sudden it appeared almost as if there were a conspiracy to *forget it* and escape into a bunch of trivial issues and trivial affirmations. It was a disservice to the morality of belief (to borrow your phrase or adapt it). Recently, Paul Meyer gave the Shaffer lectures here and reminded us, in his usual gentle but stern fashion, of the unfinished agenda. I'm encouraged because you're doing likewise, and doing it with great force. There may be a community of us recalling theologians to some of their central topics. I'd like to be able to help at least that much.[8]

Paul Meyer's 1976 Shaffer Lectures mentioned here were on the topic, 'The Justification of Jesus'. There is an annotated typescript of these lectures in the Hans Frei archive, and although we have no way of knowing when Frei made the annotations, they bear an obvious similarity to the sentiments of the letter to Harvey. Scrawling across the front cover, Frei wrote,

> If a certain question is (a) unfashionable, partly (but *only* partly) because (b) it is thought to be insoluble, that is no reason for not tackling it, including the inquiry into its present status. The only necessary precondition is that there be a group that believes that in the long run it is inescapable. It may well be argued that the curious moratorium or silence-by-consensus on this issue is simply putting off the day when the bills fall due ... Why may a return to the question be inevitable? Because there are no criteria agreed upon for judging what is the essence of Christianity, and there is of course no theological and/or institutional authority to tell us either the criteria or the actual results of judging from given criteria. In such chaos, the focus on Jesus (the question to what extent anything about him is 'objectively' given, i.e., is – whether on theological or historical grounds – independent of or prior to 'faith' and therefore incumbent upon it, to what extent all judgments about him are simply a matter of faith) is inescapable.[9]

The brief hint contained in the letter to Harvey and echoed in the annotations to Meyer's lectures is amplified by a statement Frei made in another letter some years later, when, towards the end of his eight years as Master of Ezra Stiles College in Yale, and having written very little for publication during those years, he set to work on a long essay on David Friedrich Strauss.[10] He began work, he said later, with the fear that years of administrative work might have robbed him permanently 'of the company of the muse',[11] and in the event he spent 'three miserable years writing that and nothing else',[12] and all for the sake of 'territory I had vowed never to traverse again'.[13] The meat of the essay is an argument that Strauss's work is best seen as a crippling attack on Schleiermacher's attempt to join Christian faith and the historical Jesus without disallowing historical criticism; the main question addressed by the essay was, in other words, precisely the question of faith and history. Some time after he had finished the essay, and despite the agonies involved in writing it, Frei wrote to Patrick Sherry saying,

'Though I usually don't have much pride of ownership on my scribbling, in this case I must admit to that sin. It's probably the best thing I've written.'[14] I suspect – and I hope to demonstrate – that Frei gave this estimate of the essay not simply because of its success as a piece of intellectual history, but because, on ground he had traversed many times before, he finally believed he had produced an adequate expression of what in his letter to Harvey he had called 'the issue Strauss put before us': the question of the continuity between the Jesus of history and the Christ of faith.

In order to pursue these hints, two investigations are necessary. On the one hand, we must explore Frei's analysis of Troeltsch in his 1957 article on 'Niebuhr's Theological Background'; on the other, we must examine the content of Frei's essay on Strauss. Between them, they will help to clarify what Frei meant by the question of faith and history, and that in turn will provide us with a lens through which to look in detail at Frei's work between these two points, and beyond.

2 Troeltsch and History

Strauss put to Christian theologians a question about the continuity between the Christ of faith and the Jesus of history but, as Troeltsch and Harvey were later to affirm, it was not simply a question about the plausibility of particular matters of fact. Rather, beneath his posing of multiple questions about specific Gospel incidents, Strauss set out a broader, deeper question about the compatibility between Christocentric faith and the whole structure of historical method.

In his 1957 article on H. Richard Niebuhr's theological background, Frei explored one pole of that deeper question as it had been clarified by Ernst Troeltsch, describing in some detail the assumptions of historical method.[15] By 'historical method', he meant that family of analytical procedures designed to sift and interpret the detritus of the past, and he insisted that, for all the diversity of approaches championed and practised in the nineteenth century, there was some agreement on method: a striving towards a rational scrutiny of all the available evidence, leading to the formation of probability judgments about the nature of the events and of the relationships between them, made on the basis of analogy with known processes and possibilities.[16]

Such a method implies, Frei suggests, a certain kind of understanding of the nature of historical existence, namely that it is both *uniform* and *contingent*. It is uniform, in that the kinds of processes and connections at work in any period of history are broadly similar to those at work in another period (a necessary presupposition if any historical work at all is to be possible, just as some kind of uniformitarianism is a key presupposition of natural science); and it is contingent, in that scrutiny of particular evidence is the indispensable bedrock of history-writing: what happened cannot be deduced a priori from some abstract scheme, even for a thoroughly Hegelian historian.[17] History is a realm in which everything belongs together, yet a realm of irreducible diversity.

This interplay between uniformity and diversity is related to other questions which faced nineteenth-century history writers. For instance, Frei describes a tension between the 'particularism' for which the aim of history-writing was taken to be the minute description of concrete events, and a 'universalism' for which the aim was to set particular events in the widest possible connection, such that their significance in ever broader contexts might be grasped; a tension between the desire to present a grand narrative or overarching scheme demonstrating the coherence of history and the desire to be faithful to the smallest bit of evidence, the least trace of something disruptive.[18]

There was a similar tension between 'objectivity' and 'subjectivity'. At one pole of this tension stands the kind of strict and unadorned objectivity conjured up by the phrase 'presuppositionless scrutiny'; at the other, historical imagination, empathy, and critical judgment. Nineteenth-century history-writing found itself caught between the twin temptations of pure, shapeless chronicle and the imposition of a preconceived *Weltanschauung* over the unruly evidence.[19] Yet, for all but the most extreme positivists, this tension was seen as a productive one, and history-writing was understood as a grasp by the historian, with all the controlled historical imagination at his or her disposal, of the connection of minute facts in the broad weave of history, in which fabric the historian himself was clothed. With the exception of some positivists and progress thinkers, 'historical objectivity was a far richer and more imaginative matter' than any doctrine of pure objectivity might seem to imply: 'the investment of the past at once with all the precision and empathy and imagination that the historian and his craft could supply'.[20] Such history must be rewritten in every generation. No account by any historian exhausts the possibilities of description, even if it should happen that nothing is added by a later historian to the bare chronicle underlying these differing accounts. The constantly changing perspective and concerns of the historian will lead to ever renewed attempts to see the connection and significance of things, according to ever different resources of empathy and imagination. To put it in less active mood, each generation of historians will find history impinging on it differently. History itself, the object described, is susceptible of a multiplicity, perhaps an infinity, of descriptions, all of them disciplined and 'richly objective'. If the first tension Frei identified in nineteenth-century history-writing was that between the uniformity and the diversity of history, and the second that between metanarrative and disruptive particulars, this third is between the objective describability of history and its constant excess: an excess explored by each historian differently, according to his own perspective, constraints and concerns.[21]

The investigation and writing of history in the nineteenth century did not simply produce descriptions of particular arrangements of events, as Frei understood it; it was 'reflection of man upon mankind in its social intercourse as it develops uninterruptedly through time in its myriad forms of polity, culture and thought', and as such it was 'a particular mode of the self-understanding of man'.[22] History-writing, which involves belief in uniformity yet seeks for diversity, which constructs metanarratives yet tries to do justice to particulars, which produces objective descriptions and yet is always remaking them as it explores its own place in the historical weave, assumes and projects a definite view of the nature of historical existence, even of 'human being': 'each epoch or historical "unit" becomes to the historian its own exemplification of the mysterious, chronically indefinite and yet objectively apprehensible story in which man and culture form both the substance and the ultimate questions'.[23] To such an historical consciousness, human being appears as a profound question, the answer to which can emerge from nothing less than a constantly renewed attention to the minutiae of human behaviour, past and present, in all its social, political, and cultural contexts – attention which can never be relaxed in favour of timeless metaphysical answers. In other words, while nineteenth-century historical work may imply very definite ideas about what it is to be human, ideas which in another perspective might seem restrictive, prominent among them is the idea that human being is, as historical, 'chronically indefinite'.

Troeltsch's contribution to this tradition of nineteenth-century historio-graphy was, according to Frei, to see more clearly than others that 'the whole tendency of historical method has been to overthrow all belief in a unique "essence" or "value" that might form the internal structure of one series of events and distinguish it from all others'.[24] Other writers, like von Harnack, had placed great weight on the notion of 'essence', for it enabled them, without reliance upon a realm of ideal facts outside history, to uncover a continuous subject within an apparently diverse series of historical particulars – a normative reality by which the wild variety visible on the surface of history could be tamed.[25] For Troeltsch, such reliance upon immanent essences could only be sustained by an Hegelian metaphysics, and was simply an unsupported leftover in those who were influenced by Hegel but had abandoned his philosophical schemes. For Troeltsch himself, on the other hand, 'Christianity *is* its history and development and not a unique, self-identical idea or essence that is developed through its own history'.[26] There can be, for Troeltsch, no retreat from the variety and complexity of history, from its endless particularity, or from the contingent overlapping of causes and events that binds the whole of history into one totality, from which no one element can be separated out as normative or universal.

What could Troeltsch do, unavoidably committed, as he saw it, to the unchallenged sway of these principles of historical criticism, when faced with a theology that seems to require talk of 'a unique divine revelation focused in Jesus Christ [which] is the clue to all other history'? 'Is it possible to combine faith in an ultimate Creator and Redeemer, who limits space and time beyond all conceiving, with the "open-ended" and in its way uniform historical universe which historical consciousness presents to us?'[27] To put it another way: if our identities are given to us by the grace of God in Jesus Christ – if, that is, they are 'hid with Christ in God' – what are we to make of the identity investigated and constantly redescribed by the historian? What, in other words, can Troeltsch the theologian have to do with Troeltsch the historian's demand for uniformly applied and constantly renewed attention to the minutiae of human life?[28]

3 With Strauss against Schleiermacher

Troeltsch's questions and affirmations were interventions in a long conversation, and to a large extent he was simply repeating more forcefully a question which had been posed by many, from the eighteenth century onwards. In his undergraduate lectures on 'German Religious Thought', Frei traced the problematic connection of truths of reason and truths of fact from Leibniz and Wolff, through Lessing's famous ditch between 'necessary truths of reason' and 'accidental truths of history', and on into Kant. For Lessing, said Frei,

> You are *not* ... going to be able to indicate ... that you can account for the occurrence character of historical fact in such a way that you can thereby also indicate its relation to the realm of necessary, purely rational truth. Now if you say that Jesus is the Son of God, then no matter how much miraculous evidence you cite, that evidence has nothing to do with this supposed status of his, for *that* is a claim of a logically and metaphysically different order ... You cannot conceive historical occurrence and metaphysical being together in one concept.[29]

For Kant, 'the primordial is different from, logically ... prior to [the] historical, so that [the] "ideal" in fact cannot enter history'.[30] The normative, the essential, the universal: these stand, for Lessing, for Kant and for Troeltsch on the opposite side of a great divide from the contingent, messy, diverse facts of history and the probabilistic, cumulative and partial judgments which are all that we are authorized to make about such facts.

Against such a background, Troeltsch's proclamation of a Christ without absolutes can be seen as a reaffirmation of the problem posed by Lessing and Kant – and so as a rejection of the dominant attempts of the nineteenth century to find a way past Lessing's and Kant's ditches, attempts to find a compromise between faith and historical *Wissenschaft*.[31] Friedrich Schleiermacher was the chief architect of these attempts at compromise; he (as we shall see) attempted to force his way past the impasse by performing an idealist separation of history into outer and inner, insulating the latter to some extent from the rules governing the former, and thereby attempting to ensure that *some* part of history was still able to function as the site of the kind of absolute excluded from external history by the strictures of *Wissenschaft*. Troeltsch rejected this idealist separation (which we will be exploring in much more detail later) as a betrayal of history.

In part, Troeltsch was rejecting what Frei calls 'the all but universal nineteenth- and twentieth-century agreement in the West that religious discourse is a distinct mode that does not brook identification with "ordinary" or "objectifying" talk'.[32] For Schleiermacher and those who followed him, ordinary or objectifying talk is the kind of talk appropriate to outer, objective history; it is the kind of talk subject to the messy contingency of historical judgments. Religious discourse on the other hands seeks its sources elsewhere, in the realm of *inner* history – an inner history which is to some extent independent of outer history, and which can still serve as the site of divine manifestation. Of course, religious discourse must draw on language appropriate to outer history, because the realm of inner history transcends the particularity to which our language is fitted and so can never be adequately spoken; nevertheless religious discourse must, in the midst of outer history, point us away from the bewildering diversity of that history and gesture towards the other history, the inner history, buried within it. Religious discourse must separate itself, for such a solution, from 'ordinary', 'objective' talk; it must become an esoteric language.

Troeltsch rejected this attempt to guarantee the independence of theology vis-à-vis *wissenschaftlich* enquiry – not because he denied that in encounter with historical particulars we are also encountering something of our universal, spiritual context, but because he denied that our encounters with that religious reality can be considered exempt from the strictures which govern ordinary history. He rejected the notion that religious discourse could be so firmly separated from the messiness and complexity of ordinary language. If we encounter any universal, spiritual context, we do so as thoroughly historical beings, and the encounters cannot have a character which removes them from the realm in which we breathe: they too can only be partial, contingent, revisable and historically explicable.[33]

In all this, Troeltsch was following a path beaten by David Friedrich Strauss. By the 1860s, Strauss had already come to believe that the real enemy of historical consciousness, at least on the field of the life of Jesus, was precisely Schleiermacher's idealist solution to the problem of *Glaube und Wissenschaft*, his too-convenient separation of outer and inner history. Unlike Troeltsch, who (in Frei's account) posed the question most obviously in terms of the discontinuity between faith and the general lines of historical consciousness, Strauss focused his attack very closely on Christology. In *Der Christus des Glaubens und der Jesus der Geschichte: Eine Kritik des Schleiermacher'schen Lebens Jesu* he wrote:

> Schleiermacher's *The Christian Faith* has really but a single dogma, that concerning the person of Christ ... Schleiermacher's Christology is a last attempt to make the churchly Christ acceptable to the modern world ... The illusion, which is supported primarily by Schleiermacher's explanations, that Jesus could have been a man in the full sense and still as a single person stand above the whole of humanity, is the chain which still blocks the harbor of Christian theology against the open sea of rational science.[34]

In the face of the modern world's advance, Schleiermacher, scrabbling for a foothold for the churchly Christ, had conceded nearly everything to the historical criticism which Strauss represented. Far from fighting the growth of historical consciousness, Schleiermacher had allowed that 'all events have to be explained in terms of their causal nexus, so that supernaturalistic modes of explanation have to be rejected',[35] and had done so knowing that the full panoply of historical criticism could be quartered on this ground. He therefore allowed himself no resort to 'absolute miracle', no chink in causality's armour, which would exempt a supernatural Christ from the iron laws of development and contingency. It was within a fully *wissenschaftlich* construal of history, which he allowed could not admit the presence of the absolute within the relative tides of events, that Schleiermacher sought to preserve a Christian *Glaube* which nevertheless held firm to its encounter with the absolute in Jesus of Nazareth. He held that divine life could still somehow be manifested precisely in an event fully woven into the fabric of ordinary history.

Schleiermacher's defence was carried out in large part at the level of ontology and anthropology. He replaced classical accounts of Christ's human nature with a general anthropology in which self-conscious, subjective inwardness exists alongside or beneath an objective, bodily humanity held in the close-woven mesh of causation. Exploiting the split which Kant had opened between subjective and objective, Schleiermacher argued that Christ was raised above the ordinary not by some miraculous intervention in the objective world which would sever him from the natural order, but rather by a quality of his subjectivity.

Where classical theology articulated the connection of humanity with divinity by means of hypostatic union, Schleiermacher argued for a connection with the divine as a general feature of human being. Building a religious bridge across Kant's gap very different from Hegel's spirit-historical bridge, Schleiermacher argued that the ingredience of subjects in an objective world, which subjects register in thought and action, includes within it the impingement of the total context upon the subject; it includes within it the subject's more or less conscious butting up against his or her absolute dependence upon that total context; and so it includes within itself the subject's relatedness to the divine. With such a metaphysic in hand, Schleiermacher attempted to make sense of God's real presence to inner history even while admitting that we cannot adequately take cognizance of that presence in outer history.[36]

Instead of attempting an account of Jesus' divine nature, Schleiermacher then argued for, in Frei's words, an 'archetypal status of human God-consciousness sufficient to allow [Jesus] to *function divinely* toward the rest of us'.[37] He argued for an unprecedented development of inwardness in Jesus of Nazareth which constituted, not an absolute rupture of the laws of development and contingency, but a 'relative miracle': the emergence of something new at the beginning of a fresh stage of human subjective development. The divine impingement upon inwardness, he argued, can be so fully realized within a particular human being that we may speak of that human being as the presence of the Archetype in history, as the representative of religious consciousness raised to its highest pitch, and as the catalyst of the rise of that consciousness in others.

Strauss, however, argued that Schleiermacher's stand was doomed. The retreat into inner history only made sense as a strategy, he suggested, if subjective and objective could be separated far more than Schleiermacher – and certainly far more than Strauss himself – was willing to grant. The emergence of an unprecedented perfect consciousness of the divine in one individual's inwardness was, he argued, no 'relative miracle'; it was just the kind of absolute miracle which Schleiermacher had foresworn. It was the emergence of something for which there had been no process of piecemeal preparation, something for which there could in principle be no explanation at the level of worldly causation, something for which no properly historical account could be given. It would work only if inwardness were a realm utterly removed from externality, a world utterly ungoverned by *Wissenschaft*.

No, said Strauss. Except for a brief, abortive dalliance in the third edition of *The Life of Jesus*, he would not admit 'a "subjective" or individual historical etiology that ran counter to … "objective" or cultural explanation of all historical connections'.[38] Rather, he insisted 'that Jesus's historical particularity *was one with his outward manifestation*,'[39] – and armed with such an ontology, Strauss insisted adamantly that *no* event 'could fully manifest the divine life'.[40] All strategies built on Schleiermacher's ground, on the attempt to stand faith upon some aspect of Jesus' existence separated from his 'outward manifestation' and so from the fierce tides of history in which that manifestation is immersed, are nothing but evasions. If once we accept the sway of historical consciousness, we must accept it wholeheartedly, and 'let burn what must burn', keeping nothing back from its flames.[41]

4 A glance ahead

Frei believed that the debate between Strauss and Schleiermacher had by no means gone away in the century between their time and his. As a first approximation, it could be said that my argument in the rest of this book will be that Frei's work should be seen as an intervention in precisely this debate.[42] I will be arguing that Frei was willing to go a long way with Strauss against Schleiermacher, that he came to share something very like Strauss's insistence that 'Jesus's historical particularity was one with his outward manifestation', even that he was willing to admit something like the more general historical ontology which underwrote that claim, and that he too saw that the Gospels simply do not give the kind of portrayal of Christ we would need if our focus were upon his religious inwardness.

Thanks largely to his engagement with Barth, however, Frei's intervention in the debate between Strauss and Schleiermacher involved a reversal of the terms in which that debate had been couched, for he refused to begin by asking how Christian faith could possibly fit into the constraining grid of historical *Wissenschaft*. Rather, he committed himself to finding the proper location within Christian faith for something like the historical world of Strauss and Troeltsch. To put it all too briefly, he believed that if his affirmation that an event did and can manifest the divine life was governed precisely by the strange portrayals that the Gospels give, and so concentrated upon the outward, historical manifestation of the man from Nazareth, then he not only could but also should accept fundamental aspects of Strauss's own position, even while making affirmations that Strauss would have found impossible.

So, in his 1983 Shaffer Lectures, Frei said that 'The whole of which these lectures are part is a plodding inquiry into what it might mean to laugh, but to laugh fairly and not sarcastically, and not in a fashion that might turn to gallows humor.'[43] I believe that, although Frei was referring to his projected history of modern Christology in that statement, 'the whole' could also be taken much more broadly to apply to *all* of his work. In other words, Frei's work can be seen, without too much distortion, as one long attempt to laugh at Strauss – not because he has found a way of ignoring him, but because he has learnt to defeat Strauss with Strauss's own tools.

Notes

1. For beginning in the middle, see chap. 8, §1, and my article 'An American Theologian of History: Hans W. Frei in 1956', *Anglican and Episcopal History* 71.1 (2002). For 'finding his voice' see Frei, 'Autobiographical Notes on Self' (1983g), and chap. 8, introductory section.
2. Frei's 1957 essays on 'Niebuhr's Theological Background' (*1957a*) and 'The Theology of H. Richard Niebuhr' (*1957b*) question Niebuhr's success in holding Troeltsch and Barth together; by the time of his 1988 paper on 'H. Richard Niebuhr on History, Church and Nation' (1988d), however, Frei appears more convinced of Niebuhr's success.
3. *The Historian and the Believer* (New York: Macmillan, 1966), pp. 3–4.
4. Ibid., p. 6
5. Ibid.
6. 'Theological Reflections on the Accounts of Jesus' Death and Resurrection' (*1966a*), pp. 86–7. For Frei's explicit (sympathetic but critical) remarks on Harvey at this time, see p. 90 and 'Remarks in Connection with a Theological Proposal' (1967b), p. 31.
7. 'Theological Reflections' (*1966a*), p. 87. In a letter to Leander Keck (1975e) Frei wrote, quoting Keck's words back at him, 'I do agree that Christians cannot be "indifferent to the relation of what is history-like to history". But I also think that the way the Christian qua Christian sees the connection between them is different from the way the historian qua historian sees it.' Harvey would have seen nothing but evasion in that distinction between the theologian and the historian.
8. Letter to Van Harvey (1976e), Frei's emphasis. Harvey had sent Frei a copy of his paper, 'A Christology for Barabbases', *Perkins Journal* 29 (1976).
9. Notes on typescript of Paul W. Meyer's *The Justification of Jesus* (?1976k), Frei's emphasis. The scrawl continues:

    Even those who deny it have to argue 'Jesus' out of the way first, whether they do so in the process of claiming a set of attitudes as constituting the essence of Christianity, or claiming that Christian belief should be focused on other 'doctrines', e.g., God and the meaningfulness of God-talk, or the Holy Spirit. Sooner or later the place of Jesus in these contexts will arise, with all the discomforts of fitting him into them smoothly, and in part the reason for the discomforts will be theological, in part historical.

10. Frei had been approached to write about 'Strauss, Baur, and the Rise of Biblical Criticism' (see Curriculum Vitae, 1976b) for Ninian Smart's set of volumes on *Nineteenth Century Religious Thought in the West*; by the time the essay was finished, Frei had focused it exclusively on Strauss. The essay was finished by 1981 at the latest (see my bibliography for more details), but publication was delayed until 1985 (*1985c*).

11. Letter to William Clebsch (1981h).

12. Letter to Patrick Sherry (1983e).

13. Letter to William Clebsch (1981h).

14. Letter to Patrick Sherry (1983e).

15. 'Niebuhr's Theological Background' (*1957a*), pp. 53–64; cf. pp. 21–32.

16. Ibid., p. 55

17. Cf. ibid., pp. 22–23, 55.

18. Ibid., p. 22.

19. Ibid., pp. 22–23.

20. Ibid., p. 23.

21. In Frei's account, this multiple describability was seen in the nineteenth century as applying most obviously to intellectual history, because the grasp of the 'ideational complexes' of the past is so thoroughly dependent on 'the historian's place in time and culture' (ibid., p. 24). The historian's reading of such matters involves him in the attempt to grasp the tacit structures of the thought-world in which individual ideas and intentions make sense ('the ground that does not as such appear'), and raises the question of whether understanding comes only through demythologizing or 'transliterating' the ideas from such structures and providing them with modern homes, or whether it comes by the creative inhabiting and 'appropriation' of these tacit structures (p. 25).

22. Ibid., p. 21.

23. Ibid., pp. 22–23.

24. Ibid., p. 56.

25. Ibid., pp. 25–28.

26. Ibid., p. 57, Troeltsch's emphasis.

27. Ibid., p. 24.

28. Troeltsch's own answer has been well described by Sarah Coakley in the aptly titled *Christ without Absolutes* (Oxford: Clarendon Press, 1988).

29. 'The Formation of German Religious Thought in the Passage from Enlightenment to Romanticism' (?1981a), pp. 2–3, Frei's emphasis.

30. Ibid., p. 10.

31. Some such solution has been a necessity for modern theology. As Frei described it in his 1958 article on 'Religion: Natural and Revealed' (*1958a*), modern Christian theology has consistently made reference to 'divine self-disclosure' which is 'unique and original, and its contents unknown apart from the disclosure' but nevertheless 'embodied in and therefore inseparable from specific historic events'. The terms of the question have remained constant; it has only been the form of the 'embodiment' or 'inseparability' that has changed.

32. 'Niebuhr's Theological Background' (*1957a*), p. 54.

33. Ibid., p. 54.

34. *The Christ of Faith and the Jesus of History: A Critique of Schleiermacher's Life of Jesus*, trans. Leander E. Keck (Philadelphia: Fortress Press, 1977), pp. 4f., quoted in 'David Friedrich Strauss' (*1985c*), p. 254.

35. 'David Friedrich Strauss' (*1985c*), p. 245.

36. We shall explore this theory in more detail in chap. 2, §1.

37. Ibid., p. 254, my emphasis.

38. Ibid., p. 246.

39. Ibid., my emphasis.

40. Cf. ibid., p. 245; my terminology here is drawn from Harvey, *The Historian and the Believer*, p. 30, discussing Troeltsch.

41. On the ground prepared by this basic anthropological and ontological conviction, Strauss also – and at much greater length – disagreed with Schleiermacher at the level of exegesis and of historical criticism. Even if, *per impossibile*, we could make sense of the idea of an Archetype incarnate as a particular human being in history, and even if we were to accept Schleiermacher's dubious argument that the only way to explain the current state of religious feeling is to suppose that there has *in fact* been such an incarnation, the Gospels provide us with no reason for believing that Jesus of Nazareth should be identified as that human being. Reading the Gospels, Strauss found pictures of a supernatural saviour, not of a moral or religious Archetype; and putting historical criticism to work on those portraits did not turn the stuff of supernatural miracle into the acceptable coinage of idealist religiosity but transmuted it into the folk-consciousness of a primitive people coming to terms, in the only way they knew how, with one of their own who mistakenly believed himself Israel's eschatological Messiah.

42. Another confirmation that this is the right framework within which to view Frei's early work at least can be found in Frei's brief and enigmatic 'Autobiographical Notes on Self' (1983g), which include a summary of the main topics of his teaching after his return to Yale in the 1950s: 'Historical Jesus/Christ of Faith (Van Harvey); Strauss/Barth; Philosophy/Theology …'

43. Shaffer Lectures (1983a), p. 11.

2

For and Against Barth

Frei began his academic theological career with a group of writings on Karl Barth, most of them among his densest and most difficult work.[1] In them, he undertook a detailed conceptual examination of Barth's early theological method, and a lengthy historical exploration of the connections between that method and various nineteenth-century theologies. When read in the light of his later work, it becomes clear that Frei had already encountered many of the questions which were later to animate him, and that paying attention to the form in which those questions are raised here casts considerable light on what followed. One particularly productive way to read this early work on Barth is precisely as a clarification of the question sketched in the last chapter, the question of faith and history, and it turns out that Frei's earliest work already poses that question in a form strongly influenced by Barth's rejection of earlier attempted answers.

Theologians of the nineteenth century had not, of course, been slow in proposing remedies for the problem of faith and history suggested to them by men like Lessing and Kant – the problem to which Strauss drew embarrassing attention in the middle of the century. Each patent remedy involved a different diagnosis of what might be meant by 'history', and a different prescription for what 'faith' should be taken to mean, given that diagnosis. A central achievement of Frei's earliest work was the identification of one popular and potent type of such remedies among the mainstream German Protestant theologians of the nineteenth century; he traced this type's emergence and its efficacy in certain prominent cases, labelled it 'relationalism', and suggested that it was above all the theology associated with this type of remedy against which Karl Barth had reacted in his famous disavowal of liberalism.[2]

However, although Frei shared Barth's resistance to this strain of theology, believing that it represented a fatal reaction to the question of history,[3] he began to worry that Barth's alternative theology, at least in its early stages, ended up succumbing to a different danger, one which, despite Barth's best intentions, scuppered his attempt to do more justice to history. Frei labelled *this* mistake 'epistemological monophysitism', arguing that it was by no means Barth's alone but that, on this issue if on no other, Barth was part of a much broader academic movement.[4]

Frei's early attempts to come to terms with what he was later to call Strauss's question were decisively shaped by his awareness and analysis of these two dangers, relationalism and epistemological monophysitism. On the one hand he saw, in prominent attempts to connect faith and history, a failure to do justice either to the freedom of God, or to the freedom of history. On the other hand he saw, in the rejection of those attempts, at least the danger of a failure to find theological room for the fully historical humanity of Jesus of Nazareth, and more generally for a genuinely historical conformity of human beings to God. In other words, all the technicalities that follow (and the discussion will be more recondite in this chapter than at any other point in the book) are more or less directly devoted to clarifying the two sides of the question: may we speak of genuinely historical faith?

1 Relationalism

The solution that relationalism proposed for the problem of history and revelation was, broadly speaking, idealist. That is, its proponents accepted entirely the integrity and resilience of the objective realm observed by historical method, but suggested that the world is not exhausted by that realm. A full understanding of the world must include the observer's relation to that objective realm, and that requires of us a different form of account, a 'geography of the human soul' that can locate and describe the subjective impingement of the objective.[5] The relationalist theologian's claim was that, whatever might be true in the realm of objectivity described by historians, such a subjective geography will be found to border at its limits upon the absolute. Although by definition the absolute cannot be found among the contingent pathways of cause and effect which criss-cross objective history, the human spirit may discover that, in and through its very relationships to that objective history, it has a view out towards the absolute horizon of the world. Thanks to the existence of this inwardness, we may speak about *revelation*, about a relatedness of finite subjects to the divine.[6]

Friedrich Schleiermacher, for instance, argued that in every action per-formed, a subject encounters the world both as resistance and as enabling context; she becomes aware of herself as *having* a context, and of her dependence upon it. He argued that there is in principle no limit to the breadth of the context and the depth of the dependence which is encountered in this way; in principle, each act in which a subject relates to the objective world contains at its limits a primitive awareness of the universal context of the act, and of the actor's absolute dependence.[7] To understand fully the nature of the thinking and acting subject's ingredience in the objective world, the subject's implication in and perspective upon that world, we need to refer to that subject's indebtedness to an unsurpassable whole which utterly exceeds it, as it utterly exceeds every particular.[8]

'Awareness' is, of course, a poor name for this relation to the absolute given within all our acting, as is 'feeling', the more common term used in English translations. This relation, while continually present within all our relationships to the objective world, is one of which we can at times be more, at times less 'aware' in any straightforward psychological sense. The key element in Schleiermacher's move to subjectivity is not, therefore, some privileging of emotion or the intuitive or the psychological – not 'subjectivism' in that sense – but rather the claim that relatedness to the absolute, to the divine, is a *given* for human subjects. The subject's utter indebtedness to an unsurpassable whole, to the absolute, is not the abstract conclusion of a metaphysician, but is given directly to the subject within each and every act and thought; it is the oxygen in which those thoughts and actions breathe.[9]

There were, of course, many forms of relationalist theology in the nineteenth century that differed in detail from Schleiermacher's;[10] Frei nevertheless claimed that a wide collection of nineteenth-century theologians took their stand on an ineffable, given relatedness to God present within human being as such. For such theologians, statements about God – about the absolute which upholds the world – can only be statements about this given relatedness to God, and thus statements about God only insofar as they are statements about human beings in this given state of being God-related. Hence Frei's label, 'relationalism': such theology regards itself as reflection upon an indissoluble relation in which God is immediately present to human faith, in, with and through the human subject's relationship to the objective world. 'Revelation' (as it were, the divine side of the relation) and 'faith' (the human side) are simply artificially distinct conceptual characterizations of a nexus that is itself indivisible.[11]

2 Against Relationalism

Barth rejected this relationalist settlement.[12] He saw it, according to Frei, as a betrayal of both revelation and history. He believed that by confining itself to talk about the given God-relatedness of humanity, relationalism made itself unable to speak about God's sovereignty over all human states, about a God who is free, a God who is truly God; nor is it able to talk about a creation which is truly creaturely, a history which is truly historical. Relationalism proposed what Frei calls an 'organic' relationship between revelation and human historical life, a relation which allows neither truly to be itself. God becomes a predicate of a human state called faith, and that state is itself isolated from the contingency and boundedness of history.[13]

The two sides of this problem are intimately linked. Barth, when he sought in response to articulate the objective rule of God beyond all organic confusion with humanity, found himself simultaneously asserting the creatureliness of creation. He claimed that the revelation of God's utter sovereignty is also a revelation of the world: it reveals God as God and in doing so reveals the world and everything in it *as* the world, as not-God. The revelation of God reveals the 'completely radical contingency' which characterizes life 'between origin and death'[14] and shatters the 'temptation of humanity to transform the positive scene that lies between these two borders, the historical ebb and flow, into a more or less positive clue to what lies beyond it and to our relations with it'.[15]

Frei most frequently puts both sides of Barth's insistence in terms of freedom.[16] That the concern to articulate God's sovereignty is a concern to do justice to *divine* freedom is clear enough, but Frei's couching of the demand for creatures' creatureliness in terms of *human* freedom needs more careful handling. The problem of human freedom has been so much debated in theological and philosophical contexts that the mention of it immediately brings out a welter of assumptions about what it is that is to be discussed, most of which are irritating distractions in this context. Frei was not concerned with determinism or foreknowledge; he did not investigate the anatomy of human decision-making. He was instead interested in the fully human, historical reality of the receipt of God's grace on the part of human beings. He was interested in the question as to whether human beings can be the recipients of revelation precisely as human; precisely as creaturely and particular; precisely as historical.

Barth was faced, according to Frei, with the task of avoiding both an ebionite understanding of the relationship of faith and revelation for which the divinity of the revelation is questionable, and a docetic understanding for which the humanity of the faith is in doubt. In other words, Barth's task was to 'found the doctrine of revelation solely upon the doctrine of God ... without violating the freedom and subjectivity and spontaneity of man'.[17] He was faced with the task of proclaiming that 'God as God, in his sovereignty and without becoming absorbed into the relation, addresses the free subject without cancelling its freedom.'[18] He sought to articulate the way in which God's sovereignty 'encompasses and founds, but does not transcend or absorb the irreducible subjectivity of the person (or community) that becomes the object of God's revealing act'.[19]

Frei sometimes describes the question as if Barth saw himself faced by two equal demands: the demand of divine freedom, and the demand of human freedom. In reality, however, Barth found himself in a situation in which the recent history of theology had made the former a far more pressing issue than the latter. Frei puts this in a broader historical perspective. The nineteenth-century relationalists had themselves reacted against an eighteenth-century Protestant orthodoxy which they perceived as having simultaneously made God an object alongside other objects in the world and denied human freedom. In such theology, 'just as individual beings are related to other individual beings in a purely external manner ... so the relation of God to his creation is external. The relation of finite mind to God is that of conceptual knowledge ... apprehending a being other than the knower.'[20] The 'externality' of this relationship was both an objectification of God and a denial of human 'subjectivity', of 'freedom-filled selfhood'[21] – a denial that the human knower must appropriate and interpret what he or she receives internally, subjectively and freely, rather than having the truth of God placed (by deductive reason or by propositional revelation) on the *tabula rasa* of the mind; a denial that we must have an internal relatedness to any datum if that datum is in any sense to be given to us. It is a denial, in other words, in part of the transcendence of God, but more particularly of the genuinely human nature of the Christian's relation to God. However, if such eighteenth-century theologies had erred by conceiving of the relationship between revelation and history as external (or 'mechanical', to use Frei's favoured term), Barth held that the relationalists of the nineteenth century had erred by making it 'organic'; if the eighteenth century with its mechanical relationship between revelation and history strayed more towards the denial of *human* freedom, the nineteenth with its organic relationalism strayed more towards the denial of *divine* freedom.[22] There is no doubt that, although Frei frequently called attention to the two sides of the question facing Barth, he was also aware that it was the error of the nineteenth century which remained most clearly in Barth's view.

God's freedom was the key issue, the issue requiring a new and strident articulation, and Barth was not so passionately concerned to articulate human freedom or the nature of historical existence clearly. We shall see that, even so, an account of human freedom does emerge from the underside of his proclamation of God's freedom – yet it is Frei's concern, rather than Barth's, to bring the question of history, the question of human freedom, to the fore and to trace its career through the various stages of Barth's theological development.

If relationalists argued that theological statements were always of necessity statements simultaneously about revelation and about faith (objective and subjective poles of the one indissoluble reality: the ever-present impingement of the absolute upon the human spirit), Barth argued that theological statements must be primarily statements about God, and only secondarily and derivatively statements about human beings and the states in which they find themselves – even if this calls into radical question our ability to make any theological statements other than paradoxical proclamation of God's freedom over us, and even if it means that renewed force is given to the question as to whether and how God and history can be said to be related at all.

Frei traces three successive attempts which Barth made to chart this course: the attempt of the first edition of *Der Römerbrief*, the attempt of the second edition of the same book, and the attempt of Barth's later, more properly dogmatic work, particularly the earlier volumes of the *Church Dogmatics*.[23] In all three stages, there is no doubt that it is the desire to articulate God's freedom rather than the desire to safeguard human freedom which dominates the landscape of Barth's post-liberal work, and in the earlier stages this dominance is absolute. Through all changes of approach and style, Barth's preoccupation is not primarily with method, nor with the precise description of faith, but with the sovereignty of God; all else is subordinate to that.[24] When Barth moves from the world of *Der Römerbrief* to that of the *Church Dogmatics*, a change often seen as a major methodological shift, Frei emphasizes that it is as much a change in the (Trinitarian and Christological) conceptualization of God's sovereignty as it is a change in method, and that the central theme remains the same.[25]

In the first edition of *Der Römerbrief* Barth, according to Frei, eschewed methodological and epistemological sophistication, and instead turned to preacherly proclamation, much influenced by the Biblical Realists, of the newness and power of God's Kingdom as it arises unexpectedly and potently in the midst of the old world. The focus is very much on the power of God, and although Frei criticizes Barth (perhaps unfairly) for teetering on the brink of a new relationalism in which the Kingdom of God would be *identified* with the ever-present organic growth within society of radical (socialist) justice, the focus is not at all on the clear exposition of the joint between divine initiative and human reception, but entirely on the proclamation of the coming kingdom.[26]

The second edition of the same book was a different animal. Barth tried to push the proclamation of God's transcendence and judgment of human presumption to a radically new level, all but abandoning the preacher's register, and turning to a distinctive, almost expressionist style full of tortured paradox and geometrical metaphors. Barth's aim was still, however, the positive one of proclaiming the gratuitous condescension of God relating Godself to human beings without ceasing to be God in so doing. This good news, however, is to a large extent to be proclaimed by means of bad news, because it is only good news if God is not, to use Frei's language, 'absorbed' into the relation, becoming indistinguishable from some human state or historical reality, something on our creaturely plane which can henceforth substitute for God. Such an absorbed God can neither judge nor save, can neither call into question creaturely reality nor bring about that which is new. Such a God is no God. Only if God can come to human beings in such a way that all creaturely reality is shown to be not-God, if creaturely reality is cast into relief in all its distance from God, can we rely upon God for salvation. Only if God comes as a 'No' pronounced over the world, can the 'Yes' of salvation be a word spoken by one who truly has power to save.[27]

Barth claims that no human path to God – no feeling or state, no set of practices or mental exercises, no forms of prayer or of observance, no humility or service, no attitude or cry for help, not even any dramatic dialectical theology – coincides with God's path to humanity.[28] All of those human paths are thoroughly human, thoroughly historical, thoroughly not-God. There is no organic and immediate unity, no relationalist unity, even by the grace of God, between any human state, act or process, and the action of God.[29] All supposed points of contact (if by 'point of contact' we mean some humanly accessible reality within which relatedness to the divine is a given) are 'similarly distant from the Word of God'.[30] Human endeavours to see God, even the most rigorously ascetic and negative ascent of the mind from crude material things to higher and higher apprehensions of being, or Schleiermacher's penetration into the ever broader contexts of our thinking and acting, can only result in a sight of 'the flexible and constantly receding limits of finitude in all their exasperating vagueness'.[31] The coming of God to humanity is not, in this sense, a coming of humanity to God.

Revelation and history are linked here, but in what appears to be a wholly negative way: revelation shows what history is not, it evacuates history of its pretensions. Seen in such a light, the nineteenth-century relationalists had, by their mapping of internal and external, subjective and objective, been seeking to isolate an element of human being from history, to propose an element within history which was not tied by history's bonds. Barth's focus on the sovereignty of God was at the same time a rejection of this move: for him, only a wholesale acceptance of the utterly conditioned creatureliness of every element of human being, however internal or external, objective or subjective, would do.

In the face of this stinging proclamation of God's freedom, the question is bound to arise: is there any room for faith? Or rather, can faith be anything other than the startled realization that God has nothing to do with us? Barth certainly claims that faith, as the human reality which corresponds to revelation, is a reality, but his talk about it is thickly hedged about with qualifications, for it only corresponds to revelation in a very restricted sense.[32] Faith, he says, is a creature of God's revelation, a miracle – but it is a reality which does not contain within itself a grasp upon revelation. It is the event in which the believer finds himself or herself converted – but it is not some stable state which emerges from that conversion. Faith is, in Barth's early post-liberal work, simply the acknowledgment of the terrifying and gracious fact that God's lightning has struck the recipient, an acknowledgment which bears the blackening caused by that lightning, but does not contain or mirror its brilliant flash. One cannot understand God by looking at faith, but only by looking away from it, in the direction in which its shaking finger points. In Frei's words:

> Faith is purely in process of being created, and in order to understand it one must turn not toward *it* but toward the creative act that creates it. Thus faith must negate itself, point away from itself; yet not in such a way as to dissolve the reality of the creaturely act that it is, since it is human, not divine activity.[33]

In fact, Barth goes further. If, by 'faith', we mean this creation of revelation, this crater left by the impact of God's work, this shattering absence of grasp upon God which indicates negatively the arrival of the gracious judgment of God, then

> whatever may be grasped historico-psychologically and thus known in ourselves or in others as 'faith', all this is witness and symptom of that work and miracle of God upon us, of that faith which, created through 'the Word' and deepened in 'the Word' is our righteousness before God.[34]

Emptiness, awe, ignorance and humility are no more faith than are good works. Nothing which is the historical or psychological possession or activity of human beings can claim to be inherently faith, faith in and of itself. The only definition that can be given which actually captures faith, rather than symptoms and signs which may or may not in any given place be signs of real faith, is that faith is the creation of God.

This is clear, dramatic, and powerful – but is it helpful? Does it, in the end, provide Barth with any positive account of history conformed to God, of how the conditions of creaturely existence might be made to speak of God? The question raised by Barth's proclamation of God's freedom is forced home here: it is not hard to see how this account of faith puts all relatedness of revelation to history seriously in question. In one place (to which Frei alludes but which he does not quote), Barth says that the Holy Spirit, 'invisible, outside the continuity of the visible human subject and beyond all psychological analysis ... creates the new subject in the man who stands upright in the presence of God. *He is the subject of faith*, which "religious experience" reaches after and longs for, but never finds.'[35] And there's the rub. If the Holy Spirit is the subject of faith; if it is miracle, entirely the creature of revelation, outside the continuity of the visible human subject; and if all the 'historico-psychological' factors we can point to are simply symptoms and witnesses, is faith itself really anything to do with the human subject? Has Barth left himself with any positive way of explaining the claim that God creates faith *in human beings* in their existence as historical and psychological creatures? Has his account of faith anything to do with the conditions of creaturely, historical existence? Has he succeeded in reasserting the freedom of God and the creatureliness of human beings only to break any connection between the two? Is it *only* the Holy Spirit who is the subject of faith? Are human beings simply blind spectators to the Holy Spirit's possession of 'their' faith?

Frei suggests that, in part, this question was unavoidable for Barth in his early work, because he was working with an understanding of God's freedom which saw God as free *in and only in* God's revelation. That is, Barth does not attempt to give any account of God's freedom *prior* to revelation, such that revelation is something that a free God chooses to do. God is still God-in-his-revelation, and all Barth's efforts to proclaim God's freedom have therefore to be focused on showing God's freedom-in-revelation – how it is that the result of revelation is not something which allows the grasping, the curtailing of God. Having set up his task in this way, Barth's proclamation of God's freedom has to proceed largely negatively, by way of denials of any claim that revelation might link organically or immediately to any human reality, state or process with real content, such that that content could in some way be thought to define or properly name God. Those denials provide the main content of Barth's assertion of God's freedom, and he has to risk removing faith altogether from 'the continuity of the visible human subject', in order to proclaim that it is God in all his otherness and newness, God the utterly transcendent, who confronts human beings in revelation, as their *krisis*, as the one speaking from beyond the limits of creaturely existence. Attacking relationalism head on, he gets dangerously close to setting up a competition between God and humankind, with God's freedom only being asserted by means of denials about human faith. It is, according to Frei's analysis, the lack of an account of God's freedom-*for*-revelation, his freedom 'prior' to revelation, which forced Barth's hand in this.[36]

Nevertheless, Frei knew that Barth's theology at this stage was more subtle, and had more resources to respond to such criticisms, than the account so far suggests. Frei indicated several resources which, even in the astringent atmosphere of Barth's early work, stand as pointers to a more positive account of faith and of the creaturely sphere in which faith takes place.

First, we may note that even if Barth does in fact fall into the trap of failing to articulate a genuine encounter of God with real human beings, such is not his intention. Barth makes plenty of assertions to the contrary, even if he had not necessarily found the conceptual resources required to do justice to those assertions. Thus the passage in Romans which suggests that the Holy Spirit is the subject of faith continues: 'He is the subject by whom *we* are enabled to speak ... He is the presupposition of all human being and having ... [T]hrough Him, the love of God is in our hearts ... [T]here is a human "I" and "we", a human *heart*, which God is able to love.'[37] As Frei says, 'One hears Barth constantly asserting during the dialectical period that man's question, the question that *is* man, i.e., human spontaneity and subjectivity, cannot be overwhelmed by the answer' (Frei's emphasis).[38] Although there is not much that would fill out these hints, not much that would enable us to turn brief references to 'the question that *is* man' into a substantial account of creation and of human being in conformity to God, Barth does at least claim that there ought to be space for such an account.

Second, Frei says, we have to recall that Barth's theology at this point was still not primarily concerned with the human reality of faith. Barth was captivated by the sovereignty and freedom of God, and was willing to use any expressions or concepts that might allow him to proclaim this, even if they sounded dangerously like a denial of human reality. *Der Römerbrief* is a clarion call in a particular situation; a risk rather than a systematic theology. He makes his proclamation by mixing plain, unambiguous claims about revelation with statements about faith which are anything but plain. All that he says about faith is 'dialectical', in the sense that it deliberately courts paradox by pitching claim against counter-claim, never letting the reader come to any resting place, any settled conviction as to what faith consists in.[39] Knowing that he must speak about faith, but that he must not make faith out to be itself a reality worthy of attention, Barth seeks in the very way he puts his sentences and paragraphs together to undercut any desire to focus upon faith, upon the conditions and extension of human response to God's revelation, and to divert all attention towards God's revelation. The book is therefore not a systematic denial of faith, or of the relatedness of God's revelation to the human historical sphere, but a strategic performance which in method as well as content is a radical proclamation that God is not part of that sphere, that what really matters is not to be found in it. The lack of a clear, substantial account of human historical existence is therefore a strategic rather than a systemic lack. This recognition holds out the promise that, if a shift to a more dogmatic or systematic theology is possible in the light of what Barth has said (and that was certainly no easy question for Barth in the 1920s) a more substantial account of faith and of history might emerge.[40]

Third, we should note that all that Barth says about the revelation of God's judgment and grace is focused Christologically. It is in Jesus Christ that the No and the Yes of God have been pronounced, in his death upon the cross and in his resurrection that the end of all creaturely pretension, and the gracious salvation which accompanies that end, are proclaimed. This Christological focus is, as Frei points out, an element of continuity between Barth and his liberal forebears, but whereas their eyes turned upon Christ discerned one in whom subjectivity was illuminated by the deep consciousness of his unswerving relatedness to God, Barth saw only the cross, and a Saviour dying on it who refused to grasp any relatedness to God as a possession. Nevertheless, this means that everything Barth says about the distance between creator and creation emerges from attention to a point at which creator and creation are quite definitely related: a point at which we may certainly speak of the impingement of God upon the historical sphere. Of course, if we expected that Barth's account of revelation would therefore have to include within it an account of how at least one element of human historical reality is taken up into relationship to God, and hence to contain at least some pointers towards a wider account of human historical existence in conformity to God, we would be disappointed. The Christological impingement of revelation on history is, in the second edition of *Der Römerbrief*, itself hedged about so tightly with qualifications – to the extent that he can describe it as being like the infinitesimal, extensionless point at which a line touches a circle – that Barth does not, at this stage, deliver on the promise which seems to inhere in it. Nevertheless, the promise itself remains – and we shall be returning to it before long.[41]

Fourth, there are places where the very denials which make up Barth's negative verdict on creaturely existence are themselves allowed to become elements of a more positive account of faith. One of the ways Barth had of making his denials about creaturely existence was to speak of life's 'infinite contradiction'. Immediately after breaking with liberalism, Barth, according to Frei, defined his whole problem as that of 'life and the Bible', and explained that life is a problem because it consists in an 'infinite contradiction'; it makes sense only in reference to that which transcends it, the eternal – yet that eternal, that very thing which is required to make sense of life, is 'not given', it never becomes a thing we can inspect.[42] Nevertheless, in Barth's early work, this 'infinite contradiction' of life can itself be pointed to by philosophy, even if only in a limited way. Philosophy can point to a certain kind of questionability or incompleteness in life, to the relationship of life to that which is not given with it. The abstract transcendence which such philosophy posits correlative to the questionability it uncovers is certainly not the same as the concrete eternal one who actively limits creation and who is the object of theology, and there is no way to ascend from the questionability noticed by philosophy to contemplation of God, nor to identify that questionability with the infinite contradiction under which creation stands in the face of God's limiting decree (for that decree is not an abstract transcendence or an empty philosophical sign, but is the concrete word spoken by God over creation in the event of Jesus Christ). *Nevertheless*, Barth is prepared to say that the knowledge which we can gain of the questionability of life, of our existence, is a kind of 'negative parable' of the knowledge of God: it is a parable of that emptiness under which we stand in the face of God's judgment.[43] This is a tiny glimmer of light: the allowing of this thin and constricted form of resemblance between historical human life and God's revelation, but it does allow that some graspable content of human thought might, while remaining neither knowledge of God, nor knowledge of God's verdict on creation, nevertheless resemble in some way that knowledge – as a parable. Barth concedes no more, at this stage, but in view of what was to come later, with Barth's shift to an acceptance of analogy, Frei finds it significant.

Frei analyses this structure in Barth's thought quite carefully.[44] He points out that what Barth has in mind by 'philosophy' is itself complex. On the one hand, he has in mind an idealist dialectics (of a kind not unlike Schleiermacher's) which points to the implication of every particular in a context which transcends it, ultimately pointing to the transcendence of every particular by its infinite and absolute ground. The kind of transcendence which is pointed to by such philosophy is 'sheer formal possibility' – an entirely abstract, empty minus sign standing beside each particular, disallowing any attempt to regard that particular as complete in itself.[45] Yet Barth was also influenced by a different kind of philosophy, one which gave a different account of finite reality: the radical scepticism of Franz Overbeck. Overbeck's scepticism pointed vigorously to the limits of historical existence, yet did so in a way which was less smooth, less abstract, than the idealists. He pointed to the concrete impingement upon human life of the limits of origin and death: the confinement of human life in a radically finite and contingent span. Contingent historical reality provides no clue to what is beyond it; we have no clue to what lies before or after the limits which press in upon us, for there is a 'final, tragic, and total incompatibility' between life and that which limits it – yet we are mesmerized by the dark gulfs beyond those limits.[46] This move, a rejection of relationalism as strident as Barth's, enabled Overbeck to see history as 'a ceaseless movement' from origin to death unmuddied by relationalist ameliorations, a ceaseless decay, an 'indefinite connectedness of secondary instrumentalities'.[47] Barth applauds this sceptical but profoundly historical vision of creaturely existence, an existence without ladders to the divine, limited and contingent, and affirms that it is knowledge of this very limitation and contingency – more clearly even than the idealist's knowledge of the incompleteness – which is a negative parable of the knowledge of God.[48] As I said, this is a small glimmer, but it contains the suggestion that, if we are to see a more positive account of human conformity to God's revelation within Barth's theology, it might bear a paradoxical resemblance to the most sceptical and thoroughly historical of philosophies – and that in turn might at least *resemble* the understanding of history found in a Troeltsch or a Strauss. To note more than this hint of a resemblance would be to go further than Frei, at this stage, allowed himself: nevertheless, this small start is, as we shall see, the beginning of something considerably more substantial.[49]

In response, then, to relationalism's confusion of God and creation, revelation and history, Barth attempted to orchestrate both an account of revelation which preserved God's distinction from creation and, concomitantly, a less clear but no less emphatic account of creation's distinction from God. A negative version of the latter, the proclamation that creation is not God, can be heard throughout Barth's work, but we have to listen hard for hints and promises of a more positive account, and particularly for any substantial affirmation that this creaturely reality can be made to correspond to God. As it stands, Barth's account of human freedom – of the nature of human historical existence under the impingement of God – is deliberately minimalist, and any account of the relationship between revelation and faith is deliberately muted in favour of the trumpeting of God's sovereignty. Promises of further development can certainly be found, but they stand at this stage as no more than question marks in the margins of Barth's score.

3 Analogy

Frei found an important development in Barth's response to these questions in the shift from *The Epistle to the Romans* to the *Church Dogmatics*. This shift involved both a recasting of the terms in which the questions were posed, and the development of new resources for answering them.[50] The heart of the development, however, is not in methodology or questions of religious epistemology, but in the doctrine of God. According to Barth's new perspective, God is being in act. That is, God is who God is by virtue of a determination to be Father, Son and Holy Ghost, a determination which is free, in that it is beholden to no prior necessity. God demonstrates God's freedom further, by repeating this act of self-determination in a different key in the economy of salvation: in the Incarnation of the Son and the sending of the Holy Spirit.[51] This economy is the opening up of God's triune being for the participation of creatures, an act in which creation is brought into being in order to be caught up in the relations of Father, Son and Holy Spirit; it is God's demonstration that God is free *for* creation. Any attempt to explore the relationship between divine and human freedom cannot any longer simply be cast in terms of the relationship between God on the one hand and humanity on the other: it must be described in terms of the place of humanity within this complex Trinitarian economy of salvation.[52]

This shift leads to a dramatic change in the way in which Barth thought about the conformity of creatures to the creator. Barth (according to Frei) suggests that we think about it in two ways, corresponding to the two sides of the economy of salvation.[53] On the one hand, we must think first of God freely giving himself to be an object for the human act of apprehension, becoming a Word which can be encountered and known by human beings. On the other hand, we must not think of this human act of apprehension as being achieved independently of God, as if it were an independent human response to the purely external donation by God of his Word. It is a human act, yes, but (says Barth) it is also, and more fundamentally, an act of God working as Spirit, working as it were from within the apprehending human being.[54] In other words, we must think about human freedom for God, *in the context* of God's freedom for humanity, God's relating of Godself to human beings in Word and Spirit. Frei suggests that this is a strategic advance: by making space for thinking about human continuity and activity *in the context of* divine freedom (rather than *in contrast to* divine freedom) the polemical pressure on human freedom was thus lifted, and this reduced polemical pressure allowed Barth to speak more boldly about a genuinely human correspondence to God.

In itself, and described briefly, it is not clear whether this strategic advance was also a substantive advance. Indeed, the obvious question arises whether in his shift to this more Trinitarian position, Barth has lost hold of the gains he made against relationalism. Is 'reduced polemical pressure' code for Barth's having come to terms with relationalism? If this is to be a substantive as well as a strategic advance, we still have to see how Barth fortifies this new position against, on the one hand, the temptation so to describe the economy of salvation that humanity is seen as no more than a predicate of the divine act – something with no reality of its own, simply a puppet of God's Spirit, corresponding to God only insofar as it is removed from the constraints of creaturely existence – and, on the other hand, against the temptation to take Barth's description of the human apprehension of God's objective Word to mean that creaturely reality stands over against God as one being against another, in such a way that relations between the two are 'external' and mechanical. We must still negotiate, in other words, the familiar dangers posed by 'organic' relationalism and eighteenth-century 'mechanical' orthodoxy – but we now have more space in which to do so.

At this stage, the description which Frei gives of Barth's substantive advance is purely theoretical: it is given by way of a dense conceptual analysis of Barth's use of analogy. As we shall see later in the book, Frei was to find alternative and more successful ways of approaching this question (that is, of displaying how Barth's new theological framework allowed him to portray creaturely existence in conformity to God) by means of paying attention to Barth's figural exegesis.[55] Nevertheless, some important themes are touched upon in Frei's earlier, more abstruse analysis, which I think is worth exploring here.

When we ask how Barth occupied the space opened up by his Trinitarian development, and how he overcame the twin dangers besetting it, the key move (according to Frei at this stage) is the deployment of a doctrine of analogy.[56] Building, perhaps, on his earlier description of a 'negative parable' of the knowledge of God in sceptical philosophy, Barth developed an account in which not only does creation have its own order and integrity by the will of God, but in which that order can also, by the same act of God, be one which God makes to correspond analogically to God, as a true apprehension of God's Word. The primary form of correspondence that Frei analyses at this stage is *intellectual* correspondence – that shaping of human minds by God which can count as genuine human apprehension of God. Barth claims, of course, that he is not relaxing his insistence that human beings are incapable of apprehending God: as creaturely, the apprehension of faith necessarily remains apprehension of that which is not God. Yet, by the grace of God, Barth now claims that the apprehension can be of something which is, in all its utter dissimilarity from God, nevertheless in some respect similar to God.[57] Such apprehension can remain an act which is appropriate to the creaturely nature of the knower, rather than being a transcendence of creatureliness in which the knower would step over the line separating creature and creator.[58] This intellectual relationship, though – this catching up of human minds into correspondence with God – clearly rests upon the existence of that in creation which can be apprehended by human minds yet which is 'in some respect similar to God'. Barth's success in deploying a doctrine of analogy in the epistemological realm can only be as successful as his identification of that prior similarity.

In older theology (at least as it is understood by Barth) claims about the analogical nature of human talk about God arrived on the back of certain understandings of creation and its relation to the creator. In particular, they were bound up with the understanding of creation as a hierarchy of being, in which all things had being, and possessed perfections, just to the degree that they participated in the being and perfections of God. This was a hierarchy created by God in creation, and was fully visible only to eyes wiped clear by faith in Christ, but it was an inherent and stable feature of the way the world was. In such a scheme, talk about God could proceed on the basis of an analogical application to God of those perfections perceived in creaturely realities. The knowledge was inevitably *only* analogical, because those perfections applied to God in a way which was wholly unknown to us (we can only conceive of partial creaturely possession of them), but it was *genuinely* analogical, because of the divinely instituted hierarchy of being. To Barth, this smacked of too easy a marriage between philosophical ascent (the human mind's ability to find and follow the analogical ladders built in to all things) and revelation (the source of all true knowledge of God).[59]

Rather than the natural participation of all things in the perfections of God, Barth's understanding of analogy is based on creation's participation in the concrete act of God in which God is Trinity – and in which the Son becomes flesh. It is creaturely reality insofar as it is caught up by the Spirit in that specific act of God that can be said to correspond analogically to God, to be arranged into concentric ripples whipped up by the Spirit around the impact of God's active Word, rather than creaturely reality considered as possessing likeness to God in some static state of being. This new understanding of analogy still enables talk of God's perfections and the participation of creatures in them, but now as a catching up of creaturely reality into the active, particular economy of salvation. It is a doctrine of analogy which no longer suggests an ascent through higher and higher levels of abstraction, leaving the battered complexity of created flux further and further behind, but suggests instead a constant return in the power of the Spirit to the concrete, objective act of God in the midst of the creaturely, finite world.[60]

Frei, at this stage, sticks to the intellectual, epistemological realm for his description of that act. We may say that, in his inner-Trinitarian relationships, God has self-knowledge in God's Word. This self-knowledge is literal and fully adequate: it is God's perfect self-knowledge. In the incarnation and sending of the Spirit, that self-knowledge is, as it were, repeated in the creaturely sphere, but now in a hidden way appropriate to creaturely existence. Jesus Christ is the creaturely reality in which this takes place.[61] Other human beings can know God analogically to the extent that they are in Christ, to the extent that they are conformed to him and so become co-participators with him in his relationship with the Father. It is in such conformity, the obedience of faith, that human creaturely knowledge can become analogical knowledge of God, by the grace of God.[62]

Barth's claim, then, is that God brings it about by God's Spirit that there is creaturely reality which corresponds to God in a creaturely way. Jesus of Nazareth is the creaturely reality in which that primarily takes place, but it is also true of all who are drawn by the Spirit into participation in Christ. This correspondence occurs without violating the nature of the creature, and so is always only analogical; but by the grace of God it *is* a genuine correspondence. If we consider faith as intellectual apprehension (which is not all that faith is, for Barth), then to the extent that our apprehension is truly apprehension of the humanity of Christ, it is conformed to God analogically: it is knowledge of that which is not itself God, but is chosen by God to conform to him. On the other hand, to the extent that it is true knowledge of God, it is an act of the Spirit: it is God who brings it about, in God's providence, that in creation there is and can be true apprehension of Christ's humanity.[63]

In other words, Barth's later work contains a more definite and more positive account of the nature of historical existence and its relationship to God. Without going back on his assertion that it is entirely contingent and finite, that it contains no inherent ladders by which the mind may ascend to God, he has affirmed more clearly than before that it is this very contingent and finite historical existence which can be and has been taken up by God into correspondence with Godself. Creation, the human historical sphere, is given its own order by God as that which is not-God, yet it is nevertheless also ordered by God as that which, in Jesus Christ, can correspond to God. This is at least the technical outline of an account which holds together God's utter sovereignty, history's complete contingency and finitude, and a positive relation between the two which preserves the nature of each without confusion.

4 Epistemological Monophysitism

Perhaps because this was, as he analysed it at this stage, a largely technical solution, Frei was not satisfied. He was happy to accept that Barth had made conceptual space for a positive account of the unity of faith and history, but he was not yet sure that Barth knew how to fill that space out with real content.[64] Everything that we have just analysed is really no more than a complex, abstract pointer to the site where we might expect to find a rich and particular account of humanity in conformity to God: Jesus of Nazareth. In order, therefore, to understand the questions which remained for Frei in Barth's account, we need to look more closely at the Christology which lies at the heart of it.

In the second edition of *The Epistle to the Romans*, Barth's theology was no less Christocentric than was his later work. The Word of God which is spoken to humanity as judgment and salvation, which is the effecting of his double predestination to damnation and salvation, is spoken in Jesus Christ. Concerning that Word, we must speak (as Frei analyses it) on the one hand of *eternal revelation* in Jesus Christ and on the other of the eternal revelation *in Jesus Christ* – or we might say 'the formal element' and 'the concrete element', without separation or confusion between these elements.[65] On the one hand, what is spoken in Jesus Christ is a revelation of 'the other side' of all creaturely, finite, contingent reality: the limit faced by and underlying everything that is. On the other hand, one can only speak of this by speaking of Jesus of Nazareth. In the words of Barth, this means we must pay attention 'to the scandal of the historical revelation of the Christ. God is not "apodictic truth of reason". His eternity is not the harmless, non-paradoxical and directly affirmable constancy of universal ideas ... and his omnipotence is not the necessity of a logico-mathematical function.'[66] In other words, Barth wants to affirm the relation of every particular and contingent human and worldly reality to God: he wants to make it clear that creation is creation, and finds its origin and judge in God. But he wants to do this through and only through the scandalous particularity of Jesus Christ.

Nevertheless, Barth did not at that stage have the rest of the theological machinery necessary for filling out these Christological promises, according to Frei. His inability to speak positively of a human freedom for revelation based on divine freedom for humanity meant that, although he proclaimed that God's Word of judgment and salvation was spoken in the historical Jesus of Nazareth, he did not know how to pay attention to that humanity as humanity, in all its contingent and historical reality, without falling back into a new relationalism in which creator and creation would be confused, and the human reality of Jesus of Nazareth would be taken for divinity. Jesus' humanity too could only be relevant as the percussion point of God's revelation, as the blackening of history around God's lightning bolt, as a void which was a negative indicator of the miracle of God's Word.

In his later work, as we have seen, Barth did develop the theological resources he needed to allow him to talk more positively about human historical reality without being in danger of confusing that human reality with divine reality. Jesus Christ, human and divine, is at the very centre or pinnacle of that account of the relationship between God's action and human action; he is the foundation upon which all the other aspects of that account depend. And Bruce McCormack's description of Barth's whole theology of this time as conducted 'in the shadow of an anhypostatic–enhypostatic Christology' is quite appropriate:[67] it is the hypostatic union in this particular form, the unity of the two natures in the person of the Word, which lies at the heart – not of Barth's *system*, for he is not a systematic theologian, but – of Barth's achievement. Yet for Frei, reading the earlier volumes of the *Church Dogmatics*, so great is this absolute concentration upon an account of the hypostatic union in Jesus Christ that little room is left for the contingent and irregular details of Jesus' human life, for those particular thises and thats which make up the visible continuity of this human person.[68] Barth remained, thought Frei, as willing as he had ever been to adopt a very sceptical attitude to what can be known about Jesus of Nazareth. That Christ had a fully human nature is, of course, regularly acknowledged, and the fact of it is vital to the whole of Barth's theology. Yet, about what can or should be known of the content, the winding course of that human nature as it was lived out in ancient Palestine, Barth is disastrously silent. He is guilty, Frei says, of 'epistemological monophysitism': rigorously a duophysite in the structure of his theology, when it comes to what we may actually dwell upon and know about, what we may actually explore in the context of dogmatic theology (and thus, in this sense only, in 'epistemology') he is a monophysite: what is significant for our salvation is neither a fully human reality, nor an exclusively divine one, but a diagram, a Christological scheme. That the Word took flesh is relevant, supremely so. What flesh the Word took is not. The doctrine of anhypostasis–enhypostasis, which should (by clarifying and deepening the theology of the hypostatic union) secure and enable attention to the contingent details of Jesus' fully human life as themselves the possession of the Word, appears to do no such thing in Barth. His explanation of enhypostasis is 'all too easy'.[69] Or so Frei claimed, with regard to the earlier volumes of the *Church Dogmatics*.[70]

So, although we have seen Frei tracing Barth's development of a negative, anti-relationalist account of historical existence, and although we have seen his tracing of Barth's development of a framework for a more positive theological account of history, one which provides room for an account of creaturely correspondence to God by participation in Christ, without any erosion of the strong account already achieved of creatureliness – although, in other words, we have seen the beginnings of an account of the relationship of revelation and history which would respond to the rise of historical consciousness in the nineteenth century in a way which was both more thoroughly theological and more thoroughly historical than nineteenth-century relationalism – although we have seen Frei uncover all this in Barth's developing theology, there is, nevertheless, one remaining lacuna. Frei found in Barth's account too little attention to the details of Christ's humanity, too little attention to the contingent course of wider history; he found an account which ultimately undermined itself by failing to perform what it prescribed: conformity of its concepts to the humanity of Christ. Barth's theology in the early volumes of the *Church Dogmatics*, Frei argued, is in danger of conforming itself so closely to a Christological *system* that it 'does not actually know what to do with Jesus Christ at all' – a move 'detrimental to genuine objectivity', because it passes over 'every concrete content' of human existence.[71]

Frei did not believe that this was an isolated technical problem in Barth's theology: he believed that here Barth was one representative of a broader failure in the early twentieth century, a failure to do justice to Christ's humanity. In his 1957 essays on H. Richard Niebuhr, Frei explored the history of this 'epistemological monophysitism' more closely. In nineteenth-century relationalism, the inseparable relation in which God is present to human faith is also, in some way, found to be brought to explicit consciousness or raised to its highest pitch by encounter with Jesus of Nazareth. The indissoluble, always-given relation with God is also, for Christians, in fact a relationship with Jesus of Nazareth. No apologetic arguments were adduced for why it should be Jesus of Nazareth through whom this takes place; it was simply held to be a fact that, in relation to this man, the relation of revelation and faith is 'actualized'. In this way, 'history' is drawn into the relationalist nexus of faith and revelation; the impact of history (i.e., Jesus of Nazareth) upon us is united to the rise of faith within us, in such a way that the hiatus between external impact and internal response is overcome: 'the Christ outside us is the Christ within: efficacious history is effected faith'.[72]

Although the terminology is more appropriate to some nineteenth-century relationalists than others, we may say that the believer's consciousness of God, in which God is present, is most fully awakened or made explicit by a relation to the perfect God-consciousness present in Jesus of Nazareth.[73] The uniqueness of Jesus is not a metaphysical or 'suprahistorical' uniqueness, but an 'historical' uniqueness: a raising of historical possibilities to their highest pitch, without the boundaries of creaturely possibility being transgressed.[74] He bore within himself humanity's highest possibility: uncomplicated consciousness of God, or rather, a relation in knowledge and action to himself and to the world in which God is constantly a felt and determining presence. The relation that the believer bears to this God-consciousness of Jesus is one that is mediated by witnesses to the Saviour's external history, but it is one which transcends that external history. The inner relationship to God shines through the external surface of Jesus' history in such a way that it can become the catalyst and mould of the believer's own relation to God.[75] That this does in fact happen is the testimony of faith; that it can happen is the testimony of an analysis of human selfhood as always potentially religious, and an analysis of history as bearing an inwardness beneath its apparent exteriority. In the relationalist vision, inward God-consciousness resonates to inward God-consciousness across the vast distances of external history in a hidden harmony which has to be experienced to be believed.[76]

In the nineteenth century, such an emphasis clearly had a distinct competitive advantage. When the fires of historical criticism were banked up high, this focus on Jesus' inward God-consciousness became essential to his retention as the real source of the Christian religion. Any detail of Jesus' historical life could be doubted or re-described, because such things were only the extrinsic expressions of that inward God-consciousness, which itself remained secure. The *external* history of Christianity, with all its changes and chances, could be reinterpreted as one 'continuing, shifting series of religio-cultural syncretisms in the context of others'[77] without the constantly renewed *inner* linkage between Christian piety and the piety of Jesus being severed. Clearly there was a limit beyond which historical criticism could not go – the relationalist could not follow Arthur Drews into the denial of Jesus' existence as the founder of Christianity, for instance – but so long as the existence of Jesus and the broad character of his moral action were preserved, relationalists could in principle be happy to see much else consigned to the flames; they would still have sufficient material for their 'lives of Jesus'.

The details of such relationalist Christology changed over the century: the portrait of Jesus altered, the philosophical machinery by which the possibility of Christ-awoken faith was analysed and confirmed altered; but the broad outline remained the same. The scheme had one crucial historical linchpin, of course, for the supreme God-consciousness of Jesus must be affirmed, but that pin seemed secure to all but the most radical sceptics – secure, that is, until Wilhelm Wrede called into question this very point. As Frei tells the story, Wrede's attack on claims about Jesus' 'messianic consciousness' struck a blow against the heart of the relationalist Christological tradition more severe even than that levelled by Albert Schweitzer. The relationalist theologian faced with Schweitzer's challenge could still claim that the tragic eschatological cast of Jesus' message was an external clothing, a husk surrounding an inner kernel of pious God-consciousness. Wrede's attack, on the other hand, suggested that any approach to that inner kernel made on the basis of the Gospels was doomed to failure.[78] There was, of course, no sudden capitulation of relationalist liberalism; its proponents had many escape-routes and counter-measures available to them. Nevertheless, in the atmosphere of the early twentieth century the escape-routes and counter-measures became increasingly strained, relationalism was forced onto the back foot, and its attempts to bolster its claims about the historical Jesus began to take on the character of a rearguard action.[79]

In the face of this rout, retreat along one arm of the arch which relationalism had tried to build between the historical Jesus and contemporary faith led to Bultmann – and to a form of epistemological monophysitism which differed from Barth's. Bultmann, according to Frei, concentrated entirely upon 'the encounter that each generation experiences in its particular contemporaneity within the historical stream'.[80] For liberal relationalists, it was the encounter with the historical Jesus which provoked the growth of faith; for Bultmann, it is encounter with the kerygma, with Christian proclamation, which fulfils this function. Bultmann stepped back from the claim that this encounter tells one anything about, or relies in any substantial way upon, a figure standing in history at the beginning of the kerygmatic tradition. There is such a beginning in time, to be sure, and the fact that encounter with God's grace through the encounter with this kerygma has indeed begun and has continued to occur in time is vital; but the precise *occasion* of that beginning need bear no serious relationship to the *content* of the kerygma. So, says Frei:

> we can assert nothing clearly about Jesus Christ: all that a 'contemporaneous decision' needs is the completely formal, positivistic claim that Jesus Christ did once exist in human particularity. This sheer epistemological agnosticism with regard to Jesus of Nazareth is the necessary compliment to the monophysitism of which we have spoken, for which the eternal revelatory act is in our history, illuminating the relation between faith and history, but giving no noetic content to the revelatory act as history.[81]

Jesus' specific history, which took place in a certain period and place, in interaction with certain others, in a public and identifiable world, is simply the impetus for, rather than the content of, a tradition of preaching and listening through which human beings, wherever and whenever they might be, are encountered by God's call. As James F. Kay has pointed out, for Bultmann 'Jesus', the mythical figure proclaimed in the kerygma, is *occasioned* by Jesus, the historical person who lived in first-century Palestine; nevertheless the *referent* of the mythical 'Jesus' is not in any sense the historical figure, it is the *Christus praesens* – in Bultmann's words 'he in whom God acts in the present',[82] and in Kay's, 'the acting agent, the performing subject, the very *condition* of the eschatological event'.[83] As Kay says, 'Other than the relation of occasion to condition – a relation established by the electing will of God and to which the human will contributes nothing (and which, therefore, outside of faith, may only appear arbitrary) – there is no connection' between the eschatological 'agent' and the man Jesus from Nazareth.

Bultmann's theology differs radically from Barth's, and Frei did not mean to deny this when he diagnosed both as suffering from epistemological monophysitism. Barth's understanding of salvation, of the electing will of God, of the eschatological event, are all thoroughly different; nevertheless, Frei believed that despite those differences Barth's account in his earlier work shared one key feature with that of Bultmann: while it is not possible to give a proper account of the encounter between God and humanity without speaking of the *fact* of Jesus of Nazareth, it seems for both to be possible to give such an account without detailing the *content* of that fact, without paying attention to the contingent details of Jesus' historical life.[84]

However, whereas the possibility of epistemological monophysitism was grasped and affirmed by Bultmann, Frei sees it only as a *danger* in Barth's later, and then-unfinished, work. There had been a stronger dalliance with it in Barth's earlier work, but by the time Frei had reached the end of *CD* II, he saw the danger as a spur to further investigation and elaboration, rather than as a reason for rejecting what Barth had done. He still thought that he had found the conceptual *beginnings* of a proper account of human historical existence and a proper account of Jesus' humanity bound together in Barth's work, and simply suggested that such a foundation was weakened to the extent that it had not yet provided an impetus toward paying more detailed attention to the actual *content* of Jesus' humanity.

5 Conclusion

In the early 1980s, Frei described his work in progress as an attempt to laugh at Strauss's question. In the last chapter I argued that, for Frei, that question concerned the possibility of the manifestation of divine life in history, of a positive relation of human historical existence to God, and suggested that the whole of Frei's work could be seen as a struggle with Strauss; I argued that Frei was so pleased with his late 1970s' essay on Strauss precisely because it clarified for him a question with which he had been wrestling for decades. In this chapter, we have seen that Frei's reading of Karl Barth, right at the beginning of his academic career, opened up for him something very like Strauss's question. Both Barth and Strauss had criticized Schleiermacher and his followers for their confusion of divine and creaturely reality – Strauss, because he saw Schleiermacher marking out an implausibly protected reservation within history where an unhistorical absolute could reside; Barth, because he saw Schleiermacher neutering the divine by absorbing God into God's relationship with creatures. Strauss rejected Schleiermacher, and in so doing proclaimed the impossibility of any Christian theology; Barth rejected Schleiermacher, and yet argued that in so doing he was at last retrieving the long-submerged possibility of a *truly* Christian theology. Treading parallel paths, Barth and Strauss nevertheless found themselves at opposing destinations. If we may give the Frei of 1956 the benefit of his 1970s' analysis, we may say that Barth's theology represented for Frei at the beginning of his career a way in which Strauss's question – the question of God and history – could be taken seriously, and yet a way in which the question could be given the ringing positive answer which Strauss had thought an impossibility.

Barth had combined the negative insistence that history is not God (an insistence which Strauss could have shared) with the positive proclamation that history can be caught up into conformity with Christ by the Spirit (a proclamation utterly beyond Strauss). If history can indeed be positively related to God while remaining history, it is because it can bear this conformity to Christ; Christ is the ground and paradigm for creaturely existence being caught up, precisely as not-God, into relationship with God. Barth's answer to Strauss's question, to the question of God and history, is given in the language of Christology.

Yet Frei remained dissatisfied with Barth's theology, as it stood at the end of volume II of the *Church Dogmatics*, because he could not find in it the delivery of a Christology which thoroughly proclaimed Christ's creaturely conformity to God, and so could not find in it the delivery of the account of history as related to God that he believed it promised. Barth had not yet provided the resources we need if we are to say that Jesus of Nazareth's complex, contingent, particular, creaturely humanity, which is utterly and entirely not-God, is nevertheless united with God so as to become God's humanity. It allows, of course – and more than allows – the *formal* assertion that Jesus' humanity is united to God, but it does not allow that assertion to be substantially shaped by the rich and complex content of that humanity. If we are truly to answer Strauss along Barthian lines, we will have to find a way of speaking about incarnation that will not ignore the content of Jesus' particular humanity, but will make constant and constitutive reference to it. Indeed, if we are to defeat Strauss, we will have to find a way to allow talk about the incarnation to be constituted by reference to that humanity, in such a way that it *cannot* dispense with talk about the complex and winding course of Jesus' life. If we are to answer Strauss along Barthian lines, we must first overcome epistemological monophysitism.

Notes

1. Namely, his doctoral dissertation *The Doctrine of Revelation in the Thought of Karl Barth, 1909–1922: The Nature of Barth's Break with Liberalism* (1956a); an unpublished paper titled 'Analogy and the Spirit' (?1960a); a pair of articles in Paul Ramsey's festschrift for H. Richard Niebuhr: 'Niebuhr's Theological Background' (*1957a*) and 'The Theology of H. Richard Niebuhr' (*1957b*); and (in passing) in his article for *A Handbook of Christian Theology*, 'Religion: Natural and Revealed' (*1958a*).

2. See, e.g., 'Summary of Dissertation', *The Doctrine of Revelation in the Thought of Karl Barth, 1909–1922*, (1956a) p. ii. Although Frei used the term very little once he had finished his dissertation, the idea remains a target of his; even as late as 1979, he could criticize Ebeling's dogmatics for being too 'relationalist' (letter to John Hollar, 1979a).

3. In his 'Notes for an Oral History' (1975g), Frei spoke of developing, in the 1940s and 50s, 'an ambiguous relation to Hegel and Friedrich Schleiermacher'; 'liberal Protestantism was one of the most magnificent technical accomplishments' and at the same time one of the profoundest errors in theology', making three 'errors of faith: first, that the starting point of theology is anthropology; second, the belief that the proper mode of anthropology was to analyze man as self-consciousness; and, third, that out of this one could derive Christology' (p. 4).

4. Frei subsequently argued that the later volumes of the *Church Dogmatics* escaped this charge.

5. *The Doctrine of Revelation* (1956a), p. 32; cf. pp. 27–28.

6. Although relationalists accepted 'a properly "scientific" method in history which, when it is applied to historical events of any sort, must brush aside any event's claim to qualitative uniqueness', they nevertheless had a method which allowed them to speak of 'an absolute relation to absolute history' – an absolute relation which at least some relationalists

approached by means of 'a critique or phenomenological description of consciousness' (ibid., pp. 36–37).

7. Or at least, he argued that this kind of dialectical investigation of thinking and willing *pointed towards* a primitive awareness of absolute dependence, the awareness itself being beyond the grasp of formal analysis. The relationship between the philosophical, dialectical account, and the actual awareness of sin and redemption in Christ which is the proper subject matter of theology, is a subtle matter in Schleiermacher – one to which Frei was to return in the 1980s, in 'Barth and Schleiermacher: Beyond the Impasse' (1986d).

8. Cf. *The Doctrine of Revelation* (1956a), pp. 236–55.

9. Ibid., pp. 238–41. In 'Religion Natural and Revealed' (*1958a*), Frei speaks of 'a total sensitization of the human being, mind, will and psyche in the presence of the totality of the universe, impinging on him from without and within' (p. 311).

10. See *The Doctrine of Revelation* (1956a), pp. 255–361. In 'Remarks in Connection with a Theological Proposal' (1967b), Frei gives a slightly different exposition of relationalism, beginning not with Schleiermacher but with Kant, who 'substituted a Christology of action for the doctrines of Christ's person and work. In the unity of the original event with the contemporary appropriation of it, two different acts, each in its own integrity, join in one action, divine and human. More than anything else, it is an action in back of the outward, visible scene – be it that of nature, history, or the moral life' (pp. 28–29). For Kant, of course, the original event is not historical but archetypal; for later theologians it is the unity of divine and human action in the (historical) self-consciousness of Jesus. For both, though, that historical or archetypal action must be seen in unity with an 'action' deep in human self-consciousness – the conversion which is our act, but which we understand or represent as (also) the act of God.

11. *The Doctrine of Revelation* (1956a), pp. ii, 1, 27. Such theology is deeply ambivalent about its own status. The subject's relatedness to God is not an object alongside the other objects in the world, nor a disruption of historical continuity which might yield to the empirical scrutiny of the historical method. It is, rather, an aspect of or accompaniment to the subject's relation to any and every finite object. The mode in which God has given Godself to us is, therefore, a mode that eludes the grasp of human words and concepts, which are properly only tools by which particular relations to finite objects are negotiated. Of course, such finite words and concepts may become part of the informal ways in which people express the relatedness at the heart of their faith, but theology is what happens when one tries to use these flat-footed words and concepts away from their home territory, to speak formally about the subject's ineffable relatedness to the absolute. Such speech is necessary, if we are to probe into the limits of our speech about the objective world, and if we are to hold ourselves accountable to our relatedness to the absolute, but nevertheless it is and can only be secondary and distorting. Cf. ibid., pp. 12–33, 77.

12. As did Frei – and not just when writing his thesis. See, for example, 'Notes for an Oral History' (1975g), p. 4 (quoted in John Woolverton, 'Hans W. Frei in Context', p. 384): 'Through the Middle Ages people believed that their self-consciousness was mediated to them through God. Their self-consciousness was mediate, not immediate. The problem of the modern Christian is that his consciousness is directly of himself. He hopes his self-consciousness will mediate God-consciousness to him. Despite Tillich and Schleiermacher, [I would say that] *God as the ground of being is simply not there! ... Man has no self-consciousness in which a God-consciousness is present.*'

13. *The Doctrine of Revelation* (1956a), pp. 87–202, particularly pp. 174ff. (reproduced with small changes in 'Niebuhr's Theological Background' (*1957a*), pp. 40–53).

14. *The Doctrine of Revelation* (1956a), p. 170.

15. Ibid., p. 470. Frei notes the criticism voiced by Hans Urs von Balthasar that Barth presents the relationship of God to creation as one of such eschatological immediacy that the distinct reality of all particulars is crushed or sublated. Frei demurs, pointing to the concreteness of God's revelation; the act by which God stands in judgment over the world and all that

is in it is one focused in a particular concrete event: it sets concrete and insuperable limits to the world, but it does not eliminate it. See also Appendix 4.

16. E.g., ibid., p. 173.
17. Ibid., p. vii.
18. Ibid., p. 173.
19. Ibid., pp. 172–73.
20. Ibid., p. 222.
21. Ibid., p. 206.
22. 'The chief inheritance bequeathed by nineteenth-century theology to the present discussion is that … the Christian faith arose and developed in a genuinely historical matrix.' ('Religion: Natural and Revealed', *1958a*, p. 317.)
23. *The Doctrine of Revelation* (1956a), pp. 87–105.
24. Ibid., p. 555.
25. Ibid., pp. 197, 564–66.
26. Ibid., pp. 136–67.
27. Ibid., pp. 167–75.
28. Ibid., pp. 184–85, 111–13.
29. Cf. n. 10 above.
30. *The Doctrine of Revelation* (1956a), p. 113.
31. Ibid., p. 111.
32. Ibid., pp. 185ff.
33. Ibid., p. 519, Frei's emphasis.
34. Barth, 'Antwort Auf Herrn Professor von Harnacks offenen Brief', *Christliche Welt* 37, col. 249, quoted in *The Doctrine of Revelation* (1956a), p. 522.
35. Karl Barth, *The Epistle to the Romans*, p. 158, my emphasis.
36. *The Doctrine of Revelation* (1956a), pp. 557–61.
37. Barth, *The Epistle to the Romans*, p. 158, my emphasis.
38. *The Doctrine of Revelation* (1956a), p. 567–68.
39. Ibid., pp. 504–36.
40. Ibid., pp. 568–70.
41. Ibid., pp. 570–77.
42. Ibid., pp. 136ff.
43. Ibid., p. 191.
44. Cf. Appendix 4.
45. *The Doctrine of Revelation* (1956a), pp. 474–76.
46. Ibid., p. 371.
47. Ibid., p. 470.
48. Cf. ibid., pp. 476, 480–82.
49. See, in particular, chap. 7, §2.
50. Frei discusses these resources briefly in *The Doctrine of Revelation* (1956a), pp. 193–202 but at far greater length in an unpublished paper entitled 'Analogy and the Spirit in the Theology of Karl Barth' (?1960a).
51. 'Analogy and the Spirit' (?1960a), p. 9; cf. *The Doctrine of Revelation* (1956a), pp. 197–98.
52. *The Doctrine of Revelation* (1956a), pp. 557–61.
53. 'Analogy and the Spirit' (?1960a), pp. 1–2.
54. Ibid., pp. 10–11.
55. See chapter 7.
56. 'Analogy and the Spirit' (?1960a), *passim*.
57. Ibid., p. 5.
58. Ibid., p. 2.
59. Ibid., pp. 4, 23.
60. See my later discussion of Barth's figural vision in chapter 7.
61. 'Analogy and the Spirit' (?1960a), p. 20.

62. Ibid., pp. 20–21. The bulk of 'Analogy and the Spirit' is taken up with technical questions. Do the concepts which Barth has borrowed from Idealism allow him to distinguish the Spirit from faith? How does Barth articulate the undoubted difference between his doctrine of the Spirit and Idealism's Absolute Spirit? At one stage, however, Frei turns from this more philosophical analysis to a more properly *dogmatic* analysis, and asks what relation Barth's deployment of analogy has to his Christology, and to his doctrine of providence. On the one hand, in the doctrine of the Word's (enhypostatic) assumption of (anhypostatic) humanity, the fully human nature of Jesus is taken on by the fully divine Word, without there being any confusion or diminution of either nature, and yet with the divine Word having absolute priority. The human nature is not 'necessarily, essentially or internally' connected to the divine Person (although it has no prior existence, or existence outside this relationship), but the divine Person is, by divine election, the 'sufficient ground' of the (full and real) humanity. This provides a paradigm for an understanding of faith whereby faith has God's act as its 'sufficient ground', but is not thereby simply made a necessary addendum of the divine act (pp. 8–9). On the other hand, Barth claims that God's predestinating action is the 'indispensable ground and enabling context' for human freedom: it is only by God having taken the human person away from the mastery of sin and placed him or her on a sure footing that that person is truly free: God's decision in election is the ground of human freedom. This parallels Barth's understanding of faith which would see God's liberating act as its enabling context, the necessary presupposition for the human act of faith to be considered free from bondage (pp. 9–10). This focus on predestination and election is one to which we will return when we examine Barth's figural vision in chapter 7.

63. To avoid possible confusion, one further point should be made: whereas in relationalism, intellectual apprehension was secondary to the immediate relationship with God which took place in human internality, in Barth's analogical theology there is no aspect of the relationship between God and humanity which is 'better' than the analogical relationship which can be true of apprehension. There is no site in the 'geography of the human soul' where this analogical relationship is transcended and immediacy is achieved; *fides qua* is just as creaturely and distinct from God as is *fides quae*. The relationship between God and humanity is analogical all the way down, even though that must be understood in more complex ways once we have broadened our view beyond apprehension.

64. It is worth stressing already that Frei eventually shifted from this conclusion. We will see in the next chapter that he found a response to his questions in *CD* IV/1; in chapter 7 we will see that he then returned to earlier volumes, and found even in II/2 everything he needed for a fuller solution.

65. *The Doctrine of Revelation* (1956a), pp. 478–79.

66. Barth, *The Epistle to the Romans*, pp. 259f., quoted in *The Doctrine of Revelation* (1956a), p. 478.

67. *Karl Barth's Critically Realistic Dialectical Theology* (Oxford: Clarendon Press, 1995), part III; cf. n. 62 above.

68. *The Doctrine of Revelation* (1956a), pp. 574–77.

69. 'The Theology of H. Richard Niebuhr' (*1957b*), p. 111.

70. Which volumes? 'In his *Prolegomena* [Vol. I] it seemed that there was a tendency toward [epistemological] monophysitism ... which is balanced by, but not easily harmonised with, what he later has to say concretely in his anthropology about Jesus the man [volume III.2], and in his doctrine of redemption about reconciliation accomplished through the gospel history and the words and deeds of Jesus [IV.1 and 2]' (ibid., p. 111). Cf., however, n. 64 above.

71. *The Doctrine of Revelation* (1956a), p. 571.

72. Ibid., pp. 72, 78; cf. p. 47.

73. In 'Religion: Natural and Revealed' (*1958a*), Schleiermacher is presented as the builder of a powerful compromise between natural religion and revealed, but it is stressed that 'there was no religion in general, for religion, without a specific historic content, was merely an

empty form. Thus ... Christian faith had no other content than the historic event, Jesus Christ' (p. 313).

74. Strauss, of course, would disagree; see chap. 1, §3.
75. 'The Theology of H. Richard Niebuhr' (*1957b*), p. 112.
76. *The Doctrine of Revelation* (1956a), pp. 36, 78–80.
77. 'Niebuhr's Theological Background' (*1957a*), p. 28.
78. 'The Theology of H. Richard Niebuhr' (*1957b*), pp. 110, 114.
79. The later history of these endeavours, as renewed after the Bultmannian hiatus, is described by Frei (in the days before the Third Quest of the historical Jesus) as having become 'ever more complex, esoteric, and abstruse' ('Theological Reflections', *1966a*, p. 88).
80. 'Niebuhr's Theological Background' (*1957a*), p. 111.
81. Ibid.
82. Bultmann, *New Testament and Mythology* (Philadelphia: Fortress Press, 1984), p. 32, as translated in Kay, *Christus Praesens* (Grand Rapids: Eerdmans, 1994), p. 93.
83. Kay, *Christus Praesens*, p. 119.
84. The *fact* of Jesus Christ is understood differently in each theologian: for Barth, a high Christology is necessary in describing this fact; for Bultmann this is not so. It is equally true that the *content* which Bultmann is consciously eschewing differs in kind from the content which Barth did, eventually, give (in later volumes of the *Church Dogmatics*); for Bultmann, had there been any content to give, it would have been the assured results of historical criticism; for Barth, it is, as we shall see, something rather different.

3

Paying Attention to Jesus

1 Two Hints

Frei found the first hint of a solution to the problem of epistemological monophysitism in the course of his struggles with the work of H. Richard Niebuhr. He devoted his first two academic publications to Niebuhr's work, attempting to understand and evaluate the theology of the man who had first attracted him to academic theology, and who had been a mentor in his PhD studies. Unlike the assessment of Niebuhr's work that he was to give right at the end of his academic career, however, the tone of Frei's early engagement at least with Niebuhr's technical theology was primarily negative. He believed that the 'value theory' which lay at the heart of Niebuhr's theological method was thoroughly relationalist (thoroughly aligned, that is, with the liberalism which Barth had done so much to discredit) and although Frei spent considerable time looking at the ways in which that value theory was qualified and ameliorated by other aspects of Niebuhr's work, it is clear from the essays that Frei considered himself to stand on the Barthian side of the divide.[1]

Nevertheless, in the midst of this critical assessment, Frei was struck by what he regarded as 'so far ... an isolated moment in [Niebuhr's] technical theological writing':[2] the section in *Christ and Culture* called 'Toward a Definition of Christ'.[3] In that section, Niebuhr simply ignored the questions of historical criticism, and chose instead to dwell on the portrait of Jesus painted for us in the Gospels. The Jesus portrayed there cannot, he suggests, be captured by some list of excellences, and particularly not by the claim that he exhibited, above all, some single defining virtue. 'Love', for instance, cannot on its own be made the clue to Jesus' identity without reducing the portrait to the level of an illustration or a diagram; all the rich life of the Gospel portrayals is drained by any such procedure. Rather, we must look to the particular *shaping* which love (or any other proposed defining virtue) receives in Jesus' life: it is love for God and love for humanity in God; it is a love that takes Jesus to the cross. The Jesus depicted in the Gospels is not an exemplification of a virtue or any set of virtues; rather he is the bearer of a life in which virtues are held together in irreducibly particular shapes and patterns, for particular ends. We may, of course, re-describe that portrait in more abstract ways – saying with Niebuhr, for instance, that Jesus is both wholly God-directed as a man, and wholly humanity-directed in unity with his Father – but only if we recognize that such abstractions are simply aids to following the contours of Jesus' manifest teaching and action, not inferences about his inwardness, the simple truth of his identity lying somehow behind the shifting shapes of external history.[4]

Frei saw in these brief hints the germ of a response to epistemological monophysitism without a return to relationalism.[5] Admittedly, Niebuhr does not explicitly pose the question of historical reference, which might be thought to be central to Frei's problem; nevertheless, he claimed that his 'definition' amounted to a new Chalcedonianism, a new approach to high Christology, now grounded in 'moral' rather than 'metaphysical' description.[6] This is a high Christology which tries to establish itself on the ground of Jesus' actions and interactions, a Christology which Niebuhr believes emerges from attention to the details of the complex and contingent story of Jesus' life before God and before his fellow human beings. Frei, worrying away at a Christology which, he thought, achieved its Chalcedonian orthodoxy 'all too easily', with scant attention to the details of Christ's human life, must have found Niebuhr's approach peculiarly enticing – in particular since Niebuhr eschews both a focus on a consciousness lying behind the story of Jesus' public actions, and a reliance upon the description of any existential impact which the depiction of Jesus might have for the faithful, and so avoids the paths which lead most directly to relationalism.[7] This was enough for Frei to declare that this Christological contribution might well 'be one of the most important individual contributions Niebuhr has made to technical, systematic theology'.[8]

Another hint came from Barth himself. By the time that Frei wrote his 1957 essays on Niebuhr, he was already able to say that Barth's tendency to epistemological monophysitism in the earliest volumes of the *Church Dogmatics* was 'balanced by, but not easily harmonised with, what he later has to say concretely in his anthropology about Jesus the man (vol. III/2), and in his doctrine of redemption about reconciliation accomplished through the gospel history and the words and deeds of Jesus (vols. IV/1, IV/2)'.[9] By the time of *The Eclipse of Biblical Narrative*, which Frei completed in 1973, but on which he had been working for considerably longer, he could speak of himself being

> most deeply indebted not to the famous commentary on Romans, nor to *The Doctrine of the Word of God*, the methodological introduction to [Barth's] *Church Dogmatics*, but to the later volumes of that monumental enterprise, beginning approximately with vol. II/2, on the doctrine of divine election. It seems to me that Barth's biblical exegesis is a model of the kind of narrative reading that can be done in the wake of the changes that I describe in this book ... Simply as good instances of this procedure I want to cite, from a vast number of other examples, Barth's remarkable use of figural interpretation of the Old Testament in *Church Dogmatics* II/2, pp. 340–409, and his narrative treatment of the Gospel story in IV/1, pp. 224–28.[10]

We will examine the first of the exegetical passages to which Frei refers in chapter 7. If we turn for now to the second passage we find Barth exhorting us to 'consider this history [i.e., the Gospel history, leading to the passion] carefully once more: how radically puzzling and therefore significant it is just as it stands, factually and without any great attempt to draw attention to it, in its simple character as history'.[11] We find him seeking to explicate his doctrine of the occurrence of reconciliation in Jesus of Nazareth precisely by examining 'the picture of the sayings and acts of Jesus Christ ... within the wider and narrower circle of his disciples, the multitudes, and the spiritual and (on the margin) political leaders of the people'.[12]

> Jesus Christ as he exists in this history cannot ... be merged into all the significances which do, in fact, come to him, or disappear in them. He cannot, therefore, be identified with them or forgotten by reason of them or shamefacedly relegated to the sphere of the purely historical beginning and cause of the thing which really matters, proclamation, faith, fulfilment (and, if possible, the Church and sacraments). He himself is the thing which really matters. He is always Lord over and in everything that has its beginning and cause in him ... He himself and his history as it took place then and there is identical with the Word of God, not with that which may result from the Word of God in the way of proclamation and faith and fulfilment in and through and from us men who hear it. The relationship between the significant thing which he is in himself and the significances which he may acquire for us is an irreversible relationship.
>
> On this basis and in this sense we say and must say, as when we tell a story: It came to pass that Jesus Christ, the Son of God, as man, took our place in order to judge us in this place by allowing himself to be judged in our place. In saying this, and saying it in this way, we keep to the Easter story as the commentary on the Gospel story in the unity and completeness of its first two parts: to the affirmation made in the event of Easter that in and for itself, and in and through the existence of the One who acts and suffers in it, and therefore objectively for us, this Gospel story is the story of redemption.[13]

That Barth is, as he had said himself in the Foreword to this volume, 'in an intensive, though for the most part quiet, debate with Rudolf Bultmann';[14] that he proceeds by insisting on (and, in the rest of the volume, performing) a close reading of the details of the story of the man Jesus of Nazareth;[15] that Barth's response is therefore a direct assault upon Bultmann's epistemological monophysitism; that it is also at the same time a continuation of his assault on relationalism – all this is quite clear, and should make it no surprise that Frei found here a rich resource for answering the question which Barth's own earlier work had thrown up for him.

2 The Gospels and Demythologization

In response to hints like these from Niebuhr and Barth, Frei began in the late 1960s to develop his own constructive Christological proposal.[16] His task, I have suggested, was to produce a Christology (in the narrow sense of an account of the relationship of humanity and divinity in Christ) that was not neutral with respect to the details of Jesus' humanity. Frei did not approach this task in the way one might have expected. He did not analyse and develop a Christology like Barth's, and then show how it was that the details of Jesus' humanity could fit into that scheme; nor did he follow his doctoral thesis with another book on Barth showing how the richer material on Jesus' humanity in the later volumes cohered with and improved upon the Christology of the earlier volumes. Rather, he was determined to strike closer to the root of epistemological monophysitism than that: he decided to *begin* by paying attention to the Gospels, to their complex and multi-faceted depiction of Jesus of Nazareth, and *then* to ask what kind of Christology might fit with these texts.[17] Only by tackling the question in this order did he believe he could develop a Christology that constitutionally avoided epistemological monophysitism. At the risk of being ignored by both systematic theologians and historical critics, Frei resolved that his own first constructive writing would not be a Christology that happened to make good use of the Gospels along the way, but an analysis of the Gospels that succeeded in pointing the way towards a high Christology at the end.

The most important claim with which Frei emerged from his study of the Gospels was that they themselves resist any epistemologically monophysite reading, any reading which feels able to talk about the significance of Jesus without paying close attention to the detailed narratives of his life. He put it most clearly in his 1966 article, 'Theological Reflections on the Accounts of Jesus' Death and Resurrection'. The Gospels themselves are characterized by an 'urgent insistence that the story of salvation is completely and exclusively that of the savior Jesus from Nazareth in Galilee ... [T]he pattern of redemptive action exhibited in Jesus is so identical with his personal story that he pre-empts the pattern. It is *his* story and cannot be reiterated in full by the story of anybody else.'[18]

How Frei believed that this urgent insistence is present in the Gospels will only become clear in the remainder of this chapter. For now, we simply need to see that, for Frei, only by pushing against the grain of one of the Gospel's most 'urgent insistences' could one possibly suggest that the message of the Gospels about salvation, about human flourishing, is something detachable from the messy and complex details of the story they tell. The story told in the Gospels is indeed told as the story of salvation, but this story is identical with the story of one particular human being. The Gospels overcome epistemological monophysitism.

Elsewhere, instead of using this 'two story' terminology, Frei spoke of the holding together in the Gospel depictions of unsubstitutability and cosmic scope. That is, on the one hand Frei believed that it did not make sense to think that the 'same' story of salvation as that related in the Gospels could be told of anyone else, or of any other place and time; the particularity of the story (its configurations of events and circumstances in a given locale) is constitutive for its meaning.[19] Yet on the other hand this story is, precisely as it is told as a story of one particular human character, told as a story of a salvation of cosmic scope, and therefore in a sense as everybody's story. It is a story in which the action of God and the relations of other characters to God are constitutive elements, and a story which leads us to think differently about the relationship between God and ourselves, wherever and whenever we might be – yet without ceasing to be a story which is made up decisively from particular concatenations of events and circumstances among human beings in one particular time and place.

Lastly, as well as speaking of the unity of two stories, and as well as speaking of unsubstitutability and cosmic scope, Frei gives the same point a more obviously theological cast by speaking of Jesus' power and power-lessness, or the 'pattern of exchange'. Because the story of salvation is the story of Jesus of Nazareth who went his way to Calvary, we must say that the story of Christ's power to save is in some way identical with his path to and through death, to and through utter powerlessness.

The task which Frei set himself was to demonstrate, by following the Gospels closely, the existence, the order, and the unity of the two stories, of unsubstitutability and cosmic scope, of power and powerlessness. His task was, in other words, to exhibit, by reading the Gospels, the ways in which Jesus is portrayed as Saviour, not by virtue of some separable and repeatable content illustrated in him, but by virtue of his singular and unsubstitutable life, death and resurrection.

One of Frei's main approaches to this question was a tracing of what happens to generalized descriptions or predictions of Jesus' power to save in the course of the Gospels. Focusing particularly on Luke amongst the Synoptics, Frei first of all suggests that at the start of that Gospel, in the nativity and childhood stories, Jesus is very largely identified by the prophecies he fulfils, by the events of Israel's history which are re-enacted in and around him, and by various epithets drawn from Old Testament sources. He is overwhelmingly identified by the attribution to him of descriptions drawn from elsewhere, which state or hint at his saving significance. Yet, at this stage, there is little sense of a distinguishable, unsubstitutable individual whose identity is manifested in these things which are attributed to him, and whose particularity shapes and configures them. Jesus does not emerge to view as a character who holds all these attributes together in a particular way.[20]

In the next stage of the Gospel identification of Jesus – the ministry – he emerges a little more sharply to view as an unsubstitutable character, but nevertheless largely appears as the representative or embodiment of the Kingdom of God which he preaches and enacts: 'He is now, far more than in the infancy stories, identified in his own right as the son of Joseph of Nazareth, whom everyone knows. However, it is also true that *who* he is is defined by his proclamation of the fulfilment of promise of deliverance to the captives.'[21] The texts are no longer so aptly described as 'mythical' or 'legendary'; rather, in such a way that it is difficult to separate out the elements, they are 'partially stylised and representative and partially focused on the history-like individual'. The particular identity of Jesus of Nazareth still seems secondary to the more general nature of the salvation which he preaches and embodies – i.e., that salvation appears to make sense in a way separable from Jesus himself – yet the emergence alongside the stylized description of a more individuated description begins to raise questions. How is *this* particular man the saviour?[22]

In the third stage, which begins with Jesus setting his face towards Jerusalem, Jesus becomes more and more sharply individuated:

> The connection between Jesus and the Kingdom of God becomes loose, and the figure of Jesus emerges more and more as one whose mission it is to enact his own singular destiny – while the Kingdom of God and the Son of Man who embodies it and its authority fade into the background.[23]

From now on, all more generalized, representative descriptions are called into question by the particular course that this man takes through a set of peculiar circumstances. All thoughts of the coming Kingdom of God, or of the Messianic titles, are unsettled by the strange course into powerlessness that this man takes. The redefinition through which these titles and expectations are put begs a host of questions. How can the one who dies here be the same one who will save Israel? How can this weak one be the one who bears cosmic power? How can the one whose body lies in the grave be the one who was identified as the bearer and fulfilment of Israel's hope of salvation? Individuation comes to the fore – but only, apparently, at the expense of salvific power.[24]

It seems at this point as if the 'story of salvation' and the 'story of Jesus' are in competition: that when the story of salvation is clear, the story of Jesus as an unsubstitutable and particular human being is pushed into the background, and that when Jesus comes to the fore as a fully individuated character with his own particular and unexpected course towards the cross, the story of salvation is rendered obscure and problematic. The Gospels, when they arrive at the cross, have posed for us the question as to how the story of Jesus and the story of salvation cohere, and have asserted that they do; on the cross, however, that assertion seems questionable. *That* the general descriptions of salvation are true of Jesus has been claimed; *how* he reconfigures and transforms them – how they apply to *him*, specifically – has not yet become clear.

Before exploring the answer which the Gospels give to this question, Frei suggests in other, more detailed ways that the Gospel stories themselves constitute a 'demythologization' of the general attributes which are ascribed to Jesus. In the process he places the particular story of Jesus in the foreground, and allows the question of cosmic scope, the story of salvation, the true extent and nature of Jesus' power, to slip temporarily out of view. He begins by suggesting that we should pay careful attention to the form in which the Gospels, particularly the Synoptics, present Jesus' identity to us. They do so, particularly in the passion sequences, by presenting us with a story of public actions and interactions, sayings and incidents. They do so by describing Jesus' climactic public actions as the enactment of crucial intentions, and by depicting the actions of others upon him.[25] To take the Gospels seriously, we must take this form of portrayal seriously, Frei says, rather than automatically regarding it as a secondary and distorting form of identity-description. That is, we must assume that we are not settling for second-best when we settle for the kind of identity-description given of a person in such a story. If we settle for this kind of identity-description, we are in effect assuming *the priority of a kind of identity that can be gained and achieved over time in public*, rather than regarding such public, timely manifestations as the secondary and dispensable display of an identity inherently more private.[26]

Frei knows that there are other ways in which the Gospels present Jesus' identity, and he tries not to deny that plurality. He nevertheless insists that this kind of portrayal of public action and interaction has a certain priority – not in the sense that all other ways that the Gospels have of identifying Jesus for us can be reduced to this level, but in the sense that no other form of identity-depiction offered in the Gospels finally trumps this: no other form of depiction renders this form purely illustrative. For instance, we may be used to describing people's identities by adumbrating the abstract qualities that a person shares: he is kind, she is refined, he is faithless, she is devoted. One temptation we might face is to think that, if the Gospels can be made to yield such a description of Jesus, that set of virtues might turn out to be the real referent of the stories, and the public actions and interactions be seen to be accidental, anecdotal illustrations of that referent. Frei tackles this possibility head on by showing how, although the Gospels do in certain places lend themselves to just such a description of Jesus by a key abstract quality, a closer inspection demonstrates how even there they require us to privilege the story of the intentional actions in which this abstract description is given a particular shape and content.

Frei argues, for instance, that, on the basis of the Gospels and other New Testament material, *obedience* is a better candidate than love if we are seeking for a central defining characteristic of Jesus. He argues that the Gospels do not allow us for a moment to focus on obedience as an abstract deportment, however – as the sort of deportment that would be *illustrated* rather than *constituted* by the specific lines of action, the specific history, in which it is seen.[27] In the first place, 'obedience' is a relational term, and we are unable to describe Jesus' obedience without speaking of the one to whom he was obedient. Even when considered in abstraction from particular stories the idea of obedience always implies a referent, some compulsion or authority that can be obeyed. The description of Jesus as obedient therefore pushes us to consider the relationship between Jesus and the one to whom he is obedient, the one he called Father. Far from taking us away from the detailed story of the Gospels, a focus on obedience will therefore push us towards an attempt to show how Jesus' relationship to the Father is depicted in the Gospels, and we will find that what we learn of Jesus' identity in tracing that relationship is more irreducibly complex than can be grasped by any abstract definition of obedience as a deportment or stance.

In the second place, Frei indicates the extent to which the Gospels as they stand get in the way of our attempt to focus on obedience as an inward deportment. The climactic and most revealing sequence of the story when it comes to understanding obedience as a deportment is in Gethsemane.[28] It is only really here in the Gospels that the passage of intention into action is clearly depicted; only really here that we are given an almost novelistic insight into the nature of Jesus' intentions in tandem with his determined enactment of them. Yet if Gethsemane is a space in the narrative where we might find footing for a focus on obedience as an inner deportment, separable from its specific enactment, the waters swiftly close over the possibility, and we are returned to a description of actions and sufferings, of trials and beatings, which provide scant clues to Jesus' piety or inner life. Gethsemane points forward to the cross, and the narratives surrounding the cross give scant quarter to those on a quest for Christ's inner life.

> The glimpse we are provided within the story of Jesus' intentions is just sufficient to indicate the passage of intention into enactment. And what is given to us is neither intention alone nor action alone, neither inner purpose alone nor external circumstance alone. Rather, he becomes who he is in the coincidence of his enacted intention with the train of circumstances in which the story comes to a head.[29]

In the face of these narratives, those who speak of Christ's obedience are bound, according to Frei, to realize that they are producing a commentary upon what Jesus does and undergoes in this narrative sequence – a commentary, which, however good and appropriate it is, is secondary to that narrative sequence. The Gospels do not let us tarry in Gethsemane, but urge us on towards the cross. To privilege a kind of description that wishes to settle on Jesus' inwardness in Gethsemane is to push against their flow.

So, having started with what he regards as the best candidate for a description of Jesus in terms of a general deportment, Frei has shown how it plunges us into the description of public actions and interactions, of characters in relation, requiring us to tell the story of Jesus' mission, tell the story of the precise form in which Jesus' obedience was enacted. It is not, of course, the case that Frei allows no commentary or conceptual clarification of this story: he is very happy to use 'obedience' as a concept that illuminates a significant aspect of the Gospel narratives. He argues, however, that such concepts, however useful they might be, have to be used in such a way that they point back to the rich and complex narrative which they seek to clarify, rather than being used in such a way as to substitute for the narrative. We are led away from any idea that we might be able to come up with an ahistorical, un-narrated explanation of the coherence of Jesus' identity, and towards the recognition that, if there is such a coherence, it will only be found by telling a story of unfolding action and interaction in time, which includes the unfolding story of Jesus' relationship with the one he called Father. This is, in the case of the Gospels, the shape that unsubstitutability takes.

3 Power, Powerlessness and Resurrection

After his analysis of 'obedience', Frei looks at the particular ways in which the concepts 'power' and 'powerlessness' can illuminate the Gospels, and can help us to grasp something of their intractable shape.[30] Once again, he shows that investigation of the meaning and appropriateness of the concepts 'power' and 'powerlessness' as applied to the identity of Jesus leads us directly into consideration of a complex narrative that configures and specifies them. He notes, first of all, that Jesus' obedience involves, at both the level of intention and the level of action, a *transition* from power to powerlessness. We move from a strong, continuous narrative line in which it makes sense to claim that Jesus' identity is gained and displayed in climactic actions, to a sequence in which those actions are more and more pushed into the background, superseded by the actions of others. Jesus submits to having the initiative taken from him; his obedient intention is one that eventually renders his ability to intend and act deeply problematic. There are hints, certainly, of abiding power (particularly in the Fourth Gospel) but Jesus eventually allows himself to become powerless.

Second, this transition from power to powerlessness, seen in Jesus' increasing enmeshment in circumstances which he did not initiate, is seen as a submission to the Father. There is a strange identification of the 'historical circumstances' which overtake Jesus with God: Jesus submits his will to the Father's in the Garden, and it is God who allows and even initiates all the circumstances which overtake Jesus; it is God who remains in control and from whom any control which other characters may seem to have has come; it is God, not the soldiers, to whom Jesus calls out in the cry of dereliction. The depiction of Jesus' obedience to the Father in the Gospels requires us to look at the complexity of the narratives' identification of the Father whose intentional action is hidden in the deeds of the betrayers, the crowd and the crucifying soldiers.[31]

Third, however, Jesus retains his own distinct identity to the very end. Jesus' identity does not, in the passion narrative, become submerged by God, even when his intentional actions have disappeared under God's.[32] Jesus remains in view. For a long time, of course, he continues to act, and 'his intentions and actions ... retain their personal quality and weight', but even when that ceases to be true, he does not stop being himself. We are not presented with a sequence in which the Gospels' focus finally slips away from the man, Jesus of Nazareth, and on to God.

In other words: the Gospels force upon us the question of the relationship between Jesus' power to save, and his powerlessness as one creaturely being among others who in his particularity is buffeted by the actions and intentions of others. When we pay attention to that question, and ask how the relationship of power and powerlessness is *narrated* in the Gospels, we find that we are forced to consider the irreducibly complex relationship between Jesus and the one he called Father, and we find that the cross is the point at which the question of the relationship of Jesus to the one he called Father becomes most difficult and most urgent. This should, by now, be no surprise: we saw that it was on the cross that the question of the identity between the story of Jesus and the story of salvation, the question of the 'demythologization' of generalized expectations by their specific attribution to Jesus of Nazareth, was repeated most sharply. We saw that the cross forces upon us the question as to whether and how this handing over to death relates to the mission of salvation to which Jesus declared obedience in Gethsemane.

It is on the cross that all these questions become unavoidable – but the story does not stop at the cross: Jesus appears again in the resurrection.[33] It is in the resurrection that the Gospel writers begin providing answers. Of course, the resurrection accounts do not provide neat *explanations* of how this powerless man is truly powerful, of how Jesus is the Saviour, of how his unsubstitutability coheres with cosmic scope – they appeal to no theory which would explain how it is that items of this nature can be held together. Nevertheless, the affirmation that this man is indeed powerful, that the crucified one is indeed the Messiah, rings out again. Here, more than anywhere, our gaze is prevented from turning away from Jesus to some more general referent of his message, or towards his Father: our attention is caught and held tightly by the resurrected man from Nazareth. There is a repeated insistence that this is the same Jesus who went his way to the cross (he is the one, after all, who bears the scars of crucifixion; he is the one who can forgive Peter who had betrayed him; he is the one who can allow the disciples to recognize him). He is able now, as the bearer of a complex and unexpected identity, to show how it is that he is indeed the one long expected: 'Beginning with Moses and all the prophets, he interpreted to them in all the scriptures the things *concerning himself*.'[34] Whatever the dynamics in earlier portions of the Gospel narratives by which Jesus pointed away from himself to his message, or pointed away from himself to his Father, or handed initiative over to that Father, here he himself becomes the focus in his identity as the one who was dead but is now risen. There is, says Frei, an 'absolute coincidence of his manifestation with his unsubstitutable individuality'.[35]

It is also in the resurrection accounts that the final, decisive complexity is added to the Gospels' account of the relationship between Jesus and the one he calls Father. In the passion narratives Jesus' obedience to God, his handing over of his intention to God, led to the gradual submersion of Jesus beneath God's hand hidden in the opaque material of history. Now, Jesus is raised from the dead by God[36] – and yet in the Gospel narratives of the resurrection God does not appear. This is, in this narrative, God's climactic action, and yet only Jesus appears. The focus in these passages on the manifestation of Jesus' particular identity means that a kind of reversal has taken place, a reversal foreshadowed by the baptism and transfiguration narratives: at the climax of Jesus' mission of obedience to the Father, at the climax of his being handed over, and handing himself over, to the Father, it is not the Father who appears but Jesus. Instead of effacing himself in favour of the one to whom he points, the Gospels culminate with Jesus becoming most fully visible, most fully the focus of attention.[37] The Father is, curiously, left somewhat in the background in the resurrection narratives: God acts, but Jesus appears.[38] It is in *this* reversal, Frei claims, that the story of salvation and the story of Jesus are fused into one.

4 Conclusion

I have argued that tackling the question of epistemological monophysitism without falling into relationalism is the move Frei believed he must make first, if he were to attempt an answer to Strauss – an answer to the question of faith and history – along Barthian lines. That is, Frei needed to show that we can make sense of the claim that Jesus' historical humanity is caught up into relationship with God without losing its character as historical. Following hints from both Barth and H. Richard Niebuhr, Frei approached this question from an unexpected direction: arguing that the Gospels, read precisely as stories of Jesus' public actions and interactions rather than as stories of his religious inwardness, are stories about God: precisely *as* historical, these stories are stories of divine manifestation. The story of God's decisive action on behalf of humanity is not a deeper meaning, an inner meaning, to which this story of outer history points, but is this story itself. God's decisive action on behalf of humanity *is* Jesus of Nazareth: God acts, but Jesus appears.

Of course, in order to turn this claim about the Gospels into a response to Strauss, more is needed. On the one hand, something needs to be said about the connection between these stories and the kind of history to which historical-critical endeavour seeks to gain access: 'What really happened?' On the other hand, something needs to be said about how it is that readers of this story may take account of it. Frei, as we shall see, does go on to seek an answer to both these questions. What he does not do, however, is provide a theory to *explain* what has been asserted here. At no point in the chapters that follow will we find Frei presenting some mechanism by which God was able to arrange for Jesus' history to take the shape that it took, or some argument demonstrating that history has sufficient malleability to allow for that shaping. Frei will not, for instance, discuss Quantum Mechanics and argue that the indeterminacy of history at the quantum level allows sufficient leeway for God to make a portion of history bear a divine stamp without seriously violating its natural integrity. Strauss had not, after all, asked whether God could manipulate history without damaging the bonds which held it together, but had asked whether it was possible to speak of divine self-manifestation in history without automatically falling into *nonsense*, without automatically saying that the history involved ceases to have the character of history. The heart of Frei's answer is that the Gospel's way of speaking about divine self-manifestation in history does not give that question purchase, because the Gospel's claim is that God has spoken precisely in the language of history – the language of contingent, finite, complex and messy public actions and interactions. How God 'managed' to do such a thing is a mystery which Frei refuses to probe; what it means to claim that God has in fact worked in this way is the question which occupied him and will occupy us in the coming chapters.[39]

Notes

1. It was, perhaps, the publication of this critique that led to Frei's 1957 'falling out' with Niebuhr, described in Woolverton, 'Hans W. Frei in Context', p. 389.
2. 'The Theology of H. Richard Niebuhr' (1957b), p. 116.
3. Niebuhr, Christ and Culture (1952), pp. 26–43.
4. See 'The Theology of H. Richard Niebuhr' (1957b), pp. 107–16; Niebuhr, Christ and Culture (1952), pp. 26–43.
5. He introduces it in explicit contrast to his account of epistemological monophysitism ('The Theology of H. Richard Niebuhr', 1957b, p. 107) and spends considerable time distinguishing it from the kind of relationalist Christology discussed in the last chapter (pp. 114–16).
6. Although 'Niebuhr is right in saying that this portrait needs to be complemented ... by historical and metaphysical portraits' (p. 116); cf. Appendix 3.
7. Niebuhr's approach avoids both epistemological monophysitism and 'the psychologizing view' which sees the unity of divine and human in Christ as taking place in a 'substratum disconnected from or at best inferentially connected with his moral, historical acts'. 'It seems to me that in the avoidance of the two extremes outlined and in the actual countersuggestion of an understanding of Jesus' personhood significant for Christology, we have the core of the real importance of Niebuhr's essay.' 'In this brief outline of Christology, Niebuhr takes a new and suggestive departure, and goes beyond the question of methodology to actual theological content' ('The Theology of H. Richard Niebuhr', 1957b, pp. 114–16).
8. Ibid., p. 116.
9. Ibid., p. 111.
10. Preface to The Eclipse of Biblical Narrative (1973f), p. viii.
11. CD IV/1, p. 224.
12. Ibid.
13. Ibid., p. 228.
14. Ibid., p. ix.
15. See, for example, Barth's astonishing discussion of Gethsemane in ibid., pp. 259–73.
16. The first version of Frei's constructive Christology is found in an article published in the winter of 1966 Christian Scholar: 'Theological Reflections on the Accounts of Jesus' Death and Resurrection' (1966a). Soon afterwards, in the first and second quarters of 1967, a much longer version of the same proposal was published in Crossroads, an adult education magazine of the Presbyterian Church: 'The Mystery of the Presence of Jesus Christ' (1967a). Later in that year, in December, Frei delivered a paper at Harvard Divinity School in which he commented upon the proposal: 'Remarks in Connection with a Theological Proposal' (1967b). Some years later in 1975 the Crossroads version was republished in book form, with minor changes, as The Identity of Jesus Christ (1975a). The book form added to the original text a final reflection (?1974f), and a critical 'Preface' (1974i). Frei also published in 1974 the much more substantial Eclipse of Biblical Narrative (1974a), on which he had

been working throughout the period in which these various versions of his constructive proposal had appeared; although very different in approach and focus, *Eclipse* is closely related to Frei's constructive proposal.

17. Note: with these *texts*, *not* with the 'historical Jesus' lying behind these texts and reconstructed by historical criticism.
18. 'Theological Reflections' (*1966a*), p. 46.
19. Ibid., pp. 46, 48.
20. Ibid., p. 77; cf. *The Identity of Christ* (*1975a*), pp. 128–30.
21. Ibid., p. 131, Frei's emphasis.
22. 'Theological Reflections' (*1966a*), p. 78; cf. *The Identity of Jesus Christ* (*1975a*), pp. 130–32.
23. Ibid., pp. 133–34.
24. 'Theological Reflections' (*1966a*), pp. 78–82; cf. *The Identity of Jesus Christ* (*1975a*), pp. 132–35.
25. Ibid., pp. 102–15.
26. See chap. 5, §2 for more detail.
27. Ibid., pp. 105–11.
28. Ibid., p. 111.
29. Ibid., p. 104.
30. Ibid., pp. 112–25.
31. We will see in chapter 5 how this passivity begins to raise questions for Frei's intention–action scheme for identity description, most particularly when the Gospel accounts finally reach the grave, where it is only others who have intentions and actions: Jesus is dead, and has none.
32. Frei also very briefly mentions an extent to which Jesus' 'intentions and actions become increasingly identified with those of the very God who governs the actions of the opponents of Jesus who destroy him' (ibid., p. 118), but does not elaborate at this stage. Cf. Appendix 3.
33. Ibid., pp. 139–52; 'Theological Reflections' (*1966a*), pp. 80–82.
34. Luke 24.27, quoted in ibid., p. 81, Frei's emphasis.
35. Ibid., p. 81.
36. Frei stresses that the resurrection does not appear in these stories as organically connected to the cross – as, we might say, the other side of the cross's coin. Rather the transition from the cross to the resurrection is presented as genuinely contingent. That is why we must speak of God raising Jesus from the dead rather than of Jesus raising himself, and rather than speaking of the resurrection following as a natural concomitant to the cross.
37. That is, the Gospels themselves perform the transition from 'proclaimer' to 'proclaimed'.
38. Ibid., p. 81.
39. As I have already suggested (chap. 1, §4), Frei is interested in exploring Christian theology on its own terms, and seeing where the claims of history might fit within that theology. We will be discussing this method in more detail in chapter 8.

4

The Mystery of Christ's Presence

For Frei, any attempt to tell the story of salvation in such a way that it could be separable from the story of Jesus of Nazareth – or to tell the story of Jesus of Nazareth in such a way that a separable story of salvation could be derived from it – brushes against the nap of the Gospel narratives. Yet although we have traced the arguments by which Frei justified his claim that the Gospels insist upon the unity of the story of Jesus and the story of salvation, we still need to turn more squarely to face the question of the nature of that story of salvation. How does the story which Frei has told, the story of Jesus of Nazareth, turn out to be a story which includes its readers, a story of salvation? How does this story of how one part of history was defined by its relationship with God give rise to an account of how history more generally might conform to God?

1 The Presence of Christ

In the Gospels, Frei argued, we at first see Jesus interpreted in terms of the people of God, as that people's representative and that people's Saviour. In the body of the Gospels this identification is called into question by the particular identity which this unsubstitutable person gains. He acquires a specificity and density which is not easy to see as the stuff of recapitulation or representativeness. Yet, in the final sequence, the one Jesus has pointed to as his Father points back to him in a strange reversal, and directs the people's eyes to the resurrected man from Nazareth. God acts, but Jesus appears. Frei puts this in an unexpected way:

> [W]hereas at the beginning, in the first stage of the account, it was the community which served to identify him, the reverse is now true. He, Jesus, provides the community and its whole history with his identity, just as he imposes it on the mythical savior figure.[1]

More fully:

> He, the Christ, can now interpret to them 'in all the scriptures the things concerning himself.' ... Jesus of Nazareth ... as that one man, is the redeemer undergoing in obedience all that constitutes the climax and summation of Israel's history ... His identity is so unsubstitutable now through the event of resurrection that he can

79

bring it to bear as the identifying clue for the community that becomes climactically focused through him. Indeed, the New Testament will ask just this of all men: To identify themselves by relation, not just to a universal hero or savior figure, but to Jesus of Nazareth, who has identified himself with them and for them.[2]

From being the one whose general identity was imposed upon him by the people of God, using the materials that lay to hand, Jesus has become the specific one to whom they are called to look for a transformation of their identity. In the resurrection, it at last becomes clear that the Father has not allowed Jesus to be the bearer of a separable message about salvation, about the calling and identity of the people; the Father has not sent a messenger who can fade into the background once the message has been delivered. In the resurrection, God ensured that the focus fell on the manifestation of Jesus' identity. On reaching the end of the message, the people are directed to look up again from its pages, and see the one who delivered it: if anything, the message now fades in favour of the messenger's face. Far from allowing Jesus to efface himself, the Father in these narratives hides himself in Jesus. If the people will know their salvation, their transformed identity, their renewed relationship with YHWH, they must henceforth understand it in relation to the particular identity of the man from Nazareth.

And yet: the identity of Jesus Christ to which the people are pointed is precisely an identity which does not lend itself easily to 'use'. Jesus' identity is unsubstitutable, and it is no simple matter to read it as the identifying clue for a people. If the people of God are to understand themselves in terms of this identity, they will not be able to do so simply by generalizing from this identity, or by repeating it. How, then?[3]

The strange logic of the resurrection stories suggests that the manifestation of Jesus' identity takes place as the enactment of God's climactic intention: God acts but Jesus appears. In the light of this manifestation, we can no longer think of God except by thinking about Christ, and we can no longer think about Christ except by thinking about God. On the one hand, to think about Jesus at all is to think about the complex relation he has to the Father that is a constitutive and climactic part of his identity. On the other hand, the Father has declared himself for the Son; enacting in the resurrection the intention indicated at the baptism and the transfiguration, God makes it impossible any longer to think of God without being drawn to look at Christ. To think, therefore, about the God who is present, who creates, sustains and draws us, is also to think about Christ. We may not think about God's presence without also thinking about Christ. To the extent that 'presence' is an appropriate description to use for God's relationship to the world, we may say that God's presence is a Christ-shaped presence, a presence which we cannot think of as taking place apart from Christ or remotely from Christ.[4]

Yet Frei points to the fact that God has raised Jesus from the dead, so that Jesus is no longer dead but alive. For Frei, this means that the one of whom God requires us to think when we think of God's action for our salvation is, by the very same act of God, one who continues to live, continues to be active, continues to have what Frei calls his own, 'self-focused presence'.[5] The one of whom we must think when we think of God and God's impingement upon the world, of whom we must think when we think of God's action on our behalf, cannot be thought of as a finished fact of the past, but must be thought of as living and active. We may not think of God's presence to us as not being Christlike, and yet may not think of its Christlikeness as its qualification by an isolated past fact: we must think in some sense of the presence of God as being qualified by the continuing life of Jesus of Nazareth.

However, if we try to step from this to thinking about this presence of God as being directly and straightforwardly the presence of Christ, we run into difficulties. If such a presence of Jesus is to be the presence of the one who is identified in the Gospel accounts, then it is not a presence which we can think of primarily as the presence of inwardness to inwardness behind the alienated objectifications of the public world. Affirmations of such a presence would swim against the flow of the portrayals we have of the one who is present. Faced with portrayals like this, the kind of presence which makes sense is more public manifestation than it is inner communion, and to order things differently is to make a break between presence and identity, to turn away from the Gospels in order to think about religious significance. If we are to think about a *continued presence* of Jesus in any way, and have it still as a continued presence *of Jesus*, we will have to think of the kind of presence that works by means of the public mediations through which selves manifest what they are. Yet after the ascension, that is clearly no straightforward matter.

As well as being forced to think of Jesus' presence (if we think of it at all) as in some sense public, we must think of it as in some sense *embodied*. We must think of the presence of Jesus as the presence of the same one who was born of the Virgin Mary, who suffered under Pontius Pilate, was crucified, died and was buried. We must think of it as the presence of the same one who, being raised, walked among the disciples, and was eventually raised in their sight, leaving them behind. We may not think of his presence in such a way as to leave these things behind, as if they were simply the disposable chrysalis from which the true Christ bursts at the resurrection. Any presence which we deem Jesus to have is the presence of one who is still, in some sense, embodied and particular: one whom we must think of as still bearing the scars of his crucifixion, bearing his physicality transformed but intact. The presence of God to us is a presence which we can no longer think apart from, disunited from, this embodiment.

And we must think of any continuing presence that can be affirmed of the Jesus of the Gospels as being an *active* presence. If this presence is to be the presence of one who has his own 'self-focused' life, one who is alive, then it is not the power of the believer's imagination which makes thoughts of Christ's presence true. It is, Frei wants to say, Christ's ability to present himself, his ability as one who is still a living and unsubstitutable individual to share himself with us as his own free act, which allows the claim to be true. We are constrained to think of Christ's presence, if we think of it at all, as an active bestowal.

So: if the resurrection narratives require us to think of the presence of God to us in terms of Jesus of Nazareth, they also prevent us from thinking of Jesus in any other way than as one who has his own continued identity as an unsubstitutable human being. We have no way of thinking about the continuing presence of Jesus without thinking of it as public, embodied, active; to think of it in other ways is to leave behind the Gospel identifications of Jesus. We may not, as Frei has stressed time and time again, think of Christ as detached from this public, active particularity.

The best that Frei could do, when trying to summarize his conclusions, was to rely upon a double negative. We may not, he said, think of Christ as *not* present; we may not think of this continued active embodiment as *not* impinging upon us – but, just as surely, we find we cannot directly conceive of Christ as directly present. How could we grasp such a presence? How can we understand a presence which is not, in our liturgies, our experience, our affirmations, any longer confined by the ordinary rules of physical location, yet one which must be thought of as the active manifestation of one who is embodied? Our imaginations break down when we try to hold all these elements together: we cannot imagine this continued existence (if we try to imagine it at all) without imagining some kind of locatable spatial existence as a body among other bodies, yet it seems that we cannot do justice to the God-sized scope of this presence if we do imagine Christ's continuing life in this way.[6]

In the face of this complexity, Frei turns to talk of the Holy Spirit.[7] Christians, he says, have long acknowledged the complexity of the Christ-shaped presence of God, and have long acknowledged the ambiguity of describing this presence directly as Christ's presence. They have avoided sheer contradiction by talking about the Holy Spirit as the one who mediates this complex presence, a presence which is God's presence and which is Christ-shaped, and which both is and is not the presence of Christ. When we speak simply of the 'presence of Christ' in what follows, it is (following long Christian usage) this complex Spirit-mediated presence to which we refer.[8]

2 Christ and the Church

We are still some way from discovering what the story of salvation is that Frei thinks is identical to the story of Jesus. All that has been said so far simply clarifies some of the ground-rules, the *grammar*, which the story of salvation must respect.[9] Frei goes on, however, to provide brief but suggestive accounts of how the identity of individual believers, and the identity of the people of God, is constituted by this complex presence of Christ.

At the level of the individual, the affirmations about which we have been speaking are, we might say, 'self-involving'. To understand the identity-description presented in the Gospels is to be faced with a claim that God cannot be thought of without thinking of Jesus of Nazareth, and that Jesus of Nazareth is the one to whom God has directed our gaze. This is not a person who can be kept at arm's length. If the Gospels are an apt identity-description, then Jesus of Nazareth has become unavoidably significant for each of us.[10] The Gospels present us, in other words, with a challenge to any idea or practice which we had previously understood *remoto Christo*.

To be won by the identity-description given by the Gospels is first of all, Frei claims, to be drawn into a 'strange unity of factual affirmation with commitment and love'.[11] Such commitment will involve a transformation of our action in the world, for now it is re-presented to us as the world for which Christ died. Other people are re-presented to us as our brothers and sisters, our neighbours. '[C]oncerning Jesus Christ and him alone, factual affirmation is completely one with faith and trust of the heart, with love of him, and love of the neighbors for whom he gave himself completely.'[12] The story is, in this sense, 'overwhelmingly affective', 'an absolute personal impingement'.[13] Accepting the description of any other identities need have no such consequence: there will always be somewhere we can go to escape from the limited impingement they imply; with this identity, and with this identity alone, we find that the central claim made for the one described – the linchpin around which the rest of the identity depiction is arranged – is the inseparability of this identity from the one presence which we cannot escape, even in the grave.

It is important to be cautious when presenting this point. Frei insists both that this unity of factual affirmation and commitment is a gift of the Spirit, and that its existential impact is a consequence of the particular identity description given in the text – and should be governed in its scope, intensity and kind by consideration of that particularity. This is not, in other words, simply another example of the existential possibilities opened up by reading texts, to be governed by a general account of what can and does take place in the activity of reading. This is not a *hermeneutical* account of self-involvement. In fact, it may well be that if we seek to do some justice to the God-sized significance of what is depicted in this particular text we will find that any broader, more generally applicable ideas about existential appropriation and about hermeneutical possibilities are exceeded and transformed – or 'scrambled', to use Frei's word – when we bring them to this particular text.[14]

In any case, Frei's concern is far less with this individual transformation, which he appears to mention almost solely in order to call into question the kind of hermeneutical account which would take it as paramount, and far more with the nature of the Church.[15] While what he has said about individual self-involvement could be read as the unfolding of an implication of what he has said about Jesus' identity and presence, what he goes on to say about the Church does not have the same deductive logic to it, but rather starts in the middle. Rather than asking what understanding of the Church might be *derived* from the account he has given, he uses his complex account of Christ's presence and identity to criticize existing claims about the Church: in part confirming them, and in part calling them into question.

He begins by showing that the account he has given can provide a good deal of support to a high ecclesiology. The details of Frei's account are not altogether clear to me, but something like the following seems to be involved.[16] We may think of Word and Sacrament as means by which the unsubstitutable particularities of Christ's identity are made known in the world, and made known aptly, not in a necessarily distorted fashion. Here is where the stories of Christ are repeated, and aspects of his engagement with others are re-enacted. Here is where the Church proclaims and displays the unsubstitutable identity of its Saviour, and refuses to replace that identity with some more tractable idea or programme.[17]

Word and Sacrament cannot be a presentation of the Gospel identity of Jesus, however, if they are treated as actions in control of the Church, such that the Church metes out the presence of a Christ whose identity is fundamentally finished, and therefore manipulable. Only if they are thought of as in some sense Christ's own act, through the Holy Spirit, can Word and Sacrament be presentations of the identity of the risen, Gospel Christ. Word and Sacrament must be thought of, if we are to do justice to the Gospel identification of Jesus in what we say about them, as Christ's *active* bestowal of his identity. If we do this, then Word and Sacrament cease to be simply memorials of Christ's identity, and become something like a verbal and a physical basis for his continuing presence, a basis in some ways similar to the verbal and physical basis which ordinary interpersonal presence involves. Believers may take Word and Sacrament to be the word of Christ and the body and blood of Christ, and instead of being an act in which they take the Word and the Sacrament to be something which really they are not, or an act in which they transform those words and objects into something new, they may (without breaking Frei's strictures) affirm that this act of imagination genuinely and truly responds to a prior act of Christ. Such an affirmation does far more justice to the complex nature of Christ's presence, Frei suggests, than any relationalist affirmation of a presence-to-inwardness: Word and Sacrament are sufficiently public, sufficiently embodied, that they may appropriately present to us, and refer us to, the public and embodied presence of Christ, and yet also show, sufficiently clearly, that they are not straightforwardly identical with it.[18] If by 'Church' we mean that body which is *constituted* by Word and Sacrament, we may say that, in a sense, the Church *is* the continued self-bestowal of Jesus of Nazareth.

Frei affirms all this before insisting upon a serious qualification. He suggests that such an affirmation is still in danger of taking us too far from the unsubstitutable identity of Jesus' presence. Frei emphasized again, as he has emphasized all along, that the Gospel narratives render the identity of Jesus as an unsubstitutable individual with his own historical specificity and density, his own (continuing) life – and therefore as an individual who is not exhausted by any narratives about him, nor by any acts of bestowal. While we might be able to affirm that the identity of Jesus can be truly bestowed in Word and Sacrament, we cannot claim that his identity is wholly bestowed in this way. Jesus may not be transformed into the Church without remainder. The Church can neither claim to be an identical repetition of Jesus, nor claim to have control over his presence: Jesus is free.

If we try to do justice to this, we can only qualify our high claims about Church and Sacrament by saying, in the next breath, that nevertheless the Church can only be a 'following after' with its own specificity and historical density[19] whose re-presentations of Jesus' identity are secondary to that identity. Jesus and the Church are not identical: he is his intention–action pattern with others through history; the Church is, in turn, its own intention–action pattern with others through history.

And this is not all. There is another complexity of proper talk of Christ's presence which we also need to allow to qualify any affirmation that the Church is in some sense the indirect abiding presence of Christ. That is the claim that Jesus' significance is found in his inseparability from the presence of the God of all history. A direct and exclusive identification of the presence of Jesus with the Church's performances of Word and Sacrament, which are not the whole of history, would make this presence something other than the indirect presence of Jesus in unity with the God of all history. It would, in effect, be a denial of Jesus' and his Father's 'presence in and to the shape of public events of the world and of human history'.[20] Therefore, Frei says, we need to balance any claim that the Church embodies Christ's presence by the power of the Spirit, not just by a recognition of the Church's and Jesus' unsubstitutability, but 'by saying that the Church is simply the witness to the fact that it is Jesus Christ and none other who is the ultimate presence in and to the world'.

3 Christ and the World

This last comment brings us to the doctrinal locus where the weight of Frei's account of Jesus' presence rests: the doctrine of providence. We may no longer think of God without thinking of Jesus of Nazareth; that is, we may no longer think of the one in whom the whole of history is providentially ordered without thinking of the one who lived and died and rose again in first-century Palestine. History is, in some sense, 'providentially ordered in the life, death, and resurrection of Jesus Christ'.[21] To put it another way, Jesus Christ is the truth of the world: he is the one whom God, who orders all things, has given as his promise to the world. And he is this promise precisely as the one whose identity is not hidden but manifest, and given to us in the unsubstitutable portrayal which it has been Frei's concern to acknowledge. The way that Frei understands providence, then, is from the beginning located with respect to the complex shapes of the Gospel depiction of Jesus of Nazareth.

For instance, Frei had argued that the 'pattern of exchange' is one of the fundamental shapes which these narratives take: that strange reversal by which Christ's power to save is submerged entirely beneath his powerlessness, and then declared in the resurrection in such a way that the powerlessness is not simply removed but is made the material of his power. It is this powerless–powerful one who is given by God as his promise to the world; and Frei claims that, in that case, the pattern of exchange is an aspect of the truth of the world, not just of this one particular identity. On this basis, believers may search for 'events in the history of mankind at large that may parabolically bespeak the presence of Christ':[22]

> Jesus Christ, precisely because he is not only an individual but an individual in a narrated story, serves as a parable. Hints of the pattern of union through the agonised exchange of radical opposites do break forth in history. In the story of Jesus itself this stage is not simply transcended by his resurrection. Unlike the dying and rising savior myth, Jesus' death remains a once-for-all and significant occasion that has its own final and ineradicable 'thereness', after the fashion of all historical events. The same is true of all terrible sacrifices dimly setting forth the same pattern. The pattern itself looks toward reconciliation, redemption, and resurrection, but as yet there is no full realization of it for the creatures of history, though the hope is there.[23]

To put this another way: Frei is able, on the basis of the narrative of Christ's death, burial and resurrection, to see the world as awaiting resurrection – not as the organic consequence of its powerlessness, but as the fulfilment of the promise of God in Christ, fulfilled in such a fashion that the powerlessness itself becomes the material of the resurrected life. The identity of Jesus Christ helps him both tentatively to identify much in the world which calls for resurrection, and, more boldly, to specify the kind of hope which Christians may have in the face of such things.

> Surely the pattern of this agony and hope may be discerned in such instances as a nation of brothers fighting a civil war to purge itself of the curse of slavery and so achieve concretely a union previously little more than a contractual arrangement. One may dimly discern the same pattern in the equally agonised and uncertain fight of the same nation to complete the unfinished task of reconciliation of those who have lived in estrangement from each other because of racial discrimination. Dare we hope that the terrible suffering inflicted on a small East Asian people by the defensive provinciality of a large power may someday in retrospect exhibit the same pattern of reconciliation of extreme opposites, instead of mere aimless and terrible futility?[24]

Frei is very cautious about pushing this argument too far, however. 'Hope' is the keynote of his understanding of Christ-like providence, rather than 'optimism'. He advocates no less than hope, because he is not suggesting a pious wish for nice things, but a robust theological vision which funds and shapes action. He advocates no more than hope, however, because the illumination which shows us that hope is of a particular kind. First, Jesus Christ cannot be for us a diagram or a principle: he is a person. His passion and resurrection, for example, are, 'in the first place, not a parable at all, but an event climactically summing up a series of events'.[25] Any understanding of Jesus' significance which thinks it can read off from him a grid to lay across the messy tapestry of history is relegated to a secondary and subordinate place by this recognition. The clue we have been given to the truth of the world is an unsubstitutable person, and is worked out in a world which has its own unsubstitutability.

> The providential action of God over and in his creation is not that of a mechanical fate to be read off of one occasion. God's work is mysteriously, abidingly mysteriously, coexistent with the contingency of events. The history of his providence is one that must be narrated.[26]

Second, we must also do justice to the complex unity between the unsubstitutable identity of Jesus and the presence and action of the Father. The two are 'given together indissolubly'.[27] When talking of 'the presence of God as the determining impulse of the providential course of history', we must 'abide by the New Testament's complex rather than simple identification', and that means that the future summing up cannot be thought to be

> simply a recapitulation in more enormous scope of the events of the story of Jesus. Beyond this confession the believer cannot go. Either to affirm that it is simply Jesus Christ as he was in past history, or to affirm that it is simply God manifest in Jesus rather than Jesus Christ himself, who will stand at the latter end, is an unwarranted short-cut of the New Testament's complexity and therefore an illegitimate dissolution of its mysteriousness.[28]

Frei expresses this twofold reservation by means of a carefully stated eschatology, which gives to all statements about providence and the truth of the world an eschatological provisionality.

> The parabolic application of Christ's passion and resurrection is limited. It does not light up all history. (It is, in the first place, not a parable at all, but an event climactically summing up a long series of events.) This is the clue it provides: There will be a summing up of history, a summing up of the history of the church together with the world. It will be a summing up in which not only the events we find significant by the use of certain parables but all events will find their place.[29]

We can perhaps use our own parable to make the shape of Frei's point clearer. It is not one he himself offers, although it springs from the parallel he draws between Jesus' 'individual and climactic summing up, incorporation, and identification' of Israel at his first advent, and his 'as yet undisclosed historical summing up' to come. We have referred before to Jesus' words to the two men on the road to Emmaus: 'And beginning from Moses and from all the prophets, he interpreted to them in all the scriptures the things concerning himself.'[30] Perhaps the best way to think of the future summing up of the whole of the history of the world is to think of Jesus Christ, in some unguessable mode in the future, beginning from creation and the various cradles of history, and interpreting to us in all our stories, in all our tellings and retellings of the complexities of history as well as in all the things left untold, the things concerning himself: finally and comprehensively, but without explaining them away or denying the diversity of description appropriate to them; without denying the reality, density and irreducibility of those events, any more than Jesus on the road to Emmaus explained away Moses and the Prophets.

4 Conclusion

Frei's arguments represent further important steps in his quest to answer Strauss. On the basis of a re-description of the identity of Jesus Christ which takes absolutely seriously its contingent and particular shape, Frei has sketched an ecclesiology which, although it can see the Church as constituted by Christ's active bestowal in Word and Sacrament, nevertheless insists upon the Church's thoroughly historical nature; and he has sketched a doctrine of providence, which sees history as illuminated by the 'parabolic application' of patterns of Christ's life, death and resurrection, and yet, because it acknowledges that this illumination is qualified by the always-greater richness of Christ's identity, insists upon the enduring intractability of history. In other words, he has begun to show in more detail that a theology which begins with the Gospel depiction of Christ's identity will hold that Jesus is the manifestation of the divine life without denying either his fully historical reality, the fully historical reality of the Church which follows him, or the fully historical reality of the world the Church interprets by him. Instead, by sticking close to the Gospels, Christians will find that the fully historical reality – the contingency and finitude and particularity – of all three is not just allowed but insisted upon.

It is worth, I think, raising a query at this point to which we will not be returning until the final chapters of this book. These sketches and hints of a broader dogmatic theology have an ambiguous status in Frei's work. By the time that *Identity* was published in 1975 (some years after the bulk of the material we have been examining was written, in 1967) Frei was already unsure whether he had taken quite the right approach.[31] He felt both that he had placed too much reliance upon the category 'presence', and that he had taken too thoroughly an intellectual approach. I think the problems he identifies are no more than *dangers* in his work at this stage, rather than actual failures – Frei had a tendency to be too harsh on his earlier work once he had made some clarifications and restatements later on. Nevertheless, Frei's main aim in the section of *Identity* which has been our main source in this chapter can seem to have been to see what happens to the concepts we use to describe God's relationship to history if we run them through the mill of the Gospel identification of Christ. What goes in is a concept, 'presence', most obviously suited to the Idealists' theoretical account of that relation;[32] what comes out is a collection of conceptual doctrinal fragments – hints of a pneumatology, an ecclesiology, and above all a doctrine of providence, by means of which Frei tries to give a richer conceptual description of God's impingement upon the whole historical world in Christ. So, although the Gospel mill has certainly done effective work in pressing any relationalism out of these fragments, and the very process of using the mill has done away with epistemological monophysitism, we are nevertheless left with what looks like a primarily conceptual response to the Gospels: a set of conceptual clarifications and constraints upon what Christian theologians may or may not say. These sketches may well contain a fuller answer to Strauss, but it will be an answer on a largely theoretical level. Frei, it seems, came to believe that to concentrate in this way on the attempt to find an appropriate *conceptual* articulation was to get the cart before the horse. One should rather be asking what believers should and should not *do* in response to the Gospels, what shape of life, what practices are appropriate responses – and then make greater efforts to keep the conceptual work subordinate to that practical reality, as its clarification and support. If I understand him correctly, Frei became increasingly convinced that the proper relation of faith and history was something which needed to be *shown* rather than *stated* – or at least that the stating and the showing should always go hand in hand. Just as Frei found a hollow at the centre of Barth's early theology, in its failure to demonstrate its Christological assertions by attention to Jesus' humanity, so he later detected a hollow at the centre of his own early work, in its failure to focus firmly on the practices to which believers are called by their acknowledgment of Christ in the Gospels.

Nevertheless, even though Frei came to believe that he was in danger of making his exploration of presence too speculative an account of God's impingement upon the world in Christ, and so felt he should no longer make these comments in quite the same way, and even though he became more wary about using the term 'presence' in particular, he did not budge from most of the convictions which were expressed in his conclusions. Much of the rest of this book will be taken up with an exploration of Frei's understanding of providence, and we will find that even when Frei shifts to an approach more deeply grounded in practice, his understanding of providence never ceases to bear the stamp which it already bears here – even if he does recast it in such a way that the unfolding of theological concepts is made more obviously secondary to the Christian practice of figural reading and political action which is the primary proclamation of God's providence, and the primary way in which the connection between God's action and history is repeatedly shown.

Before we turn to examine what else Frei said about providence, however, we need to pause and take stock. Frei's attempts to answer the question of epistemological monophysitism had already involved him in assumptions about history, and in suggestions about the way in which theology relates to history, which we have so far passed over in silence. On the one hand, he made some complex assumptions about the historicity of the Gospel stories of Jesus; on the other hand, he made some more general claims about the nature of historical existence which point towards the fuller account that his investigation of figural interpretation allowed him to give. Both those topics are the subject-matter of the next chapter.

Notes

1. 'Theological Reflections' (1966a), p. 82.
2. The Identity of Jesus Christ (1975a), p. 149. In a review of Identity in the Journal of Theological Studies 27, Maurice Wiles complained about Frei's 'cumbersome and at times obscure' language, then cites this passage as an egregious example (p. 262). On his own photocopy of the review (1976d), Frei wrote 'Yep! Very true' next to the general complaint, but after the citation of this passage writes 'Now that's not really difficult. Typology is reversed. At the beginning, Jesus is identified by applying to him crucial identifying marks from the history of the community. At the end, the community is identified by being referred to the specific marks of his story. These now become the clue to a discernibly teleological pattern in the community and its story.' See Appendix 2, though, for the suggestion that there is indeed a missing link in the argument at this point.
3. For what follows, see The Identity of Jesus Christ (1975a), pp. 149–65.
4. For the relation of these conclusions to classical Christology, see Appendix 3. Frei chooses, in Identity, to push this question in terms of 'presence'. In part, his choice was polemical: the idea of Christ's presence was vital to various forms of relationalism, and Frei decided to tackle relationalism head on by seeing what happens to the notion of Christ's presence when it is approached down the long road of Christ's identity, rather than directly (see chap. 5, §3).
5. The Identity of Jesus Christ (1975a), p. 149.
6. As well as the passages cited above, see The Identity of Jesus Christ (1975a), pp. 17–34.
7. See Appendix 2 for more on this transition in Frei's argument.
8. The Identity of Jesus Christ (1975a), pp. 155–57.
9. For more on 'grammar', see chap. 8, §7.
10. The Identity of Jesus Christ (1975a), pp. 158–59. The significance which we find inherent in Jesus' identity as portrayed in the Gospels is strictly unlimited. This is part of what Christians have meant by the doctrine of Christ's descent to hell: 'In Christian confession what remains constant through all such changes is that all reality – whatever its shape – imaginable and unimaginable, good and evil, is referred to Jesus, God's own Word, whose life and death on our behalf are adequate to protect us from the abyss'; 'Jesus Christ is so real – and therefore his cross so efficacious – that he defines, undergoes, and overcomes whatever it is that is absolutely and unequivocally hellish.' ('On the Going Down of Christ into Hell', 1987d, p. 2). As Frei put it in his Cadbury Lectures (1987a[i]): Jesus, 'unlike you and me ... was of universal saving significance or scope. This universality was not merely a qualitatively or geographically larger extension of effects consequent upon what he said, did and underwent than other people's resonances. No: the universal scope of his being what he was was as much of a defining quality of his person as his specific identity' (p. 3).
11. The Identity of Jesus Christ (1975a), p. 156. It is also to be won over to trust in the Gospel accounts. In 'Historical Reference and the Gospels' (?1981c), Frei confirmed that, even at the risk of sounding naïve, some such trust must be affirmed as one of the substructures supporting his discussion in Identity of 'what is involved in belief in the resurrection': 'Until better instructed I believe Scripture to be of unique divine inspiration, a miraculous grace for which no independent external evidence or a priori reason can be adduced, though some

a posteriori support can be given, e.g., the extraordinary fitness of Jesus' attitude in the story to a vision of life and salvation infinitely richer than that of Mr. Moon [an example Frei had discussed earlier in his reply], to the extent that I am acquainted with the latter's life and attitudes' (pp. 10–11).

12. *The Identity of Jesus Christ (1975a)*, p. 157.
13. 'Theological Reflections' *(1966a)*, p. 83.
14. For Frei's debate with general hermeneutics, see chap. 5, chap. 8, §4, and my article, 'Hans Frei and David Tracy on the Ordinary and the Extraordinary in Christianity'. For fear of imprisoning his conclusion within a general account of what is possible and appropriate when reading a text, Frei refuses to give any theoretical hermeneutical comments at this point – without denying that such an account might possibly be given in a way which is sufficiently modest. Frei allows that 'in another context' it might be necessary to underscore the fact that 'existential appropriation' is the only way to grasp the meaning and truth of this text, and implies that the 'elaborate description' of such existential appropriation might be part of such underscoring ('Theological Reflections', *1966a*, p. 84).
15. I have some difficulty with this transition in Frei's argument. See Appendix 2 for more details.
16. I am drawing on *The Identity of Jesus Christ (1975a)*, pp. 157–63, and pp. 12–34.
17. As he put it in the 'Meditation for the Week of Good Friday and Easter' (?1974f) appended to *Identity* when it was published in 1975, 'the sense of recall, re-enactment and identification in the retelling of this story gains from its association with ritual performance. The passion story and the Lord's Supper belong together. Together they render present the original; each is hobbled when it is separated from the other' (p. 169).
18. Clearly, this affirmation is true in some way such that the bread does not cease to have all of the obvious properties of bread, the wine wine, the words human words, but more than this 'in some way' believers cannot say. Frei presents no *explanation* of what is going on in preaching or the Eucharist; and he certainly would not claim to have justified these statements about Christ's presence to a sceptic. He has simply tried to specify the logic of Christian claims: to pinpoint the mystery of Christ's presence in relation to the constraints he has identified on Christian affirmations about Christ's identity.
19. *The Identity of Jesus Christ (1975a)*, pp. 66–73, 159–60. In 'Religion: Natural and Revealed' *(1958a)*, Frei had noted that 'Nineteenth-century theology discovered that Christianity is not a ready-made eternal constant but a genuine product of historical change, and that therefore the truth of Christianity cannot be separated from its history' (p. 318); here, Frei is (for his own reasons) trying to be more faithful to this insight than relationalist theology allowed nineteenth-century theologians to be.
20. *The Identity of Jesus Christ (1975a)*, p. 157.
21. Ibid., p. 161. It should be clear by now that this providential ordering is not produced by the way believers think of Jesus' significance; their thinking of the God in whom the whole of history is providentially ordered in unity with the unsubstitutable Jesus of Nazareth is a witness to what they hold to be true on the basis not of their action but the action of God in Christ.
22. Ibid., p. 162.
23. *The Identity of Jesus Christ (1975a)*, p. 162. If this seems an intolerably abstract or irrelevant way of stating the truth of the world, another way of seeing the world through the same counter-intuitive lens of the pattern of exchange is more familiar: 'Blessed are the poor in spirit, for theirs is the kingdom of heaven. Blessed are those who mourn, for they will be comforted. Blessed are the meek, for they will inherit the earth.'
24. Ibid., pp. 162–63. Cf. 'Meditation for the Week of Good Friday and Easter' (?1974f), p. 169: 'There are multitudes of crosses in the world. But it is because of *Jesus'* cross that we apply the term to all the others.' For a more detailed discussion of this claim, see chap. 7, §3.
25. *The Identity of Jesus Christ (1975a)*, p. 163.
26. Ibid., p. 163.

27. Ibid., p. 155.
28. Ibid., p. 164.
29. Ibid., p. 163.
30. Luke 24.27.
31. For more on Frei's shift in direction, see chap. 8.
32. See the 'Preface' to *The Identity of Jesus Christ* (1974i), and chap. 5, §3.

5

Paying Attention to History

In the last two chapters we have concentrated on Frei's attempt to defeat epistemological monophysitism by sketching a dogmatic theology which has its basis not just in the bare fact of the incarnation, but in the rich and complex content of Jesus' humanity as portrayed in the Gospels. We noted that, along the way, Frei bracketed other aspects of Strauss's question, the question of faith and history, and it is the task of this chapter to see what happened when Frei removed those brackets, and asked more closely about the historical nature of the foundations upon which he had built his dogmatic evidence. We will see him asking first whether and to what extent these foundations – the Gospel portrayals of Christ – are of the right kind to make questions about historical reference appropriate; and then asking whether and to what extent we may claim that they do refer historically.

This imposing and removing of brackets is not due to a purely pragmatic decision about the order in which topics might best be presented. I said at the end of the first chapter that Frei had 'committed himself to finding the proper location within Christian faith for the historical world of Strauss and Troeltsch', and noted that this was a deliberate reversal of Strauss's procedure. Where Strauss had asked where, on the ever-shifting sea of history, there could be room for a supposedly immutable Christian faith, Frei had asked where on the sea of faith we might find history. He wished to allow the question of history to be theologically situated.

Frei gave three main answers to this question in his Christological project. First, he argued that the *form* of the Gospel accounts is profoundly historical (in contrast to a primarily mythical or legendary form) – and historical in a particular way. If we make the wrong kinds of assumptions about the nature of history, our ability to make sense of these texts, to take account of what they say and do not say, will be drastically limited. We will be exploring this question for the bulk of the present chapter.

Second, the historical *form* of the Gospel accounts allows the posing of the narrower (but still urgent) question of historical *reference* – the 'Did it really happen this way?' question. Having argued that the Gospels are of a kind to allow us to read and make sense without having first decided upon the question of reference, Frei then argues that the question is nevertheless pressed upon us urgently by the sense that these texts make – and that it becomes unavoidable precisely at the point of the resurrection. We will be exploring this question in the final section of this chapter.

Third, Frei argues that the Gospels, by telling this historical story of Jesus of Nazareth, tell the story of salvation, and tell it in such a way that the world which Christ saves is shown itself to be historical. We have already seen hints of this argument at the end of the previous chapter, but will be devoting considerably more time to the doctrine of providence and the practice of figural interpretation which are its main components in the next two chapters.

All in all, these arguments amount to the claim that Christian faith has an historical consciousness of its own, which has some striking *ad hoc* resemblances to the historical consciousness explored and championed by Strauss and Troeltsch, but which has its own peculiar configuration – a configuration which allows Frei to acknowledge, and then to laugh at, Strauss's question.

1 Repeatable or Unsubstitutable?

We have seen that Frei believed epistemological monophysitism to be a betrayal of the Gospels. It was not, he thought, merely his own prejudices and sensibility that led him to dislike epistemological monophysitism: the Gospels themselves insist that the story of salvation, of God's ways with the world, is inseparable from the story of Jesus of Nazareth's particular and contingent human life. On the basis of the Gospels, Frei argued, we must reject any theology which seeks to tell the story of salvation without allowing it to be decisively shaped by attention to Jesus' particular story. The Gospels do not lend themselves to a separation of these two stories; they do not tell the story of Jesus in such a way that it can be rendered down into the stuff of epistemological monophysitism.

The mainstay of Frei's clarification of this Gospel insistence was his tracing of the complex shapes of the narrated identity of Jesus Christ, but he accompanied this tracing with a reflection on the frame of reference which that tracing assumes and projects.[1] He demonstrated that one's ability to do justice to the Gospels' strange insistences is decisively affected by the hermeneutical, anthropological and ontological commitments one makes, such that those commitments can in turn be disrupted and reordered by the attempt to read these texts attentively. In the course of the various versions of his Christological project, he makes a series of conceptual distinctions, one side of each of which favours an epistemologically monophysite reading of the Gospels for which the contingent particularity of Jesus' story can eventually be converted into some other currency, and argues that the Gospel narratives consistently stand on the *other* side of each of those distinctions. In other words, Frei draws a map of theological possibilities, and shows that epistemological monophysitism and the Gospels stand on opposite sides of several important boundaries.[2]

The importance of these distinctions is not, however, purely polemical. The distinctions enable Frei to build up an account of the Gospels as thoroughly historical in form – as history-*like* – and therefore provides the ground on which he stands when he revisits the question of historical reference. Were it not for the historical *form* of the Gospels, the question of historical *reference* would be a distraction.

We would be mistaken, however, if we thought that Frei had begun with a general methodological description and only later proceeded to substantive issues. He drew his map of these distinctions only in the process of charting his own path through the territory described, and the map simply attempts to make explicit the sense of the wider landscape which emerged as he pursued particular paths. The material addressed in the current chapter, therefore, represents neither a methodological prolegomenon to the specific work of interpretation described in the previous two chapters, nor the real fruit for which those chapters were a preparation. It is an *accompaniment* to the more concrete reading of those chapters, which is secondary to that reading, but which serves to support and clarify it. In separating out the material of this chapter from the last two chapters and presenting them in sequence, I have risked ironing out the complex back and forth motion of Frei's essays, presenting as a cumulative argument what was originally spiralling and ruminative.[3]

We can begin with a distinction which was very close to the surface in the analyses of chapter 3: the difference between mythic discourse and its opposite, a kind of narrative which has certain formal similarities with historical or novelistic writing. Frei defines 'myth' as a narrative the referent of which is not the 'finite, particular occurrences' of which it superficially appears to speak but some 'broader and not directly representable psychic or cosmic states' which transcend those occurrences.[4] Myth is, in other words, about that which is not tied to a specific time and place – even if the mythic expression itself is a culturally and historically limited objectification of an unobjectifiable, unlocatable content. The telling of the myth takes place in the public, historical world; that which it is about does not.

Frei suggested that there are 'tenacious and often haunting qualities' in the Gospels which 'do not easily fit the patterns of other ancient accounts of dying and rising gods', not simply in terms of the details of content, but also in terms of the form of the accounts. He does not deny that myth is an important element in any account of the development of the earliest depictions of Jesus of Nazareth; he accepts, perhaps too readily, that whatever took place with Jesus Christ did so against the background of a plethora of 'dying-and-rising saviour' myths, among which parallels can, perhaps, be found for any individual element of the Gospels. This mythic vocabulary was inevitably, he admits, used to talk about whatever it was that had happened to and through Jesus of Nazareth. However, Frei claims that the form which the Gospels take cannot be accounted for if we only say this – or at least that such an account misses something crucial. As the myths were used to describe what had taken place in and through Jesus of Nazareth, they were, Frei claims, 'demythologized': they were tied irrevocably to a particular name and, to a certain extent, reinterpreted in terms of the history and fate of that particular individual. They ceased to have as their referent 'broader and not directly representable psychic or cosmic states' and instead were drawn into a depiction of 'finite, particular occurrences'.

In order to clarify the qualities in the Gospels which he thought put up this resistance to characterization as 'myth', Frei introduced a distinction between 'unsubstitutability', a word he uses constantly throughout the article,[5] and its opposite, for which he does not have a consistent name, but which we might call 'substitutability' or 'repeatability'. He used the term 'unsubstitutability' to name the anti-mythic quality in the Gospel depictions of Jesus, contrasting the repeatable, common or universal referent of myth with the more unyieldingly particular referent of non-myth.

Contrast the approach of Rudolf Bultmann. We saw in the second chapter that Bultmann's emphasis fell upon ever-renewed present encounter with the *Christus praesens*, whose connection with the specific history of Jesus of Nazareth remained at best tenuous. Bultmann, in other words, concentrated upon that which happens time and time again, in place after place, rather than upon that which happened once, in one specific time and place. He acknowledged that the form of the message which elicits present kerygmatic encounters will change with the shifting seasons of culture; nevertheless he was adamant that the ultimate but unobjectifiable kerygma behind those penultimate changing forms remains always and everywhere the same. Now, if the emphasis of Christology falls on what is *repeated* time and time again, then its connection to the specific content of a particular, *unsubstitutable* human life is bound to become problematic. If that life appears at all it will tend to be seen as simply the embodiment of a repeatable content which transcends it and bears no constitutive reference to it. 'Repeatable' Christology is, in other words, bound to be epistemologically monophysite Christology.

In chapter 3 we saw quite clearly the kinds of reading which Frei felt called for a distinction like this, and followed his analysis of the unsubstitutable content which the Gospels give to 'obedience', for instance, or to 'power'. Frei felt, however, that his distinction between unsubstitutability and repeatability became most urgent at one specific point in the story of Jesus above all others. The force with which mythic forms were pressed into the service of describing Jesus of Nazareth led to the joints of those forms being forced apart precisely at the key juncture of the story: the transition between Jesus' death and resurrection.[6] This transition does not, in the Gospel depictions, have the quality of myth; it above all is the stone over which myth stumbles. In every account which takes myth as having priority over the particular occurrences and transpirings of Jesus' life, from Gnosticism to Bultmann and beyond, the move from cross to resurrection is an organic transition, because it is an expression of a structure deeper than itself, not a contingent transition in a story. In some forms of this organic transition, the process of the Saviour's dying is in unstoppable and natural continuity with – or perhaps even identical to – the process of his returning to life; in others the emergence of resurrection faith is naturally and organically united to the event of crucifixion. In the Gospel accounts, despite the use that is made of elements drawn from mythic accounts, the logic is different: there is a genuine hiatus between cross and resurrection.

> [I]n the case of the Gospels the figure of the cosmic redeemer was indeed so completely identified with the human being Jesus of Nazareth, and he in turn was so completely at one with his human brethren, that *he* the *savior* became just as helpless as they ... There is no natural, organic transition from his need for redemption to his being redeemed. The divine figure suddenly stands before us without his divine power, especially as that power would affect himself. Indeed, there was truth in the sarcastic remark that he could bring salvation to others but not to himself.[7]

The implication of Frei's claim is clearly that certain kinds of appeal to myth in accounts of New Testament Christianity are called into question, and that modern theological positions which draw inspiration or justification from such appeals are thereby destabilized. Yet instead of turning immediately to an analysis and dismissal of a list of modern theologians, Frei first turned his critique upon the 'Christ-figures of some modern novels'.[8]

At first glance, Frei appears to have made this move because the Christ-figures represent a pitfall *opposite* that presented by the proponents of myth. The modern novelists Frei has in mind take seriously the utter weakness of Jesus on the cross, his inability to save himself; they try to take seriously the human story of their protagonists. What power these figures have to save can only be found along the path of their utter desolation, their real submersion under the hostility of the world. The Christ-figure's identity as the redeemer is depicted as mysteriously congruent with his utter powerlessness, a powerlessness which organic and mythic accounts of the transition obscure.

However, despite doing more justice to this transition than do the mythical accounts to which Frei has been referring, the novelistic Christ-figures which he has in mind are ultimately beset by exactly the same problem. The very starkness with which the novelists treat the transition from cross to resurrection is all too often recruited into the service of a portrayal of Christ as the embodiment of a paradox of power and powerlessness. When that happens we have swung towards a new mythologization, a new stylization – a new repeatability. 'The embodiment of a paradoxical coincidence of opposites' is not the stuff of which unsubstitutable identities, firmly ingredient in their particular times and places, are made. To make the Christ-figure out to be such an embodiment of opposites is to make him substitutable all over again.

The process by which this happens in the modern novel is itself a paradoxical one, because it arises as the writers (inevitably and properly, says

Frei, given that they are writing novels) seek to interpret or demythologize those elements of the Gospels which are stylized, or still couched in mythical terms: God, miracles, salvific power. In trying without reference to these stylized elements nevertheless to capture what is going on in the crucial transition from cross to resurrection, and to see its relationship to some kind of salvation, they are forced precisely to re-stylize the Christ-figure by taking the paradoxical coincidence of opposites as the real content of the cross and resurrection stories. Such re-stylization once again makes his identity repeatable: this paradoxical and tragic love is constantly re-emerging and sinking again beneath the waves of history, and its bearers are always depicted as something less than fully individuated, so dominated are they by this repeatable deportment.

When the Christ figures do achieve substance, it is by means of their enmeshment in specific transpirings and occurrences which differentiate them from one another – and from the figure of Jesus in the Gospels; it happens, in other words, precisely to the extent that they do not try to *repeat* Christ. To the extent that such individuating enmeshment is missing, the modern novelists too are left with a kind of monophysitism: a Christ-figure who, rather than being saviour because of the connection of his full humanity with God, has saving power because he is the not-quite-human embodiment of an idea not quite divine.

Of course, Frei did not mean to restrict his critique to modern novelists. As we have already heard, he followed Niebuhr's hint and held that *any* attempt to portray Jesus simply as the embodiment of any virtue or set of excellences, even as the embodiment of love, is to dehydrate his personhood. Such a strategy betrays Christ unless the virtues in question are given specificity and richness by their subordination to a story which organizes and configures them. And we saw that, in the case of the Jesus depicted in the Gospels, the specific configuration in which he held and shaped his virtues and excellences – even love – cannot be understood without reference to precisely those elements which the modern novelist has eschewed: God and the mission of salvation.

> The unity of his personal being depicted in the Gospels, we are saying, is not to be seen directly, by adumbrating the personal excellences discernible in him and then choosing the most noticeable in comparison to the others as the first. That unity is seen more nearly as the shaping of all his personal qualities in conformation to his mission or aspiration in obedience to God.[9]

Quietly, but decisively, Frei's target has broadened. It is no longer simply the Bultmannian type of epistemological monophysitism which is in view; nor is it simply the Christ-figure novels of the nineteenth and twentieth centuries. The same kind of analysis which Frei applies to the modern novelistic Christ-figure applies just as easily to the relationalist Christologies of the nineteenth century against which the epistemological monophysites had supposedly reacted, and whose *Lives of Jesus* are so far from the modern Christ-figure novels. The kind of picture which liberal relationalist theologians presented of Jesus was of the perfect embodiment of a universal human possibility, the bearer of a piety which is significant precisely insofar as it can be shared or repeated. Just like the novelists, the relationalists of the nineteenth century arrived at such a portrait of Jesus precisely by trying to do greater justice to his humanity, and with precisely the same embarrassment about some of the 'stylized' elements of the Gospel portrayals. By deploying the distinction between unsubstitutability and repeatability, Frei was able – quietly and unobtrusively – to unite Gnostic saviour myths, Bultmannian epistemological monophysitism, novelistic Christ-figures (at least to the extent that they are taken as Christ-figures, rather than as characters in their own right), and nineteenth-century relationalism, and to claim that all of these, whatever differences there might be between them, were defeated by the Gospels. All of them had made the same Christological mistake: they took the real meaning of the Gospel accounts, and particularly the transition from cross to resurrection, to be some repeatable content (whether it be the kerygma, a paradox of opposing characteristics, or messianic consciousness) rather than a specific and contingent concatenation of public circumstances and events. All of them had missed the *history-likeness* of these texts.

Before we turn to the second of Frei's distinctions, two further clarifications are in order. First, it is important to note that Frei is not claiming that the non- or anti-mythic quality of the cross-resurrection transition counts as *evidence* that the resurrection (or, for that matter, the cross) 'really happened': it can equally well characterize fictional narratives, and Frei presents no argument for or against the fiction-writing capabilities of the early Christians.

Second, we must also avoid another common mistake: Frei's work has repeatedly been misread by those who prematurely turn his specific comments into general theories. Frei focuses his counter-claim to epistemological monophysitism very closely. Whatever else may be true about other portions of the depiction of Jesus in the Gospels (and Frei is willing to concede a great deal), the claims of the epistemological monophysites do not do justice to the passion narratives and the transition between cross and resurrection. All that is initially at stake is that one portion of the Gospels. The Synoptic Gospel telling of at least this transition, whatever mythic elements are built into it, can be seen to fall on the opposite side of the unsubstitutable/repeatable divide from that on which myth and its variants fall. It is true, of course, that Frei is interested in something more than a minute clarification of the narrative logic of one point in the Gospels. He does not, however, go by way of a general or a biblical hermeneutics. Instead, he argues negatively that doing conceptual justice to this one key transition in the Gospels helps us at very least to see that some of the categorial structures which we have commonly used for understanding these texts, their subject matter and their significance (and much else besides) are questionable because they cannot account successfully for what goes on just here.

2 Alienation or Manifestation?

If Frei develops and deploys the idea of 'unsubstitutability' in order to clarify the kinds of literary portrayal we do and do not find in the Gospels – and so clarify 'history-likeness' as a hermeneutical quality – the second distinction we are going to examine moves more clearly from the hermeneutical to the anthropological realm. What assumptions about human identity do we need to make in order to claim that the Gospel narratives, characterized as they are by unsubstitutability, are indeed identity descriptions? What will our claims about the nature of human identity begin to look like if we allow that the Gospels do indeed portray Jesus' identity aptly?[10]

When describing Bultmann's theology earlier, I said that for him 'the form of the message which elicits present kerygmatic encounters will change with the shifting seasons of culture; nevertheless ... the ultimate but unobjectifiable kerygma behind those penultimate changing forms remains always and everywhere the same'. Something like this picture is present more or less explicitly in all the versions of repeatability which we have mentioned: the proponents have to have some way of looking behind the obviously diverse and contingent facts of history and culture in order to find a message which can be everywhere the same. The message must somehow transcend objective history, even if that means that it can never directly appear in its pure form, but only through a penultimate diversity of objectifications.

The second distinction which Frei makes is aimed at elucidating precisely this logic. On the one hand stands any description of the identity of a person – particularly any description of the identity of Jesus – which regards itself as looking for the identity which stands 'behind' its objectifications in the public world; Frei calls this kind of self-description, 'subject–alienation description'.[11] On the other hand he places descriptions which look for the identity of the self 'in' or 'in unity with' its manifestations in the public world, descriptions which see a person's identity as given in, rather than hidden by, the messy details of his or her public interactions with the world. Such description assumes a self inextricably entwined with the world in contingent and particular ways; it assumes, in a word, unsubstitutability. Frei describes two versions of this kind of description, the first called 'intention–action description', the second called 'subject-manifest-in-difference description' (or, in *The Identity of Jesus Christ*, 'self–manifestation analysis').

The anthropology of alienation coheres naturally, Frei claimed, with the substitutability or repeatability side of the first, more hermeneutical distinction, whereas the anthropology of manifestation coheres more naturally with unsubstitutability. Frei's opposition to alienation anthropology is thus presented as an implication of his opposition to misuse of the category of myth. In this way, having been led from Frei's earlier concerns about Bultmannian epistemological monophysitism to the recognition that far wider tracts of modern theology suffer from a similar deficit of attention to the particular human identity of Jesus of Nazareth, we are now brought to the realization that very broad issues about human being are caught up in the same conflict. The question of human freedom or of human historical existence which had animated Frei's thesis turns out once again to be the companion of the question of Jesus' humanity.

For proponents of the subject–alienation scheme, the self stands 'behind' its objectifications in the public world in the sense that those objectifications emerge from the self but are not the self, there being an inherent tendency for them to misrepresent and distort the self, for the self to be hidden by them – hence 'alienation'. Nevertheless, although it is a constant temptation, these schemes do not necessarily posit a 'ghost in the machine': the self is not some other thing alongside its objectifications, a thing which could be located, inspected and used to adjudicate the objectifications. Frei claims that the self in such a view exists as a 'basic self-reflective stance' accompanying expressions of the self as they pass into objectification and distortion. The self is ultimately, in Frei's rather awkward phrase, 'non-objectifiable self-reflexiveness'.[12] In hermeneutics in particular, this structure shows itself in two assumptions:

> (1) That the written word ... represents not the proper expression but the 'frozen objectification' of the mind that lies behind it;[13] (2) that the proper way to grasp one's own intention, indeed identity, as well as that of others, is by entry into the basic self-reflective act of the self, into that which is never 'merely given'.[14]

Frei's claim is that attention to the Gospels allows us to imagine a different way of describing identity, or to see that their authors operated with anthropological assumptions which do not sit easily in a subject–alienation scheme. Attention to the Gospels allows us, in other words, to call into question the primacy of subject–alienation anthropology, and by so doing call into question a central feature of a major tradition of modern theology. Once we have made the distinction between repeatability and unsubstitutability, seen on which side the Gospel depictions lie, and then seen the intimate connection between that hermeneutical distinction and the current anthropological distinction, Frei thinks us forced to deprecate subject–alienation views of the self in favour of subject–manifestation views – at least for the purposes of providing an account of the portrayal of Jesus in the Gospels. The Gospel texts are, at least when it comes to the passion–resurrection sequence, simply not describing Jesus' identity in a way that is well grasped by a subject–alienation scheme.

Part of the problem with the earlier distinction was that Frei's preferred side, unsubstitutability, did not emerge clearly into view. Its silhouette was visible against the contrasting colours of the opposing side, repeatability, but its own details were difficult to discern. With the new, anthropological distinction, however, Frei paints in considerable detail the forms of talk about identity that fill out the subject–manifestation scheme, as well as marking out its distinction from a subject–alienation scheme.

The subject–alienation scheme assumes a dialectical relationship between the private self and its objectifications in the public world. We may, for such a scheme, talk about the self 'behind' its objectifications, not because there is a 'ghost in the machine' (some separable private entity manipulating a public body entirely distinct from it) but because public manifestations emerge from the self, are all that is visible of the self, *but are not the self*: the self is that always-hidden point from which they emerge, and which they inevitably cloak.

Frei does not question the idea that we need to assume some kind of dialectical relationship between the self and its objectifications or mani-festations in the public world. To reject the 'self' side of the dialectic, he implies, would be to opt for purely behavioural description, or to reject the possibility of biography and autobiography; to reject the 'manifestation' side would render us completely unable to see that there were any identities requiring description.[15] Yet where a subject–alienation scheme sees this dialectical relationship as inherently uneasy and contested, with the self standing 'behind' manifestations or objectifications which imprison it, a self–manifestation scheme sees the relationship as ordinarily and properly peaceful. The self is present 'in' its objective manifestations; descriptions of the self are possible which focus upon objective realities caught in the contingent flux of history, because they do not thereby fail in some basic way to depict a person's real identity. In fact, rather than speaking of a self and its manifestation, we should think of the self as a dialectical relationship of, as it were, 'inner' and 'outer'.

Frei suggested two differing ways of colouring in this basic anthropological sketch, each of which marks the line between 'inner' and 'outer' in a slightly different place.[16] In the first of the schemes, the 'inner' is intention, the 'outer' action in the world. Following Gilbert Ryle, Frei observes that to act intelligently is to do one thing and not two:[17] intention and action are not two separable realities, so that we might get back to the intention from the action by a process of inference (and arrive at, or closer to, the real self in the process). Rather, to see behaviour as an action is to see it as explicit intention; intention is similarly implicit action.[18]

Frei offers a catena of instances in which we grasp the immediate connection between intention and action. Even when introspecting, we do not normally or without special effort *infer* our intention from our action or our action from our intention: we are simply aware of ourselves as acting intentionally. When reading a novel, we are presented with a character who acts intentionally, not normally with the description of behaviour from which we are meant to infer an underlying intention. When interacting with others, Frei claims, we normally perceive their actions *as* action; we do not first see behaviour and then, in a subsequent reflective act, infer an intention. Only in the case of the critical historian is Frei willing to concede that it might be necessary to take behaviour as evidence on the basis of which to infer intention, although he prefers to leave even that as an open question. In other words, if we need to make an assumption about the unity of intention and action, about a certain kind of unity between inner and outer, in order to make sense of the Gospels as successful identity-descriptions, we are not thereby doing something that is utterly counter-intuitive or implausible; we are doing something familiar and widespread.[19]

Frei claims that only if one works with an anthropology in which there is this immediate connection between intention and action is it possible to describe a person's identity by describing his or her patterns of activity, and hence by telling a story of the public, or at least potentially public, transpirings in which he or she is involved. Jesus, in the sequence from Gethsemane to the cross, is identified largely through the significant occurrences in which he takes part, through the actions and interactions in which he engages: he is the one who heals and eats, who preaches and prays, who argues and remains silent. One does not need to look away from these things, or regard them simply as promissory notes to be traded in once we reach some different level on which we would approach Jesus' *real* identity: they are already themselves the ingredients of a successful identity-description.

Focusing on 'intentional action' provided Frei with a set of concepts in which 'inner' and 'outer', construed more or less in terms of the distinction between 'mental' and 'physical', are dialectically related, and in which the self is found in the unity between the two. Some such scheme of concepts appears, said Frei, to be required of us if we are to allow that an identity can be presented to us through the story of a series of unsubstitutable public transpirings. Intention–action description, however, points beyond itself. The kind of description which presents a person as an agent is frequently – perhaps inevitably – mixed unsystematically with description which presents a person as a patient: as undergoing the intentional actions of others. If such accounts assume that a person's identity can be given through the depiction of objective actions, and so assume a fundamental unity of intention and action, they also assume that a person's identity is given – perhaps less straightforwardly – in a description of what they suffer. Yet it is far harder here to speak of this in terms of a dialectical relationship of 'inner' and 'outer' without shifting attention away from the sufferings themselves and on to their subjective appropriation (the way they are 'refracted through [a person's] own response'),[20] and Frei does not want us to do that. The Gospels describe much that Jesus suffers; they barely hint at Jesus' subjective appropriation of that suffering. To assume that only a focus on subjective appropriation would allow us to consider Jesus' sufferings as ingredients in his identity is to assume that we miss or obscure Jesus' identity when we simply describe what was done to him, when we describe him as the patient of the passion. If we take the Gospels seriously, says Frei, then we must accept that simply to describe Jesus' climactic sufferings alongside his climactic actions can still be a description of his identity, rather than the description of secondary clues which we might subsequently use to reconstruct his identity.

We can clarify this point by going a little beyond Frei's comments, and pointing to the death of Jesus. Jesus is the crucified one, not just the one who faces death authentically – and if we are able to say that then we are clearly moving away from an understanding of identity which insists that its linchpin is subjective appropriation, the basic self-reflective stance which accompanies objectifications in the public world. The dead body of Jesus represents the end of identity from the latter perspective, yet Frei tries to understand forms of description of a person's identity which can include descriptions of his death, and descriptions of him dead. What happens to our anthropology when we see a *Pieta* not as the depiction of an absence of identity – a depiction of an identity that has been absolutely swallowed beneath the waves of objectification – but instead as the depiction of one of the forms which Jesus' identity took? What if pointing with Grünewald's John the Baptist to the dead body of Christ on the cross is one of the central ways of answering the question, 'Who is Jesus of Nazareth?'

Such questions begin to go beyond the intention–action scheme, and Frei soon qualifies it with another form of talk about identity, one which he allows to bear more of the weight of his explicit opposition to subject–alienation anthropology.[21] He calls it both 'subject-manifest-in-difference description' and 'self–manifestation' description, and I will stick to the latter, less clumsy designation. Frei wished, with this scheme, to move away from the ways in which a person's identity is given through the story of actions and interactions, and to look instead at the phenomenon of attestation: those instances in which a person identifies herself, or is identified by others, with some enduring objective reality – not exhaustively, so that the person would be nothing other than this particular enduring objective reality, but truly: this reality genuinely manifests the self.

Frei's focus is not now on the rendering of a person's identity by the description of the various changing episodes of her action and interaction; rather he is interested in the ways in which a person's identity over time, her continuity and persistence, are grasped. Yet he is not interested in turning away from a person's manifestations in the shifting public world and towards some safe internal source of continued identity; he refers instead to objective, 'external', historical realities: bodies and language. He urges us to consider the strange way in which my body is both 'me' and 'mine'. My body is an item in the objective, historical world, yet it is one by and with which I can be identified, one by which my identity is manifested publicly. A subject–alienation scheme must assume that the body is a cloak for and a distortion of the self, that a true approach to grasping one's own or someone else's identity must eventually leave bodies behind; a self–manifestation scheme finds no such problem in speaking of identities by means of talking about bodies, and feels no pressure to move behind them to some true, internal source of identity. To talk about my body is, in such a perspective, to talk about me; find my body and you have found me; describe what I do in and through my body, what is done to my body, where my body ends up, and you are describing me. The body is a worldly reality that is able to provide continuity in the description of a person's identity. Some such assumption, at least, is operating whenever we pursue identity-description by means of descriptions of bodily performances and locations, without qualifying those things as fundamentally distorting.[22]

Frei also points to the language with which a person can identify herself. We might think, in a biblical context, of the 'I am' sayings of Jesus, or similar sayings in Exodus and deutero-Isaiah.[23] A person is not simply these words, but we may say (if we do not assume that they are necessarily distortions) that they can be the apt manifestation of a person's identity in a medium different from herself, a manifestation by means of which we may grasp 'who she is' – that is, through which we may truly grasp something of her persisting identity. One who follows a subject–alienation scheme must eventually leave behind such public acts of communication and move behind them in search of their source; self–manifestation descriptions will be far readier to grant that such words and designations can truly represent and communicate a person's identity; that we may rest content with them.[24]

One of the parts of language with which a person can be so identified is a name, a word generated by others and applied to the self. In subject–alienation schemes, names provide a source of great anxiety, the link between the externally donated name and a person's true identity being at best questionable. In a self–manifestation scheme a person may be truly identified in a name; may truly identify himself, and allow himself to be identified, by a name. The public world in which he lives and moves can be the scene in which his identity is gained and manifested, not the scene in which it is necessarily betrayed or hidden. To read a narrative which allows names to be, or to become, true manifestations of the characters' identities, is to read a narrative which makes some kind of self–manifestation assumptions.

All this would be reasonably clear, I think, were it not for the confusing fact that, whereas the link between Frei's technical description of intention–action description and his actual exegetical performance as described in chapter 3 is reasonably clear, the links are far less clear when we come to self–manifestation description. His multifaceted theoretical description is complex enough, but when Frei actually gives an account in self–manifestation terms of the portrayal of Jesus' identity in the Gospels, his focus shifts. It is in this connection that he points to Jesus' identification 'in terms of the identity of the people of Israel' and in terms of the Kingdom of God, and Jesus' eventual emergence as a fully individuated figure who questions and transforms those descriptions in the process of owning them. That is, instead of pointing to Jesus' name, or Jesus' body, Frei points to the identification of Jesus in terms of what we can think of as stories of salvation which are, to an extent, public property, and the ways in which the Gospels pose for us the question of *how* these generalized identity-descriptions fit the one to whom they are applied. He is interested in the ways in which such identifications are pressed home: ways in which such identifications are rendered particular and specific; ways in which they are shaped by being pressed into the service of identifying this unsubstitutable human being.

In his actual practice, then, Frei's self–manifestation description turns out to be about how specifications of Jesus' true identity are, in the Gospels, linked to his particularity: how they are deployed in such a way as to become manifestations of his identity rather than impositions upon it. Taking an example which Frei does not discuss, we could trace how the title 'Messiah' is used in the Gospels: how it is deployed to identify Jesus, but how his story first calls it into question and then gives it a new meaning. The use of the title in the Gospels serves to help identify who Jesus is, to manifest his identity, but it does so only as it is slowly called into question and then reshaped by being forced up against the intractable surface of Jesus' story.[25] Frei is interested, in other words, not simply in attestation or manifestation as a static fact, but in the *process* by which it is achieved – even if what is achieved in this process is the manifestation or attestation of the persistent identity of a person.[26]

Frei was obviously never completely happy with his formulations of this scheme. Having presented one version in the *Christian Scholar* article, he presented another in the *Crossroads* version of the same material, and another in his 'Remarks' on that double project.[27] He clearly found it hard to render his thoughts on this point precise. Nevertheless, although we may have trouble in clarifying exactly what he meant, we can make a far more confident attempt to say why it was that he thought something like this worth saying. For Frei, something like subject–manifestation description is necessary if we are to do justice to the depiction of the resurrection. In the accounts of the resurrection, the portrayal of Jesus' identity through the relating of enacted intentions falls somewhat into the background, and the focus shifts on the one hand to the empty tomb and the reappearance of Christ's body, and on the other hand to Christ's self-identification through giving and accepting the name by which he had been known: the resurrected Christ witnesses to the fact that he is one and the same Jesus. In other words, Christ's identification in the resurrection accounts has to do precisely with those things which subject–alienation description finds it difficult to articulate: the identity of a person with his or her flesh, the identity a person finds bestowed and revealed in a name, and the demonstration that a person can now be properly identified through descriptions hitherto generalized and external. For subject–alienation descriptions, such things fall on the side of 'frozen objectification': they fail to approach the heart of a person's true identity, being rather its cloak. Yet in the Gospels it is precisely in these things that the resurrected Jesus is identified, and it is precisely through these things that the obscurity of his previous identification is overcome.

In the sequence from Gethsemane to the cross Jesus is identified primarily through the continuous narrative of specific and climactic enactments as, fundamentally, the crucified one; we understand this by a process of following the story of climactic transpirings in ancient Jerusalem. In the resurrection he is identified through a scattering of illuminating appearances and self-attestations as the Messiah and Saviour; and we understand this more through a process of 'crucial insight' than by following a story. We grasp that this one who appears is identical with the one whom we had previously identified in the narrative from Gethsemane to the cross; and more than that we grasp the true identity of the one whom had endured and enacted all these things: the Saviour.

The distinction between 'repeatability' and 'unsubstitutability' enabled us to clarify history-likeness as a hermeneutical quality – helping us to see that the *prima facie* subject-matter of the Gospels is the specific and contingent concatenation of public circumstances and events about which they clearly speak, rather than some hidden, repeatable content to which those realities refer. The distinction between alienation and manifestation helps clarify some of the anthropological assumptions underlying that hermeneutical distinction. These texts are, in crucial ways, history-like because they portray identities that are gained and displayed historically – that are gained and displayed in specific concatenations of public circumstances and events. It is not, of course, that identities are exhausted by their public manifestations, nor that the forms of identity description appropriate to such public manifestations are the only ones which Christian theology will need to use – but in order to do justice to the Gospels we will need to have categories which allow us to do justice to this history-like nature of their portrayal of identity, which do not prevent us from agreeing with Strauss that 'Jesus's historical particularity was one with his outward manifestation.'[28]

3 Presence or Identity?

In *The Identity of Jesus Christ*, Frei made use of a third distinction which summarized and recast the other two and which begins to move us from consideration of the history-likeness of the Gospels themselves to the historical nature of our relationship to them. On the repetition and alienation sides of the previous two distinctions, he placed theologies for which the basic datum was the relation or *presence* of Christ to the believer, and for which the identity of Jesus Christ must be described (if at all) in ways which cohere with and support prior claims about that relation. On the favoured unsubstitutability and manifestation sides of the earlier distinctions, he placed those Christologies which allowed their understanding of the relation or presence of Christ to the believer to be governed by a prior tracing of the *identity* of Jesus Christ, a tracing which tries to bracket out prior assumptions about the kind of significance Jesus might have in order to prevent them from clouding clear perception of that identity itself.

The main virtue of this third distinction is that it makes even more obvious the link between Frei's theological proposal and his earlier discussions of the 'relationalism' which characterized so much liberal theology, for relationalism was precisely that theology which took presence (that is, the given relation of

God to the believer) as its starting point and norm. In the Preface to *Identity*, Frei wrote that, in his use of the concept 'presence', he 'was obviously still very much preoccupied and trying to come to terms with a philosophical and theological tradition that had been dominant in Protestant theology since the early nineteenth century; and in the concept of "presence" I was trying to sum up what all the variants had in common'.[29] Frei used 'presence' as shorthand for a concentration upon the self as primarily a perspective-upon-the-world, and upon the present as the moment in which this intuiting of the world takes place, and as the only point at which the self truly exists. In relationalist theology, some such concentration is central. Elsewhere, Frei traces this concentration back to Lessing's discussion of proof in 'On the Proof of the Spirit and of Power', saying 'The arguments are those of Hume, concerning tailoring belief to fit the evidence. But something is different. There is an emphasis on the *present* and on the time interval that Hume doesn't have: *Now* is when I want to be in the presence of such proofs.'[30]

Frei had himself given a version of this concept some prominence. In his 1958 article on 'Religion: Natural and Revealed', he had said that 'revelation as divine self-disclosure in history may become intelligibly significant for its human recipients'; it 'must come to present recipients as a present event'.[31] Indeed, Frei's emphasis in his doctoral thesis precisely on Barth's doctrine of *revelation* speaks of something of the same focus. In *The Identity of Jesus Christ*, however, he argued that the concept should only play a thoroughly secondary role in Christian theology (rather than being the hinge around which the whole turns), and later he was to criticize even the restrained position which *Identity* allowed to 'presence'.[32] 'Presence', if we allow our use of it to be disciplined by our attention to the portrayals of Christ's identity in the Gospels, turns out to be a rather misleading concept to use.

Frei's disciplining of 'presence' is simply a continuation of his assault on repeatability and alienation. For the relationalist, Jesus' presence has to be taken as something which is repeated: it must become real for each believer in his or her own place and time, yet is claimed to be the same presence, or the presence of the same one; it is a repeatable occurrence beside which the unrepeatable content of Jesus' identity is secondary. Similarly, this repeatable presence is not itself something which takes place in the public world (even if it is linked to or occasioned by some public occurrence) – were it such a public transpiring, then it could have nothing to do with Jesus of Nazareth, because in terms of the public world of events and circumstances he is two thousand years and many miles distant. Rather, it must be something which takes place in our inwardness, behind the public scene, where Lessing's ditch can be bridged, in a realm where distance and proximity are not relevant terms, and where there can be some kind of contact between that which Jesus embodied and our true selves.

On the other side of the distinction from this Christology which begins with presence, stands a Christology in which Frei does not, of course, give up all talk of Christ's relation to or significance for believers (such a move would involve abandoning Christology completely), but one which allows all it has to say about presence, or about any connection that there might be between Jesus of Nazareth and later believers, unbelievers or pilgrims to be governed by what it has to say about the unsubstitutable, manifest identity of Jesus Christ – even to the point of calling into question the propriety of a concept like 'presence' for describing that connection. It is a theology which approaches Jesus' relationship to us by way of attention to him as he stands at a distance from us: attention to the specific one that he was in his own time and place – which are not our time and place. As he says in the 'Meditation for the Week of Good Friday and Easter' which was added to *The Identity of Jesus Christ* on its publication in 1975:

> [T]his story by its very nature *does* recede, it does not annul time. Ultimately therefore its capacity to be re-enacted in your sensibility and your imagination cannot be the criterion of its significance for you. And surely, the followers of Jesus Christ have recognised this from the very beginning. For whomever it becomes the truth it does so not by imaginative obliteration of time but by hammering out a shape of life patterned after its own shape. That does not mean that we repeat the original events literally in our lives, and certainly not completely, but it means that our lives reflect the story as in a glass darkly. The shape of the story being mirrored in the shape of our life is the condition of its being meaningful for us.[33]

The history-likeness of the Gospels – their unsubstitutability, their focus on manifestation – means that they do not 'annul time'. This is the bite of Frei's delineation of history-likeness: if we are to read these history-like texts, and are to be captivated by the history-like identity portrayed in them, and are to do so without neutralizing that very history-likeness, then we must relate to them in ways which themselves are history-like. There can be, for us, no retreat from history.

4 The Gospels as History-like

Making the distinction between repeatability and unsubstitutability, between subject–alienation and subject–manifestation anthropology, and between a focus on presence and a focus on identity, is not Frei's main aim. It allows him to call into question the appropriateness or viability of the kinds of theology he is rejecting, given the use they make of the Gospel narratives, but he had no wish to erect in its place an alternative general anthropological and hermeneutical theory. He is not going to erect an alternate general theory of history-like relations to history-like texts. His alternative to the theology he rejects is only provided by the more concrete and detailed depiction of Jesus traced in the last two chapters, and he tries at all times to keep the more abstract distinctions I have been tracing secondary to that particular story. This is a necessary comment, because this chapter might well have given the wrong impression: although I have tried to avoid making the usual mistake of presenting Frei's theological proposal as largely concerned with something called 'hermeneutics', and have tried to avoid the idea that Frei's attack on liberal theology and its heirs is based upon the development of a hermeneutical theory, or the opposition of a special biblical hermeneutics to their general hermeneutics, I may well have given the impression that Frei's work is largely about another, equally general topic called anthropology. There is a certain truth in that, yet this anthropology is (at this stage) only a by-product of Frei's exposition: his main aim is to retell the story of Jesus, and to see where that leads.

Nevertheless, if we refuse to detach the conclusions we have been examining from their roots in Frei's narration of Jesus' identity, they do turn out to be important. Frei believes he has shown that the Gospel depictions of Jesus are *history-like*: that they depict a public world of action and interaction, of character and circumstance – a world in which there are no idealist reservations of the spirit cut off from the ceaseless ebb and flow of contingent events. The high Christology and wider dogmatic theology which Frei has claimed are appropriate readings of these texts rest on foundations which are, in that sense at least, utterly historical.

In order to be a little clearer about what Frei thinks he has achieved at this point, we need to look at some of his brief methodological comments. At the beginning of the *Christian Scholar* article, he said that 'Without some perspective of our own the story has no discernibly significant shape for us; but on the other hand we must not imprint either our own life problems or our own ideological analyses on it. The proper approach is to keep the tools of interpretive analysis as minimal and as formal as possible.'[34] And again, later in the article: 'we must approach the Gospels with some conceptual tool in hand, otherwise we understand nothing at all'.[35] In the 1967 lecture, 'Remarks in Connection with a Theological Proposal', in which he discussed the *Christian Scholar* article, Frei added to this the idea that 'the text may force a scramble of our categories of understanding, even though we must always keep those categories clean and distinct in the abstract, and therefore can never know (in the abstract) how on earth they may be scrambled'.[36] Frei suggested, therefore, that although we must always approach the Gospels with our own categories of understanding, it is possible to approach with sufficient reserve that the Gospels can force us towards different categories. The categories will still be ours, will still be our 'conceptual tools', a 'perspective of our own', but need not be thought of as sheer imposition.

Frei claims that the categories of identity he uses are ones which, in a sense, derive from the New Testament itself, or at least he claims to have shaped those categories by paying attention to the New Testament depiction of Jesus of Nazareth. He clearly wants to convince us that he has learnt what the Gospels teach on this in a way in which his opponents have not, and that once we have understood the distinctions which he has made, we will be enabled to see with new clarity what is going on in the Gospel depiction of Jesus, and to see that it is not what dominant modern Christologies have implicitly or explicitly claimed is going on. Nevertheless, it is clearly not the case that Frei's categories and claims have been read direct from the New Testament. It has been clear in the course of this chapter that the distinctions Frei has made have involved him in philosophical discussion with the likes of Gilbert Ryle, or with the German idealist and existentialist tradition, and that he has produced in their favour some dense and complex passages of technical argumentation which make no claim to be biblical exegesis. These are clearly not 'New Testament concepts', and they are clearly not elements of an esoteric language open only to Christians. They are elements of public language, open and available to anyone – and yet they are learnt, according to Frei, from the New Testament.

There is, of course, no contradiction in this. Frei claims that it is possible to approach the Gospels with a certain reserve, a certain ascesis, which we might think of as an openness to finding that they do things differently there. As we can see from Frei's work, this ascesis might well be a matter of hard conceptual work, but it is also a certain kind of humility, one which recognizes that the text is too various and too sudden to be covered by our conceptual schemes: we can only hope to find a variety of descriptions fit for particular small-scale purposes, which may enable us to see more clearly something of what is there. Approaching the Gospels, we are not given a wholly un-precedented language incommensurable with other human languages. Rather, the elements of our existing languages are reordered.

Frei knows that this openness cannot be a matter of becoming purely passive in the face of the Gospels. In that case we would, paradoxically, receive nothing. Nevertheless, he believes it is possible to retain sufficient modesty to feel some of the resistances which the Gospels put up to the ways we have of interrogating them. If we recognize such resistances, the text can enable us to think differently, to question assumptions which we have brought to the texts and to explore new configurations of categories.[37]

Frei's claim that our method in reading these texts can be governed by the texts themselves, and that we do not need to develop a hermeneutical method prior to our encounter with these texts, is ambivalent. Sometimes it seems to be Frei's general counsel for approaching texts of any kind, that we should pay attention to the ways of reading which are inherently appropriate to any text before reading it. At other times, it appears clearer that this is a counsel in this case only. Whatever may be the case with other texts, the resistances which the Gospels put up are such as to allow us to be guided by them in method as much as in content. The Gospel narratives are, in significant part, *history-like* – they are characterized by unsubstitutability, by the portrayal of public action and interaction and their assumption of subjects' ingredience in the public world, and by a concentration upon identity rather than presence; they portray an historical world, and as such they demand to be read in ways which allow that world to unfold in its own time and space. This kind of writing, more than most others, has a robust enough form to resist any number of over-hasty methods of reading. This kind of writing has the power to resist some of the largely unquestioned assumptions of modern theology, and to force us to realize that other ways of accounting for human being, for human life in history, might be necessary if we wish to do justice to these Gospels. This kind of writing slows us down in our headlong rush to find the text's significance, and requires us to travel by the winding path of unsubstitutable identity.[38]

Admittedly, Frei was later to retreat from this form of argument. He stopped claiming that his method was justified simply by the form of the texts themselves, and started giving a more thoroughly theological and ecclesiological grounding for his conclusions. We shall examine that retreat in chapter 8, and discover that it is a complex matter – by no means a rejection of the whole structure of his argument about *Identity*. For now, however, we can turn back from this relatively abstract material about the general quality of the Gospel texts, and concentrate again on the specific content which provided the real focus of Frei's claims.

5 Alienation and Resurrection

For most of his presentation, Frei brackets the question of historical reference in order later to be able to ask where and how it is most appropriately posed. As we shall see in more detail in the next section, he eventually argues that it is at the resurrection that the question becomes most urgent. In order to clarify Frei's point, however, it is worth turning back to relationalist Christology, and to the very different conclusions about the resurrection and historical reference which turn out to be appropriate in its case.

It is, at first reading, a strange fact that the most rhetorically effective passage in the various writings which make up Frei's Christological proposal is that in which he describes the kind of Christology which one finds on the 'repeatability', 'alienation' and 'presence' side of the divides we have been examining. The kind of description he analyses is one which begins with the conviction that Christ is present to us as a decisive and transformative illumination of our situation, and which, consciously or unconsciously, allows its rendering of the identity of Jesus to be governed by that conviction. Everything in the Gospel depictions of that identity which does not prove so illuminating is reinterpreted: its outer layers are peeled back until its true import for us can be grasped.

Inevitably, this kind of Christology has found any number of different expressions as ideas about the plight and possibilities of human being have changed over the years. The particular example which Frei gives (and he means it only as one example of a wider structure) we might call a Christology of alienation.[39] In this example, Jesus illuminates precisely the fact of our alienation, of our homelessness:

> Jesus is the archetypal man, or the pattern of authentic humanity. He is the *stranger* – as we all are – in this harsh and hostile universe. Our spirit's longing is infinite, our capacity for good and evil – though seldom fully exploited – is likewise unbounded.

We have no destiny on these alien shores other than death. Where our essential home is, since it is not in this world, we do not know. All we know is that it is neither here nor in a superworld of immortality and eternal personal life – a world in which miracle originates and which is miraculously similar to this world. In just this wandering estrangement, Jesus is our embodiment or representative.[40]

This truth about ourselves – and a paradigm of the way in which one can live authentically with such a devastating insight – is the illumination which Christ brings; the encounter with this truth is the presence of Jesus Christ.

In the Gospel depictions of Jesus of Nazareth, stories of the virgin birth are apt symbols of this homelessness: even in birth, he has no anchoring in this world by way of a secure genealogy. The moment he is born, he is forced to flee, and from that time on he is the one who has no place to lay his head. He is rejected and abandoned even by those with whom he has shared himself most fully; in the end, they simply do not understand him and they leave him. He is the one who dies outside the city, dying a death which was not qualitatively distinct from all others, but is paradoxically unique only because

he, unlike others, surrendered all claim to uniqueness by his act of dying and so became one with all of us. He surrendered all false security of reputation by which men try to escape from their true humanity and its ultimately anonymous quality ... That is why his death speaks to men in such an elemental way, and why they can identify with him in sympathy and even in antipathy.[41]

Even in death, he occupied at best a stranger's grave – or, even more strikingly, found no known resting place on earth, but is represented only by a tomb left empty.

This revelation of our true nature is one which grasps us, but which we try to reject. We look in any number of fruitless directions to find something which might count as an identity, a security against the hostility or indifference of the universe. Wherever we run, however, the figure of Jesus always stands in judgment over our efforts, and if we ever allow ourselves to be captivated by him, we will feel that judgment fall – and in it, our salvation arriving.

The rhetorical power of Frei's account of this Christology (which I have done little to capture here) is, it turns out, deeply appropriate. Such a Christology convinces by captivating us with an image of Jesus of Nazareth as Everyman, as the embodiment of the truth which lies within us all. Unless we can be drawn into seeing in this distant mirror our own true faces (or our own true facelessness), such a Christology gains no grip. When it does work, however, there is a shock of recognition, the dawning of a light. As Frei says, 'By contrast, moral substitution, an innocent Saviour dying a unique and unshared death on behalf of the guilty to satisfy the wrath of a literally offended deity, looks like poor fare.'[42] This kind of Christology must speak directly and persuasively (or, as Frei would say, 'concretely')[43] of Christ's presence, for it stands as midwife to the birth of an illumination.

Such a Christology does not allow the question of the historical reference of the resurrection stories any purchase. In fact, if the accounts of the resurrection were to be considered as making a factual claim, Frei suggests that the whole scheme would be put in jeopardy: it would, from the point of view of this account of Jesus' significance, be at best a distraction from his real message, at worst yet another way of running headlong away from the truth which Jesus has to tell us. How could one who has had something happen to him that is so extraordinary, so 'out-of-this-world', so inhuman, continue to be a fit representative of our essential human situation?

> The manner in which he would then confront us has about it the eeriness that accompanies the story of the raising of Lazarus. It is as though we were being stared at with blank eyes capable of evoking in us only that inner terror that bespeaks our reaction to the presence of an absence ... [Such a] Jesus is as inaccessible to us, whose lives are confined to this one lifetime and one lifespace, as if he were on another planet with which there is not even the minimum communication of undecipherable radio signals.[44]

Nevertheless the resurrection can be a fitting climax to the story of the one who is representatively homeless – if we take it as a symbol. Jesus is the one who never gains a location which is his own. He never has even the corner of a stranger's tomb as a possession. As a fact-claim, the resurrection accounts serve only to remove him from our sphere, to cut off the illumination which his identity can cast on ours; as a symbol, they are the starkest judgment upon our desires for immortality. For a Christology of alienation (and, Frei implies, for many other versions of the same logic) Christ can be more nearly 'present' if it is not claimed that he has been factually raised from the dead.

6 The Resurrection and History

If, to begin with, we refuse with Frei the question of historical reference (in order to be able to raise it more pertinently later on), what do we find?[45] What sense can we make of these texts? We have seen Frei's main answer to this already. Without having decided the question of the historical reference of the name 'Jesus', or the kind of reference appropriate to the term 'God', these texts lead us to say that God raised Jesus from the dead, and that this resurrection is constitutive of Jesus' identity – at least, constitutive of the identity of the Jesus of the Bible. The Jesus of the Bible *is* the risen one, whether he is a fictional character or real.[46]

In other words, this Jesus cannot be thought of as not risen. To think of this Jesus as not having been raised is to deny that these texts depict his identity, because it is there that they focus that identity. The resurrection is, in these texts, the climax that organizes and confirms all else that can be said about his identity. If it is denied, the rest of that identity is reduced to a selection of unordered anecdotes, the unity of which will have to be sought in a way which is not depicted in the text but imported by the reader. A Jesus who has not been raised is not *this* Jesus.

Frei very deliberately phrased this claim in a way which resembles Anselm's ontological argument for the existence of God.[47] God, for Anselm, is that than which nothing greater can be conceived, and nothing which bears that name can be conceived of as not existing; Jesus, for Frei, bears the name given him in the Gospels, and one who bears that name cannot be conceived of as not having been raised. This does not mean that the resurrection is 'conceivable' any more than the existence of God is 'conceivable': it remains profoundly mysterious, and any direct imagining of it is soon questionable. Nevertheless, to deny it is to reject the name given to Jesus in the Gospels; it is to talk about a different identity. Frei finds this logic symbolized in the sequence in Luke, when the women are told by the angels at the tomb, 'Why do you look for the living among the dead?' One who had remained in the grave would *by definition* not be the one for whom they were looking.

How does this conclusion relate to the question of historical reference?[48] On the one hand, we have seen Frei argue that these texts are history-like, in particular in the passion sequence *and* the resurrection sequence. If Frei is right in his characterization of the Gospels, the resurrection episode too is depicted with the use of primarily non-mythological or demythologizing techniques apt for the depiction of an unsubstitutable, manifest identity, a character who is formed by and takes his place among the complexes of event and circumstance which make up the public world. The question of historical reference is *allowed* by these texts in a way in which it is not allowed – is, indeed, rendered irrelevant – by most kinds of mythological depiction. To Frei's mind, however, the question is less obviously applicable in, say, the birth narratives, because they have a form closer to the legendary; by the time we have reached the passion narratives, the question has become thoroughly applicable, and it does not cease to be applicable when we reach the resurrection.

In the second place, the question of historical reference is not merely possible, it is *attractive* – and it is attractive here. Frei has, elsewhere in his argument, taken it for granted 'that a man, Jesus of Nazareth, who proclaimed the Kingdom of God's nearness, did exist and was finally executed'.[49] Whether or not that belief is true, anyone who shares it is bound, given the nature of the texts just described, to become curious as to whether the Jesus depicted by these texts is like or unlike the historical Jesus of Nazareth. The place where that question should grip most tightly is precisely where the textual depiction of Jesus has its focus. Most fundamentally, these texts say, Jesus was the crucified and risen one; the question of historical reference, if we let it arise, will find as its first form: 'Did the historical Jesus die and rise again?'

In the third place, however, the question is not merely possible; it is not merely attractive; it is *forced* by these texts, and forced precisely at the resurrection. We have seen that the identity which the texts describe becomes, at the resurrection, the identity of one who (in whatever complex ways) impinges upon our world absolutely. At the resurrection, the depiction we are given is of one who is now unavoidable – who puts the identities of us and of our world to the question. The identity depicted here is of one who, to put it sharply, asks us to place all of history relative to him. How can we, faced with such a claim, avoid the question as to whether the world is truly like this? And if we have that question of truth forced absolutely upon us, how (given the character of the texts in which it is forced) can it be forced without including within it the question of historical reference? To be told that our historical world has unavoidably to do with one who gained and manifested his identity publicly in a particular time and place *requires* us to ask the historical question. A believer, one who believes that the claim that the Gospel depictions make on us is a true claim, a just claim, will have to go on to say that the resurrection is constitutive of the identity of the Jesus of Nazareth who lived on this earth two thousand years ago. The only alternative, from the point of view of the believer, is to reject these texts completely – to take them to be depictions of a fictional world which is absolutely and irrevocably divorced from our own.

The question of history is, then, forced upon us – but this does not mean that our only recourse is naïve literalism. In particular, Frei does not believe that we are pushed towards that kind of literalism which tries to find a harmony of the various resurrection accounts, and tries to present a smoothed out version of 'what really happened'. The ambiguity, mystery and complexity that have been keynotes of Frei's discussion of the resurrection are not abolished now. Instead, Frei settles for a careful statement of his conclusion: it is 'more nearly correct to think of Jesus as factually raised, bodily if you will, than not to think of him in this manner'.[50] On the one hand, Frei finds himself compelled to affirm *that* the resurrection happened – that these texts refer; on the other hand, he finds himself unable to say *what* happened except by telling the story: he has no description available of that to which these texts refer other than that provided by the curious, fragmentary, confusing and mysterious story which they tell – and he has no desire or need to deny their mystifying nature. Frei affirms the resurrection, but he does so with a deep reserve.[51]

Frei gives more content to the two-sidedness of his affirmation by saying on the one hand that we should not expect the resurrection to be amenable to direct proof in historical-critical terms (that is, it is not of a kind to be rendered probable by the accumulation of historical-critical evidence). On the other hand, decisive evidence that the resurrection did not happen would indeed be evidence against the truth of this claim – and hence against the truth of the Christian faith. If it were somehow to be shown that there was a body still mouldering in the grave then, despite all his analogical reserve, Frei would hold that the limits of his affirmation had been breached, and that the structure of his belief would be destroyed. Frei's claim about the resurrection is thus in principle a falsifiable claim: or at least, he finds the description of this claim as falsifiable the best way of conveying the kind of insistence that he finds to be the thrust of these texts, once the nature and the content of their depiction of Jesus' unsubstitutable identity has been taken into account. To say that such a falsification is in practice implausible, or even that it is impossible to think of anything that might count decisively as such a falsification, is not necessarily a serious criticism of Frei's position: he has not made this comment in order to describe a procedure by which Christainity could be attacked or vindicated, but in order to show what *kind* of affirmation he takes himself to be making.[52]

Frei has argued that the Gospels are historical in form, and that they refer historically at least at this particular juncture. Nevertheless, he is not saying that our conclusions about what did and did not happen historically must be based solely upon historical-critical investigation, and he is still allowing himself to say that something has happened in history which isn't simply one more historically explicable occurrence. On the one hand, he is still relying upon a trust in the appropriateness of the biblical witness which, from the point of view of a Harvey or a Strauss, must appear excessive. As he puts it in *Identity*, the affirmations he has made rest on a belief in 'something like the inspired quality of the accounts' – a belief that these texts are trustworthy guides.[53] On the other hand, he has committed himself to belief in an event which does not fit anywhere within the normal categories of imagination. Frei has not, in other words, made any compact with Troeltsch's insistence upon the probabilistic weighing of evidence, or the assumption of a fundamental uniformity in history. Clearly, Frei's answer to Strauss is not going to involve any convergence on the question of historical *method*. On this point, his answer to Strauss is a bold denial. He will not start from where Strauss wants him to start, and he will not regard himself as bound by the rules by which Strauss believes he should play.

Nevertheless, on another level, and for thoroughly theological reasons, Frei is able to respond to Strauss far more positively. He has argued as strongly as Strauss that there can be no retreat from the messy public world to some artificially isolated realm where we can step outside our finitude. So far, he has argued this in the case of Jesus of Nazareth, claiming that what takes place in Jesus takes place in the world of contingency and complexity, of actions and interactions, of characters and circumstances. Yes, Frei boldly claims that something unprecedented and unparalleled has taken place within that world, but he is adamant that the world in which that has taken place is an historical world, and the characters among whom it has taken place are historical characters, and that its taking place does not rest on the existence of any aspect of historical existence which is not itself truly historical. By unashamedly proclaiming a miracle in the midst of history, history is freed of the intolerable burden of somehow being *naturally* the home of the absolute, and so is allowed to be itself again.

In the next two chapters, we will examine another aspect of this insistence towards which we have seen Frei gesturing with his distinction between Christologies of presence and of identity: the claim that the world in which believers acknowledge the impact of this act of God in Christ is and remains an historical world, and that our relation within this world to Christ must be understood, in some sense, historically. We will see that Frei believes he can continue to affirm the finite, contingent and creaturely nature of historical existence (indeed, that he must affirm it more strongly than before), precisely *because* one part of that historical existence has been given by God a status utterly unique, and is held by believers parabolically to illuminate the whole. In order to understand how that can be so, however, we need to turn to Frei's doctrine of providence, and to his description of the practice of figural interpretation.

Notes

1. To use the terms which John Milbank uses in one of his critiques of Frei, we can say that Frei accompanies his 'syntagmatic' tracing with 'paradigmatic' reflection; see *Theology and Social Theory* (Oxford: Blackwell, 1990), pp. 382–88.
2. Chapter 8 describes Frei's later retreat from the form of this argument.
3. Note how the central sections of 'Theological Reflections' (*1966a*) are arranged: a section on 'The Central Enactment of Jesus' Identity' which tells the story of Jesus from Gethsemane to the Resurrection is followed by a section on 'Formal Elements of Identity Description', which in turn is followed by 'Identity Description and the Story of Jesus in the Gospels' which retells the story of Jesus from beginning to end.
4. Ibid., pp. 46–47.
5. See, e.g., ibid., pp. 46, 56, 59, 76, 82.
6. This very precise focusing is far clearer in 'Theological Reflections' (*1966a*) than in *The Identity of Jesus Christ* (*1975a*).
7. 'Theological Reflections' (*1966a*), p. 49.
8. Ibid., pp. 46, 51–56; cf. *The Identity of Jesus Christ* (*1975a*), pp. 63–84.
9. 'Theological Reflections' (*1966a*), p. 51.
10. We should be careful, once again, not to misunderstand the task in which Frei was engaged, nor to lose sight of his insistence that we stick close to the Gospel stories. He did not set about developing a new anthropological theory under cover of which he could launch an attack on an alternative anthropological theory. Rather, he set himself the task of asking what kinds of assumptions about human identity allow us to make sense of the Gospel stories as depictions of Christ's identity. What conceptual framework allows us to take these texts as seriously as possible?
11. 'Theological Reflections' (*1966a*), pp. 68–70.
12. Ibid., p. 89. Frei tended to trace this schema back to Kant. In his lecture notes for 'The Formation of German Religious Thought in the Passage from Enlightenment to Romanticism' (?1981a), he writes that, after the self's near-disappearance in Hume, 'Kant's revolution was to bring the self back, but now *in a manner in which it no longer fitted into the world of substances/things*' (p. 5, my emphasis). For Kant the 'Self is not simply a substance like other realities in the world but [is] a slant on the world. Now ... Kant posits ... that *this* self, this unitary perspective on the world, the *whole* self, is split against itself. Hence the beginning of [the] Christology ... of all subsequent theology worth speaking of, until the present time, [which] takes its departure from this point, the unitary self split against itself which must become one' (p. 11). In attacking this subject–alienation view, Frei saw himself in line with Barth, who 'denied that human existence is primarily inward' ('German Theology', *1974b*, p. 103).
13. In his Greenhoe lectures, 'On Interpreting the Christian Story' (1976h), Frei makes explicit the link between a concentration upon symbolic language and theologies of alienation, linking theologies of manifestation to a concentration upon realistic language.

14. 'Theological Reflections' (*1966a*), p. 88. When it comes to naming names, Frei refers not just to the early twentieth century and to Bultmann, but to the last century and a half of (largely) German theology, first Idealist then Existentialist, from Schleiermacher onwards (ibid., pp. 88, 91 n. 12). He mentions Schleiermacher, Schelling, Hegel and Marx; existential phenomenologists and many psychologists; Tillich, Bultmann, and some of Bultmann's students; he dubs Kafka alienation's pre-eminent muse. This is far from being a minor border squabble over the classification of one portion of the Gospel texts.

15. Ibid., pp. 63, 65.

16. In fact, although I present both schemes as different specifications of Frei's general claims against the subject–alienation scheme, their presentation in Frei's work is somewhat more complicated. The first scheme, 'intention–action' description, he presents more or less independently from his polemic against subject–alienation schemes, even though its basic structure clearly reflects that polemic. The second scheme is the one which he refers to as 'subject-manifest-in-difference' description or 'self–manifestation description' proper. In presenting them both under the rubric 'subject–manifestation', I have risked confusing the terminology in order to make clear the logic of Frei's position. However, from now on, we will speak, with Frei, of 'intention–action' description on the one hand and 'self–manifestation' description on the other, recognizing that while both are united in opposition to subject–alienation schemes of description, it is the latter which Frei lets bear the fullest weight of that opposition.

17. *The Identity of Jesus Christ* (*1975a*), p. 92. Frei was drawing on Gilbert Ryle, *The Concept of Mind* (London: Hutchison, 1949), with which he had become more closely acquainted when supervising Robert H. King's dissertation, *The Concept of Personal Agency as a Theological Model* (Yale, 1965).

18. Frei describes 'intention–action' description in 'Theological Reflections' (*1966a*), pp. 62–64 and *The Identity of Jesus Christ* (*1975a*), pp. 91–94.

19. 'Theological Reflections' (*1966a*), p. 64.

20. *The Identity of Jesus Christ* (*1975a*), p. 93.

21. See 'Theological Reflections' (*1966a*), pp. 64–73; *The Identity of Jesus Christ* (*1975a*), pp. 94–101; 'Remarks in Connection with a Theological Proposal' (1967b), pp. 36–37.

22. *The Identity of Jesus Christ* (*1975a*), pp. 97–98.

23. 'Theological Reflections' (*1966a*), p. 70.

24. *The Identity of Jesus Christ* (*1975a*), pp. 96–97.

25. It is relatively easy to see how this relates to what he said about 'names': we can see that, to the extent a name is regarded not simply as an empty signifier but as a title or description, both Frei's theoretical account of self–manifestation and his actual practice of it are interested in the way that a name which is given to Jesus from outside, which is a public possession, can nevertheless manifest rather than cloak Jesus' identity. It is somewhat harder to see the connection between what Frei said before about bodies and what he says now. Frei appeared to be aware of the instability of his theoretical account at this point: in 'Remarks in Connection with a Theological Proposal' (1967b) he distinguished between 'self–word' or 'self–culture' descriptions and 'self–body' descriptions, and instead of making the latter simply another form of self–manifestation description, he connected it with intention–action description. Nevertheless, it seems to me that these details are relatively unimportant. What matters are, on the one hand, the contrast between self–manifestation and self–alienation schemes of description (in the service of which contrast it makes sense to consider bodies under the heading of manifestation as much as under intention–action) and, on the other hand, Frei's more detailed indication of how the Gospels identify Jesus in ways which outstrip intention–action categories (in which context 'body' plays a more ambiguous role).

26. John Milbank is right to describe this as being 'akin to the circular plot of a detective story, in which something is gradually disclosed to both fictional characters and to the reader that has really been the case all along. Here it is the truth about the identity of the central character, Jesus.' However, it should be clear by now that Frei would absolutely reject

Milbank's continuation: 'Moreover, this identity does not actually relate to his "character",
but rather to his universal significance for which his particularity stands, almost, as a mere
cipher' ('The Name of Jesus', in *The Word Made Strange* (Oxford: Blackwell, 1997), p.
149).

27. In the Preface to *The Identity of Jesus Christ* (1974i), Frei wonders whether the form in
which he had presented it 'may suffer from ... too heavy an infestation of the vagaries
and dogmas of its Idealist parentage' (p. x). Frei's final return to these topics can be found
in one of his drafts for the 1987 Cadbury Lectures, (1987a[i]), in which he says that, in
contrast to intention–action description, 'subject–predicate' description is 'important in
our context because the almost midrashically flexible extendability or porousness of the
texts about Jesus of Nazareth, allowing every age to discover in him its particular vision
or ideal type of humanity, is a function of a subject–predicate description of him, rather
than a description of his identity as the intentional agent constituted by his passion, death
and resurrection. Predicates unlike subjecthood or agenthood are – precisely as the word
indicates – predicable. They may be shared by many subjects. They are communal, as well
as inter-personal, and as such they foster shared identities.'

28. See chap. 1, n. 39.

29. 'Preface' (1974i), p. viii.

30. 'The Formation of German Religious Thought in the Passage from Enlightenment to
Romanticism' (?1981a), p. 1. Frei continues, 'One mustn't forget (1) that Lessing was
himself (like Goethe!) a pietist believer once, and that he prefers this with its orthodox rather
than Rationalist leanings always to the brittle, intellectualistic and dishonest compromises
of the Neologians; and (2) that he's talking about proof of spirit and power, i.e. of a here-
and-now inward strength that gives *certitude*, not simply a weighing of evidence for and
against the facts. And that's where the gulf or time interval becomes so important: Past
so inexorably a dimension I cannot experience, a past occasion cannot be immediately,
inwardly–certainly present to me: *Reports* of prophecies fulfilled, of miracles done, are not
the same as prophecies fulfilled and miracles done. "Those ... done before my eyes work
immediately ... the others are supposed to work through a medium which robs them of all
power"' (pp. 1–2, Frei's emphasis); cf. 'Religious Transformation in the Later Eighteenth
Century' (1974c), pp. 34–36, 40 and 'Religion: Natural and Revealed' (*1958a*), p. 318.

31. 'Religion: Natural and Revealed' (*1958a*), p. 310.

32. See chap. 8, §4 for Frei's rejection of 'presence'. His shift away from presence parallels the
shift which he believed the later volumes of Barth's *Church Dogmatics* display away from
'revelation' as a central concept.

33. 'A Meditation for the Week of Good Friday and Easter', 1974f, pp. 170–71.

34. 'Theological Reflections' (*1966a*), p. 46.

35. Ibid., p. 58.

36. 'Remarks in Connection with a Theological Proposal' (1967b), p. 32.

37. In 'Historical Reference and the Gospels' (?1981c), Frei wrote, concerning *The Identity
of Jesus Christ* (1975a), 'I must stress however that the exegesis was of extraordinary
importance to me, and that I tried to make the hermeneutical instruments as minimal and
non-interfering as possible ... I tried to allow the text to influence not only the content,
i.e., the application of the rules of thought to my re-rendering of the descriptions given in
the texts, but to influence the rules of thought by which I was proceeding, "the conditions
for the possibility of understanding" the texts, as our phenomenological friends would
say. Not that I believed there is no "pre-understanding" (to quote another set of friends),
that there are no formal rules for making intelligible statements as well as claims, no rules
covering various types of argument. But I believed and still believe that I ought to leave
open the possibility that a reading of the texts might actually and in principle influence,
modify, change these preconditions, rules, or what have you ... I hoped that coherence
between the content of the exegesis and the description of the formal rules under which
it took place – both, and not only the former, being referred to the text – might actually
constitute an argument against those who argue that exegesis is simply governed by the

theological design that goes into it. Obversely, it was to de-rigidify those who know a priori and with absolute confidence all the rules under which texts are understood' (pp. 5–7).

38. Of course, we should beware of a premature generalizing. Frei does not immediately apply universally what he has found here, as if he should claim that because a subject–alienation account is resisted by these texts at this point, we must abandon it across the board. To rush to that conclusion would be to locate the significance of the Gospel depictions of Jesus as located directly in the *general* quality of unsubstitutability, or in the general nature of the relationship between the self and its manifestations which is suggested here, and would be once again to locate their significance in something repeatable, which could be and is born equally well by any number of other depictions. (This would be closer to Herder than to Frei. In his notes for a 1973 undergraduate lecture [1973b], Frei said that for Herder, 'The *meaning* of these stories is the gradually developing realistic spirit evident in them' [p. 5]). Frei is not going to approach any more general affirmation of historical consciousness by that route. If the Gospels say anything about the general nature of our world (and Frei will argue that they do), they say it by means not simply of their *form*, but by means of their winding and complex content.

39. *The Identity of Jesus Christ (1975a)*, p. 51.

40. Ibid., pp. 29–30.

41. Ibid., pp. 30–31.

42. Ibid., p. 31.

43. E.g., ibid., p. 33.

44. Ibid., p. 28.

45. It is Herder, not Frei, who refuses the question of historical reference permanently. In a lecture on Herder (1973b) Frei quotes C. Hartlich and W. Sachs, *Der Ursprung des Mythosbegriffes in der modernen Bibelwissenschaft* (Tübingen: Mohr, 1952), p. 57: 'Herder wants to return to the original naïveté of the Bible, appropriate it completely and *live* within it as one lives within a poetic work. He does not want to be tempted either by the question of the factuality of what is narrated there, nor by the question of the necessary reshaping of the temporally conditioned biblical meaning.'

46. For this, and for what follows, see 'Theological Reflections' (1966a), pp. 82–87; *The Identity of Jesus Christ (1975a)*, pp. 139–52.

47. For more on the connection with Anselm, see Appendix 1.

48. For what follows, cf. 'Historical Reference and the Gospels' (?1981c): 'I may put the argument like this. Suppose someone who believed (1) that Jesus Christ did live, (2) that this is essential for the religion named after him, and (3) that the accounts describing his life state some things that are more important than others for the affirmation of (2), then, I want to say, the crucifixion and resurrection are the most important. On this a non-believer and a believer should be able to agree.'

49. *The Identity of Jesus Christ (1975a)*, p. 51.

50. Ibid., p. 150.

51. It is important to grasp that this reserve does not imply that Frei secretly knows better. He knows that the affirmation is inadequate, and yet he knows no other way of making it, and believes that the other ways of making it available to him are still more inadequate – including the other way which would say, 'I have to say that it is factually true, but I know that it isn't really.'

52. For Frei's later clarification of these matters, see chap. 8, §7. Such falsifiability may seem to sit ill with the presentation of Frei's argument as an Anselmian *proof* of the resurrection of Jesus, but Frei does not mean his Anselmian argument as a proof which must convince the unbeliever. The unbeliever is quite at liberty to regard this account of Jesus' identity as fictional, and to regard the claim which it makes to factuality as part of the fiction, seeing the texts therefore as a kind of 'hyperfiction claiming to be self-warranting truth' (ibid., p. 143). The believer, however (one who believes that these texts are an apt depiction of the man from Nazareth) is compelled to affirm the resurrection in this way.

53. Ibid., p. 150.

6

The Eclipse of Providence

I said at the end of chapter 4 that the main way in which Frei filled out the lines of his sketched 'story of salvation' was by elaborating a doctrine of providence, and I suggested that it was most of all his exploration of figural interpretation which provided him with the materials he needed for this filling out. At the end of the last chapter I suggested again that it was Frei's exploration of the parabolic illumination of history by Christ that allowed him to establish the form of historical consciousness proper to faith. As we have seen, Frei hinted at these matters in the final chapter of the 1967 articles which were later published as *The Identity of Jesus Christ*; his fuller account can be found in, among other works, his paper, 'Karl Barth: Theologian' (1969a), in *The Eclipse of Biblical Narrative* (1974a), and in an unpublished paper from the early 1980s, 'History, Salvation-History, and Typology' (1981f). We will begin, however, with an examination of one of the major influences on Frei's development of this material: Erich Auerbach.

1 The Divine Illumination of History

Like Frei, Erich Auerbach took a rather winding route from Berlin to Yale. He was born in the former city thirty years before Frei, in 1892, 'a member of the humanely liberal, financially comfortable, Prussian-Jewish haute bourgeoisie'.[1] He gained a doctorate in jurisprudence in 1913, was drafted into military service, and on his return studied Romance Philology at the University of Berlin. He moved to Marburg in 1929, and there wrote a book, *Dante als Dichter der irdischen Welt* – that is *Dante as Poet of the Earthly* (or, as the book's American translator rendered it, *Secular*) *World*; while there he also began work on a project on the meaning and philological history of the term 'figura'. A Jewish academic in Nazi Germany, he was dismissed from Marburg in 1936, and moved to Istanbul, where he published his findings on 'figura' in an article of the same name, and, more famously, wrote *Mimesis: The Representation of Reality in Western Literature* – a sprawling, episodic history of Western literary realism from Homer to Virginia Woolf, written from the geographical margins of the West, at a time when it seemed like the achievements of that tradition were being buried. After the war he moved to Pennsylvania State University, then to Princeton, and finally to Yale, where he stayed until his death in 1957 – the year after Frei completed his doctoral thesis.

123

The story he tells in *Mimesis* starts long before Dante, and continues long after him, but Auerbach's reading of Dante is the pivot on which the book turns – and the key to Frei's use of his work.[2] Auerbach thought he had found in Dante the point in Western letters where a fully appropriate literary form had at last been found for the representation of the contingent, complex, everyday, historical world: a literary form which allowed that reality to be represented not now as necessarily comic, nor as necessarily idyllic, but with real seriousness. As such, Auerbach's Dante stands at the beginning of that tradition of secular realism whose maturity we see in the Western novel – and as such, Auerbach's Dante became for Frei a pivotal figure in his attempts to understand what it meant to do justice to that historical world.

It might, on first hearing, sound strange that it should be Dante who provides Auerbach's key to the representation of secular reality. Auerbach is, after all, speaking of Dante's *Comedy*, a vision of an other-worldly inferno, purgatory and paradise; yet his argument is not simply that Dante somehow overcomes this other-worldly setting in order to produce his worldly vision; he argues that Dante's achievement was *made possible* precisely by a long Christian and Jewish theological tradition of the portrayal of everyday reality in the light of God's eschatological judgment. The relevance of Auerbach's account to Frei's wider concerns should be clear: Auerbach provides, in his reading of Dante, an account of the mutual implication of a theology of God's eschatological judgment and what we might call 'secular realism' – obviously meaning by that not a realism without God, but rather the realistic portrayal of the world of the *saeculum*: the messy human world between fall and eschaton.

Mimesis begins with a contrast between Homer and the Old Testament, in which Auerbach teases out the differences between their approaches to the representation of reality, to realism.[3] Auerbach believed that there is a strong relationship between Hebrew monotheism and the ways in which the Old Testament's style of narrative history differs from Homer's narrative style. In Homer, 'Even on occasions when gods appear suddenly and briefly, whether to help one of their favorites or to deceive or destroy some mortal whom they hate, their bodily forms, and usually the manner of their coming and going, are given in detail.'[4] By contrast, Hebrew monotheism is characterized by a prohibition on idolatry, an emphasis, says Auerbach, on God's 'lack of form, his lack of local habitation, his singleness'.[5] In the story which Auerbach selects as his example, that of Abraham's journey to sacrifice Isaac, 'God appears without bodily form ... coming from some unspecified place – we only hear his voice, and that utters nothing but a name.'[6] Abraham does not respond to a clearly illumined divine character, placed in the limelit foreground of the narrative; instead his 'words and gestures are directed toward the depths of the picture or upward, but in any case the undetermined, dark place from which the voice comes to him is not in the foreground'.[7]

This does not mean that we are given a portrayal of a fully realized, brightly lit human foreground, with hints of divine mystery glimpsed only in its occasional gaps: rather, things, places and people are portrayed primarily in the moments in which they are drawn into encounter with this divine darkness and strangely illuminated by it, albeit briefly. The presence of God in the narratives in Genesis is like repeated flashes of lightning, blinding when one looks towards them, but capable of throwing stark, momentary illumination on the surrounding terrain. Much of the creaturely world is left mysterious, its connections and reasons not fully displayed. Whereas Homer, according to Auerbach, 'represent[s] phenomena in a fully externalised form, visible and palpable in all their parts, and completely fixed in their spatial and temporal relations',[8] Abraham's journey to Jeruel is 'a silent progress through the undeterminate and the contingent'.[9]

The narrative technique of Genesis is determined by this brilliant darkness of God, and the brief illumination and deep shadows which it allows to human affairs; it is characterized by

> the externalization of only so much of the phenomena as is necessary for the purpose of the narrative, all else [being] left in obscurity; the decisive points of the narrative alone are emphasized, what lies between is nonexistent; time and place are undefined and call for interpretation; thoughts and feelings remain unexpressed, are only suggested by the silence and the fragmentary speeches; the whole, permeated with the most unrelieved suspense and directed toward a single goal ... remains mysterious and 'fraught with background'.[10]

As a result, characters can, far more clearly than in Homer, have complex and intractable depths. Precisely because their thoughts and feelings are less cleanly displayed, the psychology underlying the contingencies of the narrative remains problematic, a matter for tentative explanation, always liable to lose its way.

It is in this light that Auerbach makes a distinction between a literary form he labels 'history' and a literary form he labels 'legend'.

> [O]nly seldom does a more or less plain situation, comparatively simple to describe, arise, and even such a situation is subject to division below the surface, is indeed almost constantly in danger of losing its simplicity: and the motives of all the interested parties are so complex that the slogans of propaganda can be composed only through the crudest simplification – with the result that friend and foe alike can often employ the same ones. To write history is so difficult that most historians are forced to make concessions to the technique of legend.[11]

With this distinction in mind – rather than a distinction between factually accurate and factually inaccurate accounts – Auerbach argues that the monotheistic atmosphere of Hebrew narrative makes for something which is in form closer to 'history' than to 'legend', at least when compared to Homer, and that this is so precisely because of, rather than despite, the presence of encounters with God throughout the narrative.

In other words: Hebrew monotheism goes with a certain kind of realism in depiction which grants that history is not straightforwardly explicable. Because straightforward and easily graspable causal connections cannot be sustained in a narrative that has the inscrutable will of a God like this as its constant reference point, the kind of straightforward and easily graspable connections that gloss over the complexity of real human history are broken too: room is made for a more question-begging picture of human action, a picture of history which is repeatedly obscure, which repeatedly and systemically calls for interpretation. To reject idolatry, and to write narratives like this, go together – indeed, for Auerbach the shape of Hebrew monotheism is as much a consequence of the Hebrew form of story-telling as it is its cause.[12]

Auerbach notes various other aspects of this alliance between theology and literary representation: aspects of the kind of portrayal favoured in Genesis which are at the same time aspects of Hebrew monotheism. First, he suggests that there is a significant social difference between Homer and the Old Testament. Homer, he says, 'seems more limited and more static in respect to the circle of personages involved in the action and to their political activity'.[13] '[I]n the Homeric poems life is enacted only among the ruling class – others appearing only in the role of servants to that class'; 'they are unmistakably a sort of feudal aristocracy'. 'As a social picture, this world is completely stable; wars take place only between different groups of the ruling class.'[14] Auerbach acknowledges that the patriarchal narratives of Genesis are also focused on leaders and rulers, but suggests that the nomadic context does not allow for the same political stability as the Homeric picture, and claims that, in any case, in the later narratives of the Hebrew Bible, and especially in the prophets, matters become more socially and politically complex.

> As soon as the people completely emerges – that is, after the exodus from Egypt – its activity is always discernible, it is often in ferment, it frequently intervenes in events not only as a whole but also in separate groups and through the medium of separate individuals who come forward.[15]

In another sense too, the Old Testament depicts a world in which the isolation of the ruling classes is far less complete than it is in Homer. The members of Homer's ruling class are 'far more untouched in their heroic elevation than are the Old Testament figures';[16] the Old Testament characters can appear with much less dignity; scenes of great import take place in the midst of the domestic and the commonplace, whereas for Homer the domestic is always and only the 'peaceful realm of the idyllic'.

> In the Old Testament stories the peace of daily life in the house, in the fields, and among the flocks, is undermined by jealousy over election and the promise of a blessing, and complications arise which would be utterly incomprehensible to the

Homeric heroes ... [T]he perpetually smouldering jealousy and the connection between the domestic and the spiritual, between the paternal blessing and the divine blessing, lead to daily life being permeated with the stuff of conflict, often with poison. The sublime influence of God here reaches so deeply into the everyday that the two realms of the sublime and the everyday are not only actually unseparated but basically inseparable.[17]

The brilliant darkness from which God rules does not rest on top of a finely graded hierarchy, or shine more brightly on a single class of people. Rather, when the lightning of encounter with God flashes, the illuminated landscape is to an extent flattened: the everyday and the lowly receive their share of this light just as do the exalted and proud. Yes, there is plenty that is patriarchal and monarchical, hierarchical and aristocratic, in the Old Testament narratives; nevertheless, Auerbach suggests, the literary form of the biblical narratives renders that stratification questionable.

The same 'mixture of styles' which Auerbach had identified in the Old Testament comes even more clearly to the fore in the New Testament literature, which he analyses in the second chapter of *Mimesis*. There Auerbach examines on the one hand Petronius and Tacitus who, like Homer, 'reveal the limits of antique realism and thus of antique historical consciousness';[18] and, on the other, the Gospel of Mark, which

portrays something which neither the poets nor the historians of antiquity ever set out to portray: the birth of a spiritual movement in the depths of the common people, from within the everyday occurrences of contemporary life, which thus assumes an importance it could never have assumed in antique literature.[19]

Every occurrence in the New Testament

is concerned with the same question, the same conflict with which every human being is basically confronted and which therefore remains infinite and eternally pending. It sets man's whole world astir ... What we see here is a world which on the one hand is entirely real, average, identifiable as to place, time and circumstances, but which on the other hand is shaken in its very foundations, is transforming and renewing itself before our eyes. For the New Testament authors who are their contemporaries, these occurrences on the plain of everyday life assume the importance of world-revolutionary events, as later on they will for everyone.[20]

The plain of everyday life, the plain on which the mighty and the lowly both stand, is caught up as a whole and in all its parts in the great drama of God's providence. Only literary representations of the world which ignore classical barriers between lofty and comic, sublime and lowly, can properly flourish in this atmosphere.

The second additional feature of Hebrew realism which Auerbach notes is that the world displayed in Genesis is also a world which takes time. In

Genesis, God chooses and forms the patriarchs 'to the end of embodying his essence and will – yet choice and formation do not coincide, for the latter proceeds gradually, historically, during the earthly life of him upon whom the choice has fallen'.[21] The patriarchs are only slowly 'differentiated into full individuality', shaped by their repeated encounters with and reactions to God. The stark lightning flashes by which the story of Abraham is illuminated do not obliterate his temporality: they simply punctuate it, and we are shown a man who mysteriously grows and changes. Whereas in Homer, individuals are to a large part explained by their unchanging character, their actions emerging from the virtues and vices which define them, a figure like Abraham in Genesis is only defined by his story: we see him as he encounters God moving him and moulding him, and we are given access to no underlying clue, no psychological profile, which would enable us to explain all his appearances as emanations of an inviolate core. He is what he is only in the successive, cumulative encounters with God (and, to a lesser extent, with others) which are the substance of the narrative. The world of Genesis takes time to unfold.

The third additional feature of Hebrew realism which Auerbach notes is that the narrative is imperialistic. Homer can present to us, he says, a uniformly illumined world that, precisely as such, is self-contained: its reasons and connections are fully displayed, fully consistent, and require no support from and make no claims about realities outside the narrative's light. The Old Testament, however, does not allow such a distancing: by portraying the world in relation to a transcendent and ineffable height – in relation, we might say, to its overwhelming judge and universal crisis – Genesis does not present a distant, self-contained world for our entertainment, but seeks to overcome the whole world, to unravel the strings of connection and explanation with which we thought we had surrounded ourselves, and to tie them in to the story being told. The Scripture stories 'seek to subject us, and if we refuse to be subjected we are rebels'.[22] '[W]e are to fit our own life into its world, feel ourselves to be elements in its structure of universal history.'[23] This is no pleasing virtual reality into which we can, in an idle hour, imagine ourselves: it is a portrayal of our whole world broken open in encounter with an inescapable God.[24]

According to Auerbach, then, the narratives of the Hebrew Bible portray a world which is allowed to emerge as mysterious, complex and contingent – as historical – *because* it relates to a transcendent ground; a world in which the lowly as well as the mighty are called before the same throne of God; a world in which the plans of God take time to become all that they have been chosen to be; and a world which is no entertaining fiction, but the crisis and judgment of the one world in which we live. The very form of the narratives suggests a theology of the One God who creates and calls, who elects the lowly, who providentially orders the whole world, and such a theology is a condition of the possibility of this kind of narrative. Only because God is seen in this way can human history be taken so seriously.

2 Figura and History

The story which Auerbach tells of the development of Western representations of reality from the Old Testament to Dante is a complex one, with many episodes. For our purposes, however, there is only one other major element which we need to explore before we turn to Dante himself: Auerbach's account of figural interpretation, found both in chapter 3 of *Mimesis* and in an earlier long article which Frei found particularly generative – a piece simply entitled 'Figura'.

Christianity inherited the Hebrew Scriptures, but their preservation within the Christian Scriptures was not a straightforward matter. It would not be too difficult to tell a version of the story of that preservation which saw the realism, the materiality, the history-like quality of Hebrew narrative precisely as the element which was overcome, undermined or abolished when Christians adopted these texts. Christians, such an account might say, could only form a united canon of Old and New Testaments when they had found ways to cloak the literal sense – the realistic sense – of the Hebrew narratives in a spiritual sense which overcame the embarrassment of Judaism's historical world.

Auerbach argues that this is not so; or at least, not the only or the most important strand of the story. The form of adoption of Hebrew Scripture which ultimately triumphed in early Christianity was the *figural*, and the form of figural interpretation which Christians adopted has a more complex and more interesting relationship to the literal, realistic sense of the Old Testament. What then is figural interpretation? A figural interpreter, says Auerbach, might take an occurrence like the sacrifice of Isaac and interpret it 'as prefiguring the sacrifice of Christ, so that in the former the latter is as it were announced and promised, and the latter "fulfils" ... the former'. This is not because the interpreter has identified any earthly causal link or process of development linking the two; rather the connection 'can be established only if both occurrences are vertically linked to Divine Providence which alone is able to devise such a plan of history and supply the key to its understanding'.[25]

How does such a figural interpretation relate to the realism that Auerbach has identified as characterizing the Old Testament narratives themselves? Auerbach suggests that this very question was a source of contention in the early centuries of the Christian era. He pits Origen against Tertullian, suggesting that for Origen Christian interpretation does undercut the realism of the Old Testament texts: the spiritual meaning which the Old Testament texts bear is one which they have *despite* their apparent reference to a concrete, contingent history.[26] Even if that reference is still affirmed (perhaps as providentially arranged for the edification of the hermeneutically uninitiated), the connection between the deeper Christological meaning and the surface historical meaning is severed. For Tertullian on the other hand – a 'staunch realist' in Auerbach's opinion[27] – it is more often precisely the historical reality aptly depicted in the Old Testament text which is the figure of Christ; both figure and fulfilment are fully historical, carnal realities: the figure is a 'phenomenal prophecy', its fulfilment an incarnate reality.[28] The figural interpretation of the Old Testament text is for Tertullian *dependent* upon its literal reading.

In the West, it was a compromise between Origen and Tertullian which prevailed; Auerbach identifies Augustine as the main architect of the deal. Auerbach argues that pure allegory was *not* the mainstay of Augustine's interpretation of the Old Testament. Rather, for him, 'the Old Testament was pure phenomenal prophecy';[29] it described a concrete history of events and observances that were a promise of what was to come, and that have now been overtaken by their fulfilment, a fulfilment which is itself a clearer and more complete promise, equally historical and concrete. For Augustine, the promise-fulfilment scheme is now threefold rather than a simple binary opposition: the new promise, the fulfilment of the old, still looks forward to a final, eschatological fulfilment.

If we accept, for a moment, Auerbach's characterization of the various authors he cites, we must say that Origen's interpretation cannot be called 'figural' in Auerbach's sense, insofar as the reference to Christ he finds in the Old Testament is all too often independent of the literal, historical scenes portrayed there; on the other hand, Tertullian's and Augustine's *is* figural, whenever it is clear that it is precisely the historical scene portrayed in the Old Testament text, or some part of it, which is, in the providence of God, a shadow of things to come. Only these latter authors assume a genuine theology of history, a genuine doctrine of the providential governance of history.

A further question still remains to be asked, however. Granted that figural interpretation could support rather than abolish the historical reading of the Old Testament narratives, does it, in doing so, support or undermine the specific character of the Hebrew historical vision, as identified by Auerbach? To use the labels with which Auerbach provided us, Hebrew narrative was, in literary terms, closer to 'history' than to 'legend' – i.e., it projected a view of history which, precisely because all was seen in connection with an ineffable God, allowed for a fundamental complexity and mysteriousness about events and persons, rather than requiring that everything be nailed down under the uniform light of legend. Is this 'historical' rather than 'legendary' character of the Old Testament histories acknowledged or ignored in their Christian appropriation?

Auerbach certainly believed that it, or something very like it, was preserved. Just as it was precisely the Old Testament's referral of the world to God that made space for its portrayal of the world as contingent and historical, so, he argues, figural interpretations' claims about phenomenal prophecy themselves *require* a view of the world which is closer to 'history' than to 'legend'. Of course, the practice of figural interpretation varied enormously, and it is certainly true that for some figural interpreters, perhaps for many, the rich density of the world projected by Old Testament narrative was dissolved. Nevertheless, Auerbach argues that this was not always so, and that it need not have been so: such solubility is not implied by the nature of figural interpretation itself. Figural interpretation, he suggests, itself projects a vision of the world which is 'historical' rather than 'legendary'. This is particularly true once the eschatological provisionality of the reality to which figural interpretation points is taken into account – that is, once Augustine's more complex threefold pattern of promise, renewed promise, and eschatological fulfilment triumphs over the simple twofold pattern of promise and fulfilment. Auerbach says:

> Figural prophecy implies the interpretation of one worldly event through another; the first signifies the second, the second fulfills the first. Both remain historical events; yet both, looked at in this way, have something provisional and incomplete about them; they point to one another and both point to something in the future, something still to come, which will be the actual, real and definitive event ... Thus history, with all its concrete force, remains forever a figure, cloaked and needful of interpretation.[30]

It was just such a need for interpretation which characterized the understanding of history sustained by the Genesis narratives: the illumination provided by encounter with the brilliance of God was not such as to illumine all the causal connections of events and characters; rather, it cohered with a presentation of history in which much was left in darkness, inviting but always exceeding our tentative interpretations. History read figurally displays something of the same intractability: the light in which history is to be understood is now more precisely specified as the light of God's providence in Christ, but this is a providence which has yet to draw things to completion, and which awaits its eschatological fulfilment: 'In this light the history of no epoch ever has the practical self-sufficiency which, from the standpoint both of primitive man and of modern science, resides in the accomplished fact; all history, rather, remains open and questionable, points to something still concealed.'[31]

Far more briefly, it is worth noting that the other features of Hebrew realism identified by Auerbach are also found in figural realism: the world projected by figural interpretation is a world which takes time – not the time of slow evolution, the time of cumulative causal chains, but the time of the unfolding of God's plan, the time taken by God to form the world according to his election. The world projected by figural interpretation is also a flattened world: all reality, however lofty or lowly, is caught up into God's providential ordering, and there is nothing which cannot speak of Christ. Lastly, the world of figural realism is also an imperialistic world: we are promised Christ not simply as the interpretation of Old Testament history, but as the judge of all history, including our own: we, too, are rendered questionable because the key to our meaning, Christ, is not yet fully visible; we too await eschatological unveiling.

It is time to take stock. Firstly, we noted that, in the book of Genesis and elsewhere, Auerbach found a symbiosis between a certain kind of vision of God's election, providence and judgment, and a certain kind of realistic narrative. Logically, the theology generates the possibility for the narrative (even if, for Auerbach, the theology was more likely a back-formation from the narrative form). The theological claims disrupt the possibility of a more legendary form of narrative, the disruptive presence of God making the smooth surface of legend an impossibility, and thus negatively opening up the possibility of a kind of narrative which has a rougher surface. This theologically sustained possibility is indeed positively realized in Hebrew narrative.

When we turn to Christian interpretations of history, and in particular to Christian figural interpretation of Hebrew narrative, Auerbach claims first of all that, despite the persistent temptation to allegorical interpretation, figural interpretation need not simply ignore the claim of Hebrew narrative to portray a concrete historical world. Second, he claims that figural interpretation itself could also *actively militate against* a 'legendary' reduction of such history: once again, by referring all things to a God who does not fully appear, whose final judgment awaits eschatological revelation, it disrupts any form of narrative which too easily claims to have history sewn up. In at least this negative sense, figural interpretation allowed for the possibility of narrative portrayals as 'historical' in form as those of the Hebrew Bible.

We must, of course, remember that possibility is not the same as actuality: the disruption of legendary forms of narrative in a figural vision is not the same thing as the actual, positive generation of historical forms of narrative. Remembering that we are looking at a period of Christian history *after* the writing of the Gospels and Acts, we are left with the question whether the possibility of historical writing which Auerbach sees in the figural vision was in fact actualized. Do we find a Christian flourishing of 'historical' as opposed to 'legendary' narrative? (Once again: remember that this is a question about literary form, not about factuality.) This is precisely the question which the remainder of Auerbach's *Mimesis* is dedicated to answering. He seeks to demonstrate that the possibility is indeed actualized to a certain extent among the Fathers themselves, and in various ways in medieval literature and drama. Auerbach's major claim, however, is that it is in Dante that we see this possibility most fully realized, and at last find a form of historical narrative emerging from figural soil which matches and even surpasses the historical seriousness of the Hebrew narrative.[32]

3 Dante and the Fulfilment of History

Auerbach began his career as a literary historian with a book on *Dante as Poet of the Secular World*; his article on 'Figura' was intended in large part as an attempt to uncover the roots of an aspect of Dante's procedure;[33] and *Mimesis*, as I have said, is arguably a pre- and post-history of the kind of realism found in Dante's vision.[34] For Auerbach, the *Comedy* is the most profound embodiment of the figural vision of history. According to this vision

> Earthly life is thoroughly real, with the reality of the flesh into which the Logos entered, but ... with all its reality it is only *umbra* and *figura* of the authentic, future, ultimate truth, the real reality that will unveil and preserve the *figura*. In this way the individual earthly event is not regarded as a definitive self-sufficient reality, nor as a link in a chain of development in which single events or combinations of events perpetually give rise to new events, but viewed primarily in immediate vertical connection with a divine order which encompasses it, which on some future day will itself be concrete reality; so that the earthly event is a prophecy or *figura* of a part of a wholly divine reality that will only be enacted in the future.[35]

What Dante encounters on his way through the inferno, purgatory and paradise is this 'true, concrete reality, in which the earthly *figura* is contained and interpreted'.[36]

There is at first an apparent paradox in his achievement:

> Imitation of reality is imitation of the sensory experience of life on earth – among the most essential characteristics of which would seem to be its possessing a history, its changing and developing ... But Dante's inhabitants of the three realms lead a 'changeless existence' ... Yet into this changeless existence Dante 'plunges the living world of human actions and endurance and more especially of individual deeds and destinies'.[37]

The figures from earthly historical life whom Dante encounters in the changeless context of the *Comedy* are, we might say, recognizably themselves, only more so: as Auerbach puts it, 'it is precisely the absolute realization of a particular earthly personality in the place definitively assigned to it, which constitutes the Divine Judgment'.[38] In the light of God's judgment, the position of each creature in divine providence stands revealed, but not in such a way as to obscure or sublate that creature's earthly, historical particularity: Dante's portraits are startling in their power and movement; they clearly stand, in literary terms, on the side of 'history' rather than 'legend'; yet precisely in the arrangement and full revelation of each creature as the creature it is, the great plan of God is laid bare. God's providence, election and judgment are displayed clearly and definitively in the three realms precisely in and through the judgment of each creature: the heightening of each individual's rich complexity and individuality.[39] '[T]he individual figures, arrived at their ultimate, eschatological destination, are not divested of their earthly character. Their earthly historical character is not even attenuated, but rather held fast in all its intensity and so identified with their ultimate fate.'[40]

Virgil in the *Comedy* is not, according to Auerbach, an allegorical figure; he is neither 'reason nor poetry nor the Empire. He is Virgil himself';[41] better: he is the concrete, fulfilled reality of which the historical Virgil was the figure. The Virgil of the *Comedy* is *more* real, and more really Virgil, than the Virgil of history, because he is a Virgil whose position in God's plans is now made fully clear, and who is now most fully able to play his allotted role in demonstrating God's justice. The historical Virgil known of by Dante had predicted the *Pax Romana*, had inspired future poets, had prophesied Christ in the Fourth Eclogue, had described the pathway to the dead, and was a man of justice and piety; living before Christ he nevertheless stood on the threshold of Christianity, pointing towards it; living as a pagan, he could approach but not cross that threshold. It is precisely as the fulfilment of this historical figure that the Virgil of the *Comedy* is elected as Dante's guide, but 'can lead him only to the threshold of the kingdom, only as far as the limit which his noble and righteous poetry was able to discern'. Virgil is now all that Virgil was then; only now the full meaning, the full grandeur and limitation, of Virgil's existence is made clear. The *Comedy*'s Virgil is a concrete, living figure who interprets for us the concrete, living Virgil of history. Virgil in the *Comedy* is more Virgil than Virgil.[42]

With Beatrice, the situation is more complex. Beatrice was in Dante's own life always understood as 'a miracle sent from Heaven, an incarnation of divine truth'.[43] We need not bury ourselves in discussion of how the Beatrice constructed in Dante's poetry and imagination, the Beatrice of the *Vita Nuova*, relates to the particular Florentine girl who later married Simone de' Bardi;[44] her fulfilment in the *Comedy* is the fulfilment of the figure of Beatrice experienced by Dante in his own life and depicted in his poetry. Beatrice in the *Comedy* is the fulfilment of this genuinely, if not straightforwardly, historical reality.[45] The Beatrice of the *Comedy* is therefore an incarnation of (not an allegory of) revelation: an incarnation of 'that part of the divine plan of salvation which precisely is the miracle whereby men are raised above other earthly creatures. Beatrice is incarnation; she is *figura* or *idolo Christi*'.[46] This is what the experience of Beatrice had been to Dante in life; this is now what the *Comedy*'s Beatrice is more fully and clearly. Once again, the Beatrice of the *Comedy* is more Beatrice than Beatrice, precisely because her position in God's plans is made fully clear, and because she is enabled to play fully the role in displaying God's justice which the Beatrice of Dante's earlier life had played only in part.

In the *Comedy*, then, it makes sense to say that history is displayed as judged, displayed according to its position in the great providential order of God; it is not displayed, however, stripped of its concreteness and particularity; it is not portrayed simply as a diagram of God's justice. It is only by the accumulation of living portraits of concrete persons that Dante is able to display God's judgment.

Dante's vision is not simply a vision of the eternal fulfilment of history, however; it also implies a vision of the history that is fulfilled. Far from evacuating this world of significance by locating real meaning in a realm beyond, the figural vision lends a sharpened urgency to historical affairs:

[S]ince the human world receives the measures by which it is to be molded and judged from the other world, it is neither a realm of dark necessity nor a peaceful land of God; no, the cleft is really open, the span of life is short, uncertain, and decisive for all eternity; it is the magnificent and terrible gift of potential freedom which creates the urgent, restless, human, and Christian-European atmosphere of the irretrievable, fleeting moment that must be taken advantage of; God's grace is infinite, but so also is his justice and one does not negate the other.[47]

Or again:

The perception of history and immanent reality arrived at in the Comedy through an eschatological vision, flowed back into real history, filling it with the blood of authentic truth, for an awareness had been born that a man's concrete earthly life is encompassed in his ultimate fate and that the event in its authentic, concrete, complete uniqueness is important for the part it plays in God's judgment. From that center, man's earthly, historical reality derived new life and value.[48]

In Dante, we finally see fully realized the possibility of an historical vision generated by figural interpretation.

For Auerbach, however, Dante's *Comedy* is not simply a culmination and realization of the figural vision: it is a turning point. 'Dante's great art', he says,

carries the matter so far that the effect becomes earthly, and the listener is all too occupied by the figure in the fulfillment. The beyond becomes a stage for human beings and human passions ... [W]ithin the figural pattern, [Dante] brings to life the whole historical world and, within that, every single human being who crosses his path! To be sure, this is only what was demanded from the first by the Judaeo-Christian interpretation of the phenomenal; that interpretation claims universal validity. But the fullness of life which Dante incorporates into that interpretation is so rich and so strong that its manifestations force their way into the listener's soul independently of any interpretation.[49]

The living movement of Dante's portraits is, despite all that Auerbach has said about its origin in the figural vision, barely containable within the ordered eschatological framework of the *Comedy*. The 'turbulent new forces' of this dynamic, contingent, particular history beat against the walls of the inferno, purgatory and paradise, and it should come as no surprise that Dante stands at the threshold of Renaissance literature, in which those forces 'violently break loose',[50] fatally weakening the very figural vision on which they had been nurtured.

In other words, Auerbach suggests that the figural vision contains the seeds of its own destruction: that it makes for but cannot finally contain a thoroughly historical vision. He suggests that Dante's historical vision, for all that it is genuinely fostered by the figural vision, might contain the seeds of that vision's destruction. Auerbach's Dante is, as the subtitle of his 1929 book suggests, *poet* (we might say, prophet) *of the secular world*. By means of the figural, eschatological vision, he produces a vision of a rich, contingent, complex, historical world which unwittingly outstrips the figural frame; a faithful Christian author, he nevertheless gives birth to a secular, sceptical vision.

4 The Exhibition of Providence

Although he accepted gratefully a large part of Auerbach's analysis of the nature and significance of *figura*, Frei had none of Auerbach's residual Hegelianism, and did not accept his narrative of *figura*'s demise at the very moment of its triumph. Characteristically, he found himself tracing a rather more complex and confusing story of *figura*'s decline, of its relationship to a secular vision, and of the place of both in the developing shape of modern theology, shifting the scene from Dante's late medieval world to the world of seventeenth-, eighteenth- and nineteenth-century hermeneutics. At the same time that his Christological proposal was going through its various stages, Frei was working on a history of modern European biblical hermeneutics in England and Germany from the seventeenth to the nineteenth centuries, a project he had apparently started at the beginning of the 1960s or earlier. After extended labour, the work was finally finished in late 1973, and published, as *The Eclipse of Biblical Narrative*, early in 1974.

Eclipse is a much longer work than *Identity*, and it operates at a far higher level of detail. It has also stayed continuously in print far longer than *Identity*, and reached a far wider readership: *Eclipse* was reviewed not just in the predictable theology journals, but in the *Times Literary Supplement* and in the *New York Review of Books*, by such people as George Steiner, Alasdair MacIntyre and Frank Kermode.[51] Yet, despite the differences in character and substance, each project implies the other and requires to be read in the light of the other. Frei hints at this in the preface to *Eclipse*, where he says that '[t]hose who might want to know how I would put my thoughts to an exegetical test I refer to ... a brief theological experiment I tried some time ago, to be published ... under the title, *The Identity of Jesus Christ*'.[52] On the other hand, the preface to *Identity* refers to *Eclipse* as having identified a category error which bedevils modern reading of the Gospels and suggests that *Identity* 'is the endeavour to show how exegesis *can* be done – and hopefully done better – if the error is avoided'.[53]

The story told by *Eclipse* is, in brief, as follows. In the period before the rise of modern critical scholarship, readers of biblical narratives (particularly those narratives found in Genesis and in the Gospels) normally assumed, if they found a passage that appeared to describe a public, historical sequence – that is, a narrative that was 'history-like' – that the sequence described truly happened in history, and happened just as described. There could be various kinds of exceptions to this norm (indeed, there were many) but this was the default position underlying most other exegetical moves which readers made with such texts. With the rise of various kinds of critical thinking in the eighteenth century, particularly in England and Germany, however, the assumption that there was no significant gap between narrative text and the historical referent fell apart. Much of *Eclipse* is taken up with a detailed examination of various ways in which readers tried to salvage the integrity of the authors and the religious meaningfulness of their texts from this divorce, and with the demonstration that none of those attempts managed to take the 'history-likeness' of the narratives seriously as a constitutive factor in the way that these texts make sense. In other words, the character of certain central portions of biblical narrative was 'eclipsed': it was persistently missed, ignored or denied. The book strongly suggests that it will be possible to retrieve something of the pre-critical acknowledgement of the history-likeness of biblical narratives, without simply turning the clock back on the findings and methods of historical criticism, but does not make it very clear what such a retrieval will actually look like.

Frei invites readers to see *Eclipse* as a tale about hermeneutics: about a hermeneutical mistake which was, for various reasons, made by modern biblical interpreters; he also invites readers to see *The Identity of Jesus Christ* as an example of a rectified hermeneutical procedure. This is the connection between the two books which Frei suggests in the prefaces to each, and it is confirmed in the subtitles of both books: *Eclipse* is 'A Study in Eighteenth and Nineteenth Century Hermeneutics', and *Identity* concerns 'The Hermeneutical Bases of Dogmatic Theology'. Nevertheless, this suggestion can be misleading. At the start of the preface to *Eclipse*, Frei says

> This essay falls into the almost legendary category of analysis of analyses of the Bible in which not a single text is examined, not a single exegesis undertaken. Faced with certain puzzles that demanded *historical, philosophical, and theological* explanations, I tried to provide them as best I could; but there is no denying the odd result of a book about the Bible in which the Bible itself is never looked at.[54]

We are misled if, guided by the way in which the term 'hermeneutics' is often used, we assume that Frei was seeking primarily 'historical' and 'philosophical' explanations, and that the 'theological' explanations he mentions are secondary matters. This is not true: if we miss the theological story that Frei has to tell, we miss the heart of the book.

It would, of course, be pointless to deny that the book is substantially concerned with historical and philosophical explanations. Most obviously, the book tells a complex historical story about developments in biblical hermeneutics, and it brings to that historical story a series of illuminating philosophical and hermeneutical concepts. Frei acknowledges the influence of Gilbert Ryle's 'demystification of the concept of intentional personal action',[55] and acknowledges that Auerbach's *Mimesis* and 'Figura' provided many of his concepts. It is, however, as a *theological* essay that *Eclipse* is most interesting. The story which Frei has to tell about the change in modern hermeneutics is not simply a story about changing interpretive procedures, nor simply a story about the changing hermeneutical concepts which were deployed by those using these procedures; it is also a story about profound theological alterations which underlie those conceptual changes: changes in the understanding of providence, of history, of God's ways with the world. It is that theological story which we must follow.

The story does not begin simply with a pre-critical hermeneutical procedure. It begins with a set of pre-critical hermeneutical assumptions that were themselves grounded in particular theological claims: Frei repeatedly makes the point that pre-critical interpretation made sense on the basis of a set of claims about God's providence. It is not that one can extract from pre-critical interpretation any *explanation* of providence. Frei found no account of how it is that God manages to manipulate, intervene in, or otherwise guide the processes of history. Rather, he found a practice of reading that *assumed* and *exhibited* God's providential ordering of history,[56] a practice which responded to the question 'How then does God order the world?' with the answer, 'We do not know; but look – he has.' It is not even the case that the practice of reading to which Frei points sought to *prove* that God's providential ordering had taken place. It did not, for instance, proceed by accumulating convincing cases until the balance of probability swung in favour of the existence of a certain kind of divine activity. Rather, it was a practice whose proponents regarded themselves as having been led by the Spirit to see again and again what was simply the case: that God had indeed ordered history, and had exhibited his ordering to their gaze in the Scriptures.

For the pre-critical readers described by Frei, the Scriptures made history accessible, and made its providential ordering legible. History was selectively re-presented to the reader in the biblical narratives in such a way that he or she could follow its course, and in such a way that he or she could see the imprint of God's providential ordering uniting otherwise distant parts of that history, giving the whole *form*. Sometimes the Scriptures explicitly made the connections that exhibited providence ('all this took place to fulfil what had been spoken by the Lord through the prophet'); at other times they invited the reader to make the connections, presenting history to him or her in such a way that he or she was able to see more than the texts explicitly said.

Although providence was neither explained nor proved by the Scriptures, its character was made clear. The texts in which providence was exhibited were, in significant part, of a certain kind: more or less realistic or history-like narratives. That is, they depicted the interaction of characters and circumstances; they depicted intentional action in a public setting;[57] while depicting miracles and many extraordinary events they did so against the background of a causal, random, everyday world of credible people, ordinary events and historical forces.[58] Frei claims that pre-critical interpreters such as Calvin read such texts in the first place 'literally' or 'realistically'. That is, they began by taking the narratives to be about precisely what they appeared to be about. They saw these texts as making accessible to them a real history of characters and circumstances, rather than as presenting to them a story which spoke of characters and circumstances only as a veil through which the reader must pass if the real, very different subject matter was to appear. It is certainly true that these pre-critical interpreters often passed on to other kinds of interpretation, even that they frequently did not dwell on the literal interpretation; nevertheless Frei claims that this assumption of the direct historicity of history-like texts underlies all the other hermeneutical moves made. The fit between history-like text and historical truth was the unexamined norm, and any exception to that priority required good reason to be entertained. There was, on the whole, no gap between history-like text and historical reference, except for texts whose obscurity, or exceptionally problematic nature, required some out-of-the-ordinary account.

When it was exhibited first and foremost by such accounts, providence had to be understood as an ordering of such history: an ordering of the history of public intentional action, characters and circumstances, cumulative sequences of events, credible people, ordinary and extraordinary events, historical forces. It was the ordering of a world that takes time to unfold. It was not an ordering which was primarily discernible in the deep inwardness of humanity, nor in gigantic overarching structures of *geist*. It was the ordering of that middle-distance world which is fitly rendered to readers by the devices of history-like narrative.

If the reading of history-like texts as historical provided the raw materials of providence, it was figural reading that exhibited the actual providential ordering of those raw materials. Frei adopts Auerbach's explanation: figural interpretation takes two apparently separate incidents or characters from biblical history, and claims that one is a 'type' or 'figure' of the other. The paradigmatic pre-critical use of figural interpretation was as a means of linking together the old and new covenants in the one ongoing history of God's ways with the world. The Old Testament was preserved, and could edify Christians, precisely because it was seen to depict part of God's ongoing ordering of history that came to fruition in Christ – and figural interpretation was the means by which Old Testament characters and incidents could be demonstrated to have pre-figured, and been fulfilled in, Christ. Such figural reading exhibited providential order 'directly and without recourse to a theoretical explanation or the setting forth of temporal causal links. For figuration or typology, the cogent suggestion of a divine plan was always dependent upon its being directly exhibited in the juxtaposition of widely separated and specific occurrences and their meaning.'[59] No sequence of historical development needed to be traced between, say, Moses and Christ, no slow education of the human race proposed to link the two. For figural reading it was enough that the depictions of Moses be placed beside the depictions of Christ, so that the reader could see how God had ordained that Moses pre-figure Christ, how God's work in Christ was foreshadowed by God's work in Moses.

Moses, the historical character who lived and breathed in Egypt and Sinai, was made accessible to the reader by means of a history-like text, the

Pentateuch; he was a type or figure of another historical character, Jesus, who was made accessible in a different history-like text, the Gospels. Figural reading did not, according to Frei, claim that the Pentateuch *appeared* to be about Moses but was *really* about Jesus; 'Moses' was not simply a device employed by the authors of the Pentateuch for talking about something else entirely. Had that been the case, the relationship discovered by figural reading would have been a relationship primarily between texts, not a relationship between the historical circumstances or characters depicted in those texts. Following John David Dawson, we can use the term 'figur*ative*' for an interpretation that *denies* the literal interpretation of the Pentateuch in order to make the connection with the Gospels; figur*al* reading, on the other hand, coheres with and builds upon a literal reading that takes the texts of the Pentateuch to be about the very events and characters that they apparently describe.[60] The Pentateuch was, in this case, only about Jesus insofar as it was genuinely about Moses.

If the figural relationship was not primarily a relationship between texts, neither was it simply a connection (whether between texts or their referents) made subjectively by a reader – a pious reflection, perhaps, on the similar lessons to be drawn from Moses and from Jesus. The connection made by the figural reader between Moses and Jesus was possible because there was an objective connection between the Pentateuch and the Gospel texts, and there was an objective connection between those texts because there was an objective connection between the two portions of history to which they referred: the historical character Moses truly was, by God's design, a type of the historical character Jesus. It is true that the objective connection between portions of history only became visible as the two histories were given apt depiction in the words of Scripture; and it is true that for a reader like Calvin the work of the Holy Spirit was needed to cleanse the minds of readers so that they could rightly perceive the objective ordering presented to them. Nevertheless, figural reading was first and foremost not a means of responding to texts, but a way of reading God's objective work in history.

One of the distinguishing features of figural interpretation which Frei noted was 'temporal sequence': the texts related by figural reading, however diverse, however widely separated their referents, describe portions of a providential order which is itself a sequence, a history, a story.[61] Frei contrasted Luther, for whom a contrast only accidentally sequential between Law and Gospel was the basic distinction structuring his entire view of creation, with Calvin, for whom Law and Gospel were held together by their 'common ingredience in the storied text of the scriptural world'.[62] God's providence was an unfolding, cumulative ordering which joined the distinct phases or stages of history, and still looked forward to a final consummation.

Yet this talk of a 'single world of one temporal sequence' with 'one cumulative story to depict it'[63] might suggest that Frei's central move was to identify God's providential ordering of history with a continuous, organically connected story without significant lacunae: a strong and pervasive framework which could then be used to place any given particular. One might then assume that the 'eclipse of biblical narrative' of which Frei spoke was the death of just such an overarching, continuous metanarrative. The truth, however, is far more complex. Certainly, the broad narrative sequence of old and new covenant, of the eras before and after Christ's first advent, was very important to pre-critical interpreters. Nevertheless, in Frei's account, the overarching narrative into which figural interpretation links individual stories is not one which emerges fully to view, nor a story that exists in only one version;[64] to the extent that an overarching narrative framework is described, it is seen to be a very simple structure – a sparse scaffolding into which a bewildering diversity of particular narratives can be fitted.[65]

To the extent that ongoing, continuous narrative sequence was important to Frei, it was primarily as the appropriate form of depiction for the public sequences of characters and circumstances that stand at the poles of a figural relationship. It is only in a secondary and partial sense that narrative appears as the overarching form into which figural reading ties those individual sequences. We will therefore be closer to Frei's intentions if we say that the narrative that was eclipsed in the eighteenth and nineteenth centuries was the narration of the particular public histories that were the primary ingredients of figural interpretation, not some gigantic metanarrative in which all those particular narratives were dissolved.

This point is illustrated by Frei's analysis of the dispensationalist theology of Johannes Cocceius (1603–69). Frei regards Cocceius' work as a sign of the encroaching eclipse of biblical narrative, and yet directs attention to the fact that Cocceius has a *more* prominent overarching narrative framework than do many pre-critical interpreters. For pre-critical readers, the overarching biblical narrative was generated by the practice of figural interpretation of individual history-like narratives read historically; as a result, the overarching narrative and the individual history-like narratives cohered naturally. Cocceius, however, divided biblical history and the present into a 'temporally differentiated divine economy' of succeeding dispensations, an 'historical continuum' in which there were 'no gaps or missing links', and in so doing produced a metanarrative that was to a far greater degree independent of the practice of figuration, and independent of the historical reading of history-like texts.[66] For Cocceius, the metanarrative becomes an object of attention in its own right, and the question of how individual narratives of character and incident can be fitted into its close-woven structure begins to arise. A conceptual gap arises between the clearly perceived biblical metanarrative of God's providence on the one hand, and the clearly perceived realistic narrative of individual histories on the other. Cocceius, aware at some level of this gap and anxious to demonstrate that nevertheless the individual histories *were* tied in to his metanarrative, practised a 'constant and cramped recourse' to a 'baroque proliferation of figural reading' that has 'all the prodigality and extravagance of a late, decadent growth'.[67] The individual episodes of public history – both those described in the Bible's realistic narrative and those through which he was living – needed to earn their place, by means of this prolific figuration, in the larger narrative which is the primary meaning of the Bible. In a way that Frei believes simply was not true for earlier readers, there is here a gap between the overarching narrative and the small-scale history-like narratives of characters and events. And note: what began to go into eclipse in this process was not the biblical metanarrative (far from it!) but rather the direct ingredience in the larger story of individual history-like narratives, and the individual histories which were their referents.

There is another problem with using 'narrative' to describe the overarching structure which is assumed and suggested in figural interpretation. Individual history-like narratives are read by figural interpreters as relating directly to Christ – either as prefigurations of Christ's work or, as we shall see, as figures after the event. Figural interpreters affirmed that Christ was, in some sense, the centre of history, and exhibited this centrality by showing how God's action in earlier biblical history (in Moses, for instance) prepared for and was fulfilled in God's action in Christ. Frei does refer to Calvin's wariness about finding 'hidden specific reference to Christ' too easily in the Old Testament;[68] nevertheless, his reticence in particular cases in no way softened 'the claim that the canon is one because the meaning of all of it is salvation in Jesus Christ'.[69] However, Christ was not regarded as central in such a way as easily to allow talk about greater and lesser *distance* from Christ within history.[70] For example, Moses was not connected to Christ primarily by means of a long causal chain stretching through the intervening centuries – a longer chain than that connecting Christ to Zerubbabel, perhaps, but shorter than that connecting Christ to Adam. 'Distance' from Christ in God's providential ordering of history was not understood as being defined by time or space in this way. Frei insists that figural interpretation worked through the juxtaposition of widely separated events and characters[71] – that is, that it worked precisely by overcoming a straightforward concept of 'distance'. However, if distance is overcome, we have to be wary of placing too much reliance on talk of a continuous overarching narrative: it is precisely such a metanarrative which would allow us to regard a domain as being structured by calculable relations of distance.

The pre-critical reader did not, by means of figural interpretation, discover how many chapters separated him from Christ. Rather, he 'was to see his disposition, his actions and passions, the shape of his own life as well as that of his era's events as figures of that storied world'.[72] The reader was enabled to see what was dim, murky and confused in his or her own situation written clearly in Christ. We might say that the clear primary colours making up the palette with which God had painted the world were displayed in their full beauty only at the heart of the picture, in Christ. Once these primary colours were seen, the rest of the picture could be seen to be painted with them – albeit mingled and smeared, and only occasionally visible in anything like their proper radiance. The full possibilities of those colours, the endless combinations and subtleties to which they lent themselves, could be seen only in the ever-new combinations in which they were found in the reader's own time; the palette from which those combinations were painted could be seen only in Christ.

Although there certainly were narrative elements to the set of relations in which the readers found themselves, in that they found themselves living in the time between the advents, their discovery that they were implicated in the world opened up in the Bible was not simply a case of accepting their position in a single ongoing story. The ways in which the present could be read as a figure of Christ were more subtle and more varied than that. All that Frei will say of the process by which the Spirit awakens the reader to true comprehension of his or her own place vis-à-vis the biblical texts is that it is the 'effective rendering of God and his real world to the reader by way of the text's appropriate depiction of the intercourse of that God and that world, engaging the reader's mind, heart, and activity'.[73] What Frei does stress is that the links made between the depictions of Christ and the reader's own time neither turned Christ into a parable or cartoon, nor evacuated the present of its particularity and contingency. Both poles of the relationship retained their concrete, unsubstitutable existence.

What kind of providence, then, is assumed and exhibited by pre-critical readings of the Bible, before the eclipse of biblical narrative? In the first place, it is an ordering of history, with 'history' understood in a particular way. 'History' is that reality aptly depicted by realistic, history-like narrative: it is the public history of unsubstitutable characters in social and natural circumstance; it is ordinary, everyday history; it is particular and contingent. Yet, for pre-critical figural readers, such historical reality, precisely as real, unsubstitutable and densely particular, could by the grace of God refer to some other historical reality, for this kind of history (unsubstitutable persons and events) was, to use the excellent phrase of John David Dawson, 'the idiom in which God acts and speaks'.[74] Precisely as an irreducibly complex and abidingly particular reality, a portion of history could be understood to be spoken by God as a 'phenomenal prophecy' of Christ. Dawson explains this further, saying,

> Although one may refer to a figure 'announcing its fulfilment', it is ultimately God who does the announcing, for a person or an event is a *figura* precisely because it begins an extended divine utterance that embraces subsequent persons and events … If Jesus is the fulfilment of Joshua, that is because both Joshua and Jesus are moments within a single divine intention to signify. Discerning that intention as a literary congruence, the figural reader makes explicit the similarities by which otherwise separate events are related to one another as moments in a single, divine utterance.[75]

How could pre-critical interpreters say that concrete, particular histories are, without having their unsubstitutable density evacuated, the utterances of God? They could say it because they believed that nothing was impossible for God, and because, when they put the history-like depictions of widely separated portions of biblical history beside one another, they believed the Spirit enabled them to see what was there: a congruence, a pattern, uniting otherwise distant realities. In all the history-like complexity of his story, Moses could be and was read as a type of Christ. Figural interpretation was performed, and God's strange providence displayed. Clearly, God allowed history to be itself – to be contingent, particular, concrete, unsubstitutable, to be a history of publicly narratable characters and circumstance, to be capable of depiction in followable history-like texts; equally clearly, God had spoken these histories as proclamations of salvation in Christ. When the pre-critical combination of realistic and figural reading was eclipsed, it was this that was hidden: the possibility that public, concrete history could be understood as ordained by God to speak of Christ, and that Christ's public, concrete history could be understood as ordained by God to fulfil all history.

5 The Reconstruction of History

For interpreters like Cocceius, the history in which they lived was emerging as an object separable from the providentially unified biblical narrative; anxious about how present history could be fitted into the biblical framework, Cocceius calmed himself with a profusion of figural interpretation. Of course, Cocceius was not the first or the last in whose hands figural interpretation had seemed strained, and it is perhaps unfair to have singled him out; he was, however, working at a time in which an unprecedented development was brewing, and his uneasy practice is bound, in retrospect, to appear as an omen. It was not long before, instead of anxiously seeking to fit the problematic present world into the stable biblical narrative, a younger generation of interpreters were worrying about whether and how biblical narratives fitted into a continuous, unproblematic history which they could now see by other, more methodical means. The terms of Cocceius' anxiety were preserved, but its direction was reversed: history emerged still further as an object separable from the providentially unified biblical narratives – and it was now the latter that seemed unstable.

History was emerging as an object of study in its own right. Whatever the practical reality, the idea was now abroad that there was a relatively straightforward method for investigating history, and that this method was competent to set before the investigator a connected, probable and uniform vision of past and present. Historical method, at least in principle, provided a systematic and therefore transparent and robust way of constructing an object called history, and *that* history was the clearest context in which the investigators lived. Where did the Bible histories, or claims about strange figural links between those narratives, fit with this new, scientifically constructed object?[76]

One of the most obvious results of this shift was, according to Frei, the near universal replacement of literal reading by historical-critical reading. Faced with a passage in the Bible that appeared to describe an historical sequence, interpreters started to ask whether what *really* happened fitted the biblical description.[77] Even those for whom the answer was positive had nevertheless made this hermeneutical shift, said Frei: even for them there was a question to be asked about how historical these history-like texts were, and evidence and arguments to be accumulated in order to provide an answer. The text became evidence for use in reconstructing the historical referent, even if it turned out to be rather good evidence.

In its clearest form, derived from Locke, the Bible's history-like materials can be converted into a set of historical propositions demanding a strength of assent in accordance with the weight of the evidence – or they are nonsense. A history-like text makes sense insofar as it lends itself to historical-critical assessment.[78] The idea that the text's history-likeness was constitutive for the way it made sense – that is, the idea that, given a history-like text, the referent of the text was simply and straightforwardly the unsubstitutable characters and events described in such a text – inevitably came to seem like nothing more than naïveté, a backward-looking refusal to engage with critical questions.

Pre-critical interpretation was, according to Frei, a marriage between literal and figural reading. If literal reading gave way to various forms of historical-critical reading, what happened to its partner? Figural interpretation, which pre-critically had negotiated the connection between individual histories and the overarching narrative frame, and in Cocceius had been used to bridge the gap between the narrative framework and the problematic present, now failed. It was ill suited to act as a proof of the accuracy of the biblical histories. It was able, when God's Christ-centred providence was assumed, to spot echoes of Christ in wider history; if turned into an argument, however, it became an attempt to prove God's remarkable providence by counting unremarkable coincidences.[79]

However, just as literal reading found its successor in historical-critical reading, figural reading too gave way to new forms of interpretation. Figural reading had fulfilled two related functions in pre-critical exegesis: it had exhibited the unity of the canon, particularly the unity of Old and New Testament, and it had provided a link between the biblical history and the readers' own time. As figural reading collapsed, these functions were inherited by a number of procedures by which a consistent religious meaning of some kind could be found in the texts, for such a religious meaning could bind together the canon, and could be applied in the present.

Interpreters differed as to what kind of object the 'religious meaning' might be, and what procedures existed for gaining access to it.[80] For some whom Frei labels traditionalists and supernaturalists, the religious meaning was understood to be simply the abiding consequence of the facts described. In particular, accounts of substitutionary atonement, particularly when understood as an event within a longer drama encompassing both testaments, allowed some theologians to account for the abiding relevance of the factual history described in the Bible. Such theologians went for a root and branch affirmation of the specific historical event of original, inherited, and naturally inexpungeable guilt, the fatal moral, metaphysical, and noetic flaw which could be wiped out only by a similarly factual saving occurrence ... a return to the notion of a single overarching story, now held to be factual history, as providing the encompassing interpretive context both for biblical hermeneutics and theology.[81]

History remains providentially ordered in such a view, but the focus has shifted almost entirely to a causally connected sequence of factual occurrences and their outcomes; the more mysterious connections of a figural providence drop out of view. God still speaks in the language of characters and events, but now it is more clearly than before a language of facts and mechanisms, transactions and results.

At the other end of the spectrum, deists and rationalists found that the biblical stories were meaningful only to the extent that they republished the religion of nature.[82] The religious meaning of the Bible, to the extent that it had any, did not stand or fall by the factuality of its history-like accounts. Its meaning was found in truths of reason, universally accessible, and bound to no temporal framework. For some, they were truths that either bore a purely extrinsic relationship to the biblical texts – it being simply a matter of *usage* that the knowledge of these truths could be acquired or deepened by means of these texts. For others, these ideas were intrinsic to a proper understanding of the Bible: in the Bible, these ideas are found cloaked in a secondary, material, historical form – either because the biblical authors were accommodating themselves to the gross minds of their contemporaries, or because they were themselves confused as to the nature of the truths they glimpsed. For those exegetes influenced by Christian Wolff (1679–1754), the excavation of this meaningful ideational content from the biblical texts becomes a process that parallels the structure of historical-critical reading. The philosopher is able to map, by means of the ontological and psychological methods available to him, the total landscape of ideas; the task of the exegete is then to discover whether and how the problematic biblical texts succeed in referring to this landscape.[83] In such deistic and rationalistic approaches, history and religious meaning are split: they are two fields that have little to do with one another. On the one landscape we find a succession of contingent facts; on the other, a collection of abiding, universal truths. To the extent that God speaks it is in the language of abiding truths, and the words hover over the chaos of particular, contingent characters and events.

There were other theologians – those Frei refers to as latitudinarians and neologians – for whom some mix between the rationalists and the super-naturalists was the answer. Frei refers to the case of Conyers Middleton, for example, who regarded the first three chapters of Genesis as teaching that 'this world had a beginning and creation from God; and that its principal inhabitant man was originally formed to a state of happiness and perfection, which he lost and forfeited by following his lusts and passions, in opposition to the will of his Creator'.[84] In this interpretation, the particular story of Genesis 1–3 obviously makes sense because its real reference is a more general story with no particular protagonists, a story which is at the same time a theory about the origin of the world and the relation between the nature and destiny of man … In some unspecifiable way, the ideal truth is not merely exemplified over and over again; it is instead an actual historical sequence, though not of the specific, literal shape involving the particular times and dramatis personae set down in the account.[85]

Latitudinarians and neologians are, according to Frei, simply examples of a rather broader category of theologians we find occupying the middle reaches of the spectrum between traditionalist/supernaturalists and deist/rationalists: 'mediating theologians'. For such theologians, biblical texts refer ostensively to historical events, but those events have religious meaning only against the background of 'an indispensable moral lack or dilemma'.[86] In this way, the religious meaning of the texts requires the specific content of the Bible – historical and ideational – but also requires a 'general moral experience and religious principles' to supply the framework within which that specific content becomes meaningful.

> Redemption in history becomes intelligible from its natural context in our moral and religious experience, so that the wise man readily appreciates that rational, natural religion and morality need to be perfected from beyond themselves by a revealed religion which is above them rather than against them. The mediating version of the concepts sin and revelation may be sharper than that: the redeeming historical revelation may in large part contradict rather than perfect our natural religion and morality; but even then it remains certain that *without our antecedent awareness, either positive or negative, of such morality and religion, the revelation has no applicative meaning*. Without that antecedent context, the Bible's story of historical revelation would be religiously meaningless.[87]

Frei suggests that, for all their differences, the structure of mediating theology can be found in the work of John Locke, Samuel Clarke, Joseph Butler, Johann Salomo Semler, Johann Joachim Spalding, Friedrich Schleiermacher, Albrecht Ritschl, Wilhelm Herrmann, Emil Brunner, Rudolf Bultmann, Karl Rahner, Gerhard Ebeling, Wolfhart Pannenberg and Jürgen Moltmann.[88] Just as much as was Middleton, such theologians are, according to Frei, investing in an unstable mix between the concrete particulars of history-like texts and the expansive generalities of supposed religious and moral experience. They are, to use terminology from the previous chapter, mired in a complex and perhaps unstable mixture of repeatability and unsubstitutability: their God speaks both in the idiom of person and events, and in the idiom of overarching generalities – and Frei suspects that the latter language will eventually drown the former.

6 A History of the Human Spirit

A considerable portion of Frei's narrative is taken up with the description of a particular set of developments in biblical interpretation that dominated the German-speaking world to a far greater extent than the English. It is, for him, above all the development of romantic and idealist interpretation that provides a powerfully coherent replacement for pre-critical interpretation, and which has decisively shaped a great deal of modern theology.

Once critical thinking had taken root, the Bible was seen by many as a witness by human authors to a positive revelation that has taken place in history. God's Spirit had guided the human authors, but only in such a way as to raise them to their highest possibility: to preserve their integrity and perspicuity. A modern interpreter, perhaps having demonstrated this unusual but not inexplicable truthfulness by examining key test-cases at the bar of historical criticism, could then reconstruct the revelatory history these witnesses described by working out what they were referring to, and how they were referring to it. From such a position, it is only a short step before one is paying attention to the cultural specificity of the authors: considering the way in which their historical and cultural specificity shaped the way they had of referring to the history they described – and from *there* it is only another short step to paying attention to the *Geist*, the pervasive, developing outlook on the world discernible in the succeeding generations of biblical authors. The specific reference of the texts can come to be of secondary importance; what matters is the text's 'ingredience in and illustration of the outlook of its day'.[89]

For some, then, biblical hermeneutics became focused on the empathetic reconstruction of the outlook, *Geist*, or sensibility of earlier times.

> The peculiar disposition of this thought movement, as represented by Herder, [is] to spiritualise history by turning it into the development of the stages of collective-spiritual individualities, in large part as a result of the fact that the knowing subject occupies a distinctive, self-positioning location toward the historical world. Historicism is the rendering of mankind's unfinished story in which man, in his encounter with determinate historical situations and developments, actually encounters himself writ large. But the universal self or man he meets is never met – as a Rationalist might claim – in direct, universal, trans-historical form. The universal historical being of man is met only as the specific spirit of a specific age and group.[90]

In such a view, the meaning of the biblical texts is the empathetic reconstitution of the *Geist* from which they have emerged, by an interpreter who himself stands in the stream of this *Geist*'s development, and for whom this *Geist* is an ingredient in his own sensibility (one of the bright, primary colours from which his own complex image is painted). The interpreter's sensibility functions as the explication and fulfilment of the *Geist* exhibited in the biblical texts; it shows what this colour can be combined with and used to achieve.

In such a context, there is a kind of retrieval of figural interpretation. Herder wrote that the question was not whether this or that person in the Old Testament recognised himself clearly as a type, or whether his time recognised him as such, but whether in the sequence of times he was pointed to as an archetype ... Only later illumination, the clear succession of the developing sense in the sequence of time, together with the analogy of the whole, shows us the building in its light and shadow.[91]

Standing at a later point in the 'clear succession of the developing sense', the interpreter's subjectivity serves as a hermeneutical key which enables the identification of such archetypes *as* archetypes, and shows how what flows from such archetypes can become ingredient in more developed and complex forms.

When the understanding of biblical narratives is a matter of following the story they tell, various abilities and accomplishments are certainly necessary; it is, after all, something that one learns to do. But Frei believes these to be of a wholly different kind from the 'sensibility' that must be cultivated if what one is after is the empathetic re-experience of the *Geist* of earlier times. Only interpreters who have become sensitive to the vibrations of the human spirit can understand *Geist*; the meaning of the narratives understood will not be evident to someone of duller sensibility. To that extent, we could say that the meaning of biblical texts is, in this view, produced by the reader. Nevertheless, for someone like Herder, it is clear that interpretation is not simply invention or imposition; it is based upon the real history of *Geist*, which includes both text and reader.

Frei says of this approach to texts that it is

more than [the] insight that past forms of life develop and endure into the present, that we and our institutions – language, culture, state, family – would not be what we are without the preceding history. Rather, it referred to a distinctive mode of consciousness on which our apprehension of the human past depends.[92]

Frei uses Goethe's phrase 'the sensibility of the past and the present in one'[93] to refer to this sensibility. It is a sensibility for which the seemingly random material of external history is always riding on top of the deep waters of internal history: the history of developing sensibility, the history of the human spirit's evolution. A new figural interpretation has emerged, which seeks in the purity of earlier ages the archetypal forms of the human spirit, unencumbered by artificial restrictions. The providential history of God's ways with the world which underlay pre-critical figural interpretation has been replaced by an inward history in which the truly significant occurrences lie beneath the surface, as modulations in the rhythms in the one cumulative, evolving, continuous story of Spirit.[94]

For Frei, this approach to biblical interpretation is part of the 'preschematic sensibility'[95] which precedes and allows Kant's 'turn to the subject'. It allows for a view of human freedom precisely as the mysterious, hidden, interiority which stands behind and appears to contradict the ingredience of a human being in the causal chains of the external world. In other words, Frei has described, to use the terms of an earlier chapter, the emergence of a subject–alienation framework for understanding history, a point of view he believes fundamentally antagonistic to the interplay of unsubstitutable character and circumstance in the concrete particularities of public history. A providential ordering that naturally coheres with such public history, which is precisely an ordering of such history, has given way to a different kind of immanent providence, a providence whose home is spirit, brooding beneath the surface of the chaotic external world.

7 Conclusion

For Auerbach, figural interpretation is the glue by which Christian literature could hold together two affirmations: the relation of everything to God's universal judgment, and the contingent and particular world of history. These two, however, are ultimately in tension for him: in Dante, the depiction of contingent and particular history, though fostered by the theology of God's judgment, comes into its own independent strength and throws off its parent's cloying attentions. The theology has produced its own contradiction, and naturally (if not exactly organically) makes way for a vision which transcends it, and in which the significance of contingent particularity is finally given its proper place.

For Frei, figural interpretation is the handmaiden of a doctrine of providence, both resting upon that doctrine and displaying its character. It is figural interpretation which allows Frei to say that God speaks in the language of characters and incidents aptly depicted in history-like texts. Frei does not share Auerbach's belief that providence and history are ultimately in tension: where Auerbach has *figura*'s inevitable self-consumption, Frei has a far more complex and contingent narrative of figural interpretation's far from inevitable eclipse.[96] The eclipse was unnecessary and, we might hope, as temporary as the word implies.

Two questions are therefore left to us at the end of this investigation. On the one hand, we must ask what kind of retrieval of figural interpretation Frei believed lay open to him. On the other hand, we must ask what view of the secular world of history, so forcefully depicted by Auerbach, that retrieval would make possible.

Notes

1. Arthur R. Evans, Jr, 'Erich Auerbach as European Critic', *Romance Philology* 25.2 (1971), p. 212.
2. Cf. *Mimesis*, p. 489.
3. It is important to note that Frei was no fan of accounts of the Bible's unique outlook – the kind of accounts which would contrast the 'Hebrew mind' with the 'Greek mind', and suggest that 'The Bible ... testifies to a unique and pervasive outlook which separates the Hebrew mind and culture not only from the philosophical and abstract Greeks but from the surrounding Near Eastern peoples. Its unique content is the act of God's self-revelation

in history' (Review of James Barr's *The Bible in the Modern World* [?1975b], p. 1). He is not interested in Auerbach's insights into the Hebrew *Geist*, but in Auerbach's specific analyses of the relationship between form and content in certain biblical texts.

4. *Mimesis*, p. 6.
5. Ibid., p. 6.
6. Ibid.
7. Ibid., p. 7.
8. Ibid., p. 4.
9. Ibid., p. 7.
10. Ibid., p. 9.
11. Ibid., pp. 16–17.
12. 'The concept of God held by the Jews is less a cause than a symptom of their manner of comprehending and representing things', ibid., p. 6.
13. Ibid., p. 17.
14. Ibid., p. 18.
15. Ibid.
16. Ibid., p. 19.
17. Ibid.
18. Ibid., p. 35.
19. Ibid., p. 37.
20. Ibid.
21. Ibid., p. 14.
22. Ibid., p. 12.
23. Ibid.
24. It is sometimes thought that, when he took Auerbach's suggestions and used them to interpret Barth's language about the 'strange new world within the Bible', Frei was suggesting that in biblical narrative we find the portrayal of a complete, connected, self-contained world: an imaginative world like, say, Tolkien's Middle Earth, but one that we can choose – in an act of irrational, inexplicable, fideistic faith – to adopt as our own, to adopt as true (or even *as if* it were true). In terms of the description offered by Auerbach, this would be to suggest that, for the Yale theologians, the Bible was more like Homer, offering us a world with its own structures of plausibility, its own background and foreground, with faith as the deliberate imaginative act of entering into this world and living 'as if' the Homeric gods and heroes existed. Frei is more faithful to Auerbach and to Barth than this. There is no 'as if' here: believers are those who find themselves overwhelmed by the reality attested to in the Bible, which judges all other claims to reality, and will not let them go until they have acknowledged it – and which continues to overwhelm and exceed us. This is not our decision, but the act of the Holy Spirit – and to think otherwise, as Frei says in a different context, 'makes Pelagius look by contrast like Augustine's most devoted follower' ('Estimate of the Work as a Whole' [1983e(ii)], p. 4).
25. *Mimesis*, p. 64.
26. See, however, John David Dawson, 'Allegorical Reading and the Embodiment of the Soul in Origen', in Lewis Ayres and Gareth Jones (eds.), *Christian Origins* (London: Routledge, 1998) and *Christian Figural Reading and the Fashioning of Identity* (Berkeley: University of California Press, 2002).
27. 'Figura', p. 30.
28. Ibid., p. 29.
29. Ibid., p. 39.
30. 'Figura', p. 58.
31. Ibid.
32. We can agree that figural interpretation allows that the Hebrew narratives are portrayals of a concrete history; and that figural interpretation as a whole at least allows for the possibility that history can be seen as complex, contingent and messy in a similar sort of way to the historical world projected by Hebrew narrative; we can even agree that figural

vision is the soil in which a literary realism which inherits the mantle of Hebrew realism eventually flourishes. However, we may agree to all of this without that necessarily implying that in the figural interpretation of specific episodes of Hebrew narrative, the contingency and complexity which Auerbach had described is positively acknowledged by the figural interpreter of that specific episode. It could still be that, despite all we have said, the figural interpretation of specific episodes of Hebrew narrative does involve the trimming and tidying of those episodes' complexity and contingency: their transmutation into something more diagrammatic, something more controllable, something more 'legendary' in form. Yes, figural interpretation, in Auerbach's sense, should – because of divine ineffability and eschatological provisionality – prevent figural interpreters from offering a final and complete interpretation of an Old Testament episode, but is that negative restraint the same thing as genuinely taking seriously the positive fact of the contingency and complexity, the positive messy history-likeness, of the individual Hebrew portrayals? This is a question which we will face again when we look at Barth's practice of figural interpretation in the next chapter.

33. See 'Figura', pp. 71–72.
34. It is unfortunately unclear whether Frei ever read the *Dante* book; he was fascinated by Auerbach, and especially by Auerbach's description of Dante's vision of historical reality, and the English translation was published by the University of Chicago in 1961, but I have found no explicit reference to it in Frei's papers.
35. 'Figura', p. 72.
36. Ibid., p. 73.
37. *Mimesis*, pp. 166–67. Auerbach is quoting from Hegel's *Lectures on Aesthetics*.
38. *Mimesis*, pp. 168–69.
39. Auerbach believes that Dante is at this point a poet of Thomism, saying that for Thomas

> diversity is looked upon not as an antithesis to perfection, but rather as an expression of it; the universe, moreover, is regarded, not as static but as engaged in a movement of its forms toward self-realization, and in the perpetual striving from potency to act, diversity is exalted as the necessary road to perfection. As applied specifically to man in the Thomist psychology, that doctrine becomes a justification of the historical process with its concrete realties and dramatic tensions (*Dante*, pp. 84–85).

40. Ibid., p. 86.
41. 'Figura', p. 70.
42. Ibid., pp. 68–70.
43. Ibid., p. 74.
44. *Dante*, p. 60.
45. In the Dante book, Auerbach suggests that the encounter with Beatrice was to some extent the source of Dante's profound feeling for the figural vision:

> In many men of his time, that yearning [for transcendence and transfiguration] was so overpowering as to destroy their perception of the world; the spirit became utterly absorbed in mystical devotion to the transcendent figuration of its hope. Dante's intense feeling for earthly existence, his consciousness of power made that evasion impossible for him. He had seen the figure of perfection on earth; she had blessed him and filled him and enchanted him with her super-abundant grace: in that decisive case he had beheld a vision of the unity of earthly manifestation and eternal archetype; from that time on he could never contemplate an historical reality without an intimation of perfection and of how far the reality was removed from it; nor, conversely, could he conceive of a divine world order without embracing in the eternal system all manner of phenomenal realities, however diverse and changing (p. 67).

46. 'Figura', p. 75.
47. *Dante*, pp. 132–33.
48. Ibid., p. 178.

49. *Mimesis*, pp. 175–76.
50. *Dante*, p. 178.
51. Alasdair Macintyre in *The Yale Review* 65 (winter 1976), George Steiner in *Philosophy and Literature* 1 (spring 1977), and Frank Kermode in *The New York Review of Books*, 29 June 1978.
52. *The Eclipse of Biblical Narrative* (1974a), p. vii.
53. Preface to *The Identity of Jesus Christ* (1974i), p. xv.
54. *The Eclipse of Biblical Narrative* (1974a), p. vii, my emphasis.
55. Ibid., p. viii.
56. Ibid., p. 152.
57. Ibid., p. 13.
58. Ibid., p. 14.
59. Ibid., p. 174.
60. *Christian Figural Reading and the Fashioning of Identity*, p. 15.
61. *The Eclipse of Biblical Narrative* (1974a), p. 29.
62. Ibid., p. 21.
63. Ibid., p. 2.
64. Ibid., p. 3.
65. Cf. ibid., p. 49.
66. Ibid., p. 47.
67. Ibid., p. 49.
68. Ibid., p. 26.
69. Ibid., p. 27.
70. The Anno Domini dating system does not, after all, measure years *after* our Lord, but years *of*.
71. Ibid., p. 174.
72. Ibid., p. 3.
73. Ibid., pp. 24–25. Dawn de Vries is not, as she thinks, refuting Frei when she recognizes that, for Calvin, the task of relating the Biblical text to the present time involves 'much more than comprehending the meaning of the cumulative sequence of the narrative' (*Jesus Christ in the Preaching of Calvin and Schleiermacher* (Louisville: Westminster/John Knox Press, 1996), p. 42), finding that the histories of God's ways with the world are such, and are depicted in such a way, as to be lessons and examples for us in all sorts of ways.
74. 'Figural Reading and the Fashioning of Christian Identity in Boyarin, Auerbach and Frei', in *Modern Theology* 14.2 (1998), p. 187.
75. Ibid., pp. 187–88.
76. *The Eclipse of Biblical Narrative* (1974a), pp. 17–18.
77. Ibid., p. 10.
78. The idea of 'inspiration' underwent a related shift. It had referred to the action of God whereby the eyes of the reader are opened to the providential ordering of history depicted in the texts, and to the realization that this history positions and interprets the reader. It became a claim for which one could argue on the basis of the supposedly abnormal accuracy of the texts in certain testable areas, or on the basis of the supposedly remarkable accuracy of biblical prophecies – a claim which one could then use to support the accuracy of the texts in other, less testable areas.
79. Ibid., p. 37.
80. An early version of the account that follows can be found in Frei's 1958 'Religion: Natural and Revealed' (*1958a*), pp. 311–12.
81. *The Eclipse of Biblical Narrative* (1974a), pp. 61–62.
82. The reference is, of course, to Matthew Tindal's *Christianity as Old as the Creation: Or, the Gospel, a Republication of the Religion of Nature*.
83. *The Eclipse of Biblical Narrative* (1974a), pp. 96–104.
84. Conyers Middleton, 'An Essay on the Allegorical and Literal Interpretation of the Creation and Fall of Man', p. 131, quoted in *The Eclipse of Biblical Narrative* (1974a), p. 121.

85. *The Eclipse of Biblical Narrative (1974a)*, p. 121.
86. Ibid., p. 125.
87. Ibid., p. 126, my emphasis.
88. 'Most of them have disavowed that they were out to "prove" the truth of Christianity, chiefly the assertion that Jesus Christ is the Redeemer – the claim with which (as it seemed to them) all other Christian doctrines must harmonise. But they have all been agreed that one way or another the religious *meaningfulness* (as distinct from demonstration of the truth) of the claim could, indeed must, be perspicuous through its relation to other accounts of general human experience' (ibid., p. 128).
89. Ibid., pp. 160–61.
90. Ibid., p. 213.
91. Herder, *Briefe, das Studium der Theologie betreffend*, vol. 11 no. 39, quoted in *The Eclipse of Biblical Narrative (1974a)*, p. 194.
92. *The Eclipse of Biblical Narrative (1974a)*, p. 203.
93. *Aus meinem Leben: Dichtung und Wahrheit*, vol. 10, p. 681, quoted in *The Eclipse of Biblical Narrative (1974a)*, p. 202.
94. Among other things, such a sensibility meant that, in Germany, the novel developed in a fundamentally different direction from that which it took in England. Friedrich von Blandenburg, in his 1774 *Versuch über den Roman*, could say that 'Inner history is the essential and peculiar element of the novel' (*The Eclipse of Biblical Narrative, 1974a*, p. 211); in Germany, the *Bildungsroman*, in which the history of spirit is related at the individual level, is the paradigmatic form of novelistic narrative.
95. *The Eclipse of Biblical Narrative (1974a)*, p. 201.
96. In chapter 7 of *Eclipse*, Frei places an entire paragraph in italics, presumably to emphasize its centrality:

> *England and Germany were the two countries in which discussion of the biblical narratives was most intense in the eighteenth century. In England, where a serious body of realistic narrative literature was building up, there arose no corresponding cumulative tradition of criticism of the biblical writings, and that included no narrative interpretation of them. In Germany, on the other hand, where a body of critical analysis as well as general hermeneutics of the biblical writings built up rapidly in the latter half of the eighteenth century, there was no simultaneous development of realistic prose narrative and its critical appraisal* (p. 142).

The eclipse of biblical narrative was the result of an accidental separation – it was a contingent historical event, not a necessary outworking of the logic of ideas. Frei stressed the centrality of this aspect of his account in an abstract of *The Eclipse of Biblical Narrative* (1973d), apparently written for its publishers.

7

A Secular Sensibility

Frei recognized that the *pre-critical* practice of figural interpretation had been the most direct way in which a doctrine of God's Christ-shaped universal providence was displayed. In this chapter, we need to explore the kind of *post-critical* appropriation of figural interpretation Frei thought possible after the eclipse of biblical narrative, and analyse how that retrieved figural interpretation allowed him to account for history. For it is the retrieved practice of figural interpretation, grounded on a robust doctrine of providence, which provides both the main way in which Frei was able to give rich content to his understanding of salvation in Christ, and the main way in which he was able to describe the historical consciousness proper to Christocentric faith. Frei's reflections on the retrieval of figural interpretation and its implications are, however, deeply indebted to the theologian who all along had been his primary conversation partner, and so we begin our exploration not with Frei's figural vision but with Barth's.

1 Barth's Figural Interpretation

I mentioned in the second chapter Frei's reference, in the preface to *The Eclipse of Biblical Narrative*, to various passages in Barth's *Church Dogmatics* which he took to be examples of the kind of reading he himself was proposing. As well as the passage relating to the Gospels which we examined before, Frei suggests reading *Church Dogmatics* II/2, pp. 340–409 as one example from among a 'vast number' of 'Barth's remarkable use of figural interpretation of the Old Testament'. The passage is part of Barth's presentation of the doctrine of election, specifically the election of the individual; it is the second part of that presentation in which, after having treated 'Jesus Christ, the promise and its recipient', Barth turns to 'The elect and the rejected' with the question, 'What is it that makes individuals elect?'[1]

The answer which Barth gives is, of course, that it is God who makes individuals elect: the election of an individual is first and foremost a distinction in the way in which God stands towards that person; it is not *based* on any 'attribute or achievement' of that person. However, this election is inevitably *displayed* in such attributes or achievements; the fact that God stands towards a specific person in this particular way finds its expression or correlate in the calling, guidance, conduct and role of that person in his or her specific history.

Indeed, this is part of what election means: election to be a witness to, or a displayer of, the God who elects, and the election by which God elects.

A specific human life does not display this election by becoming subject to an external constraint (such that election would compete with freedom), nor does that life display election by meeting some formula or following some recipe for what can count as elect. Each elect person displays election in his or her own way, by being entirely him/herself. To use an inadequate analogy: it is as if God were to choose to witness to Godself by telling a story about an individual person, but could only make the story a good witness by making it the story of a full-blooded, consistent, contingent and free individual – that is, by telling the story of a being who reflected in a creaturely way God's own nature as free, as one who says 'I am what I am'. It is as if God could only witness to Godself by telling a story of an individual who was not simply exhausted by some abstract definition of witness, who was not simply illustrative of some general theological theme, but who was a free person able to respond in love to the three-personed God who loves in freedom.

To put the same point more precisely: God determines individuals to display their election in irreducibly diverse ways, in ways that are coextensive with their unsubstitutable individuality. The calling, guidance, conduct and role of the elect individual are historical occurrences that take time to unfold; they are inherently temporal. We may recall Auerbach's talk of choice and formation, and his understanding of the Old Testament narratives as displaying the identities of, say, the patriarchs precisely as constituted by the long process in which God forms them according to God's prior choice. So, although election is not *grounded* in any difference of the elect from other human beings, it is *displayed* in such a difference: it is marked by individuals having proclaimed to them, and responding in faith to, their election in and with Christ. All elect people are, in their own ways, marked out like this from those who are not elect. 'In different ways they repeat and reproduce the solitude of Christ. They are lights in the world because he is the Light of the world.'[2]

> [T]he difference of those who are chosen in him (their calling) is *the* witness to the truth besides which there is no other. There and there alone the truth is testified – there and there alone it finds expression – where in and with the election of Jesus Christ the election of man is proclaimed to him, and where he may have assurance of it through faith in him.[3]

It is not, of course, only the elect for whom '[t]he original and proper distinction of Jesus Christ ... is the truth which ... transcends, comprehends and illumines their existence'.[4] There are also the 'rejected' – or, rather, those who attempt to live in denial of this election, who attempt to live as ones rejected by God, yet who can only lie by so doing because God has allowed the role of 'rejected one' to be filled by Jesus Christ. The attempt to live as if rejected

> is evil, perilous and futile ... It is evil because it denies that God has taken sinful and guilty man to himself in eternal love. It is perilous because it conjures up anew

the shadow of the withdrawal, the disapproval, the aversion – yes, the hate – of God which inevitably menaces every man. It is futile because while it may indeed demonstrate and confirm the sin and guilt of man, and the wretchedness of his ensuing punishment, it cannot alter the fact that there is only one Rejected, the Bearer of all man's sin and guilt and their ensuing punishment, and this One is Jesus Christ. Those who undertake the attempt may indeed lie – but can only lie – against the divine election of grace.[5]

In other words, the witness to God's election in Jesus Christ which God calls into being in history, which God *determines*, is a witness that takes two basic forms: the form of acceptance and the form of rejection. Yet each individual makes this witness in his or her own way, displaying this election and this rejection in and through his or her own irreducibly complex and contingent path. The basic distinction of acceptance and rejection, each a form of witness to God's election in Jesus Christ, is worked out and displayed in forms which are coterminous with the peculiar concrete destiny of innumerable individuals.

Barth's whole discussion of the nature of election is in fact a re-description of the results of his exegesis, in particular his exegesis of the Old Testament, where the electing and rejecting will of God is displayed precisely in and through the portrayal of elect and apparently rejected individuals and groups caught up for a time in the activity of God, without any diminution or overriding of their particular individuality, without any dissolution of the 'freedom in which they are what they are'.[6] As Barth says,

> The Bible is, in fact, everywhere concerned with the election of individual men. A human name mysteriously appears and occupies the stage for a time, whose peculiar human life, doing and sufferings in relationship with those of others form for a time the secondary subject and content of the biblical witness, and therefore themselves become a witness to that which is the primary subject and content of this witness.[7]

Barth stresses that each individual person who becomes, for a time, the secondary subject of the biblical witness becomes a witness in his or her own peculiar way, but becomes a witness to the same Lord. The final word in exegesis of all these diverse figures is the same: 'Jesus Christ'. Barth does not, however, mean to take away what he has just given, and suggest that the rich contingency of the Old Testament stories ultimately reduces to sameness; the relationship of all these figures to Jesus does not work like that.

> [W]e do not recognise him in any of these types in exactly the same way as in the others, but ... in all of them we have to recognise him as he is. None of the types gives quite the same witness as the others. None simply repeats the witness of the others. The historical multiformity of individual elect and non-elect, of those placed on the right and those on the left, cannot be ignored, and no sound exegesis can afford to ignore it. It cannot be glossed over. It cannot be reduced to a formula. It cannot be simplified. But this multiformity of historical appearances is *best observed and maintained* if here too the final word in exegesis is actually the name

of Jesus Christ, if he is understood as the individual in whom we recover both the unity of that which they all commonly attest, and that which is the peculiar individuality of each.[8]

If, then, we ask what Barth means, and how he can justify his talk of election, calling and determination – how he can say that individuals display their election precisely in and through their freedom – how he can say that finding the name of Jesus Christ to the final word in exegesis, far from undercutting the history-like nature of the biblical stories, is the best way to observe and maintain their 'historical multiformity' – if we ask all this, the only kind of answer that Barth ultimately gives is exegesis. Rather than directing us to some metaphysical scheme that could ground the possibility of such a claim, he points to the actuality, to the ranks of the elect and the rejected who parade through Scripture.

After fourteen pages of dogmatic analysis, sprinkled with exegetical asides, Barth turns to an immense block of exegesis, covering fifty-five pages of small print. He begins with a brief survey, mentioning Cain and Abel, Isaac and Ishmael, Jacob and Esau, Rachel and Leah, Ephraim and Manasseh, Perez and Serah, Israel and Moab, Midian and Canaan.[9] Then he provides astonishingly detailed exegesis of three key passages: the rituals of the two birds and the two goats in Leviticus 14 and 16;[10] the story of David and Saul in 1 and 2 Samuel,[11] and the strange story of the man of God from Judah and the prophet of Bethel in 1 Kings 13.[12]

He first concentrates on two rituals in which election and rejection are enacted: the ritual of the two birds in Leviticus 14.4–7 (for the cleansing of a leper) and the ritual of the two goats in Leviticus 16.5–22 (on the Day of Atonement). He suggests that in each ritual the Israelite spectator sees 'in a picture' his own relationship to God's election and rejection, which are enacted upon the two goats or the two birds. Barth insists, however, that we look more closely at the detail of the passages, and note the differences between them. If we do so, we see that they run in opposite directions. In the ritual for the Day of Atonement, on the one hand, the 'elect' goat is sacrificed, and the Israelite sees in this both that his life is required of him, and that God will graciously take his life as an acceptable sacrifice. The other, 'unusable' goat shows in its 'surrender to an utterly distressful non-existence'[13] the fate from which the elect are saved. In the ritual of the two birds, on the other hand, the bird that is sacrificed is killed for the sake of the bird that is released. In the sacrificed bird, the leper sees that his accession to purity occurs only with the death of his impure life; in the freed bird, which is first dipped in the blood of the dead bird, he sees that he is removed from the realm of God's wrath and 'once more a free member of the congregation'.[14] Barth summarizes his findings:

> If, according to Leviticus 16, the non-elect, those who are separated and rejected, stand in the shadows in order that the grace of God may illumine and continue to illumine the elect, we are taught also by Leviticus 14 that it is to the realm of

Azazel that the light of God's grace is poured and streams abroad. Let us gratefully know ourselves to be elect in the picture of the first goat of Leviticus 16 – grateful that we are accepted to sacrifice ourselves, grateful that we may suffer the saving judgment of the wrath of God, which is the wrath of his love, as only the elect can and may do! But let us with equal gratitude recognise ourselves as the non-elect in the picture of the second bird of Leviticus 14 – grateful because there is ordained for us the life for whose painful birth the other is elected, the resurrection for whose sake the elect must go to his death![15]

Having established this interpretation, Barth raises two questions. First, he asks whether the individual Israelite may truly see himself in either the dead or the living animal. Does he really see that his life is handed over to God and found to be an acceptable sacrifice? Does he really see that he has finally been transferred to freedom? Barth suggests that life as we know it is more limited than this, both negatively and positively, and that we do not see in the biblical stories of the elect and the rejected this kind of purity, completeness or finality in their election or rejection. The rituals represent election and rejection in a heightened, extreme, 'superhuman' form which 'transcends the human reality known to us'.[16] Second, he asks how it is that the individual Israelite can see himself both as simultaneously dying a pure death by the grace of God, and being freed for true life by the same divine grace. How can the unity of the twofold picture portrayed in these rituals be achieved? More generally, looking at the Old Testament narratives of election and rejection, Barth notes that, despite all the fluidity according to which the rejected can appear suddenly as the recipients of God's favour, the elected as the recipients of his wrath, nevertheless election and rejection are finally represented always by two separate individuals or groups, and the full unity of election and rejection in one individual is not and cannot be portrayed, even though it is suggested by the interrelation between the two doves or the two goats, and hinted at in the fluidity just mentioned.

In the face of this 'twofold enigma', Barth suggests that there is a provisionality about the Old Testament witness to election and rejection. The two rituals together suggest a form of election and rejection the full actuality of which we cannot find in the Old Testament.

> These data confront us with the following choice. On the one hand, this subject of the Old Testament witness may be regarded as an unknown quantity. This might mean that for some reason it is not yet known to us, whether because it has not yet made itself known, or has in fact taken place but has somehow escaped us. But it might also mean that the Old Testament has no subject at all, that its testimony points into the void, and that in the place to which its stories and sacrificial pictures … all point, there is, in fact, nothing, so that there is nothing to see, and never will be anything to see. On the other hand, the subject of the Old Testament witness may be accepted as identical with the person of Jesus Christ as he is seen and interpreted and proclaimed by the apostles because he had himself revealed and represented himself to them in this way.[17]

Barth is deadly serious here. This is no hermeneutical conjuring trick whereby he, with a twinkle in his eye, will pull a Christological rabbit from a Levitical hat. He believes that his exegesis shows that these Old Testament texts point to an election and rejection greater and more final than any they portray; he believes that there is an eschatological provisionality even about these supposedly static Levitical texts. He believes that a recognition of this eschatological dynamism requires us to ask the further question about what kind of fulfilment will come. And he believes that his exegesis does not force the question, but allows that there could be no fulfilment, or another fulfilment, instead of fulfilment in Christ.

> The choice between these ... possibilities is not an exegetical question; it is a question of faith. It is, therefore, to be distinguished from exegesis. But it is inescapably posed by it; and in the answer to this question, whatever it may be, exegesis is forced (even in the form of a *non liquet*) to speak its final word.[18]

Nevertheless, he believes that the eschatological provisionality he has identified is part of the context in which Christ emerges, and by which Christ interprets himself and is interpreted by the apostles. The incompleteness and provisionality of the election and rejection actually found in Israel's past, and the promise of the completion and unity of election and rejection found at least in Israel's rituals, create a space which Christ occupies and transforms. Having deliberately refused the path taken by the 'old exegesis' (the kind of exegesis which sees in Leviticus and elsewhere 'prophecies of Jesus Christ, pictures and stories which find their fulfilment in him'), 'preferring to let the Old Testament text ... speak by and for itself', he has nevertheless found an enigma which, although it 'can still be explained quite differently, in spite of what we think we know about Jesus Christ', can nevertheless also be understood to be answered in Christ. Indeed, for those who believe in Christ, 'How can we believe in Jesus Christ and not *of necessity* recognise Him in these passages?'[19] How can we deny that this space was created for Christ, and that the interpretation given by Christ and the apostles was fundamentally true? The 'old exegesis', therefore – such as the figural exegesis that Calvin gave to the Leviticus 16 passage – is, at a deeper level, 'correct'.[20]

In his second example, Barth retells the whole drama of Israel's first two kings, Saul and David, turning from a passage in which election and rejection are portrayed in their purity by means of a ritual, to one in which they are displayed in the thick of human lives. Barth provides first a reading of 1 Samuel 8, in which the 'folly of the nation' demands a '*melek* of the same kind as all other nations' and God judges the nation by giving them what they have asked for, and yet saves them by revealing that his will for them (concealed until now) is a will for a different kind of king, his anointed one. Saul is both this anointed king chosen by God according to God's good purposes, and a king like the kings of the Gentiles who is given by God as a judgment; he is, according to Barth, the former concealed under the latter. This reading enables Barth to give a powerful interpretation of Saul's sin, acknowledging that '[t]o this very day we find it difficult to stifle the sympathy and approval which are more readily felt than their opposite' in relation to his 'microscopic sins'.[21] Saul's sins are precisely moments in which it is clear that he fulfils the nation's desire for the wrong kind of king, and hence shows himself to be God's judgment against Israel and to be the one whom God has rejected, and hides his character as God's salvation for Israel and the one whom God has chosen.

From Saul, Barth turns to the 'remarkable figure of David'.[22] David has the same dual character as Saul, but in his case divine election rather than rejection is uppermost. Nevertheless, both sides are still emphatically there; indeed, Saul's sins barely register when measured against David's. Barth refuses to make his reading of David too simple.

> Why, if [David] is God's elect, is he not unmistakably differentiated from Saul? For all the beauty of the story, it is confusing and disturbing that Saul's son has the leading role in their covenant before God. And it is still more confusing that the position of the king who is also the son of God is not awarded to David but to his son. It is again confusing that for no very clear reason David is debarred from building the temple. Above all, how confusing it is that in his sin he actually realises in a much harsher fashion than Saul in his sins the picture of the heathen king rejected by God.[23]

The difference between Saul and David is not based upon any comparative estimate of the weight of each man's sins. The difference between them is purely and simply that in David we see election uppermost, and in Saul rejection uppermost; God has determined his relation to each differently, and that determination is seen in the whole course of each man's life as it is displayed in the texts of 1 Samuel. Nevertheless, David only appears as the elect in such a way that the shadow of the rejected *melek* of the Gentiles looms large behind him; Saul only appears as the rejected in such a way that the light of God's anointed ruler plays constantly across his features – an ambiguity, Barth suggests, which is never absent from the subsequent sorry history of the kings of Israel and Judah.

Once again, Barth finds that there is a riddle here, an eschatological provisionality.

> It is the riddle of the fact of a religious community which is gathered and remains gathered for centuries about a text whose content is necessarily a riddle for them, in itself as well as in its relation to their contemporary situation. For in it they can find only the story of a mistake – and of a mistake which in the text itself is actually, though not explicitly, admitted. They can find only the story of a beginning ... without the corresponding development, a broken column pointing senselessly upwards, or, at any rate, a prophecy so far unfulfilled ... It is only eschatologically and therefore only as prophecy that they can read and understand these texts, if at all, as the texts of revelation.[24]

And once again, and with the same reserve, Barth finally turns to the question of figural exegesis:

[W]e can only again say that the ultimate exegetical question in relation to these passages – the question of their subject – is identical with the question of faith: whether with the apostles we recognise this subject in the person of Jesus Christ, or whether with the Synagogue both then and now we do not recognise Christ. The question obviously cannot be settled by the Old Testament passages as such. The final result of the passages as such is the difficulty. Again, it is naturally impermissible to accept the reply of the apostles solely because we cannot solve these difficulties in the exegesis of the text itself, or because, on the other hand, we share with them an idea that Jesus Christ is supremely fitted to occupy the place where we are pulled up short. The apostles themselves did not reach their answer as a possibility discovered or selected by themselves, or as a final triumph of Jewish biblical scholarship. They did so because the Old Testament was opened up to them by its fulfilment in the resurrection of Jesus Christ, and because in the light of this fulfilment Old Testament prophecy could no longer be read by them in any other way than as an account of this subject.[25]

There is no need to describe Barth's third example in the same detail. He examines the strange self-contained tale of the man of God from Judah and the old prophet of Bethel found in 1 Kings 13, and finds that similar questions to those which he has raised in the priestly context of the Levitical rituals, and the kingly context of Saul and David, are raised in a story of prophets and men of God; once again he finds that the story points to a resolution which is not contained in the Old Testament itself, and once again he argues that a Christian can find that resolution nowhere else than in Jesus Christ.

In all three examples we see the same movement. Barth begins by practising an exegetical ascesis: he refuses to begin by finding Christ in these Old Testament stories. Instead, he begins by paying careful attention to the texts as they stand, to their details and their dynamics. He is even perfectly willing to pay attention to the textual history and the subsequent use of these passages.[26] He deliberately and explicitly brackets out his Christology, and approaches the texts in the first instance *remoto Christo*; he then deliberately and repeatedly reminds us of this ascesis even while he is reintroducing the Christocentric frame at the end of his exegeses.[27] Only once the passage has been carefully interpreted *remoto Christo* is the hermeneutical restriction lifted, and only then does Barth's interpretation become thoroughly figural. He finds that the Old Testament portrayals, in all their rich detail, both illumine and are illumined by Jesus Christ, not because there is some process of development linking the two, but simply because God has provided in Christ the answer and fulfilment to the reality that he established in the Levitical rituals, or in the rise of Saul and David. 'Fulfilment' is seen in the specific ways in which it turns out that these passages point beyond themselves, and Jesus Christ is seen by faith to occupy the space at which they point; it is seen in the always particular ways in which each Old Testament character is made a witness (whether positive or negative) to Jesus Christ.

In all this, we have an analysis of the significance of Jesus of Nazareth for history that does not rely upon an account of his spreading historical influence, nor upon the existential impact of witness to him, nor upon the secret tides of his influence pulling upon an inwardness hidden below the surface of history. We have instead a theological account of the ordering and interpreting of history in Jesus of Nazareth which tries to do justice to depictions of the messy surface of history – the contingent and particular actions and interactions of characters in complex social circumstances.

2 Barth after Dante

In order to understand something of what Frei made of this exegetical performance, we need to look at a piece he wrote several years before the preface to *Eclipse*. In January 1969 he spoke at a memorial colloquium held forty days after Barth's death, and talked about the 'energetic and logically consistent Christ-centredness' shown in Barth's 'conceptual unfolding of a rich variety of beings and relations, all of them good and right, and all of them real in their own right, and all of them referring figurally to the incarnate, raised and ascended Lord who has promised to be with us to the end, and at the end'.[28] 'In casting about for a comparison' to Barth's achievement in the *Church Dogmatics*, Frei said, he found himself 'invariably drawn to some things Erich Auerbach has said about Dante': there is a 'Dantesque element in Barth'.[29]

> For Barth, the Bible was, in a manner, Virgil and Beatrice in one. The Guide who took him only to the threshold of Paradise, it was at the same time the *figura* in writing of that greatest wonder which is the fulfillment of all natural, historical being without detracting from it: the incarnate reconciliation between God and man that is Jesus Christ.[30]

Barth saw in the Bible a portrayal of creatures who have their own concrete particularity, but who are portrayed in the context of divine providence, and in that fuller context are shown to be both *witnesses* to the reconciliation of God and humanity and the *embodiment* of that reconciliation – both Virgil and Beatrice. Virgil is, after all, one concrete historical figure among all others, who nevertheless acts as a guide who leads Dante to the threshold of that region in which the lives of men and women are made to display the reconciliation of God and creation; as a John the Baptist figure he *points towards* this reconciliation only from a distance. Beatrice, on the other hand – again as one concrete figure among others – is in her very particularity an *embodiment* of the reconciliation to which Virgil can only point: she displays the nature and glory and beauty of it.

This witnessing and this embodiment are not functions which diminish, annul or override the concrete particularity of the creatures portrayed in the Bible, and neither are they roles which are external or accidental to that concrete particularity: rather they are the confirmation and fulfilment, the establishment and preservation of that particularity. As such it is misleading to use terms such as 'function' or 'role': the witness or embodiment which the Bible displays to us in its characters is a matter of their identity rather than of something ultimately distinguishable from them. They *are* witnesses and embodiments, precisely as the unsubstitutably particular individuals that they are.

Frei insists that Jesus, as portrayed in the Bible, is both fulfilment and figure, for Barth. As *figured*, the reconciliation of God and humanity in Jesus of Nazareth is and will be the fulfilment of 'all created reality': all the creaturely reality depicted in the Bible (and, indeed all other creaturely reality, when seen in the light of God's Word) finds its true meaning when it is shown in all its particularity as a witness, as a reality which points away from itself and towards Christ. As *figure*, however, what we see displayed concretely in Jesus is also found repeated in every other concrete form of the divine–human relationship: in each of those concrete forms the incarnation is as it were republished and filled out, split in the prism of diverse creaturely reality into a rainbow of incarnate reconciliation.

The comparison with Dante allows Frei to specify the ways in which Barth's figural imagination was at the same time an *historical* imagination. On the one hand, recognition of Barth's Christocentric vision as a figural vision allows Frei to describe Barth's imagination of fulfilment in Christ as anything but 'Christomonist': it suggests a vision of the fulfilment of history according to which each particular is seen in relationship to Christ, and has its very particularity established and accentuated in that relationship. This is a fulfilment which does not involve the annulment or loss of any figure's concrete particularity; it does not involve the abolition of any figure's creatureliness; it does not involve the erasure of any figure's difference from Jesus of Nazareth. In this fulfilment all figures find their full reality as the individual creatures they are, in unity with Christ, and only in Christ.

On the other hand, however, the comparison with Auerbach's Dante allows Frei to highlight another way in which Barth's figural imagination is an historical imagination, by pointing to a kind of shadow that his figural imagination casts, which Frei refers to as Barth's 'sceptical and secular' sensibility. We have already seen that figural interpretation does not make connections based on straightforward causal links between the poles of the figural relationship, nor on any process of evolution that includes both poles; rather, it finds and displays relationships which are grounded solely in God's providential plan. This means that when a figural relationship is displayed, there is no further evidence which can be presented to explain *how* this relationship works: the only things that one can do by way of explanation are first to refer to the mysterious freedom of God for creation which allows him to call and form witnesses in the midst of creation, and second to portray both figure and fulfilment in such a way as to highlight the resemblance or contrast between them. A figural relationship cannot be explained; it can only be displayed.[31]

In other words, the figural relationship is not an expression of some deeper worldly relation between the events, which could be exposed with the right analytic techniques; there is no hidden variable to which the displayed figural relationship is epiphenomenal. What God does in Christ is not the activation or fulfilment of some prior potential within history, a potential that also lies behind the apparently diverse figures of Christ in history. In that case, to establish the existence of the prior potential would be to find the real relationship between figure and figured, a real relationship of which the figural relationship was a secondary form. If, for instance, we were to hold that Abraham was a figure of Christ because he partially fulfilled the human possibility of God-consciousness which we see perfected in Christ, then that human possibility would provide the secret, subterranean connection between Abraham and Christ at which the figural relationship merely hinted.

Barth, says Frei, resisted any move which would make the actual, concrete, historical appearance of Christ secondary to some deeper, more pervasive worldly possibility.[32] Such a move would inevitably imply that there was a point at which we could substitute the general name of that possibility for the particular name of Jesus of Nazareth. The 'possibility' of Christ's appearance as the fulfilment of all history is to be found purely on God's side, not on the world's side: there is no site within ourselves, no aspect of the 'human situation', no portion of history, no worldly reality which serves to explain the incarnation's possibility. Christology cannot begin with anthropology, or with any such generalizing discipline.

Put another way, we may say that if history is regarded *remoto Christo* we cannot expect to find any *praeparatio evangelica*, any capacity or potential for relationship with the divine which could in any way dictate the forms in which God could bring that relationship about. Speaking of Barth's 'slightly bemused and slightly amused but appreciative and even delighted' appreciation of America, described in the introduction to the American edition of *Evangelical Theology*, Frei says:

> It is not only the case, I believe, that Barth took pleasure in the vast variety of this indefinitely expansive human experience in this vast natural context – not only that he affirmed every part of it, at once in and for itself and for its potentiality as a *figura* of God's fulfilling work. Additionally, I believe he looked with a long, cool scepticism at that scene and every part of it because he believed that none of it shows that figural potential by any inherent qualities or signs of its own – either positive or negative.[33]

We can recall, at this point, Barth's refusal to find Christ too easily in the pages of the Old Testament – his insistence on approaching the texts *remoto Christo* in the first instance. Of course, the Old Testament is not simply history; it is already a witness to the activity of God in history, and it is a witness that, for Barth, holds a privileged position within the purposes of God. It is a text that has an ambiguous, questionable relationship to any historical-critical reconstruction of 'what really happened'. So, although Frei suggests that the figural interpreter will not even find a negative preparation for the Gospel by examining history *remoto Christo*, Barth allows himself to find an eschatological provisionality in the Old Testament narratives even when they are considered on their own terms: they are found to pose a question which need not be but can be answered by Christ. Nevertheless, he refuses to find more than that even here: the texts do not *require* a Christological reading. Frei's suggestion is that, when figural interpretation is extended beyond the pages of the Bible, not even a question to which Christ is the answer can be discovered without the light of Christ.

This negative constraint is, however, the source of a far more positive vision. If this constraint is taken absolutely seriously (and Frei suggests that Barth did take it seriously), history is freed from an unbearable burden: it is freed from having to be the ground of the ways of God; it is freed to be itself, freed to be properly creaturely. If Barth's figural imagination is an imagination which sees the particularity and individuality of history upheld when that history is fulfilled in Christ, it includes within itself a 'secular' vision which sees that history is, precisely, a realm of particularity and diversity, complexity and contingency – and has no need to downplay or ameliorate that vision. This is what Frei means when he says that 'there was in Barth a self-conscious secularity of sensibility far, far beyond' that shown by any apologetic theologian who seeks to find in this world the possibility which God's work fulfills.[34] 'Barth', he says,

> may have explored at once calmly and passionately, at once positively and negatively, that secularity which from a theological stance he would have thought an 'impossible possibility'. He may have explored it far more searchingly than any of his opponents, as well as any of his own modifiers with their little apologetical nostrums, either in favor of or against the 'secular situation'.[35]

Figural imagination and secular sensibility go hand in hand.[36]

Any suggestion that Barth was, in his own way, a 'secular' theologian needs very careful handling if it is not to be patently false. We must, for instance, note that Frei in no way suggests that Barth was in possession of some total secular account of the world, an account which excluded God, or graciously allowed God in at its gaps, or which could be set in paradoxical relationship with a positive theological account. The secular, sceptical vision of which Frei speaks is something rather more like an *absence* of such accounts, a willingness to pay attention to the always disruptive, never containable suddenness of things, a willingness to wait upon the particularity of the world rather than digging beneath that particularity in search of some stabilizing religious bedrock. The figural vision believes that each particular awaits its fulfilment in concrete relationship to God in Christ – and that *there is no more general way of fixing the truth or meaning of any particular*. The secular, sceptical sensibility of which Frei speaks is, we might say, a commitment to an unending *learning* of the world which does not know in advance what it will find, and which is not simply recalling or confirming general truths already known.

We should not think, either, that the secular, sceptical sensibility is some universally available default position to which all right-thinking observers would revert if only they would dare to think, dare to rid themselves of religious obfuscation. I have called it the shadow-side of Barth's figural imagination deliberately: it is itself produced by the same light of revelation that makes the figural economy visible. Barth is, in Frei's terms, able to take secularity seriously precisely because, for him, it has been made visible by Christ. In Christ, Barth finds a judgment upon all religious accounts of the world, and it is only in Christ that he finds the possibility of a non-religious account of the world. Barth's secular sensibility is a vision of a thoroughly *theological* secularity, the relationship of which to any non-theological secular vision is purely *ad hoc*.

Frei understood the *Church Dogmatics* as a portrayal of the 'fulfilment of all natural, historical being' in Jesus Christ, in such a way that the full concrete particularity and contingency of historical being is not undercut or ignored but preserved and proclaimed in its fulfilment. He understood that this kind of fulfilment was not simply asserted or described in the abstract by Barth, but that Barth had rediscovered a fitting Christian means for displaying it. If we ask what it can possibly mean for history to be fulfilled without diminution of its creatureliness, Frei will point us to Barth's exegesis; look, he will say, how Barth finds Christ to be the subject matter of these history-like stories without turning away from their history-likeness; look how he does justice to their contingency, their roughness, their intractability, and finds that they speak of Christ in and through that. Look how he finds that reference to Christ not in abstraction from Christ, but only in the relationship between concrete text and concrete text – in the relationship between the messy Old Testament history and the unsubstitutable identity of Jesus Christ. That is both a depiction and a promise of the fulfilment of historical being in Christ.

3 Figura, Secularity and Politics

Reading Frei's descriptions of figural interpretation in 'Karl Barth: Theologian' and *The Eclipse of Biblical Narrative* alongside the hints he provides about reading the world in the light of Christ in the final chapter of *The Identity of Jesus Christ* makes it clear enough that he had appropriated something very like a Barthian figural interpretation within his own work. If we wish to see that demonstrated in more detail, however, we have to turn to some of Frei's later works.[37] We could, for instance, turn to Frei's 1976 Greenhoe lectures, and note that when a member of the audience asked him for a clarification of his comments on the resurrection (comments which could have come straight out of *Identity*) Frei responded – perhaps somewhat to the questioner's bewilderment – with a brief account of figural fulfilment.

An even clearer demonstration of Frei's own figural commitments can be found, however, in a paper on 'History, Salvation-History and Typology' which he delivered in 1981, and in which he describes the Barthian figural vision as his own. He begins the paper by asking how we are to understand history; specifically, how we are to describe the relationship between the history of the 'world at large' – and that sacred history which is rehearsed by the Church.[38] This is, for the theologian, an unavoidable question: the Christian vision of God will not allow the 'world at large' to be ignored, and neither will it allow any turning away from the scandalously particular history of Jesus of Nazareth. The theologian is thus faced with a dual vision:

> on the one hand a God who endows *all* his human creatures with freedom and preserves his *full* creation from ultimate loss or absurdity; who, on the other, in the fulfilment of that creation as well as its radical redress in the face of evil has focused his providence in the person of Jesus Christ in whom the reign of God has come near, a reign foreshadowed, not embodied, in the precarious existence of Christian community.[39]

This is the basic structure of 'the Christian belief in providence'; this is what lies at the heart of 'strong Christian claims about history'.[40] To think about history theologically is to see 'Jesus Christ as the all-governing providence of God'.[41]

Yet, given the nature of God, of Jesus Christ and of the world, we cannot expect to turn a commitment to the 'world at large' and to fulfilment in Christ into a neat explanatory scheme: 'the manner of their cohesion is hidden'.[42] Certainly, Frei can speak in terms of 'a public pattern in which humankind is seen as united in destiny', and of 'the whole of human history as the enactment of a complex design',[43] but he does not regard that pattern or design as one which we can simply uncover and state. It is, rather, a patterning of the world which we can discern only fragmentarily.[44] This discernment is, perhaps, one of the key tasks of Christian theology, indeed of Christian life: the tracing of what glimpses we have of this patterning of the world in Christ.

After suggesting (in familiar fashion) that there are various common theological moves which get in the way of this kind of pattern-tracing,[45] Frei argues that the theologian will need two tools in her toolbox if she is to be properly equipped to trace those glimpses of providential patterning and point towards their eschatological completion. On the one hand, we need, 'An understanding of persons as historical subjects and historical agents who cannot be sublated by any of the available "larger force" explanations';[46] a description of history as 'the interplay of character and circumstance ... the unfinished or cumulative, confused interface of human designs'.[47] We need, that is, an understanding of history which allows that it can receive its patterning in relation to Christ, and will not secretly substitute for that patterning some deeper structure of its own. On the other hand, we need figural interpretation, for 'something like it is indispensable if we are going to give descriptive substance to the claim that history is the story of the providential governance of God the Father of Jesus Christ among humankind'.[48] We need, in other words, a history that allows for Christological patterning, and a means of tracing out glimpses of that pattern.

And where do we find these two necessities together in modern theology? In Barth's figural exegesis, of course, which combines 'complex ... reference to the person of Jesus' with a reserve about making that reference too quickly, and so both finds providential patterns in history and at the same time allows history a 'plasticity, openness or ambiguity' it would not otherwise have.[49]

Frei describes again Barth's exegesis of the Levitical rituals which we discussed above, and points to his remarkable exegetical reserve, 'unthinkable in earlier figural exegesis'.[50]

> I suppose he would claim that the reason figurative reading in the classical and pre-critical period did no such double duty was that it didn't have to, or rather that it did the double duty without intruding the differences ... But, he would also claim, the procedure is really the same under the earlier condition and under the somewhat different and perhaps temporary conditions of a world picture gradually introduced since the Seventeenth Century.[51]

Drawing attention to the 'secular sensibility' implied within the figural vision is, for Barth and for Frei, a temporary measure: it is needed in a situation in which the pervasive temptation is to find immanent patternings to history, and to allow those patterns to ground or exclude the patterning of the world we find in Christ. Perhaps in a different situation ('a new, post-modern world picture', if such arises)[52] the emphasis will change again. But for now at least it is a note that needs to be sounded.

Most of this is, by now, familiar material; it is Frei's own restatement of the Dantesque vision that he had learnt from Barth. Frei throws one more element into the mix, however. In a letter to Julian Hartt in which he reflected on the 1981 paper, Frei makes one small addition. He wants, he says, to go slightly further than Barth in paying attention to 'the history of political communities of the ordinary sort', to see them as 'variable antitype' to the biblical original.[53] In other words he wants – and believes that the figural and secular vision he shares with Barth allows him – to become a more obviously political theologian, a public theologian: one who by means of his thoroughly theological vision can contribute to wider public debate. In his earliest criticisms of Barth it was clear that, although he did not wish to water down Barth's insistence upon the freedom of God, he did wish, now that that insistence had been made, to turn more directly than Barth to the freedom of the creature. Now it becomes clear that, although Frei does not wish to water down Barth's insistence upon turning to face Christ, Frei wants to build upon that insistence by paying more direct attention to the multiple situations in which we are called to make that turn. And he believed not simply that Barth's figural vision *allowed* that, but that it *required* it. As he put it later, 'I think a Christian case can be made that we have not met the textual Jesus until we have also met him, as Søren Kierkegaard said, in forgetfulness of himself or incognito in a crowd.'[54] We can only approach the fullness of the figural vision to which Barth has recalled us – and that means the fullness of our vision of Christ in whom the world is ordered as well as our vision of the world that is ordered in Christ – if we devote unstinting attention to *both* poles. Now that Barth has sounded his strong note, and called our distracted attention to one pole, we may now turn more explicitly and directly to the other, and give more prominence to our role as theological commentators on history, society and politics.[55]

In the last year or two of his life, Frei began to take these hints further, and did so by way of a rapprochement with H. Richard Niebuhr. Returning to Niebuhr's work, he now found that it was less dominated by relationalist method than he had thought in 1957, and that there was much in Niebuhr's vision which chimed with Barth's figural vision and Frei's own desire to take that vision further in a political direction. He found in Niebuhr an account of just that tentative tracing of history's patterns called for by the figural vision, a tracing sufficient to support circumspect political action:

> Niebuhr may well have approved Karl Barth's insistence that there is no natural line of affinity from liberal politics to the witness of the church ... But he might equally well have agreed with Barth that with caution, care, forethought and luck, there might just be an affinity the other way around: that a gospel of the universal, present, governing glory of God might have more to do with a carefully circumscribed progressive politics than with either a theology of revolution or some other political theology.[56]

A 'carefully circumscribed progressive politics': Frei certainly wished to turn more directly towards a political theology, but he also believed that the figural vision which lit the way for him to do so imposed significant constraints on the kind of political theology he could attempt.[57] He displayed this reserve most powerfully at a 1986 conference in honour of Jürgen Moltmann and Elisabeth Moltmann-Wendel. He had gone to the conference with a paper prepared on 'God's Patience and Our Work', in which the questions of the limitations upon a Christian political vision were already raised. The second half of his paper was 'a plea that the Church participate in political life in limited and specific ways'.[58] The Church must so participate, for Christians 'believe that love – and justice as its closest ally – are the promise of the undisclosed future. And ... they believe that this world has been, is and will be God's world, and that God's way is best seen where pressure toward freedom and structures of justice may be discerned.'[59] The Church must, however, participate in a limited way, because 'to *believe* that God's kingdom holds the human future [is] not to *know* how it will supersede the present, in fact to know very little about the future for sure'. Christians will therefore at least be 'uneasy about thinking that the crucifixion and resurrection of Jesus are the clue to the shape of the political future. The limits of time and space remain, and yet we have the promise of God.'[60]

At the conference itself, however, Frei found that he had to state his caution more forcefully. He abandoned his prepared paper and, apparently overnight, wrote a completely new one. He explained his decision in these terms:

> There was, in this conference, a kind of touching and affecting upbeat sensibility right from the beginning ... There was an upbeat quality about ... the sureness,

the unbreakable promise of God, his covenantal loyalty, within which there is reason not only for work but ground for optimism, ground for the belief that liberation is not so much a miracle but a steady motion toward that kingdom – which will nevertheless come in as a miracle. And I suppose what I want to say more unequivocally is that the triumph of love must remain a miracle, it seems to me, in the light of the gospel. I want to say that we still see in a glass darkly now, and it seems to me more darkly perhaps than I thought I heard yesterday. We see analogically, we see brokenly, and not schematically, not even in the schema of a dialectic of history.[61]

Later in his paper, Frei gave an example which illuminates both sides of his concern – his concern both for the boldness to think theologically about concrete political situations, and for the reserve necessary if we are not to misconstrue the illumination we have been given.

Let me remind you of our second greatest (Jonathan Edwards was our greatest) American theologian, Abraham Lincoln. Go back, read and re-read his second inaugural address ... Read those soberly optimistic lines about the undefeatability of the purpose of a just God, and the puzzling, tragic course of events through which it was achieved.[62]

Lincoln's remarkable speech was given on 4 March 1865, a month before he was assassinated. Speaking of the two sides in the Civil War, he says:

Both read the same Bible and pray to the same God, and each invokes His aid against the other. It may seem strange that any men should dare to ask a just God's assistance in wringing their bread from the sweat of other men's faces, but let us judge not, that we be not judged. The prayers of both could not be answered. That of neither has been answered fully. The Almighty has His own purposes. 'Woe unto the world because of its offences! For it must needs be that offences come, but woe to that man by whom the offence cometh!' If we shall suppose that American slavery is one of those offences which, in the providence of God, must needs come, but which, having continued through His appointed time, He wills now to remove, and that He gives to both North and South this terrible war as the woe due to those by whom the offence came, shall we discern therein any departure from those divine attributes which the believers in a Living God always ascribe to Him? Fondly do we hope – fervently do we pray – that this mighty scourge of war may speedily pass away. Yet, if God wills that it continue, until all the wealth piled up by the bond-man's two hundred and fifty years of unrequited toil shall be sunk, and until every drop of blood drawn by the lash, shall be paid by another drawn with the sword, as was said three thousand years ago, so still it must be said 'the judgments of the Lord are true and righteous altogether.' With malice towards none; with charity for all; with firmness in the right, as God gives us to see the right, let us strive to finish the work we are in ... to do all which may achieve and cherish a just, and a lasting peace, among ourselves, and with all nations.[63]

What might it mean to try to read the Civil War in figural relationship to the cross and resurrection of Christ? First of all, it will of course mean that the War is allowed its own density and specificity, and that there is no way in which it can be turned into an illustration of a more general historical structure. Perhaps it might mean that we may tentatively seek to see this suffering as a participation in Christ's suffering on the cross, and therefore as a suffering which, in its own way, might give way to redemption? Given the characterization of figural interpretation which Frei has presented, even if we accept some such discernment, it can only be as a *partial* theological description, and will need supplementing by others, perhaps even by claims which run in a quite different direction. And even to the extent that we may accept it, this discernment does not make things simpler, but more complex. To interpret the suffering of the War as a figure of the suffering of the cross does not give us any easy access to blame or acquittal, for instance; it does not mean, say, that we can justify those 'by whom the offence cometh', any more than the redemptive power of the cross exonerated in any simple way the acts of Judas or of the crucifying soldiers. Nor does it give us easy answers to the question, 'Where was God in this War?' To accept the figural claim might mean that we are able to say more clearly that the horror of this War was not the absence of God; it might even mean that we can read it as (partially!) a sign or consequence of God's drawing of the nation towards himself; but it might also mean, when we remember that the transition from cross to resurrection is not an organic transition bespeaking an underlying mythical structure but a stark and contingent transition which is entirely in the hands of God, that we see the War not as an organic (and therefore, possibly, a justifiable) *cause* of any redemption which might follow from it, but as an agonized plea which requires the unmerited grace of God if any good is to result.

In other words, the illumination which results when we see history and the gospel beside one another is complex and subtle, and will require sensitivity and discernment – *and it is an illumination which will send us deeper into the complexities of each pole of the relationship.* From the point of view of unbelief, this strange overlapping analysis of two separate events is bound to seem arbitrary; from the Christian point of view it is justified only by the faith that the same Christ who died on the cross will sum up even the Civil War in himself in the eschaton, and the faith that we might therefore be able to glimpse, with the Spirit's help, some aspects of what that fulfilment will mean – if only through a very dark glass. The Christian faith in God's Christ-shaped providence is that the journey into the complexities of the War and of the cross, each seen more searchingly in the light of the other, can – by the grace of God – be a journey into truth.

When Frei turns from the Civil War to the Vietnam War,[64] and then on to the bombing of Libya which had taken place shortly before he spoke, it is clear that he is not hoping for a simple Christian vision which will tell him precisely what the Christian course of action should be – he is not looking for a clear Christian politics in that sense – but for doorways into a deep Christian engagement with the complexity of events which turns away from any easy answer, but which does not in so doing turn away from political engagement, or from the risking of fragile and fallible discernments. This is not the bold brush of Christian revolutionary activism, but, as Frei had said, a patient and 'carefully circumscribed' political theology. 'One step at a time, no more than that for the task of public theology, but always with the protest against national self-aggrandisement and idolatry in mind. It is a slim line, but a goodly cause.'[65]

4 Conclusion

On the basis of Barth's example, Frei believed that the retrieval of figural interpretation was indeed possible – but that the retrieval placed figural interpretation in a new light. Figural interpretation in Barth's hands was a form of interpretation which does not take its success in finding the relationships between Christ and history for granted, and it is a form of interpretation which, more clearly even than before, coheres with affirmations of the contingent and particular nature – the creatureliness – of the historical world.

To put it in terms rather closer to Frei than to Barth, we may say that if it is the Jesus Christ of the Gospels who is the decisive word to have been spoken in and to the world, and if figural interpretation is the primary means by which we hear the echoes of that word across the entire stage of history, our world is proved by this word to be of a kind which does not inevitably swamp and evacuate such a word, a word spoken in the idiom of characters and events, a word spoken in the idiom of public actions and interactions. We find ourselves, by this light, in a world which cannot be reduced to inwardness or to the gigantic structures of *Geist*, but is fundamentally and inherently a world of people on a public stage.

In other words, if figural interpretation is the means by which we move from reading the unsubstitutable identity of Jesus Christ to telling the story of salvation, the story of this man's cosmic scope, then we must say – not that this kind of Christocentric theology is a possibility in the kind of historical world proclaimed by Strauss, but – that something like the historical world proclaimed by Strauss, sceptical of all religious reservations within the world, is *required* within a Christocentric theology. Christian theology has an historical consciousness, a secular sensibility, of its own.

For Frei, the world is historical precisely *because* it is providentially ordered in Christ. The world is contingent, particular, creaturely and finite precisely *because* it is the world upheld by the Word spoken in Jesus from Nazareth. That Word is a revelation which makes figures of us all, without abolishing our particularity, our diversity, our sheer messy historical nature. So when Strauss declares that theology is impossible, for to follow it would be a denial of the historical world in which we all know we live, Frei can indeed laugh – and respond that, on the contrary, a theology of Christ's unsubstitutable identity and his figural relation to any and every other particular itself provides the soil on which a thoroughly historical vision can rest, and in which it can flourish.

Should Strauss's incredulity remain, however, all that Frei can do is point to particular after particular and show, with Barth, how reading that particular in the light of the Christ of the Gospels sends us deeper into its particularity, while at the same time connecting it – however tentatively the connection is made by our weak hands – to the one Christ-centred providence of God. The figural vision is only properly displayed, this side of the eschaton, in particular interpretations – whether those be exegeses of Old Testament passages, or attempts to read the pattern of Christ in the dark and twisted shapes of our world's public history.

Notes

1. *Church Dogmatics* II/2, p. 340.
2. Ibid., p. 345.
3. Ibid.
4. Ibid., p. 349.
5. Ibid., p. 346.
6. Ibid., p. 343.
7. Ibid., p. 341.
8. Ibid., p. 366, my emphasis.
9. Ibid., pp. 354–57.
10. Ibid., pp. 357–66.
11. Ibid., pp. 366–93.
12. Ibid., pp. 393–409.
13. Ibid., p. 359.
14. Ibid., p. 360.
15. Ibid., p. 361.
16. Ibid., p. 362.
17. Ibid., p. 363.
18. Ibid., pp. 363–64.
19. Ibid., p. 364, my emphasis.
20. Ibid., p. 365.
21. Ibid., pp. 369–70.
22. Ibid., p. 372.
23. Ibid., p. 387.
24. Ibid., p. 386.
25. Ibid., pp. 388–89.
26. For instance, he discusses the sources of the 1 Kings 13 story on p. 393, and he discusses the 'sacral interest with which these texts were read' on p. 386.
27. The phrase '*remoto Christo*' needs clarification. Barth was, of course, a Christian interpreter first, foremost and always, and we cannot sensibly hope to ask whether he would have been able to arrive at his exegeses, his identification of the patterns and the provisionality in these Old Testament stories, had he not been a Christian interpreter. Whoever the 'he' is in that final clause, it is not Barth. Perhaps we might say that the deliberate ascesis, the *remoto Christo* procedure we are describing, is rather an attempt to produce (as a Christian interpreter, schooled and enabled by Christian interpretation to see patterns which other eyes might miss) readings of the text which will be intelligible and might perhaps be convincing to those who do not share this Christian inheritance. It makes sense to imagine Barth in conversation with a Jewish exegete about Leviticus 14, for instance, and to imagine them

having enough to say to one another to allow the conversation to continue rather than falter; it is possible to imagine each holding the other to account for his exegesis of the passage, by constant reference back to the text, and for Barth to hope that the Jewish exegete will see the patterns which Barth points out, even while he does not accept the light by which Barth has seen them.

28. 'Karl Barth: Theologian' (1969a), p. 174.

29. Ibid., p. 168. Cf. the start of 'Scripture as Realistic Narrative: Karl Barth as Critic of Historical Criticism' (1974d), where Frei claims that Barth and Dante share 'the sense of reality being in the deepest way a divine comedy' before moving on to describe Barth's

> basic affirmation of ... a real world which everywhere manifests ... the divine grace that emerged in the history of Israel and emerged for all mankind in the crucifixion and the resurrection of Jesus Christ ... It was as if that history was the one real history of mankind, and all history ... is to be regarded as a figure of that covenant history. All other history is history in its own right, yes, and to be seen as having its own meaning, yes, but nonetheless, finally, its reality is to be understood as a figure in that one history ... This story as the vision of all reality: it was the vision of a *Divina Comedia*.

Cf. the brief mention of similar themes in 'Notes for an Oral History' (1975g), p. 3, quoted in John Woolverton, 'Hans W. Frei in Context', p. 383.

30. 'Karl Barth: Theologian' (1969a), p. 169.

31. Ibid., pp. 170–72. If we are asked how it was possible for Dante to combine his vision of the ordered judgment of God on all history with a true flourishing of attention to historical particularity and difference, the answer can only be, 'He did so: read the *Comedy*!' So with Barth: the answer to the 'Christomonism' accusation, the accusation that Barth's attention to Jesus of Nazareth does not allow any other creaturely reality space to be itself, is simply, 'He does allow this space: read his figural exegesis in the *Church Dogmatics*!'

32. Ibid., pp. 170–71.

33. Ibid., p. 172.

34. In one of his reviews of Eberhard Busch's biography of Karl Barth (*1981j*), Frei writes about Barth's secular realism:

> Those who have read Paul Fussell's remarkable book, *The Great War and Modern Memory*, will recall how the horrors of trench warfare converted the poetic as well as ordinary usage of British English rapidly from imitation-heroic and elevated Victorian rhetoric to the ironic, blunt use that grew out of World War I. There was a parallel but for various reasons much less thorough change in German. In this as in other respects Barth was completely a man of his day, fiercely rebellious against the culture that produced the First World War. His language was far more modern than (for example) the strange combination of high rhetoric, esoteric conceptuality and stylised syntax of his post-second world war liberal opponents. They self-consciously supposed themselves modern, but in contrast to Barth their language seems disconcertingly reminiscent of pre-first world war culture not only politically or culturally but linguistically. Barth at any point in his career would have been more at home with Bertolt Brecht (for example) than would someone like Martin Heidegger, early or late!

35. 'Karl Barth: Theologian' (1969a), p. 173.

36. See Appendix 4 for further details of Frei's analysis of this aspect of Barth's theology.

37. In the next chapter we will be looking at Frei's work from the mid-1970s onwards, and focusing on the changes and qualifications of his earlier work which he then introduced. Frei's attitude to figural interpretation and the secular sensibility which accompanies it, however, do not seem to have changed materially in the twenty years from 1968 to 1988.

38. 'History, Salvation-History, and Typology' (1981f), p. 3.

39. Ibid., p. 5.

40. Ibid., p. 7; Letter to Julian Hartt (1981i), p. 2.
41. 'History, Salvation-History, and Typology' (1981f), p. 7.
42. Ibid., p. 5.
43. Ibid., p. 15.
44. Ibid.
45. In his letter to Julian Hartt (1981i), Frei helpfully summarized the paper. The polemical aspect comes out like this: 'I suggested that affirming a partially evident providential pattern in the events of history involves a denial not only of historicist, existentialist and other "perspectivialisms", but also of those panentheisms which reduce specific events to instances of either natural pattern or ideal generalisation' (p. 2).
46. Ibid., p. 2.
47. 'History, Salvation-History, and Typology' (1981f), p. 13.
48. Ibid., p. 15.
49. Ibid., pp. 16–17.
50. Ibid., p. 16.
51. Ibid., pp. 17–18.
52. Ibid., p. 18.
53. Letter to Julian Hartt (1981i), p. 3.
54. Humanities Council Lectures (1987c), p. 136.
55. Elsewhere, Frei was happy to give the term 'secular sensibility' a more unqualified prominence as a description of himself than he had allowed it as a description of Barth. In a letter to William Placher (1979f), for instance, he wrote, 'I don't know at what stage my pilgrimage is right now, except that it is made up of Reformed theology, non-liturgical worship and a secular sensibility' (p. 2, my emphasis).
56. 'H. Richard Niebuhr on History, Church and Nation' (1988d), p. 232.
57. 'Our story, our inquiry as observers into patterns which we as agents may act out, goes on, here in time, on the plane where God and humans meet. It is an inquiry into not only the church's but also our country's future, an inquiry into the polarity between the two, but always under the limited contingent conditions of response for our time to the creating, judging and redeeming work of God' (ibid., p. 219).
58. 'God's Patience and Our Work' (1986c[ii]), p. 13.
59. Ibid., p. 14.
60. Ibid., pp. 10–11.
61. 'Comments' (1986c[iii]), p. 3.
62. Ibid., pp. 5–6.
63. Abraham Lincoln, 'Second Inaugural Address March 4 1865', in Don E. Fehrenbacher (ed.), *Abraham Lincoln, Speeches and Writing 1859–1869* (New York: Literary Classics of the United States, 1989).
64. Frei had made precisely the same move in *The Identity of Jesus Christ* (1975a), pp. 162–63. I rather suspect that he had Lincoln's 'Second Inaugural Address' in mind on that occasion as well.
65. 'H. Richard Niebuhr on History, Church and Nation' (1988d), p. 233.

8

Unsystematic Theology

In May 1974, Frei wrote a brief annual report on his work for Wayne Meeks, then Chairman of Frei's Department. 'This', he said 'has been a windfall year for me': *The Eclipse of Biblical Narrative* was published, *The Identity of Jesus Christ* was on its way (Frei expecting publication that fall), and that spring he had delivered both the Rockwell Lectures on Religion at Rice University in February and a lecture on Barth's hermeneutics to the Karl Barth Society of North America in Toronto. He had (as he was later to say) 'found his voice'.[1]

With the exception of some book reviews, however, no more of Frei's work was published until the appearance a decade later of his long article on David Friedrich Strauss in *Nineteenth Century Religious Thought in the West*. In part, this gap is due to the administrative responsibilities he had taken on – Frei was Master of Ezra Stiles College from 1972 until 1980, for instance; in part, it was due to the difficulty he sometimes found in taking projects all the way to publication – he was hoping in 1974 and for several years thereafter to have his Rockwell Lectures published, but never quite finished them off; in part, it is a misleading impression created by the time lag between his finishing the Strauss lecture in 1980 or 1981 and its publication in 1985, or his delivering the 'Literal Reading' paper in 1983 and its publication in 1986. There is more to it than that, however, and if some readers have been too easily seduced into speaking of Frei's 'early work' and 'late work' as if they were entirely distinct projects separated by this long silence, there is certainly an extent to which Frei spent a good deal of the 1970s re-evaluating and qualifying the approach represented by *Eclipse* and *Identity*.

The change that takes place over the 1970s and into the 80s is quite difficult to pin down precisely. It is, I think, more of a change to the scaffolding surrounding Frei's Christological proposal than a change in its most important details; nevertheless that alteration in the scaffolding does precipitate a change in the overall style and feel of his work. Yet we are hampered in our assessment of the change by the absence of any full and definitive statement of his case, for none of the materials published posthumously in *Types of Christian Theology* and *Theology and Narrative* quite convey the full scope of his proposal in its altered form. Nevertheless, if we pay close attention to these materials, and to the mass of unpublished work in the Yale Divinity School archive, it is possible to tease out some of the aspects of the change.

First, Frei deliberately pursued, throughout the 1970s, a change in the form of his history-writing, away from too purely intellectual a history and towards a more sociologically aware form of writing. This was accompanied and supported by a clarification of the ordinary, practical, ecclesial grounds of theology, a clarification which involved Frei distancing himself from some aspects of his original, more theoretical grounding of dogmatic theology, and his re-establishment of a slightly altered version of his theology on new grounds, 'cultural-linguistic' and theological. This move also enabled him to turn to a more nuanced and varied account of the nature of theological enquiry, which allowed him to relax his earlier stringent anti-relationalist polemic. All of this combined to allow Frei to restate his Christological, figural theology with a greater explicit awareness of that theology's limitations and possibilities, and of the positive but bounded role of the academic theologians who develop such theologies.

In this chapter, we will be examining that shift more closely. We will not, therefore, be going any deeper into the precise nature of figural interpretation, nor into Frei's depiction of God's providence. We will, instead, be charting Frei's simplification of the scaffolding which surrounded that figural theology. And that is what it is: simplification. For all the complexity of some of the issues which will come up, Frei's aim in all this later work was to bring theology more closely into contact with the ordinary practices of Christian communities in our world, and to clear away that great methodological thicket which too often separates theological experts from the believing communities they intend to serve. This is a paradoxical undertaking, to be sure: we will be devoting many words and considerable effort to discussions of methodology, the purpose of which is to undermine too strong a reliance on methodology. But that is the paradox of a good deal of Frei's work – the same paradox which he had noticed when in the Preface to *Eclipse* he apologized for writing an 'analysis of analyses of the Bible in which not a single text is examined, not a single exegesis undertaken'.[2] Frei's later work is, then, a deliberate and careful simplification of the supporting structures of his earlier theology, and that is why, rather than treating this later work of Frei's at the same length as his earlier work, I have given it just one chapter. In the absence of the more substantial work that Frei would have gone on to produce had he not died so suddenly, I think his later work is most appropriately presented as a commentary upon his earlier work, rather than as an independent project.

1 Writing History

During the 1970s, Frei realized that the fact that concepts have a contingent history – a conclusion which cohered with the historical vision he thought was implied by his theological commitments – affected his systematic and dogmatic work more closely than he had allowed. Concepts that seem to their users to be natural and inevitable are in fact elements of contingent settlements by which they come to terms with their world. Those settlements could have been otherwise, not in the sense that 'anything goes', but in the sense that the multiple ways in which human beings develop sustainable ways of working with the resistances of the world may not inevitably require concepts arranged, defined and related in the same way. There is nothing unavoidable about the distinctions modern Westerners have drawn between 'self' and 'world', 'individual' and 'society', or 'history' and 'fiction', for instance: those concepts and distinctions are contingent; they have a history.[3]

This is a point which Frei had already insisted upon in *Eclipse*. Perhaps the central claim in that book is that the eclipse of biblical narrative was not an inevitable outworking of the inherent logic of the Western mind, but an accident – the contingent concatenation of a whole range of factors, including the absence from Germany, at a crucial period, of a tradition of realistic novel-writing. The eclipse need not have happened; there was not an inevitable progression from naïveté to criticism.

Nevertheless, after *Eclipse*'s publication, Frei began to worry that he had not let his appreciation of historical contingency penetrate deeply enough, and that by concentrating the majority of his history-writing in a thoroughly intellectual register, he had (despite his best intentions) given the impression that the history of the eclipse, though contingent, was a history that transpired primarily in a realm of thought, by means of the collision, interaction and unfolding of ideas. As the 1970s progressed, therefore, Frei made a deliberate effort to rethink the story he had told, and the broader story of modern theology within which it was set, in order to demonstrate how the ideas which shaped that theology had a social and cultural history.

Until the mid-1970s, Frei's writing had been quite resolutely, and sometimes rebarbatively, intellectual. In large part, his 1956 doctoral thesis, for instance, had been an exercise in intellectual history, although we should not oversimplify the kind of approach he took. Even at that stage, he did not suppose that the appearance of particular configurations of ideas could be *explained*. He wrote in such a way as to imply that no unproblematic starting point can be found from which one can work forward, clearly tracing the stages of an idea's development. History is messier than that, and instead of explanation we can only hope for exploration and description. Frei steps into the midst of complexity, attempts to get a provisional sense of his surroundings, and then patiently moves backwards and forwards constantly revising his maps; what comes earlier is not guaranteed to give the clue to what comes later; indeed what comes later often serves to unlock his understanding of what came earlier. Frei began with Barth's break with liberalism and then moved forwards, then backwards, then forwards again in a stuttering, provisional exploration of an intractably complex subject-matter. He mixes up his descriptive schemes in order to position Barth's break with liberalism, throwing together, for instance, his neat opposition of relationalism versus anti-relationalism, with a threefold scheme of mechanical, organic and post-liberal, and another more complex scheme of liberalism, scepticism, biblical realism and post-liberalism. The subject-matter he was describing did not lend itself to being exhausted by any one conceptual framework, or even the multiple frameworks which he uses, but was always wriggling free, always exceeding his historian's grasp.[4] Nevertheless, despite this practical admission of history's density – we might say its 'unsubstitutability' – the history is entirely intellectual. There are few if any concessions to social history: the various characters described appear only as the writers of particular theological texts, and the tenor of the times in which they lived and the constraints under which they wrote do not emerge to view.

Eclipse, Frei's next major piece of historical writing, was equally complex. The book is, again, largely intellectual history, but it provides few easily stated conclusions, and traces its subtle subject matter through a morass of historical detail. Frei begins the book with something that looks like a thesis, or a summary that gives the whole plot away, but this relatively clear beginning is followed by a plunge into a complex historical story in which that thesis has all the simplicity knocked out of it and is shown to be a heuristic introduction to a subject-matter too rich to be so easily contained. Frei chases his quarry through all the contingencies and complexities of a geographically and temporally extended debate, following a varied and argumentative cast of characters, and seldom allowing himself to summarize, or to set out with full clarity, what has been achieved and what remains to be demonstrated. Any such summaries as Frei does allow himself – and there are several scattered across the book's pages – are always shown in the sequel to be provisional, and to acquire necessary complexity and nuance from the detail that surrounds them rather than simply being illustrated by that detail. Patterns emerge from the detail, are described and used to further the narrative, and then disappear, to be replaced at a later breathing space along the way with other, overlapping sets of patterns. This characteristic of the book is most evident in its ending: the book that started with the presentation of a bold thesis is not rounded off with any kind of definitive and final summing up. Frei's colleagues remember the anxiety with which he constantly revised the book, struggling at every stage to do proper justice to an historical subject matter that could easily be betrayed by premature systematization. His subject matter, we might say, was *constituted* by the particularity of his historical story, rather than simply *illustrated* by it; even more clearly than in Frei's doctorate, the thesis of *Eclipse* is, in the end, nothing other than the difficult story that it tells. And yet once again, the history told is almost entirely intellectual. Crucial reference is made to the presence and absence of a realistic novelistic tradition in England and Germany respectively, but that is almost the only time that we are made to look up from a battle of minds and books and see the broader cultural landscape surrounding the battlefield.

The writing for *Eclipse* was finished early in 1973, and already in the 1974 Rockwell Lectures we can see Frei's historical approach broadening – if not in his discussion of Kant then at least in his discussion of Lessing. The history is still resolutely intellectual (even though Frei insists that the heart of Lessing's intellectual significance for theology lies not in his essays but in his dramas) but Frei pays far more attention to the social landscape in which Lessing wrote, and which both constrained and enabled his writing. In particular (a foretaste of some later inquiries) he pays attention to the social locations available to writers in Lessing's Prussia, and asks what effect on the style and content of Lessing's writings his position had. We can hardly be said to be in the realm of social history, but a new note has been sounded. Perhaps partly as a result, the Rockwell Lectures are, though no less resistant to easy summary, a touch more approachable than some of Frei's earlier historical writing.[5]

As the 1970s progressed, Frei repeatedly signalled his intention to alter the approach of his historical work, particularly in his letters. In 1976, he said in a letter to William Placher, 'I am disturbed by the fact that I am making theology too theoretical in my books',[6] and in a letter to Charles Wood two years later he was more explicit: 'I am deeply persuaded that theological history, like other intellectual history, will have to be done in conjunction with more recent developments in the social sciences than we have ever attempted to take into account.'[7] This intention, however, presented Frei with a question. How can one place ideas within their social context without courting reductionism – either the reduction of ideas to epiphenomena, bobbing on the surface of economic and social history, or of social history to a decorative appendage dangling purely illustratively from the backbone of intellectual history? In earlier chapters, we examined Frei's demurrals in the face of a subject–alienation anthropology which would drive too thick a wedge between public and private; now that battle is extended in a new direction.

Frei's rejection of too sharp a distinction between public and private in the case of subject–alienation anthropologies had not been a victory won by some overarching theory strong enough to hold the two sides together, but the presentation of a looser, more methodologically mixed approach to identity-description which simply refused to see the public–private split as a problem (except in pathological cases where intelligibility in any case rests upon the priority of the non-pathological norm). In the later 1970s, we find Frei attempting a similar outflanking manoeuvre with respect to the writing of social and intellectual history. In 1978, he delivered the George F. Thomas Memorial Lecture, 'Is Religious Sensibility Accessible to Study? The Case of G.E. Lessing', in which he tackled this question head on.

After a discussion of the state of the discipline of religious studies, he noted that the study of

> experience ... has been a particular snarl for us, for ... it is not directly and publicly accessible, and yet it refuses to go away and remain a modest epiphenomenon. No matter how sophisticated we get and how much we learn to ease ourselves and our students away from misplaced, misleading questions, we still catch ourselves wondering what it was like to live in fourteenth-century Burgundy or seventh-century Ceylon and to experience the world, including its religious aspect, in that fashion.[8]

He then discussed several possible answers to this question. On the one hand, there are those who 'declare such questions out of bounds', believing that, once we have investigated all the public manifestations of religion, 'there is no private question left over' and no private language for posing a *further* question of experience.[9] On the other hand, the idealists and phenomenologists argue that 'consciousness is an Ur-phenomenon *sui generis*, and that experience ... must be got at in a distinctive way'.[10]

Frei declares himself 'sympathetic to a loose and non-technical mixture' of these two answers, 'diametrically opposed though they seem',[11] and explains that he is going to

> substitute the vaguer, broader term 'sensibility' for consciousness and experience. It is used commonly and with laudable imprecision in our day, enjoying a resuscitated life after a lapse of over a century ... We talk about individuals' responsive capacities, a combination of their various affective and mental habits as they are ordered (or perhaps disordered) into the individuals' particular hierarchical shape. But this present use is for various reasons, I think, overshadowed by the other, overlapping one: we talk about an attitude or outlook characteristic of a group, and to that extent of its individual members, perhaps a representative outlook of an epoch or a period, including both intellectual stance and emotional disposition, not so much a group's 'ideology' or 'world view' as its way of learning and using a common vocabulary.[12]

Under the heading, 'a plea for self-aware methodological looseness', Frei admits that what he is proposing is

> in a way quite superficial and – in contrast to phenomenological ambitions – merely descriptive rather than being descriptive of a formal essence that is intuited ... But precisely that 'superficiality,' that surface quality or accessibility to description allows one to place 'sensibility' in relation to other endeavors to describe the same set of data or the same phenomenon.[13]

More explicitly:

> once one reaches beyond the *purely descriptive* task appropriate to such a loose and fairly obvious phenomenon which as such does not necessitate a special language or explanatory scheme ... my own hope is that this kind of description of sensibility, of an outlook and something of its felt quality, might be combined easily and naturally with social-critical or similar accounts.[14]

'Methodological looseness'; the use of a 'vaguer, broader term'; 'laudable imprecision'; a contrast with phenomenological 'ambitions'; paying 'quite superficial' and 'merely descriptive' attention to 'loose and fairly obvious phenomenon', which can be combined 'easily and naturally' with other accounts: it is abundantly clear that Frei's aim is to show that the 'snarl' of the question of experience is not really a problem. Our philosophical schemes (whether they be idealist or Wittgensteinian) make this appear to be a problem, and in so doing have denied the possibility of something which in actual fact *we know how to do*. In practice, when we are not misled by the tight strictures of such schemes, we know how to write history in which ideas and feelings and actions and institutions go together – we may not be able to account for what we do, but we can do it. That is not to say that our writing of history is not informed by more theoretical investigations, of course: we can often be awoken by theory to elements we have underplayed, to connections we could not otherwise have spotted. But there is nothing, says Frei, stopping us from writing methodologically eclectic history which simply manages to combine aspects which theory finds it hard to connect. How does he know it is possible? He's seen it done, and he intends to do it himself.

Frei continued to use the term 'sensibility' as the focus for his descriptions of his intensions for some time, and it was soon to provide him with the scaffolding for a description of the next major project he was to undertake. At the very end of the 1970s or the beginning of the 80s, in a short lecture describing his intentions and ambitions, Frei said

> My simple, insatiable curiosity is to be able so to write about a stretch of the past that I myself and at least some of my readers may be able to get the feel of what it was like to live, work and think then and there ... to get the feel of its low culture as well as its high.[15]

And in a letter to William Placher in 1979, possibly referring to that paper, Frei wrote of his

> agreement with and admiration of several attempts I am watching to try to integrate the history of doctrine with the history of sensibility and explore the latter by way of its connection with social structures and institutions rather than by assuming it to be an expression of a general, hypostatised atmosphere of an era (e.g., 'secularity') ... My reasons for this enterprise are two: One, the sheer fascination of trying to reconstruct as accurately as possible both what it *was like* and how it *felt* in a given past. I have always shared that fascination with the historicists while doubting the way they went at it ... Given all of this agenda, you may be surprised to know that my project, if it ever materialises, will be a history of modern Christology – yes, doctrine, but in intimate association with sensibility and the appropriate explanations.[16]

Frei was going to demonstrate the possibility of a history of sensibility, a history in which public and private, doctrine and culture, faith and society were unsystematically mixed, by writing one: a history of modern Christology, from 1700 to 1950.

2 Church and Academy

Frei never wrote his projected history of Christology. He was still at work on preparatory material for it when he died in 1988. Much of what he wrote in the 1980s, however, can be seen as preparation for that unfinished project.

On the one hand, he wrote a good deal of methodological material in the mid-1980s, all in support of the methodological 'looseness' championed in the 1978 Lessing lecture – and we will return to that material later in this chapter. On the other hand, he produced some shorter pieces of historical writing, each of which put his proposals into practice to a greater or lesser extent, and each of which would probably have had counterparts in the finished project.

The long essay on David Friedrich Strauss which Frei completed at the very beginning of the 1980s is the most polished of the historical writings completed after *Eclipse*, but there is little evidence in it of this turn in his thinking towards social history. Similarly, in the 1978 lecture on Lessing described above, the introductory material on sensibility gave way to a revised version of the material he had presented in the 1974 Rockwell Lectures, and the shift to 'history of sensibility' does not seem to have made a striking difference. However, Frei had already begun to revise his undergraduate lectures on the history of modern theology, and various sets of his lecture notes kept in the Yale Divinity School archive certainly show a steadily increasing focus on social and economic conditions, and on the religious sensibilities of various groups. In his 1978 lectures, for instance, we find him describing the 'Calvinist narrative frame' which structured the sensibilities of ordinary people in the Netherlands; by 1985 we find him discussing the social institutions which undergird changes in 'the concept of individuality and of the connection between individuality and inwardness'.[17]

The most important evidence we have, however, of the kind of history-writing which Frei would have pursued in his history of Christology comes from 1987, when Frei delivered the Cadbury Lectures in Birmingham and the Humanities Council Lectures in Princeton. Each series contained a good deal of historical material, and Frei appears to have intended both as drafts for his overall project. If we are to make sense of this material, however, and judge its place in Frei's overall scheme, we need to consider one more aspect of the shift in Frei's historical work, on which we have not yet touched. That aspect is the growing ambivalence, in the early and middle 1970s, of Frei's relationship to the Church. Although he remained a committed Christian theologian, and although he was, if anything, *increasingly* committed to theology as in large part a function of the Church for the Church, he found his relationship to the Episcopal Church which had been for many years his ecclesiastical home a rather distant one.[18] His institutional home was academic far more than it was ecclesiastical, even though his theology was in principle at least as much an ecclesial discipline as an academic one.

This ambiguity, which is itself a complex matter, has two main effects on Frei's work. In the first place, it cements a shift in the mid-1970s away from dogmatic and towards historical work; in the second place, at the end of the 70s and beginning of the 80s, we see an attempt by Frei to reconnect his work to its ecclesial roots – at first (and apparently abortively) in a very direct and practical way, and later by way of renewed methodological pondering.

In a letter to an unidentified correspondent in 1977 he wrote, 'In the company of historians I always insist that I am a theologian but when thrown with theologians I identify myself as a historian';[19] in a letter to Charles Wood the following year, he wrote, 'I still have not been able to decide firmly the question whether I am an historian or a systematician. I would like to be the latter but I fear that except for the occasional systematic hints I am really more of an historian.'[20] In a 1979 letter to William Placher he wrote:

> I have for a long time now hesitated to call myself a theologian. I would be proud to be one, and it's probably the nearest definable thing I am, and still, I'm not ... A theologian ... should have an articulate view or method, a well developed statement of its application to several issues or doctrines and finally (and this is most of all the point right now) a firm contextual reference to the religious community, whether broad or narrow, within which he writes. On at least two of these criteria, possibly all three, even the first, I am simply not a theologian, no matter how much I wish I were.[21]

We should not exaggerate the agonizing that lies behind such comments. There are two sheets of enigmatic autobiographical notes which Frei jotted down in about 1983,[22] and on one of them he writes, 'Didn't find my own voice until early 'seventies.' Frei may have been unsure quite where to place himself on the list of academic specialisms, but even if he did not know how to describe it, or to relate it to what his colleagues were doing, he had nevertheless discovered the kind of work for which he felt himself best suited. He was increasingly at home with the careful and detailed description of the history of theological ideas and practices, rather than in the direct theoretical analysis of those ideas, and he found himself particularly at home carrying out that task among the figures of the English and German Enlightenment.[23] From the time that *Eclipse* was published through to the end of his life in 1988, Frei devoted a major proportion of his energies to teasing out the patterns and connections in the religious thought of Kant, Lessing, Herder, Strauss, Schleiermacher and many others less well known, and to finding in their writings and lives the roots of all the major intellectual problems which still agitated theologians.

Whatever the negative and positive motivations behind this shift in self-definition away from 'theologian' and towards 'historian', Frei made an attempt, at the end of the 1970s and beginning of the 80s, to reconnect his work with the ecclesial roots which he believed should nourish all theology. In part, this attempt was simply the outworking of the change in the kind of history he felt he should be writing; at a deeper level, perhaps, it was an attempt to find a path from his now accepted home at the historical end of the academic theology spectrum back to the beliefs and practices of ordinary Christians. If he was to reconnect his history to the Church, he seems to have thought, then his history of Christology was going to have to be more thoroughly a history from pew-level, from within the masses of ordinary churchgoers. In 1981, he wrote to Owen Chadwick in preparation for a period of Guggenheim-funded research leave which he was to spend in England:

> I am in the beginning stages of a long project, the history of Christology in England and Germany from 1700 to 1950. I have neither the training nor the ambition to become a social historian, but I would very much like to look at archives in two parishes so that I can get at least a feeling for the ways in which religion functioned in the lives of some ordinary people in the early eighteenth century. I hope at least to construct a warning sign against my own tendency to regard ideas as self-generated and as being pervasively of a high-culture sort – the way historians of theology are unfortunately prone to go about their enterprise. Specifically, I should like to learn something about life in an early eighteenth century parish that was and continued to be rural and in one which was beginning to be a commercial and then an industrial area. I would like to read some of the vicars' sermons, and I would like to look at evidences of the nurturing of the religious life, for example the kind of reading material that parsons ordered for themselves and – more important – for those of their flock who could read. I will have about a week to spend in each place. I am painfully aware not only of the brevity of the stay but of the arbitrary character of choosing two parishes regardless of such factors as regional differences. But I have to make a start, and my aims are modest.[24]

Once he had returned from his trip, Frei wrote to William Clebsch, saying that his time in England had been spent

> trying to discover whether doing social history at my advanced age is possible, and, if so, whether it tells us anything about the status of doctrine as a relatively isolated articulation of high culture. So I've been trying to discover a few things about popular religion and its social function in England in the Eighteenth Century. I spent the first three weeks of June in England, travelling from pillar to post and reading Eighteenth Century visitation returns and similar (mostly unpublished) material. If I had another semester, it might come to something, but a method for utilizing the material in the actual juxtaposition of popular and high culture religion so far eludes me.[25]

I have not been able to find any evidence that Frei made use in the following years of the material which his plunge into the social history of the English Church had yielded. It may be that he continued to find it difficult to make connections between this and the high-culture, intellectual theology which was still his primary focus; it may be that he found the sheer quantity of new work involved in becoming an historian of popular religion daunting.[26] I suspect, however, that the main reason is that, as the 1980s progressed, he found a different way forward, which absorbed his energies.

Frei believed that academic theology should serve the Church, and yet he was far surer of his academic location than of his ecclesial location. He was an academic theologian and historian who delighted in, and had amassed considerable expertise in, studying the intellectual development of modern Western theology. Instead of striving to make his academic historical work responsive to the Church by turning his focus away from that material and on to the social history of popular Christianity, he eventually decided explicitly to examine how intellectual, academic theology of the kind he had studied for so long was and was not able to serve the Church, how and to what extent theologians' ideas distanced them from the ordinary practical life of Christian communities. Rather than retooling as a social historian of popular Christianity, he decided (at least in the first place) to write a social, institutional and intellectual history of academic theology, a history which would examine the role that academics played with respect to the churches. In an undated proposal for his new project, he wrote: 'I hope to show that there is a close link between the major types of theology and the sociology of academic education in theological studies. I plan to inquire into the social context of theological study, which helps explain the very use of the term "theology".'[27]

In the Cadbury Lectures in Birmingham and the Humanities Council Lectures in Princeton, Frei produced a great deal of detailed work on the development of academic theology since the start of the nineteenth century,[28] and although we do not know what shape the planned history of modern Christology from 1700 to 1950 would have taken, and to what extent Frei would have mixed this new material on the social history of academic theology with material on low-culture Christianity and ordinary Christian sensibilities, one thing is clear. Frei's plea in 1978 for 'self-aware methodological looseness' had become, by the late 1980s, a substantive focus on the conditions for and flourishing of academic theology in its relationship to Christian communities, and an increasingly rich awareness of the limitations upon, and possibilities for, academic theologians in their complex, historically freighted, social locations.[29]

3 Theology and Christian Self-description

We have seen that, during the 1970s, Frei felt himself shifting more and more in the direction of religious studies, and more and more defined himself as one who studied Christianity primarily historically. He did not, however, lose his more systematic, more dogmatic interests. In a 1978 letter to Charles Wood, for instance, he said, '[D]espite my disavowals, I do sometimes get an itch to develop some of the material in the book on *The Identity of Jesus Christ*.'[30] And in a 1979 letter to William Placher:

> The only way I can make a systematic statement is by way of history. I wish I could do it more directly, but this seems to be the way the good Lord has made me. Thus I hope by way of the history of the doctrine to say some useful things for present theological purposes and about present theological options.[31]

The relation of his historical work, and of the change in approach in his historical work, to his dogmatic interests is, however, a complex one. In the first place, the shift to a history of sensibility was itself a continuation in a new key of the polemical moves that Frei had previously made in his more dogmatic work, so that we should see Frei's historical concentration as itself theologically motivated. In the second place, however, it was a move that made dogmatic work hard for him: the only way he could make systematic statements was, he thought, by way of history, but how can one cross from one to the other? Nevertheless, in the third place, his renewed historical work eventually led him towards a revitalization of his dogmatic work, in which the boundary between his dogmatic and historical endeavours was blurred more thoroughly than ever before. Frei's commitment in the 1970s to thoroughly historical work led directly to his championing in the 80s of a distinctive form of 'unsystematic theology'.

In the first place, then, Frei's attack upon the overly-intellectual focus of his own earlier work was a continuation of his earlier battle against those theologies and philosophies which make attention to the public world, the world of action and interaction, 'the world of sense and things',[32] difficult to connect with the feelings and ideas of Christianity. The whole of Frei's earlier work might be summarized as a call to do theology without turning away from the history that is theology's proper arena. His determination to become more thoroughly historical was a continuation of precisely this impetus. In 1979 Terry Foreman summarized comments Frei had made to him in conversation:

> He [Frei] wishes to encourage approaches to Christianity's history that displace the normal theological/intellectual focus of histories of Christianity and displace it elsewhere, especially onto the connection between normal piety and institutional/social/economic life ... Bad enough that Christianity should be thought its formal doctrine; worse it should be a function of a general Zeitgeist or just a Geist ... whose substance is primarily intellectual and, it is alleged, subject to various necessities.[33]

Frei's shift towards social history was, we might say, a continuation of his fight against repeatability (rather than unsubstitutability), against alienation (rather than manifestation); against presence (rather than identity): it was a continuation of his fight against those approaches to history which would make its surface complexity the expression of a spiritual genetic code which could provide the *real* subject for history.

In the second place, however, this theology inspired Frei's attempt to be even more serious about allowing his understanding of history to feed back into the very theological ideas and arguments which had fed that understanding. Frei's more thoroughly historical work involved him allowing a deeper penetration of historical sensibility into the systematic concepts he had used, and so went with a growing uncertainty about how one might make systematic or dogmatic theological statements at all. How can we construct an argument using concepts like 'narrative', 'meaning', 'realism' and so forth once we have realized that those concepts too are contingent, that they have a history? During the 1970s, we find Frei consciously and deliberately retreating some way from the systematic claims he had made in *The Identity of Jesus Christ*, as he realized the extent to which the things that he had said had involved too great a reliance upon ahistorical essences. As I will show later on, this retreat did not involve Frei abandoning the heart of his earlier arguments, but it did involve considerable rearrangement of the scaffolding. We shall see, however, in sections 6 and 7 of this chapter, the shift to a more historical approach to the hermeneutical and anthropological concepts on which Frei had drawn in making his earlier theological arguments also had the effect of allowing those arguments to become more thoroughly theological.

This was because, in the third place, Frei had returned during the 1980s to more directly dogmatic work; or at least to the attempt to show the link between historical work and dogmatic work. He set himself to show that it was possible to get from his now more thoroughly historical work to something like the dogmatic theology he had propounded before – or rather, he began to understand more clearly that the implication of his earlier work was not so much a turn from systematic theology to history, but the realization that his historical descriptive work was already itself theological, and that there need be no principled distinction between it and the kind of dogmatic work he had pursued before. Whereas in his earlier work he had separated historical and dogmatic work, placing them in separate books (*Eclipse* and *Identity* respectively), in his later work he deliberately and comprehensively jumbled them together.[34]

I have suggested that this mutual involvement of dogmatic and historical descriptive work was already implied in Frei's earlier work, and we can certainly find many of the building blocks of Frei's later position explicitly present in that earlier work. For instance, one of the changes that he made when moving from the 1966 'Theological Reflections on the Accounts of Jesus' Death and Resurrection' to the 1967 articles on 'The Mystery of the Presence of Jesus Christ' was an examination of the concept 'presence',[35] and he described that examination as a 'reflection within belief' which sought to clarify the logic of 'the consent of believers', the way that 'the believer will talk'.[36] In the 1974 Preface that accompanied these articles when they were republished as *The Identity of Jesus Christ*, Frei described his subject-matter as the 'logic of Christian belief', 'the logic of religious discourse', a logic which is 'odd' compared to other discourses.[37] At this stage, these comments have the character of asides, and Frei does not make it clear quite what kind of object 'Christian belief' or 'discourse' is meant to be, nor what kind of description it calls for, but that lack was made up for in 1976, in the 10th Annual Greenhoe Lectures at Louisville Seminary. In a letter to his hosts after the event, he indicated that he was trying to push the project embodied in *Identity* further, and that as well as pursuing some 'further exegesis of the parables', he was interested in taking further his methodological, 'Wittgensteinian' musings on what it means to investigate the logic of Christian belief.[38] 'One of the tasks', he said in the lectures, in fact *the* task of Christian theology is simply to talk about the way Christian language is used, by Christians, and to ask if it is being used faithfully. The theologian simply examines contemporary use of Christian language to see if it is faithful to what he senses to be the traditional use or the biblical use – usually some combination of the two: the use the Church has made of its source, namely the Bible. That is what theology is about.[39]

After a brief dismissal of the use of the metaphor of 'translation' for what one is trying to do when seeking to understand such language-use, he says:

[I]t seems to me that when one talks about God's presence, one is not trying to explain, one is trying a much more modest task; one is trying to step back and describe the use not of a technical language but of an ordinary language, and a very specific ordinary language: the specific language of ordinary Christian usage ... Christian language in meditation, in public worship, private prayer, in the obedience of the moral life; Christian language if you will in the public and private use of faith. [40]

He then paused for a discussion of one of the differences he perceived between Lutheran and Calvinist construals of the logic of belief, Lutherans having, he suggested, more of a tendency to think that there is a root form of Christian language to which all others ultimately reduce, and Calvinists acknowledging more readily that Christian language is irreducibly diverse. Frei acknowledges himself a Calvinist on this matter, then continues:

The language of the church is, I am saying, a highly various language but it is a language in use. No ... ordinary language embodied in life is simple or straightforward. It is always a language which we *learn*. But how do we learn it? How do we learn the concepts that are embodied in that language? We learn them by using them, by speaking them. One of the marvellous and – to my mind – startling and liberating little sentences that Ludwig Wittgenstein wrote was when he said, 'Don't ask for meaning, ask for use.' There are technical languages, you see, in which the concepts – say the concept 'atom' – always means the same thing: it has a fixed, stipulated meaning; and when you deal with a language like that you can ask for the fixed, stipulated concept as a general term which runs by its definition and is always connected to other concepts by its definition. But ordinary language does not work that way; that does not mean that ordinary language doesn't have its own rules, but it is very difficult, in fact sometimes impossible to state the rules apart from the use.[41]

Christian theology is, he says, in large part a teasing out of those rules, to the extent that this is possible, and to the extent that the unbreakable connection between those rules and the use which they structure can be honoured.

These themes became ever stronger in Frei's work from 1982 onwards. In a lecture delivered in that year at Haverford College, 'Theology and the Interpretation of Narrative: Some Hermeneutical Considerations', he spoke of two ways of construing theology's task. On the one hand stands a form of investigation primarily interested in locating Christian concepts against wider structures of plausibility, meaning and truth which are themselves not specifically Christian, but are established by *wissenschaftlich* philosophy. On the other hand stands theology understood as a specific practice of one particular religious community, which may or may not have parallels in other religious communities, 'an inquiry into the coherence and appropriateness of any given instance of the use of Christian language in the light of its normative articulation, whether that be Scripture, tradition, the Christian conscience, a mixture of these and other candidates'.[42] A year later he expanded this point in his Shaffer Lectures, delivered at Yale Divinity School. Theology can be

> an inquiry into the internal logic of the Christian community's language – the rules, largely implicit rather than explicit, that are exhibited in its use in worship and Christian life, as well as in the confessions of Christian belief. Theology, in other words, is the grammar of the religion, understood as faith and as an ordered community life.[43]

It may not yet be clear how this kind of Christian *self*-description relates to the kind of historical description which dominated Frei's work in the 1970s but, as he goes on, it becomes clear both that the kind of Christian self-description he is envisaging is, like the history of sensibility discussed in the previous section, a kind of description which has loose affinities with sociological and social anthropological descriptions, and that there are connections between this discussion and his earlier arguments about subject–alienation and self–manifestation description:

> Christianity is a religion, a social organism. Its self-description marks it typically as a religion in ways similar to those given by sociologists of religion or cultural anthropologists. It is a community held together by constantly changing yet enduring structures, practices, and institutions, the way religious communities are: e.g. a sacred text; regulated relations between an elite ... and a more general body of adherents; and by a set of rituals – preaching, baptism, the celebration of communion; common beliefs and attitudes; all of these linked ... with a set of narratives connected with each other in the sacred text and its interpretive tradition. All of these are, for social scientist and theologian ... not the *signs* or *manifestations* of the religion; rather they *constitute* it, in complex and changing coherence.[44]

There is, we might say, at least a strong affinity between Christian self-description and Frei's historical descriptions.

A strange reversal has taken place by the time Frei says this. The description of *theology* as Christian self-description with which Frei emerges in the early 1980s now parallels quite closely the description of *history* which he had achieved in the late 70s. That is, the description of sensibility-history which Frei had given in the context of a discussion of *religious studies* in 1978, a context in which he had been happy, on that occasion at least, to place himself, and which he had found it hard to relate to theology, is by 1982 paralleled by a description of a type of *theology*, and theology of the most 'intra-Christian' kind – theology, we might think, at its least academic. Similarly, Frei's wistful description in 1979 of a theologian as one who, unlike him, has an 'articulate method'[45] now sounds rather like the more *philosophical* theology which is simply one possible construal of theology's nature, standing at the opposing pole to theology as Christian self-description.

4 Sidestepping Hermeneutics

During the 1970s, then, Frei concentrated on historical work. In part this was a continuation of the direction set in his more systematic theological work in the 1960s: a rejection (for Christian theological reasons) of any turning away from the public world of action and interaction in favour either of a supposedly repeatable inwardness, or the overarching structures of theory. Frei had turned his gun on himself, and accused himself – as we shall see more clearly later in the chapter – of relying on ahistorical grounds for his systematic arguments; he had begun to think of himself less as a theologian and more as an historian. Nevertheless, between about 1978 and 1982, the question of how to relate his self-understanding as 'historian' to his self-understanding as 'theologian' had become transformed into a question about how to relate theology as Christian self-description to theology as *wissenschaftlich* discipline – a debate about different construals of theology, rather than a debate between theology and some other possibility. Frei's self-identification as historian rather than theologian became instead self-identification as a different *kind* of theologian. Frei did not, of course, identify himself exclusively with theology as Christian self-description, to the exclusion of all the concerns which a more *wissenschaftlich* theologian might have (any more than, in his 1970s' discussions, he had rejected all theological concerns in his acceptance of his role as historian). Indeed, one of the distinctive features of Frei's later work was his attempt to step away from too polemical or oppositional a definition of his own position. His 1960s' Christology project had been shaped decisively by polemic against alternative positions. It is at least partially true that the content of Frei's position was *determined* by its occupation of one side of a set of conceptual distinctions, the other side of which was occupied by relationalist theology.[46] This itself may have been another of the factors which gave Frei's proposal too exclusively an intellectual feel: it was developed against, and drew much of its justification from, a primarily conceptual landscape some distance from the public spaces where ordinary Christians carry on their lives. As the 1970s progressed, Frei's shift to a more historical, less purely intellectual approach was accompanied by a growing belief that he had placed too much store on that polemic, and – although he by no means abandoned the main lines of his attack – by an attempt to relax the hold which that polemic had on his constructive theological work.

On the one hand, Frei distanced himself from one of the key polemical supports of his Christology project, at least the version found in *Identity*: his attack on 'presence'. Already by 1973 he was saying of the articles which he was arranging to have published as *Identity* that 'I have retreated some distance from the views I held at that time',[47] and when the book came out the new 'Preface' explained that it was precisely his handling of 'presence' which most disturbed him.[48] *Identity* had, of course, ended up rejecting any approach to Christology which *began* with presence, and had found that, if one began instead with identity, the kind of presence which emerged was no more than a doctrine of the Spirit and the Church. Nevertheless, Frei said in his Preface that he would not want to give 'presence' even that negative prominence any more – evidently believing that the book's structural reliance on this polemic was a weakness.[49] 'Presence' may not, he suggested, be a particularly good way of thinking about Christology or pneumatology, about the Church and about Christian life, either positively or negatively; all we can say is that *if* we find we have reason to use 'presence' as a concept for describing Christ's relation to believers and to the world, *then* we must make sure that it is governed by identity. Neither the acceptance nor the rejection of 'presence' should be a defining factor in our theology.

On the other hand, Frei gave a continued polemic against the theology of 'presence' – or at least against some of its strategic allies – a new role in his later work. Despite the explicit move away from the sharp polemical lines which had been so important in his earlier work, there is much in his later work which in many respects repeats his earlier attacks. He clearly still found it necessary to do some polemical ground-clearing as a preparation for or accompaniment to the building of his own constructive solution – but he now tried much harder not to let that ground-clearing enter too materially into the building work.

The main lines of Frei's continuing polemic are, by now, quite familiar. He attacks that kind of theology which privileges subjects' dispositions towards the world (and the symbols by which those dispositions are evoked and expressed) over the public world of action and interaction. He argues that, for theologians working in that way, 'The "objective" world of "descriptive discourse" is consigned to a decidedly peripheral and ambiguous status',[50] and that Jesus becomes primarily a centre of understanding, 'not in the first place the agent of his actions nor the enacted project(s) that constitute(s) him'.[51] 'If true being is in the unity of metaphorical language, limit experience, and meaning,' he asks, 'just how do you recapture the world of sense and things?'[52] Increasingly, he focused his fire upon those hermeneutical theologies which oriented themselves by a general account of 'meaning', seen as the linkage between human ways-of-being-in-the-world and evocative and expressive symbols, the theory of which could provide a general criteriology for what could and could not be 'meaningful' to beings like us.[53]

However, familiar though this kind of polemic will be for anyone who has explored Frei's earlier work, it often seems that there is a curious lack of connection between it and the more constructive positions which he sketches in the same articles and lectures. As he sets about a detailed discussion of the assumptions and procedures of hermeneutics, the reader is led to expect that, when Frei turns to his own constructive position, he will show in detail how it answers or outdoes the hermeneutics he has so painstakingly described, just as he had carefully shown in *Identity* how a proper account of 'presence' should be developed. In his new work, however, Frei appears to try to allow hermeneutics to collapse under its own weight (possibly with the help of a shove from the Deconstructionists – an entirely *ad hoc* ally, from Frei's point of view) and then sets out his own positive stall without much of a backward glance. The polemic may point in the vague direction of the plot where Frei will build his positive account, but he no longer brings his account and his polemical targets into detailed dialogue.

In 'The "Literal Reading" of Biblical Narrative in the Christian Tradition', for instance, Frei makes a temporary alliance with Derrida and Frank Kermode in order to demonstrate the instability of hermeneutics. As soon as that job is done, however, he moves away from both, and does not attempt to show with any explicitness that his own alternative position evades the deconstructionist attacks he has just used.[54] Rather than showing that his theology can do as well, or better, the things that hermeneutical theology (or its deconstructionist opponents) set out to do, Frei appears to have a subtler intention: he hopes to show that his approach to theology (an approach which begins with Christian self-description) is simpler, less theoretically constrained, more flexible, and more resilient because more modest – that it is a breath of fresh air after the constriction and theoretical complexity of theologies that try too hard to prove themselves at the bar of *Wissenschaft*, or post-modern theologies which seek to dismantle that bar from within. He hoped to indicate that he is simply playing by different rules, even if he plays on some of the same territory.[55]

5 Unsystematic Theology

As the 1980s approached, Frei appears to have realized that thinking of himself as caught in a tension between history and theology was a mistake – one which, perhaps, itself relied upon a conception of 'theology' too wedded to those against which he had reacted in the first place. The tension was better seen as a negotiation between two kinds of theology: theology as Christian self-description (a description with strong affinities to Frei's favoured form of historical description), and theology as a *wissenschaftlich* enterprise. In order to develop a less polemically determined theology, Frei was faced with the need to sort out the proper relationship between these two forms of theology – and to avoid collapsing it into a too-simple opposition.

It was in this atmosphere that he returned to work on Schleiermacher, in preparation for delivering a paper on Barth and Schleiermacher at the 1983 AAR meeting.[56] Whereas in the past he had approached Schleiermacher primarily through the lens of a polemical relationalism/anti-relationalism contrast, derived from his work on Barth's break with liberalism, he now approached him with 'Christian self-description' and '*Wissenschaft*' as the categories occupying his mind. The results were surprising: he found that both Barth and Schleiermacher acknowledged the importance of theology as Christian self-description, *and that both did so without concentrating on it exclusively*. For all their differences, Frei found that, considered in this new light, they were in relatively close proximity. It was this realization that inspired Frei to construct his famous typology of Christian theology, and that may finally have allowed him to step outside the polemical constraints of his earlier work.[57]

At one end of the typology, 'type 1', 'theology is a philosophical discipline within the academy, and its character as such takes complete priority over communal religious self-description.'[58] At the other end of the typology, 'type 5' 'theology is exclusively a matter of Christian self-description'.[59] These two extremes represent the poles of the tension which I have already been describing, and without more care Frei's polemic against hermeneutics could have reduced to this polarity. Between the poles, however, stand three types of theology which, in one way or another, 'correlate' Christian self-description and external questions of meaning and truth, and it is between these three types that the really interesting debates take place. For type 2, a philosophical frame provides genuine space within which theological claims are allowed to make sense and make a difference; for type 3 (the type Frei developed for Schleiermacher), philosophy and theology each have their own integrity, but neither trespasses on the other's territory, and various *ad hoc* ways can be found to move from one to the other. For type 4, on the other hand (the type Frei constructed for Barth), Christian self-description dominates, but itself provides ample grounds on which external questions may be taken seriously.[60]

There are two things we must notice about the typology if we are to understand its position in Frei's thought correctly. First, the typology was developed on the back of Frei's re-investigation of Schleiermacher, and was always intended as a step in the direction of his history of modern Christology. While it certainly had broader theological uses, the typology was never, I think, intended to be divorced from that particular history. The typology was not a neutral, ahistorical tool which could productively be used to describe any and every theological era. Frei knew that the terms in which he had set the problem were derived in large part from Schleiermacher's championing of theology in the University of Berlin, and also in part from his own struggles to find a way forward within an academic theological system which owed a great deal to the Berlin tradition. Its application outside that tradition is questionable. This is clearest in Frei's 1987 Humanities Council Lectures:

> [W]herever appeal is made to the public character of the understanding informing theology – that is, to a generally intelligible hermeneutics – there the Berlin tradition rears its ugly head, demanding that theological instruction and its organization do justice both to church training and to principles of general explanation that hold for all disciplines; demanding, furthermore, that some sort of coordination or

correlation be effected between the two, be it a correlation between autonomous, distinctive ways of thinking and speaking, or some attempt to locate the rightful status of one through the priority of the other, or a claim that the two are in principle absolutely different and there can be no real contact between them.[61]

The typology itself, in other words, is caught in the negotiation between Frei's historical and systematic work.

Second, although the difference between the types is most easily described as a difference in the proportion to which *Wissenschaft* and Christian self-description are mixed, that is at best half the story. A closer inspection of Frei's accounts of the various types reveals both that what is being described by Christian self-description is construed differently under each type, and that the external philosophical questions or *wissenschaftlich* approach is also construed differently in every type. What is distinctive about Frei's favoured fourth type is therefore not simply the logical ordering between philosophy and Christian self-description which it involves, but its unusual construals of both philosophy and of 'the Christian thing'. The typology is, to put it another way, not purely methodological: the different methods described imply differing substantive theological and philosophical commitments.

For type 1 theology, the particularities of Christianity must be so inter-pretable that they yield a truth more universally accessible. One or other form of reduction of Christianity's particularities must take place, or their supercession by a philosophy come of age. In this type, Christian theology must die and be resurrected as philosophy. There must therefore be an esoteric and an exoteric in Christianity, with the latter accessible to the masses who think Christianity's meaning and truth are bound up with the specific history of Israel and the particularity of Jesus of Nazareth, and the former accessible to the philosophical Gnostics who have penetrated beyond appearances, and see the deeper truth, a republication of the religion of nature, a truth as old as creation. For type 1, Christianity must consist of an inner and an outer, with the connection between the two elusive, and the outer itself dispensable.

For type 2 theology, some form of distinction between 'inner' and 'outer' is still inevitable, but it will be a much softer boundary than in type 1. Christian self-description can only be fitted into the spaces provided by a philosophical framework if it can supply content to a space whose parameters are not specifically Christian, set by a philosophy which is understood as criteriology. In other words, type 2 theology assumes the ability to think of Christianity as the positive and particular actualization of a more general potentiality. Most commonly, type 2 theology will have to regard Christianity as a positive example of religiousness – although not in such a way that religiousness could ever appear naked, without some such positive filling-out, nor in such a way that the true content of the Christian filling-out can be predicted and exhausted on more general criteria. Nevertheless, for type 2 to work, the Christianity described in Christian self-description must be the outward actualization of a prior inward possibility, and Christian self-description will properly involve the tracing of the connection between the outward, Christian substance and the inner, general form.

At the other end of the typology, in type 5, there is an ambiguity. The set-up of the typology implies that for type 5 theology Christian self-description will be everything, and a more general philosophical theology nothing, but this is very far from being the case. In some ways the examples of type 5 that Frei discusses resemble type 2 more closely than any other type, in that they do assume a general philosophical framework (typically, a particular kind of Wittgensteinian theory) as the foundation upon which rests the dominance given to Christian self-description.[62] The theory provides the space within which Christian self-description can work, and rules out in advance encroachments upon that space by foreign theory, *and* excursions from that space by Christian theology. As in type 2, philosophy is understood as capable of functioning criteriologically. However, the paradigm Frei has in mind for type 2 is one in which the philosophy sets up criteria of religious truth and meaning which dictate the kinds of Christian claims and expressions that can contribute to the wider religious conversation of humanity, and so allows itself authority to distinguish between proper and improper *within* Christianity. In type 5, a different philosophy allows Christianity to be an example of the general type 'cultural-linguistic community' within which anything goes: having set up the idea of a language-forming community, the philosophy denies itself the right to distinguish (on any external criteria) between proper and improper statements within that community – although it does, perhaps, reserve the right to deny to Christian statements certain kinds of universality: Christians may talk about anything and everything, but they have no way of asking whether their ways of talking relate to, and perhaps should affect or be affected by, very different ways of talking in other communities. Christianity, in this view, is another example of a cultural-linguistic community – a community which teaches and sustains a particular language; a community which is, at least in its paradigmatic forms, sociologically sectarian (such that one knows where to go to find this language spoken well). For type 5 theology, the distinctions between first order, second order and third order are rigid. Theology as a second-order discipline makes grammatical remarks about the first order, and those remarks must be recognized as logically distinct from first-order comments if confusion is to be avoided. There may be an attempt to compare that grammar to other cultural-linguistic grammars, but that is a logically distinct and optional third-order task which must not become constitutive for second- or first-order statements. The first order, in other words, is complete in itself: Christianity speaks an achieved and completed language, and the role of the type 5 theologian is to prevent that completeness being betrayed.

Type 3 is the most complex, and Frei's explanations are never divorced from his struggles to understand Schleiermacher. For Schleiermacher, two things converge. On the one hand, his understanding of Christian doctrine circles around a basic contrast between the experience of sin and the experience of redemption. He thinks that this is the centre around which all of Christian theology circles *on its own terms*, and that it is not reducible to any external language. On the other hand, his understanding of philosophy also contains elements that approximate to that centre, and that are harmonious with it. We may, therefore, borrow propositions from various *wissenschaftlich* disciplines which will allow us to provide an account of self-consciousness, and of pain and pleasure, which *resembles* the Christian theological account of sin and redemption. The two are not identical, and (according to Frei) neither are they *systematically* related: the philosophy does not provide the precise terms within which the theology is allowed to function. Rather, the philosophy is allowed to lead one to a point where one is able to *see* the way in to theology, where one can grasp how the world described by theology works, and enter into it – learning, from that point on, its irreducible and specific language. The transition is not a technical matter but a case of 'a little introspection'.[63] Philosophy and theology have their own integrity here, and neither can control the other. In order for this to work, however, Schleiermacher must believe that there is something like a systematic centre to Christian theology, and that it is a systematic centre which can stand this kind of close approach to philosophy – which can closely resemble, without being identical to, something that can be talked about in properly *wissenschaftlich*, general terms. So Schleiermacher is *both* willing to admit that the meaning of Christian understandings of sin and redemption is indissolubly bound to specific Christian stories and practices, *and* insistent that the heart of that meaning can be approximated by a general philosophy. And Frei believes that the latter tends to capture the former, pulling Schleiermacher away from the particular identity of Jesus Christ, and towards some repeatable content that Jesus represents. So, for type 3 too, at least in anything like Schleiermacher's form, there will be something like an 'inner' and an 'outer' to Christianity, for there has to be a heart to Christianity that does not look too parochial when viewed from the perspective of a *wissenschaftlich* philosophy. Nevertheless, for the type 3 theologian the distinction between 'inner' and 'outer' will be one to which Christianity naturally lends itself, and will itself be capable of presentation in irreducibly internal Christian terms.

Despite the arrangement of the typology, type 4 is that type which Frei believes gives Christian self-description most sway. For, unlike type 5, it does not let philosophy set the boundaries of the universality appropriate to Christian truth claims; that, too, is a matter that cannot be decided without asking inner-Christian questions – questions about what kinds of truth-claim are Christianly defensible. For type 4, the way in which we make distinctions between 'inner' and 'outer', the ways in which we use words like 'truth' and 'meaning', the ways in which we compare and contrast Christian claims with external claims, the use we make of *wissenschaftlich* disciplines – all these things must be allowed to be shaped by the particularities of Christian self-description, and so shaped theologically; we cannot specify in advance how those matters must work for Christianity. For type 4, for instance, there may be ways in which it is appropriate to talk about 'inner' and 'outer' in Christianity, but that usage is likely to be complex, diverse and changing, and the 'truth' or 'meaningfulness' of Christianity does not rest on any form of that distinction being deployed that might be amenable to the philosophers.

Type 4 theologians will make all sorts of use of philosophy, but they are likely to see philosophy more as a set of intellectual skills, practices of rigour, and well-honed concepts than as a comprehensive criteriology, let alone a comprehensive worldview or a discipline that has its own distinct subject-matter. Back in 1969, Frei had expressed his scepticism about the efficacy of the kind of apologetics which rested upon some form of philosophical anthropology – not just a scepticism about the *propriety* of philosophy setting the terms of a view of humanity's religiousness, but a scepticism about the *capability* of philosophy to take on so ambitious a task.

> Look at that cumbersome heavy artillery of theological reflection about 'man' and 'human existence', so characteristic of modern theology since 1700! What does it amount to? And who is listening? Do we ever really know, no matter what anthropological model we employ, no matter to what sources of individual or cultural sensibility we appeal – do we ever really know or apprehend ourselves, our neighbors, or the process of history to be in real need of salvation?[64]

In 1973, he expressed similar sentiments in a letter to Larry Nelson:

> Has it never puzzled you that, no matter how frequently this case has been made out in almost two hundred years, it has made very little impact on morally serious philosophical people (think of Wittgenstein himself!) but has usually convinced only theologians who were already convinced?[65]

And in 1986, he expressed his scepticism most clearly, in his letter to Gary Comstock:

> I am a Christian theologian and do not regard philosophy as ever having achieved that clearly demonstrated set of even formal certainties (and agreements) in 2500 years which would allow it the kind of authoritative status you seem to want to accord it; and yet I believe theology cannot do without philosophy. Furthermore theology cannot even invest so much in foundational/anti-foundational debate as to come out (*qua* theology) *in principle* on the anti-foundational side. Christian theologians will have to make use of philosophy, whichever way philosophers decide that particular issue is to be resolved. In other words, I'm saying two things simultaneously: First, Christian theology is quite distinct from philosophy ... Second, despite their mutual distinctness, theology as a second-order discipline cannot dispense with philosophy, and their relation remains complex and has constantly to be worked out, rather than being of one invariable shape.[66]

Nevertheless, philosophy will be Christian self-description's handmaid, not because Christian self-description will ruthlessly cut philosophy down to size, but because that is the task for which philosophy, properly understood, is itself properly fitted. Philosophy understood in this more modest way will, in fact, be indispensable and pervasive in theology. As Frei had earlier said of Barth's thought 'in its language and manner of conception theology is nothing but philosophy ... [because] theology is to him the abiding mystery of God's appropriation of common and created human thought (philosophy) to his revelation in Jesus Christ'.[67]

Type 4 theology does not, unlike type 5, insist that Christianity already speaks a complete and achieved first-order language. The fluid boundaries between first-, second- and third-order language mean that first-order Christian language is, at least potentially, not just described but *shaped* by second-order theological explorations which seek to help it become more faithful than it already is, and by third-order explorations which take theology into serious dialogue with alternative visions. Christianity itself can be understood, for type 4, as an ongoing *learning* of a new language, rather than simply as the *use* of an already learnt language.

For type 4, then, Christianity is above all unsystematic, public and ambitious. Unlike type 1, this is a type for which there is no substitute for paying attention to the particularities of Christianity. Unlike types 1, 2 and (to a certain extent) 3, this is a type for which the real business of Christianity does not have to go on in inwardness, for there does not have to be any kind of retreat from the public unpalatability of Christianity to an acceptable esoteric meaning. Unlike type 5, this is a type for which Christian language can grow and alter over time. Unlike all the other types, this is a type for which there is no limit in advance to the kinds of truth-claim that it might be Christianly appropriate to make. Among other things, then, this more than any other is the type for which both 'truth' and 'meaning' are not themselves defined in an a priori, generic or systematic manner, but are given Christian-specific definition in the complex weave of Christian discourse.

6 Christian Meaning

Where Frei had in his earlier work claimed that an anti-relationalist theology was needed to do justice to the unsubstitutability of Gospel narratives, he now claimed that a type 4 theology is best able to do justice to Christianity understood as social, communal and historical. Putting it in these terms, however, is likely to force an important question. What is the relationship between Christianity as social, communal and historical, and the Gospel narratives? Has Frei moved from a biblically-based theology which has the power to challenge and convict the Christian Church to an ecclesially-based theology which is inherently more conservative? This question is quite proper, and in order to answer it, we need to see what Frei's new framework does to his reading of the Bible.

As his new approach developed over the 1970s and 80s, Frei had developed some qualms about aspects of his earlier approach to the Gospels. On the one hand, he realized that more detailed exegesis was needed if he were to establish the case he had tried to make in *Identity*. For instance, on his copy of a review of *Identity* by Maurice Wiles, next to a sentence in which Wiles criticized him for having artificially made *one* story out of *four* Gospels, Frei scribbled:

> This is absolutely right. I must have been blind. At least I should have *argued* the case. Luke was my central text, and I thought Mark and Matthew had a sufficiently similar underlying pattern *in those respects that I was analyzing* to allow me the notion of one story in all three synoptic gospels. Again, my 'method' should have dictated that I at least *argue* that these three stories constitute one story, without reducing their differences. *Mea maxima culpa.*[68]

More importantly for our purposes, however, he came to believe that his earlier argument had detached the Gospels from their use, and insisted that their use must be regulated by an attribute of the texts that could be identified in a neutral, ahistorical way; and that he had thus been in danger of subordinating Christian usage to a general literary theory. Put baldly in this way, this is of course not a particularly accurate description of the complex way in which Frei had gone about establishing his conclusions in his earlier Christology project, but there is clearly some truth in it. I earlier described Frei's procedure as one of discovering concepts which would allow him the better to register the resistance which the Gospel texts put up to certain kinds of reading (hardly a straightforward subordination of Christian usage to general theory), and the shift in Frei's later work might best be seen as a shift in his identification of what it is that offers resistance, and what the nature of that resistance is.[69] Frei's new starting point was a conviction that there was a strong line of continuity in *Christian uses* of the Gospels, and that it was this continuity (a matter both of established practices and of the aptness for those practices of the Gospel texts themselves) which offers resistances to theologians' hermeneutical concepts. (He also, as we shall see, believed that there was a theological justification for this continuity in Christian practice.) 'I proceed on the conviction that there is genuine continuity in the language of the Christian church as it readapts itself in every age to the paradigmatic language of Scripture.'[70] Frei set himself the task of finding hermeneutical concepts that would enable him to pay attention to this resistance and register its complexity and particularity.

Vitally, the regularity to which Frei draws our attention has a history:

> The rules – the formal or, more likely, informal rules that the members of the community follow with regard to the reading of the sacred text – are most likely to have been learned in or by application … In the process of developing these rules in the West, in Western Christendom in particular, one guideline came to be basic: Whenever possible, use the literal sense.[71]

This was no longer a pre-critical consensus lost during the Enlightenment (as in *Eclipse*); the regularity which Frei believes he has identified is more basic, and even most modern theologians have borne a kind of witness to it.

> The consensus that I think I see, tenuous and yet constantly re-emerging from the earliest days *through the Enlightenment period into the twentieth century*, East and West, North and South, is that of the literal sense in regard to the texts concerning Jesus of Nazareth, chiefly the descriptions in the Gospels, but to some extent also in the rest of the New Testament.[72]

And the history of this regularity is no longer an exclusively high-culture history – a history of the ways in which theologians and philosophers have responded to the text. Rather, Frei believes that this regularity is displayed in ordinary, communal, devotional use of the scriptures – this is as much about 'applicative use' and the Gospels' 'emblematic function for the life of the community'.[73]

Writing to Gary Comstock in 1984, Frei summarized his new approach:

> For me 'meaning' in the gospel narratives is more and more a combination of 1) the communal-religious interpretive tradition and what *it* has seen as their primary meaning; 2) the fact that the tradition has given primacy to their realistic, ascriptive sense; 3) that outside of that tradition there is no reason to think of *any* single interpretive move or scheme as *the* meaning of these stories; 4) and even within it there is room for others, provided they do not conflict with the primary, realistic or literal sense; 5) that subordination of understanding to the text, within the descriptive schema explicatio/meditatio/applicatio ... is in no way the same as the elimination of interpretive understanding and of a possible multiplicity of interpretations.[74]

(Notice that, just as before, the focus of Frei's argument is local. He does not try to deal with Christian reading in general, or the Bible in general. Rather, he treats Christian readings of the Gospel narratives; his argument is not about meaning *per se*, but about the kinds of meaning which Christians have regularly taken these particular texts to have.)

Of course, Frei has the same high ambitions as before: he believes that the regularity in Christian practice here is sufficient to allow a good deal of the rest of Christian thought and practice to be arranged around it; it is sufficient to allow him to speak of it as the 'essence of Christianity' – but the kind of essence he has in mind is not a deep truth which can be found behind every particular of Christian practice and belief, nor a Christianity-wide invariable grammar, but one specific regularity in Christian life. In one sense, this regularity is quite contingent; from the point of view of a secular historian, at least, matters could have been quite otherwise, and there could have been a different continuity, or none. Nevertheless, Frei believes that this regularity is there, and he hopes to show us that that regularity can provide and has provided a pivot upon which the whole of Christian life can turn.

The regularity which Frei believed he had identified is 'not a single thing'.[75] Typically, Frei distinguished three components: first, the *sensus literalis* was the consensus use, the communal 'plain sense', the common sense of the

Christian community; second, it was a use which assumed that these texts were a fit enactment of their authors' intention; and third, it was either (as in the Shaffer lectures) a use which assumed to some degree that these texts were a fit depiction of their subject-matter,[76] or (as in Frei's later discussions) it was a use which consistently identified Jesus of Nazareth as the primary subject of these texts ('ascriptive literalism').[77]

Two points are worth making. First, these three characteristics do not stand on the same logical level. The first is the form of which the other two are the content: the regularity in which Frei is interested is a regularity in the consensus use by the Christian community (to the extent to which such a consensus can be identified); working assumptions about fit enactment and ascriptive literalism are the particular shape which that regularity takes.[78] From the point of view of a secular historian, that a regularity arose and that it took this particular shape are entirely contingent matters. Frei presents material on Frank Kermode's interpretation of the Gospel of Mark in 'Theology and the Interpretation of Narrative' largely in order to demonstrate that, from a non-theological point of view, there are powerfully plausible ways of reading for which these different aspects do not and cannot hold together. Something else could have been the case.[79]

Second, Frei is not simply interested in identifying a certain regular kind of practice in Christianity; he is also interested in the *material* on which that practice goes to work, and in the *results* which that kind of practice can achieve with that kind of material. In other words, he does not turn from talking about the identification of Jesus in the Gospels to talking about the nurture and support of certain attitudes and skills in the Christian community; he turns to talking about the kinds of practice which allow Christians to make some kinds of stable reference to and identification of Jesus by means of the Gospels. It is this stable identification of Jesus which remains central. Faced, in Charles Wood's book, *The Formation of Christian Understanding*, with an argument which concentrated more exclusively on Christian attitudes and skills at the expense of their material and results, Frei said (according to Bruce Marshall) that

> The aspect [Wood] treats well is the *exercise* of Christian understanding ... The aspect he does not really treat is the *content* or *object* of Christian understanding, viz., what it is about, and the relation of the latter to the exercise of that understanding. While there may not be any theory which adequately conceptualises that relation between exercise and content, one responsibility of both theology and hermeneutics is to insure that the integrity of both is preserved, and that the appearance (or worse) of making one a vestigial appendage of the other at any point is avoided.[80]

The change in Frei's approach is a shift towards use, certainly, but it is not a reduction of his theological arguments to arguments about Christian habits; his arguments are also about that which Christian usage uses, and what results from the combination of the two. Indeed, following the quote from Frei's letter to Comstock given above, we could say that although Frei's argument begins with Christian usage, that usage is one which involves a 'subordination of understanding to the text', and so one which gives priority *not* to usage but to that which is used. Christian usage is, at its heart, of such a kind as to hand over control to another, and to stand open to judgment.

Frei's more detailed explanations of the particular shape which Christian usage of the Gospel narratives has taken show in detail how this is a kind of use which hands itself over to the texts, and which allows (as other kinds of use might not) these texts to stand over against Christian use and understanding. In the first place, Frei claims that Christian usage has tended to see the Gospel narratives as the fit enactment of their authors' (or Author's) intention. In other words, the primary kinds of use which Christians have made of these particular texts (i.e., the passion–resurrection sequences in the Gospels, if no others) have not been ones in which the reader hunts for a hidden intention which will open an esoteric meaning behind the façade of the apparent meaning. Readers may make and frequently have made some kind of reference to the intention of the author who lies behind these texts, but not (at least not primarily) to an intention which runs counter to the surface meaning of the texts. These texts (and remember that we are speaking primarily about the Gospel narratives – indeed, primarily about the passion–resurrection accounts) have been taken to be, in the first place, apt for conveying what they were intended to convey; their meaning is, in the first place, exoteric rather than esoteric – and any esoteric meanings that they also have will be congruent with their exoteric meanings.[81] Frei refers to this as 'descriptive literalism':

> the *descriptive* function of language and its conceptual adequacy are shown forth precisely in the kind of story that does not refer beyond itself for its meaning, as allegory does, the kind of story in which the 'signified', the identity of the protagonist, is enacted by the signifier, the narrative sequence itself.[82]

This was the same resolve that Frei had identified in Barth, whose 'ambition was, to be a reader of the text and not of some hypothetical subject-matter behind the text'.[83]

In the second place, Frei claims that these texts have been taken to be, precisely as fit enactments of their authors' intentions, texts about Jesus of Nazareth. For the majority of Christian readers down the centuries 'there was no question that Jesus was the subject of the gospel texts, that is to say the particular person whom these texts are about, with an identity as specific as yours or mine'.[84] This is 'a very simple consensus: that the story of Jesus is about him, not about somebody else or about nobody in particular or about all of us; that it is not two stories ... or no story and so on and on'.[85] Particularly if we do not exclude Enlightenment and post-Enlightenment readers, this consensus cannot be said to extend to estimates of the 'reality status' of the Jesus so depicted: the stories are stories about Jesus of Nazareth, and were intended to be so, but they have sometimes, and in varying degrees, been taken to be fictional stories, so the consensus which Frei describes is not so much about truth as it is about meaning, and not so much about reference as it is about sense – or at least, those distinctions are relatively useful in this particular circumstance for pointing out what this consensus does and does not involve.[86]

Frei did not think that this consensus use was self-justifying, as if there were something unavoidable about this kind of use of this kind of text. There are other ways of reading texts like this that do not make the same assumptions. Nevertheless, neither did he think that this use was simply the arbitrary decision of the Christian community, paradoxically exercising its right to do what it wants with these texts by handing itself over to them. He believed that the kind of reading he had identified possessed a deeper Christian appropriateness: it made a kind of Christian sense which was not, when considered on Christian terms, at all arbitrary. It coheres with, even relies upon, the Christian doctrine of the incarnation.

Frei's earlier arguments about the Gospels had frequently, and not altogether misleadingly, been compared with the literary theories of the New Criticism. Like them he took an *aesthetic* approach to the text as an object complete in itself, and subordinated questions of its production, its reference and its impact to the tracing of its internal structures and dynamics. In his 1983 essay, 'The "Literal Reading" of Biblical Narrative in the Christian Tradition', he treated this comparison explicitly:

> As for the New Criticism, a literal reading of the Gospels is appropriate under its auspices, but only because and to the extent that it is in fact *a disguised Christian understanding* of them and not a reading under a general theory, not even a more low-level theory of meaning than the general hermeneutical scheme.[87]

At the least interesting level, the 'disguised Christian understanding' is simply the New Critical willingness to treat texts as something like inspired sacred objects:

> Theories of realistic narrative ... are not likely to be highly plausible except in tandem with an informal cultural consensus that certain texts have the quasi-sacred and objective literary status of 'classics', which form the core of a broader literary 'canon'.[88]

However, at a deeper level, a New Critical approach to the Gospels assumes a disguised doctrine of the incarnation.

> Endowing the text with the stature of complete and authoritative embodiment of 'truth' in 'meaning', so that it is purely and objectively self-referential, is a literary equivalent of the Christian dogma of Jesus Christ as incarnate Son of God, the divine Word that is one with the bodied person it assumes. Here is a general theory about texts of which the paradigm case is not only in the first instance not textual but, more important, is itself the *basis* rather than merely an *instance* of the range as well as cohesion of meaning and truth in terms of which it is articulated.[89]

Frei makes it clear in what follows that although he rejects the New Critical generalization from this rule, and the forgetting of its basis, the rule itself still holds good. The Christian use of Gospel narratives has, as its basis, a doctrine of the incarnation. This echoes (deliberately, I think) Barth's doctrine of the threefold word of God: the incarnate word, the scriptural word and the preached word (or, we might say, the word of conceptual redescription).[90] In his 1986 essay, 'Conflicts in Interpretation', Frei strengthened these echoes, using the category 'witness' to describe the relationship between Word and word:

> [T]he Reformers ... propose that even though the text is 'sufficient', we ought not to worship it. And so it is I think rightly proposed that they also implied that the text is 'witness' to the Word of God and that its authority derives from that witness rather than from any inherent divinised quality. And is that Word which is witnessed to, is that not the truth, at once ontologically transcendent and historically incarnate?[91]

He also made it clear that this correspondence is a matter of God's condescension:

> Any notion of truth such that that concept disallows the condescension of truth to the depiction in the text – to its own self-identification with, let us say, the fourfold story of Jesus of Nazareth taken as an ordinary story – has itself to be viewed with profound scepticism by a Christian interpreter. The textual word as witness to the Word of God is not identical with the latter, and yet, by the Spirit's grace, it is 'sufficient' for the witnessing.[92]

In other words, Frei began to reinsert his understanding of realistic narrative, now arrived at by way of Christian self-description, within a more or less Barthian doctrine of the Word of God. The grounds for a narrative reading of the Gospels like that which he pursued in *Identity* are intra-Christian, but they are not simply the accidental whims of the Christian community: they are supported by, and make sense within, the framework of Christian doctrine.[93] *The Identity of Jesus Christ* had been subtitled *The Hermeneutical Bases of Dogmatic Theology*; with these changes, we might more properly say *The Dogmatic Bases of Hermeneutics*, if 'hermeneutics' were not too general a term. To put it in other words, Frei's focus on Christian 'use' of the Bible does not assume that Christians hand themselves over to text, still less that they make of the text what they will, but rather that they find themselves handed over to the texts' witness to and repetition of the Word of God.[94]

7 Christian Truth

Just as with 'meaning', Frei argues that the concept 'truth' must be treated with caution by theologians, and needs to be used in ways that are consonant with the particularities of Christian confession. We have seen some hints of this already, both in the description of type 4 theology and in the discussion of the incarnation at the end of the last section, but it is now time to examine it more directly. We will look first at Frei's use, in the 1980s, of the language of 'first' and 'second order', which points us in the direction of his fuller account of truth, and then at the explicitly theological account of truth which Frei began to develop as the 1980s progressed.

Theological discourse is not the same thing as ordinary Christian language; it is a language at one remove, which comments upon the first order discourse of Christianity – its worship, its scriptures, its ordinary usages – in much the same way that a good English grammar will comment upon ordinary English language-usage. This language of orders was something Frei shared with his colleague George Lindbeck. Discussing *The Nature of Doctrine*, Frei said that, for Lindbeck 'Academic theology is that second-order reflection which is an appropriate, albeit very modest instrument in aid of the critical description and self-description of specific, religious-cultural communities, in our case the Christian church.'[95] Theological discourse is, in other words, *dependent*. Frei repeatedly emphasized the modesty that this picture suggests for theologians. They must be wary of letting their technical concepts and theoretical structures outstrip the 'common sense' upon which they are dependent. The achievement of Lindbeck's book was, at least according to Frei, that in seeking to find a set of concepts able to do justice to a widespread ecumenical common sense, it

> never pushes the common sense beyond its limits, into that realm where sensibility is constrained because aid to reflection has imperceptibly turned instead into guidance by a technical guru or therapist ... The cultural-linguist theory ... is there solely for the service it can render to the ongoing description or self-description of the Christian community.[96]

Frei insisted upon three caveats in his own use of this language of 'orders', however.[97]

In the first place, he insisted that although the distinction between levels was itself a useful concept, it should not be allowed to become absolute: 'the really important thing is to know that even such distinctions are not *prescriptive*, that their sometimes quite natural violation in practice says nearly as much about them as the distinctions say themselves'.[98] When he briefly discusses the Chalcedonian formula in his 1987 Princeton Lectures, for instance, he argues that it is at once a first-order Christian statement, a second-order piece of technical theology, and a commentary upon the Christian Scriptures. It cannot, in other words, easily be assigned simply to 'first order' or to 'second order', nor is it easy to tease out its *use* as second order from its *use* as first order.[99]

In the second place, Frei refused to invest too heavily in the idea that the first order was constant over time, and so had some persistent grammar that could provide some kind of essence to Christianity[100] – a picture which would very easily go with an assertion of a rigid distinction between 'external' and 'internal'. He did think that there was something constant in Christian discourse over the centuries, it's true – but (as we saw in the previous section) his candidate was a specific, substantive set of commitments to which Christians have adhered, and which have been worked out in very different ways as the rules and language of Christianity modulated over time. This continuity is, at least from the historian's and philosopher's point of view, a contingent fact, not an example of some more general persistence of grammar in cultural-linguistic communities.

A more important caveat, from our point of view, is that Frei liked to add talk of a 'third order' alongside first and second. There is first-order Christian language, and then there is second-order theology, theology as Christian self-description, which devotes itself to a modest tracing of the patterns of that first-order language. So, for instance, there are Christian practices of praise and prayer in which Christians call upon 'God', and there is second-order Christian self-description in which the Christian 'grammar' of the word 'God' is elucidated. But this is not enough. There are also questions about the truth, the meaningfulness, the reference of that word, for 'whereas "God" is very much a concept governed by the community's language, it is asymptotically related to other senses of the same word, including some that are the fruit of philosophical speculation'.[101] This 'asymptotic' relation is not a matter of the academic theologian having commitments beyond those he owes to first-order Christian language, but is itself something forced by that language.

> The concept 'God' has customarily been *used* referentially and not simply as one concept related to others in the complex of Christian language, the Christian community, and the Christian life. Christian discourse, *because* it is not merely a coherent abstract of specific linguistic conventions but the discourse of persons using them, has hauntingly elided 'God' as concept, as proper if elusive name, as designating 'real' presence ... 'God' and God and, cognately, first-order and second-order technical discourse have become elided.[102]

So, even in theology understood as Christian self-description, we are pushed towards a third-order use of language, 'a kind of quasi-philosophical or philosophical activity ... which consists of trying to tell others, perhaps outsiders, how these rules [i.e., the grammar of Christian discourse] compare and contrast with their kinds of ruled discourse'.[103]

Just as Frei could not, for more personal reasons, rest content in the 1970s purely as an historian, but looked for ways to keep hold of his systematic theological concerns, so in the 1980s, he believes he cannot rest content with theology purely as Christian self-description: to define himself that way, in polemical opposition to theologies which subordinate Christian self-description to, or regulate it by, some more general discipline, would be to constrain himself within a straitjacket he did not want or need. One of the tasks which faces the type 4 theologian is the development of a peculiarly Christian account of truth.

Certainly that account of truth will be peculiar. Its peculiarity will be due both to the *object* about which Christian theology speaks, and to the peculiarity of the *sources* that enable Christian theology to speak. In a letter to Gene Outka, Frei said: 'We make truth claims, but in view of the fact that God is not within genus and species as ordinary referential truths are, they have to be logically odd and not so much backed as illustrated by a *mix* of truth theories, each qualifying the other.'[104] In the letter to Gary Comstock mentioned in the previous section, he put it differently:

> I want to avoid *both* the reduction which A.J. Ayer and Christian fundamentalists share on the one hand *and* the ontologically non-realist dissolution of New Testament realistic narrative that you and Ricoeur undertake on the other.[105] That kind of straightforward philosophical revision of New Testament truth claims is simply not open to me; *the mode of New Testament truth claiming has to be more complex for me*, i.e., more complex at the second-order philosophical-theological level, not in the first-order religious confession.[106]

However, although the shape of Christian truth will certainly be peculiar, Frei insists upon the Christian unavoidability of some such account. He is adamant that Christian theology does not allow fideism. His clearest statement of this point comes in a letter to Patrick Sherry, commenting on a dissertation he had been asked to assess:

> The dissertation was the most perfect specimen of the local ('fideistic'?) brand of Wittgensteinianism I have so far seen, so it was my – reluctant – opportunity finally to face up to the view and take a clear stand on it. It is not often in academic life that one says of an outlook, 'This speaks directly and forcefully to my conscience, and yet it is absolutely wrong.'[107]

'Absolutely wrong': Frei reserves for fideism one of the strongest direct condemnations to be found anywhere in his writing.[108]

Frei's primary example of such complex but imperative truth-claiming which is required of Christians is the resurrection. He had not changed his mind about the necessity of allowing truth-claims about the resurrection to be governed by the nature of their Gospel depictions.

> [W]hat these stories *refer to* or *how* they refer remains a philosophical puzzle, but it has to be in a way congruent with their realistic, history-like character (and history-likeness of course means that the ministry, death and resurrection narratives are the chief topics, not the 'mystery of the Kingdom of God' which is not a realistic, fictional or historical, item in the same sense as these others).[109]

Frei had, however, became bolder in his explanation of the kind of truth-claims which Christians are warranted to make about the resurrection. In a 1976 letter to William Placher, Frei admitted that he needed in general to be clearer about truth-claims, and in particular about the extent to which Christian theologians are committed to 'ontological' truth-claims, and responsible for articulating some of what they mean by the claim that God acts. The resurrection is the central example, and Frei speaks of 'a kind of agnostic affirmation of at least this miracle as *having a good deal in common with ordinary events*, without being one in the same way as they are'.[110] In an incomplete but detailed reply to a critique of *Identity* which I have been unable to identify, Frei spoke of his 'perhaps too strong statements about the unverifiability in principle of the resurrection claims, a matter on which I find it difficult to sort out my options'.[111] Most clearly, in the letter to Gene Outka already mentioned, Frei writes:

> Of course we think something happened, but how it transpired we won't know in this life or history. All we know is that it is coherent with God's being and faithfulness in creating, sustaining and saving us in life and death, and therefore to be described in terms consonant therewith, as resurrection of the fullness of our being as that counts in God's eyes. What that will be, again, we don't know, but analogously 'body' is the best term I know (i.e., cheers for the tradition).[112]

Some further clarification is provided by Frei's attack on an alternative position. Responding to Gary Comstock, he wrote:

> If true being is in the unity of metaphorical language, limit experience, and meaning, just how do you recapture the world of sense and things? Just what *is* that secondary world which is referred to by the other part of the 'split' reference, the part that does not refer realistically? How is it different from that sublation of realistic reference in which the latter is at once stored up and left behind, that *Aufhebung* which seemed to be the triumph of ontology under Hegel's auspices? And if I am at least partially right in my suspicion at this point, would you tell me what 'God's *action*' really means in such a context? And would you really want to tell me that *this* is how Christians intend to refer when they greet each other on Easter morning with 'He is risen'? You tell me that I wrongly interpret that statement purely intramurally; but even if you were right (which you are not), I don't think that's any more incorrect than your apparent identification of the meaning of that text with the statement, 'Jesus's life reveals the mystery of the Kingdom of God', especially when that phrase may be little more than a literary code for a full-orbed Idealistic-ontological use of 'truth', and its residual realistic element is reduced to the level of some kind of 'powerful (poetic) presence.'[113]

In one or two places, Frei hints at a more thorough reinsertion of this discussion of truth into a dogmatic framework. The clearest example of this is a 1986 letter to William Placher, in which Frei sets out a Trinitarian framework for thinking about Christian truth, a framework which appears to gather together many of the fragmentary things which he says elsewhere.

Frei suggests to Placher that 'theologians may have a *range* of possibilities for relating theological (or Christian) to other instances of rational argument and other instances of "truth", and not simply *one*'. In terms now familiar to us, he continues:

> Can one not say that 'Christian religion' is a distinctive form of discourse, that even the concept 'truth' becomes remolded in it, i.e., becomes part of 'propositions *borrowed from* ...' as our mentor Schleiermacher would have said (*did* say),

without thereby cutting all ties to – and possibilities for discovering parallels in – other fields?[114]

This is the core conviction of type 4 theology again. 'Truth', like other formal and methodological concepts used by theologians, will have to be approached Christianly, theologically, rather than being settled philosophically before Christian self-description can begin. Frei suggests to Placher that, among the varieties of Christianly appropriate ways of thinking about 'truth', we will find something like the following:

> A) Our language *refers* to a real God, and that fact clearly implies a correspondence view of truth[115] ... B) At the same time, we can't talk or read intratextually except by taking our texts, our 'narrative', not only to *refer* translinguistically or representationally but to *be* the textual world in which we live. The text is adequate; it is a 'witness' by virtue of that indirect coherence in it of truth and meaning, which is directly present in the gift of grace incarnate in Jesus. Hence the literal sense is the articulation of the identity of the ascriptive logical or narrative subject 'Jesus Christ' with the real subject Jesus Christ. At that point of ascriptive literalism which is the reading of the Lord's identity, and at that point only, the *truth* affirmation is logically entailed by the text's meaning. To understand *who* the textual Christ is, is to affirm *that* he is. ... I am *not* saying that such ascriptive textual literalism and the coherence view of truth consequent upon it can *take the place* of a correspondence view of Christian truth; I am saying that the two must co-exist, without reduction or priority of one to the other. I would plead the tradition's complex unity here ... C) Doesn't the same irreducible complexity go for the pragmatic or subjective or existentialist view of truth in Christian faith? To know that these statements are true is truly to live (and to be forgiven for not living) them, to learn to use them as instruments of grace.[116]

Finally, Frei redescribes all of this in Trinitarian terms.

> By a use of the doctrine of appropriation we have to say that 'the one God is *the Truth*' is a statement in which: A) 'The Father is true' is a statement about God *qua* real existent being; B) 'The Logos is true' is a statement about the same, real God *qua* ground and guarantor of the adequacy of descriptive Christian language, paradigmatically that of the Bible – the indirect parallel to the unity of linguistic creativity and real world in the incarnation of the Word; C) 'The Spirit is true' is a statement about the same real and linguistically articulable God *qua* guarantor and initiator of performative certainty or ground of living Christian truthfulness, the Enabler of our conceptual capacities through Christian nurture to be true to God's grace, to enact in our lives what we depict narratively and assertorially, and in all these ways God as Subject/Spirit and not only Object/Exister. But in all of these (A, B, C), it is the same God – inconceivably? – being true.

The coherence of these aspects of truth is not given by any theory which manages to hold them together, or shows that they are all variants of some master-form of truth. It is a coherence which is given as a gift from God, and is seen in the faithful lives which are sustained by that gift.[117]

8 Conclusion

Throughout the 1970s and 80s, Frei shifted to a view of Christianity which was more thoroughly social, a view in which ideas were more firmly tied to the world of characters and institutions – a view which was, in that sense, more thoroughly historical. All the more theoretical work which he did in the 1980s, which has attracted considerable attention in its own right, was an attempt to ask what changes were necessary to his earlier dogmatic and methodological work if that more historical view of Christianity were allowed to percolate fully through all his concepts and procedures.

Changes were certainly necessary. Instead of arguing for his theology on the ground that it could do better justice to a formal feature of Gospel narratives, Frei now argued on the grounds that his theology could do better justice to a pervasive and continuous, if relatively modest, Christian usage, which latched on in a particular way to the Gospel narratives, and for which those narratives turned out to be amenable. Frei was still attempting to do justice to a feature of the Gospel narratives; now, however, he was only claiming that it was important to do so because that feature is picked out and valued by Christian usage. And that picking out and valuing were not simply matters of accidental practical habit, but on the one hand can themselves be made sense of in Christian confessional terms, and on the other can be shown to be ways in which Christian practice hands itself over (or, rather, is handed over) to something which it does not control, and which has, in the context of this practice, an objectivity which stands over against that very practice. The criterion for Frei's theology is neither Bible alone nor use alone, but this complex combination of doctrinally informed practice and that which provides the practice with its material and its stability.

Nevertheless, although this is a definite change in the scaffolding surrounding Frei's theology, it did not materially alter the main thrusts of the theology that this scaffolding supported. His later work was a 'continuation as well as a revision' of *The Identity of Jesus Christ* and *The Eclipse of Biblical Narrative*,[118] and remained committed to 'the central persuasion of Christian theology, not so much to be defended as to be set out ... that Jesus Christ is the presence of God in the Church to the world',[119] a conviction which is best set out by means of a doctrine of providence and a practice of figural interpretation.[120] He remained committed to something very like his earlier Anselmian argument about the resurrection: 'It is contrary to Jesus's very identity in these stories to be conceived of as not having been raised from the dead; therefore he *really* – and not merely in the stories – lives';[121] 'If you think of me [i.e., Jesus] in the past tense, gone even if not forgotten, with my memory still celebrated among you, you are not thinking of *me*.'[122] And much of the technical apparatus supporting this claim remained in place: it is still said that there is 'something very specific about the original portraits' and that Jesus '*is* what he *does* and *undergoes*';[123] Frei still refers to descriptions of intentional action and 'subject-predicate' descriptions.[124] To read his article 'On the Resurrection of Christ', his drafts for the Cadbury Lectures,[125] and his third Humanities Council lecture, is to find oneself unmistakably in the territory of *The Identity of Jesus Christ*: Frei is still concerned to trace the unsubstitutable identity of Jesus of Nazareth portrayed in the Gospels in such a way as to confirm that 'he is – or is representative of – all persons'.

> When Christians want to describe human nature ... they look to this man, as though true humanity could never be explained, never be generalised about or abstracted from concrete, specific description, but as though the description of this specific man, like all good fictional description, included far more than this person – in fact, the whole race, each one of us in her or his specific and different being, doing, and undergoing.[126]

Frei's new focus on Christian *use* of the Scriptures, then, must not be taken as an abandonment of his focus on the objectivity of the Gospel depictions of Jesus of Nazareth, which if registered provides the foundation for a high Christology and a doctrine of providence. In his presentations of the typology of Christian theology, the primary question Frei poses is not so much, 'Which type of theology allows us to pay most attention to Christian practice?' as, 'Which type is most able to do justice to the Jesus of the Gospels, the Jesus whose identity is fitly rendered in a pattern of public action and interaction, who stands over against Christian practice with enough stability to be a constant stumbling-block for that practice, and to whom that practice has faithfully pointed, sometimes despite itself, over the centuries?' Type 1 must turn from the Gospels' specificity to some universally accessible residue; type 2 must find the meaning of Gospels in the particular actualization of religious potential depicted in them or aroused by them; type 3 has to find the meaning of the Gospels in the connection between inward repeatability and external particularity, with emphasis finally on the former; and type 5 must stop short of taking the Gospel depiction of Jesus' cosmic scope with final seriousness. It is type 4 theology – unsystematic theology – which Frei thinks is the type able both to start without reservation with the Christian, descriptively and ascriptively literal reading of these texts, and without reservation commit to the high Christology and providential, figural vision to which that reading leads. Frei's later work is indeed a continuation and clarification of his earlier work.

Notes

1. Autobiographical Notes on Self (1983g), p. 3.
2. Preface to *The Eclipse of Biblical Narrative* (1973f), p. vii.
3. In order to see this deliberate shift taking place, we have to look beyond Frei's published writings. In 1974, he delivered the Rockwell Lectures on Religion at Rice University, speaking on 'Religious Transformation in the later Eighteenth Century' (1974c) with

a focus on Lessing, Kant and Herder; in the same year he had an article on 'German Theology: Transcendence and Secularity' (1974b) published in a volume on post-war German culture. In 1976 he delivered the Greenhoe Lectures at Louisville Seminary, 'On Interpreting the Christian Story' (1976h), a good deal of his material historical; and in 1978 he delivered the George F. Thomas Memorial Lecture, 'Is Religious Sensibility Accessible to Study? The Case of G.E. Lessing' (1978k); the article on Strauss (1985c) was itself largely completed by 1981. There are also numerous letters in which he lays out his intentions.

4. See my 'An American Theologian of History: Hans W. Frei in 1956', *Anglican and Episcopal History* 71.1 (2002) for a more detailed account.

5. Frei does, however, discuss Lessing's approach to the portrayal of action in ways which point to his growing interest in a broader conception of history:

> Lessing's drama was realistic because like Diderot he believed in presenting the real mix and confusion of human motivations and actions. But it was not realistic in the way that a Marxist would think of it, because even though he was very much aware of cultural and political conditions limiting and even entering into human relations ... he did not finally present social structure and the historical forces that lie behind them as the motivating power that drives human beings to do and suffer the things they are engaged in ... Character was finally a basic, as it were irreducible manifestation of humanity, no matter to how large an extent one's religion, country, climate, etc. influenced it, and dramatic portrayal was one of the ways in which one both showed forth and helped to redirect the pivot of the inevitably active outlet of human beings. (pp. 11–12)

> This interest in a more social form of realism is also visible in the 1974 Preface to *Identity* (1974i): 'I would now want to supplement both patterns [of identity description – i.e., intention–action and subject–manifestation description] by exploring the formal analytical techniques which sociologists of knowledge and Marxist literary critics use to identify the relation between individual personhood and the contextual social structures' (p. x).

6. Letter to William Placher (1976c).
7. Letter to Charles M. Wood (1978e).
8. 'Is Religious Sensibility Accessible to Study?' (1978k), p. 1.
9. Ibid., p. 2.
10. Ibid., p. 3.
11. Ibid., p. 6. He had also briefly discussed responses to the question guided by Hegel, or by a hermeneutics of suspicion (pp. 5–6).
12. Ibid., pp. 6–7, emphasis removed.
13. Ibid., p. 8.
14. Ibid., pp. 8–9. In the notes for his undergraduate lectures on 'Modern Christian Thought, 1650–1830' (?1978a) Frei writes:

> 'Sensibility' is how it felt, how people, especially ordinary people experienced life. Not consciousness writ large but rather close relation of experience and institutions ([cf.] Michel Foucault [on] 'Madness' – First, new institutional ways of dealing with it, i.e., therapeutically, educationally, medicinally (and disease), only therefrom the form it takes pathologically) – e.g., the change in family structure that allows increased spontaneity to feeling of affections, the history and institutionalization of madness, death, infant exposure, etc. all of it (a) quantitative as well as qualitative (b) going from small to large and (c) letting go of 'narrative' procedure in favour of behavioural/attitudinal/institutional patterns. (pp. 2–3)

15. 'Conceptual Clarification and Sensibility Description' (?1979e), p. 3.
16. Letter to William Placher (1979f); cf. Frei's letter to Van Harvey (1979c).

17. 'Modern Christian Thought, 1650–1830' (?1978a), pp. 3ff., and 'Modern Christian Thought, 1650–1830' (1985d), p. 2.
18. See John Woolverton's article, 'Hans W. Frei in Context' for a fuller account. See also Frei's letter to Woolverton (1980b):

> Far from wanting to confine my theological thought and writing in and to the university, I am actually thoroughly persuaded that a theologian has to write fully as much in the context of a (or 'the') church, but that reinforces my doubts, because in effect my communal Christian context simply isn't Anglican. I'll never change formal affiliation, but my heart simply isn't in the worship or ethos of Anglicanism ... I am not at all sure where I stand: I find Quaker meetings glorious right now, but it won't do in the long run and has little to do with my theological convictions. (p. 2)

19. Letter to 'Jane' (1977a).
20. Letter to Charles M. Wood (1978e).
21. Letter to William Placher (1979f). Cf. a letter to Richard Marius (1978b) in which Frei wrote, 'It's not that I don't consider myself a Christian but that I have very few answers on the plane of theoretical theology.'
22. Autobiographical Notes on Self (1983g), p. 3.
23. The deep attraction which Frei felt for this material is perhaps most evident in his 1975 article on 'The Foot Soldiers of the Enlightenment' (1975c).

> Just take the elevator up into the Sterling Library, choosing your floor almost at random. The printed remains of the intellectual revolution that seized Europe and then North America more than two centuries ago are everywhere. On the fifth floor, for instance, it will not take the browsing wanderer long to discover row on row of forbidding-looking volumes, huge, yellowed and long since forgotten by all except the specialist ... Like any other army, that of an intellectual revolution has not only its generals but its privates. Those are the tomes exhibited on Sterling's shelves as though they were on parade ... Why honor them? ... They were not generally cast in a heroic mold; they tended to be matter-of-fact and respectable, but they had a stubborn integrity which forced them to keep raising critical questions in the face of inherited opinions.

Frei spoke of 'Men like Richard Watson, Bishop of Llandaff and Regius Professor of Divinity in Cambridge, and Johann Joachim Spalding, clerical provost in Berlin in the reign of Frederick the Great' who 'tried to show that revelation is not irrational or superstitious' by using 'rational arguments which had the form and flavour of their opponents' views'. 'And so they were impressed into the army of the Enlightenment despite themselves' (pp. 1–3).

24. Letter to Owen Chadwick (1981g).
25. Letter to William Clebsch (1981h), p. 2.
26. Frei did, however, bring increasing amounts of material on popular religion into his undergraduate lecturing.
27. 'Proposal for a Study of Academic Education in Theological Studies' (?1985a), p. 1. The proposal begins by referring to Lindbeck in such a way as to suggest that it was written after the publication of The Nature of Doctrine in 1984.
28. This is obscured in Types of Christian Theology, which relegates most of the historical material to the Appendices.
29. By the end of his life, Frei appears to have been intending to publish a book on his typology of Christian theology as preparation for his longer and more detailed book on the history of Christology. It seems likely that the social history of academic theology would have dominated the former; what is not clear is the extent to which it would have provided the focus for the latter.
30. Letter to Charles M. Wood (1978e).

31. Letter to William Placher (1979f), p. 1.
32. Letter to Gary Comstock (1984e), p. 3.
33. Letter from Terry Foreman to Brooks Holifield (1979b). Foreman also mentioned Frei's interest in 'the Marxists', and in Alasdair Macintyre, William Clebsch and Michel Foucault. Frei scrawled in the margin of his copy: 'I want to argue among other things that *intellectually*, the development wasn't necessary in the way history of ideas have usually suggested it was (*Eclipse* provides an example of this).' *Eclipse* was, in other words, not the worst of offenders when it came to the real problem with intellectual historical approaches: the tendency to reduce the contingent world of public history either to an epiphenomenon of, or a cloak for, the true, inner, spiritual history. *Eclipse* had at least argued that the changes in interpretation in the modern period had not been the inevitable consequence of the unfolding of the inherent logic of an intellectual complex's; it had at least argued that it was a contingent development, even if it had argued that case in too exclusively intellectual a register.
34. See in particular the Cadbury Lectures (1987a) (noting their original arrangement, as described in the bibliography at the end of this book) and the Humanities Council Lectures (1987c).
35. See chap. 5, §3.
36. *The Identity of Jesus Christ (1975a)*, p. 4.
37. In a 1972 undergraduate lecture on Barth's understanding of revelation, Frei spoke of Barth's focus on the 'distinctiveness of biblical Christian concepts' – concepts which have 'no non-Christian cognate' ('Contemporary Christian Thought' [1972a], p. 1). Frei denies that this distinctiveness amounts to incommensurability, even speaking of their 'universal intelligibility'.
38. Letter to the Mausers (1976i). The intention to work on the parables is also mentioned in a letter to John Schutz (1973a).
39. 'On Interpreting the Christian Story', lecture 2: 'Interpretation and Devotion: God's Presence for us in Jesus Christ' (1976h[ii]).
40. Ibid.
41. Ibid. In 'The Availability of Karl Barth' (*1978g*), Frei suggests that the *Church Dogmatics* is intended to teach us Christian language, not by stating its rules, but by using it – and, increasingly, by retelling the stories which are that language's primary soil (pp. 158–59).
42. 'Theology and the Interpretation of Narrative' (1982b), p. 96.
43. The Shaffer Lectures (1983a), p. 20.
44. 'Theology and the Interpretation of Narrative' (1982b), pp. 96–97; cf. The Shaffer Lectures (1983a), p. 22. Further parallels to the discussion in his 1978 lecture on religious sensibility (1978k) emerge when Frei contrasts his approach both with explanatory reductionism, and with the kind of 'religion is sui generis' approach which he here associates with Mircea Eliade ('Theology and the Interpretation of Narrative' [1982b], pp. 98–99).
45. Letter to William Placher (1979f).
46. See chap. 5, *passim*.
47. Letter to Wayne Meeks (1973g).
48. Preface to *The Identity of Jesus Christ* (1974i), p. vii.
49. A few days after he completed the Preface, Frei wrote to Robert Krieg, (1974j), 'I wonder if Barth does not shift away gradually from the personal word or address model to narrative commentary or conceptual redescription.' His own move away from 'presence' paralleled this shift.
50. 'The "Literal Reading" of Biblical Narrative' (1983c), p. 126.
51. Ibid.
52. Letter to Gary Comstock (1984e), p. 3.
53. He also attacks, from time to time, 'story theology', a brand of theology with which his own work has sometimes been confused, but which represented everything he fought against. See Appendix 5 for more details.

54. 'The "Literal Reading" of Biblical Narrative' (1983c), pp. 133–39; cf. '"Narrative" in Christian and Modern Reading' (1984b), pp. 155-61. Despite this *ad hoc* use, Frei was no fan of deconstruction. In a letter to Bruce Piersault (1980d), he wrote,

> No, *Eclipse* was not influenced by the deconstructionists; I was far too unwashed literarily to know what they or even their predecessors were up to at that point. On the contrary, I was really naively persuaded that there was such a thing as a normative meaning to a narrative text, if not to others. Since then I've become a bit more jaded under their influence, but still feel like digging in my heels rather than celebrating Nietzsche's wild relativistic rhetoric accompanied by Heidegger's pompous obbligato.

55. In his photocopy of a review by Leslie Brisman of *The Identity of Jesus Christ* and *The Eclipse of Biblical Narrative, Comparative Literature* 28.4 (1979g), next to the reviewer's comment that Frei 'does not confront the fact that there would be no literary criticism (or only negative criticism, deconstruction of others' illusions about texts) if novels, let alone poems, were read realistically', Frei says 'Is this perhaps (figuration of experience apart) all one can do in the case of realistic narratives? Finally there is – *not interpretation – but reading*, perhaps comparison of readings' (note on p. 369, my emphasis); and later he writes, 'Is there "meaning" only where there is interpretation? "Meaning" is reading properly' (note on p. 372).

56. I am assuming that the 1983 paper [1983f] fed into Frei's 1986 paper 'Barth and Schleiermacher: Beyond the Impasse' (1986d).

57. The Cadbury Lectures (1987a[viii]), p. 70. The roots of the typology go back as far as Frei's 1958 'Religion: Natural and Revealed' (*1958a*), pp. 314–17.

58. 'Proposal for a Project' (1986a), pp. 2–3.

59. Ibid., p. 4.

60. In his initial presentations of the typology, Frei chose Gordon Kaufman as his representative for type 1, but he soon substituted rather more interesting reflections on Kant; David Tracy's *Blessed Rage for Order* was his constant focus for the second type, Schleiermacher and Barth for the third and fourth respectively, and D.Z. Phillips for the fifth. It is clear throughout that Frei favours type 4.

61. The Humanities Council Lectures (1987c), p. 118.

62. I am not here seeking to defend Frei's interpretation of D.Z. Phillips, who may well not fit neatly into the box to which Frei has assigned him; I am simply exploring the logic of type 5 in Frei's typology.

63. The Shaffer Lectures (1983a), p. 36, and elsewhere.

64. 'Karl Barth: Theologian' (1969a), p. 171.

65. Letter to Larry K. Nelson (1973e), p. 1.

66. Letter to Gary Comstock (1984e), pp. 1–2.

67. 'Religion: Natural and Revealed' (*1958a*), p. 317.

68. 'Notes on Maurice Wile's Review of *The Identity of Jesus Christ*' (1976d), p. 262, Frei's emphasis.

69. See chap. 5, §4 for more details.

70. 'Response to "Narrative Theology"' (1985e), p. 210. Interestingly enough, Frei at that point includes *figural* as well as *literal* reading in the consensus.

71. The Shaffer Lectures (1983a), p. 14.

72. The Humanities Council Lectures (1987c), p. 140, my emphasis.

73. 'Theology and the Interpretation of Narrative' (1982b), p. 110.

74. Letter to Gary Comstock (1984e), p. 5, Frei's emphasis.

75. The Shaffer Lectures (1983a), p. 14.

76. The Shaffer Lectures (1983a), p. 16.

77. E.g., 'The "Literal Reading" of Biblical Narrative' (1983c), p. 122; The Humanities Council Lectures (1987c), pp. 141–42.

78. This is a point which is clearer in 'The "Literal Reading" of Biblical Narrative' (1983c), p. 122, than in Frei's earlier discussions.

79. 'Theology and the Interpretation of Narrative' (1982b), pp. 106–10.
80. Letter from Bruce Marshall (1983d), emphasis as in original. Frei wrote 'yes' and 'right' in the margin at various points and, beside the clause 'there may not be any theory which adequately conceptualizes that relation', he wrote: 'right: there probably isn't but that doesn't mean you can take it for granted, any more than the "skills" of understanding'.
81. Frei's use of authorial intention here is, therefore, quite the opposite of the kind of reference to authorial intention attacked as the 'intentional fallacy'; rather than involving the divining of an intention which is fundamentally distinct from the text, it takes the text itself to be an intelligent performance.
82. 'Theology and the Interpretation of Narrative' (1982b), p. 112, Frei's emphasis.
83. 'Scripture as Realistic Narrative' (1974d).
84. The Cadbury Lectures (1987a[i]), p. 3.
85. The Humanities Council Lectures (1987c), p. 140.
86. See ibid., p. 143.
87. 'The "Literal Reading" of Biblical Narrative' (1983c), p. 143, my emphasis.
88. Ibid., p. 144.
89. Ibid., p. 141.
90. Carl Henry, in his paper 'Narrative Theology: An Evangelical Appraisal', asked 'what is "rendering an agent" ... other than a narrative construct of the transcendent Word Jesus Christ addressing us through the biblical words?' Frei simply wrote in the margin of his copy: 'Yes'.
91. 'Conflicts in Interpretation' (1986b), p. 163. Cf. 'Response to "Negative Theology"' (1985e), pp. 210, 212: '[B]elief in the divine authority of Scripture is for me simply that we do not need more. The narrative description there is adequate.' 'Once again, yes, "Jesus" refers, as does any ordinary name, but "Jesus Christ" in scriptural witness does not refer ordinarily; or rather, it refers ordinarily only by the miracle of grace. And that means that I do not know the manner in which it refers, only that the ordinary language in which it is cast will miraculously suffice.'
92. 'Conflicts in Interpretation' (1986b), p. 164.
93. In his Letter to Gary Comstock (1984e), Frei writes:

> I believe strongly in a careful, restrained and almost aesthetic applicability of typology or analogy to the relation between divine and more general 'truth' for Christian theological reflection. The textual universe of the gospel is that perfect coherence of reference and meaning, albeit always imperfectly and partially glimpsed, which allows us to analogize from there to the *imperfect*, secondary and analogous coherence of the two in other cases. In an admittedly exaggerated fashion one might say that this is the only perfectly 'public' case of truth which allows all our other limited and private truths to become at least semi-public. But of course, I have no philosophical warrant for this claim, since I have proposed that it is not backed by any general theory: Hence its status must remain extremely awkward, at once grandly if not ludicrously imperialistic, and yet totally mired in collectively private Christian discourse in the eyes of those for whom philosophy is a foundational and, in respect of the formal canons for meaning and truth, *the* universal, normative discipline. For me this is the risk Christian theology has to take if it is to recapture its character as theology of faith, and specifically of incarnation-oriented faith. If it aims at less, is it worth having? Does it do justice to the gospel that commands the life and language of the Christian community? Does it do anything that a good philosophy of religion – or perhaps even better a sympathetic and restrained interpretive social-scientific view of religions as distinctive religions, like that of Clifford Geertz – could not accomplish instead? (p. 7)

94. There is one other aspect of this dogmatic re-insertion of Frei's hermeneutical comments, at which Frei gestured in a 1986 paper prepared for a conference honouring Jürgen Moltmann

and Elisabeth Moltmann-Wendel. He sketched an account of God's patience, suggesting that,

> When conjoined with 'God's inexhaustible patience', 'suffering' has a richer fabric and complexity, it seems to me, than it does in Moltmann's more customary, almost automatic and – how shall I put it? – almost logical association of God's suffering with divine self-abandonment and being abandoned. I hope I am not being unfair if I pose at least tentatively the possibility that the suffering that goes with patience hints at the richness of a God whose Deity is the perfection of his or her unicity through the amplitude of each of his attributes ('God's Patience and Our Work', 1986c(ii), pp. 5–6).

The kind of response most appropriate to this divine patience is, Frei suggests, 'Meditative, participative knowledge, the knowledge of that love which lets things be themselves and loves them for the richness which they are' (p. 6). There is here a suggestion of a properly *theological* (in the narrow sense) grounding of an 'aesthetic' hermeneutic.

95. 'George Lindbeck: *The Nature of Doctrine*' (1984d), p. 278.
96. Ibid., pp. 277–78.
97. In any case, reference to 'second-order' reflection upon 'first-order' Christian language without further specification of how those orders are to be construed, would not have distinguished Frei's type of theology from other, opposing types. Even Kant, according to Frei's second Rockwell Lecture 'Kant and the Transcendence of Rationalism and Religion' (1974c[ii]), employed something like a distinction between these orders of discourse – in his case, a distinction between expressive and conceptual discourse.

> Kant ... sought to articulate a philosophy of religion that did not simply analyze religious concepts but asked what were right or useful religious concepts, right or useful religious practices – and how one used them properly ... Kant discovered among many other things that ordinary speech was inadequate to express certain facts or structures of human life, but unlike Lessing he did not have drama to help him express what conceptual descriptive language lacked. Instead he trenched, and trenched hard, upon a symbolic use of language that was to become the domain of Romantic thinkers who came after him. Yet he himself did not cross the barrier that Herder crossed between two kinds of language use, conceptual and expressive. Like Lessing, again, he found speculative theory defective for the articulation of ultimate truth. But whereas this defect led Lessing to treat such theory qualifiedly, to apply it tenuously and ambiguously, and only in the service of pedagogy, Kant judged speculative theory altogether unfit though inevitable as an instrument for the discovery of true belief and true religious practice. (pp. 1–2)

98. The Shaffer Lectures (1983a), p. 21, Frei's emphasis; cf. pp. 39–40.
99. The Humanities Council Lectures (1987c), pp. 124–25. In 'The Availability of Karl Barth' (1978g), Frei notes that Barth mixes second-order *description* of the rules of Christian discourse with the first-order *display* of those rules in use (pp. 158–59).
100. See the discussion in The Shaffer Lectures (1983a), p. 22, for example, where Frei leaves the question hanging.
101. 'Theology and the Interpretation of Narrative' (1982b), p. 101.
102. Ibid., p. 100, my emphasis.
103. The Shaffer Lectures (1983a), p. 21.
104. Letter to Gene Outka (1984c).
105. In the Outka letter (1984c), Frei says 'My own thinking goes down the middle between "fideism" ... and "rationalism".'
106. Letter to Gary Comstock (1984e), p. 4, my emphasis.
107. Letter to Patrick Sherry (1983e).
108. In the detailed discussion of the dissertation which accompanies the letter, Frei explains further that this kind of fideism, with its picture of the competent theologian exploring a

complete and clearly visible Christian theology, does not allow for a sense of the fullness of theological truth as an arena for continual exploration and discovery and revision. Christian life cannot, he says, simply be a matter of a set of skills which we can pick up and which are then fully adequate; it is a matter of exploring a gift which is continually being given, and which constantly exceeds us. In thinking otherwise, the kind of 'Wittgensteinian fideism' displayed in the dissertation 'makes Pelagius look by contrast like Augustine's most devoted follower' ('Estimate of the Work as a Whole' [1983e(ii)]).

109. Letter to Gary Comstock (1984e), pp. 5–6, Frei's emphasis. Cf. 'Conflicts in Interpretation' (1986b), p. 163: 'Of course, Christians want to live and speak truth or speak truthfully, but we ought to be careful at what point and in what way. There may be Christian reasons, if no other kinds, to exercise reticence about the transition.'

110. Letter to William Placher (1976c), p. 1, my emphasis.

111. 'Historical Reference and the Gospels' (?1981c), p. 7.

112. Letter to Gene Outka (1984c).

113. Letter to Gary Comstock (1984e), pp. 3–4, Frei's emphasis.

114. Letter to William Placher (1986f), p. 2.

115. Cf. Frei's letter to Elisabeth Hilke (1974k). Hilke had written an essay on Barth, Wittgenstein and Austin. He cautions her on relying exclusively on a grammatical model, saying 'Yes, essence is expressed by grammar, but that is because the real object fits itself to our concepts and words. In other words, Barth has ... something suspiciously like a correspondence theory of truth.' (p. 2) 'Wittgenstein, ... taken very systematically, is perhaps not a very good guide for describing what Barth does after all' (p. 3).

116. Letter to William Placher (1986f), pp. 3–5, Frei's emphasis. In his letter to Gene Outka (1984c), Frei had said, when discussing the kind of understanding of 'truth' he was working with,

> Yes, functional theory that appeals to cultural or personal experience ... but this qualified by a referential claim (it is more appropriate to say that God exists than that s/he does not), but this in turn to be qualified by the 'odd' character of 'existence' in this unique instance, and thus the (Barthian/Anselmic) appeal to describing a 'correspondence' claim through a 'coherence' scheme.

117. As Frei puts it in a slightly different context:

> To a natural or rather secular understanding, and even to some Christian minds, it seems at best odd, at worst utterly incongruous to put together a highly technical, theological formula such as Article Five [of the Thirty-Nine Articles] with a plea for patient labor toward mutual human understanding. But in the logic of the Christian faith nothing is more naturally congruent and coherent than saying 'do justice, love kindness and walk humbly with your God' (Micah 6.8) and saying 'The Holy Ghost, proceeding from the Father and the Son, is of one substance, majesty, and glory, with the Father and the Son, very and eternal God.' ('Of the Holy Ghost', 1987f, p. 7)

118. 'Proposal for a Project' (1986a), p. 6.

119. The Shaffer Lectures (1983a), p. 8.

120. See chap. 7, §3.

121. Letter to Gary Comstock (1984e), p. 6, where he describes this as 'a straightforward referential truth'.

122. Sermon on John 15.5 (1988c), p. 3.

123. The Humanities Council Lectures (1987c), p. 142.

124. In his notes on a photocopied extract from Ronald Thiemann's *Revelation and Theology* (?1985b), Frei indicates that he does not accept Thiemann's rejection of self-manifestation description (p. 139); in the Cadbury Draft (1987a[i]), Frei explains that both kind of description are needed (p. 9).

125. Particularly the draft 1987a(i).

126. The Humanities Council Lectures (1987c), p. 135.

Conclusion

Hans Frei called for a public theology because he understood faith to be historical. That is, he called for a theology which lives in the public world and engages with public reality, because it is rooted in a Christian faith which has its source in history-like narratives set in the one public world in which we live, which is learnt in particular historical communities living in that public world, and which prays and works for discernment in the world of public events and processes. His theology, though unashamedly resting upon the ground of a faith that is not shared by everyone and cannot by any tricks of the theologian be made plausible to everyone, is nevertheless public in form precisely because it speaks in the register of public history, and so draws constantly and inevitably on the ordinary resources which human beings have for speaking about such reality, and on the academic disciplines by which those resources are clarified and guided. In other words, his theology is public not because he shares methodological or substantive starting-points with religion's cultured despisers, but because the register of theological speech always and everywhere brings it into *ad hoc* contact with all those other forms of human speech that are appropriate to historical existence. His theology is public because it is not, in the first place, the expression of a religious inwardness which may be supposed to be a human universal but which too many of theology's interlocutors do not recognize, but because it rests upon the repeatedly renewed reading of a biblical witness which is open to inspection by all. And his theology is public because it inherently and urgently requires him to speak about, and work within, the wider public world in which Christian life is situated, not providing a technical analysis of some esoteric religious dimension to public events and institutions, but tracing in the light of Christ the patterns and connections which those events and institutions publicly display.

We have seen that Frei was fascinated by the many forms of the question of faith and history that have animated modern Western theology, particularly Protestant theology in England, Germany and America. He was fascinated in particular by various nineteenth-century attempts to give those questions a definite answer, whether it be the relationalist bridges built by Schleiermacher or the burning of those bridges by Strauss. And we have seen that Frei was captivated by the answer which Karl Barth provided: his insistence that

221

creaturely existence, precisely as entirely and persistently creaturely, can be caught up into relationship to God.

Jesus Christ is the paradigm of creaturely reality caught up to God, and so the foundation of any theological relating of faith and history, and when Frei turned to the Gospel witness to Jesus Christ he found that the history which God had caught up in Jesus was precisely a history of unsubstitutable characters and circumstances, a history of actions and interactions on a public stage – that it was primarily a public rather than an inward history. If the whole of history is caught up by God into relationship in *this* Christ, then it will be in the first place as public, unsubstitutable history: as a complex history of people, events and institutions which cannot be paraphrased or diagrammed but only endlessly narrated.[1]

The Christian Church is called to witness to this catching up of history, and so to re-present always and everywhere the unsubstitutable identity of Jesus Christ and to witness to the unlimited scope of Jesus Christ's significance. The Church is called to witness that the world, precisely in its unsubstitutable, public, creaturely life is ordered providentially in Jesus Christ, and that it will find its endlessly particular fulfilment in him. And the only way in which Christians can witness to this without turning it into a different kind of providence – a more abstract, repeatable providence – is to pay unceasing attention to the world, knowing that we cannot know the shape of the world or of any part of it in advance, but believing that the shapes we find can be read (fallibly and partially for now) in connection to the equally particular shape of Jesus Christ.

Instead, then, of providing Christians with any kind of pat answer which would allow them to turn away from history, or any kind of short-cut which would allow them to dispense with history's complexities, Christians are provided with a strange illumination which sends them deeper into history's intractability.[2] The illumination which Christians believe is cast by what God has done in Jesus Christ is not the flat illumination of legend, but that brilliant divine light which shows the world to be fraught with background, a world which is intricately and pervasively interconnected, a world which takes time, a world whose surface has a fractal complexity which exceeds any and all maps, including Christian maps. The world which Christians inhabit in the light cast by Christ is a world which has to be learnt.[3]

What Frei calls 'figural interpretation' is nothing more than the process by which Christians pay ever-renewed attention to the particularity of Jesus Christ on the one hand,[4] and to this thoroughly historical world on the other, and trust to find glimpses of the ways in which each worldly reality might find its own particularly appropriate fulfilment in Christ. All the technical explanations of figural interpretation that Frei inherited from Auerbach are not designed to pick out some *special* form of reading, but to point to this dual paying of attention and hope for connections, and to fight against all short-cuts. Every part of the definition of *figura* is simply another way of refusing an account of the attention which Christians must pay to Christ and to the world, and of the always particular connections which they may hope to be shown, which would make those forms of attention and connection secondary to some deeper, more directly graspable reality.

Figural reading is nothing more than having the Bible in one hand, the newspaper in the other, and refusing to put either down in favour of clearer writing – whether that be the maps of the Bible which are provided by theologians, or the maps of the world which are provided by other disciplines. Such maps may well be useful tools along the way, but Frei's insistence upon figural reading is an insistence that they be kept firmly in their place. Even the concepts and arguments with which Frei presents this figural vision must be kept in that subordinate position – they are themselves thoroughly finite and historical, the tools of a particular tradition of thinking, a service to the task of living Christianly in the public world that can only be a service to the extent that it retains humility.[5]

Only a methodologically humble theology – an 'unsystematic' theology in the sense defined in the last chapter – will be able both to read Gospels for all they are worth, and to accept the strangeness of the kinds of affirmation which turn out to be appropriate to them. Only such a theology will be able to accept that Christian concepts have to be learnt in all their diversity and complexity from the community and its confession, and that even concepts like 'truth' and 'reference' do not come in the neat packages of philosophical definition. For such theology, the essence of Christianity is not, in the end, any shared mode of consciousness or broad philosophical framework, but nothing more than constant return to the Jesus of the Gospels, and so such theology will have conceptual room for Christianity as a growing, changing, multifarious community – a public and historical reality – which has an endlessly complex and particular involvement in the world for which Christ died.

Notes

1. 'Whatever else we are and whatever may be hidden about us, our surface story has its own density, and it is the literary or narrative linguistic world that we all inhabit. We may inhabit other worlds also, and for certain purposes it may be illuminating and even essential to subvert this diachronic world of agency and suffering – by "deeper" accounts – deep synchronic structures, the unconscious, or economic infrastructures – but it will have to be *subverted*, for we must return to it again and again' ('Theology and the Interpretation of Narrative', 1982b, p. 111).

2. As Frei says in 'Conflicts in Interpretation' (1986b) of the parables: 'the best reading is the reading in which the text is not interpreted without residue, i.e., where a surd or problem of reading always remains. Does the text resist being totally resolved by any hermeneutical solvent applied to it?' (p. 165).

3. 'We have to learn in an almost Wittgensteinian way how to use the concepts that apply to the way we know ourselves because the world, the true, real world in which we live ... [t]he only way we know the world is historically' ('Scripture as Realistic Narrative', 1974d).

4. '[T]he task of the redescription of Jesus will remain unfinished as long as history lasts' (The Humanities Council Lectures, 1987c, p. 146).

5. '[M]any things are needed in the Christian church. Sound theology is not the first of them, but it sure would help a little now and then' ('Response to "Narrative Theology"', 1985e, p. 207). After all, the viability of 'literal reading as a religious enterprise' (and, we might say, of the figural reading that is its proper accompaniment) is not in the hands of theologians but 'will follow excellently from the actual, fruitful use religious people continue to make of it in ways that enhance their own and other people's lives' ('The "Literal Reading" of Biblical Narrative in the Christian Tradition', 1983c, p. 119).

Appendix 1

Frei and Anselm

Frei had a particular model in mind when he spoke of 'dogmatic theology': Barth's *Fides Quaerens Intellectum: Anselm's Proof of the Existence of God in the Context of his Theological Scheme*, a book about which Frei had written in his doctoral thesis, repeating the material in the first of his Niebuhr Essays. In his Christological project, and particularly in the introduction to the version published as *Identity*, he made it quite clear that he had adopted as his own a model or method very similar to that expounded by Barth in the Anselm book; in the description of the resurrection identity of Jesus Christ which forms the keystone of that version of his proposal, he expressed his conclusions in such a way as to make the comparison with Anselm unavoidable.

God raised Jesus from the dead. This resurrection is constitutive of Jesus' identity: he is, as self–manifestation description has helped Frei to articulate, the risen one. In other words, Jesus of Nazareth cannot be thought of as not risen. To think of Jesus as not having been raised is to deny that these texts depict his identity, because it is there that they focus that identity. The resurrection is, in these texts, the climax that organizes and confirms all else that can be said about his identity. If it is denied, the rest of that identity is reduced to a selection of unordered anecdotes, the unity of which will have to be sought in a way which is not depicted in the text but imported by the reader.

Frei very deliberately phrases this conclusion in a way that resembles Anselm's ontological argument for the existence of God. God, for Anselm, is that than which nothing greater can be conceived, and nothing that bears that name can be conceived of as not existing; Jesus, for Frei, bears the name given him in the Gospels, and one who bears that name cannot be conceived of as not having been raised. This does not mean that the resurrection is 'conceivable' any more than the existence of God is 'conceivable': it remains profoundly mysterious, and any direct imagining of it is questionable. Nevertheless, to deny it is to reject the name given to Jesus in the Gospels, to talk about a different identity.[1]

Barth describes Anselm as looking within the text of the Credo for an 'inner text' which asserts that the outward text is the truth, by showing how it hangs together, and demonstrating the necessary mutual implication of each of its parts.[2] Frei uses very similar language in his resurrection argument when he talks about the Gospels implicit claim to be 'self-warranting truth', a claim which is present in the text by virtue of its various patterns, and which can be uncovered only by considered reflection. This claim the unbeliever too can encounter, but must reject as a 'hyperfiction'.[3]

Frei's argument is, he claims, a 'reflection within belief' – by which he means something similar to Barth's and Anselm's 'faith seeking understanding'. He is not claiming that the resurrection can be made plausible to unbelievers; neither is he arguing from something Christians accept to something they do not yet accept, so as to spring upon them novel conclusions; he is (he says) simply showing how two Christian beliefs are mutually implicated, and how the priority of one qualifies what may be said about the other. In the terms of Barth's *Anselm* book, he is pursuing a demonstration of the *ratio* of faith.[4] And just as Anselm's *intelligere* issues in *laetificare* – the first purpose of understanding being joy,[5] the primary outcome of Frei's investigation is 'first of all ... a certain pleasure'[6] (even 'delight'[7]); it is for the believer 'a pleasurable exercise in ... ordering his thinking about his faith and – in a certain sense – a praise of God by the use of the analytical capacities'.[8]

For Frei, this investigation consists of an examination of the arrangement and connection of the claims that Christians have made, in ways that can be followed equally well by believer or unbeliever. At the end of the investigation, both believer and unbeliever have moved from a simple acquaintance with these claims which is already a partial understanding to a firmer grasp of how they are ordered. Nevertheless, for the unbeliever, all he has uncovered is a strange and implausible fiction. It is only the believer who believes that in clarifying this ordering of claims, she is gaining a clearer apprehension of the truth. This is no achievement of the believer; it is the gift of God, by the Spirit – in other terms, Christ's own turning to share himself with believers.

Compare with this Barth's description of Anselm, for whom theology investigates the Credo of the Church, which Credo is a 'coherent continuity that is expressed logically and grammatically, and which having been heard, exists *in intellectu*'.[9] Both unbeliever and believer can have this logico-grammatical structure *in intellectu*,[10] but it is only in faith that the *intelligere esse in re* is added to this *esse in intellectu* – and faith is a gift of God.[11] As Frei had explained when he provided in his thesis an exegesis of this very aspect of Barth's interpretation, 'the actual *res* which the symbolism signifies is present only in faith and not in unbelief'.[12] It is true that hearing this argument *might* be the path by which an unbeliever comes to faith; but such an unlooked-for consequence can occur by God's grace alone.[13]

Appendix 2

Jesus' Identity and the Identity of Others

When attempting to restate or reconstruct the course which Frei takes into the doctrines of pneumatology, ecclesiology and providence from the conclusion of his re-description of Christ's identity, one encounters at several junctures an ambiguity as to what Frei is doing. We might consider, for instance, Frei's introduction of pneumatology:

> When Christian believers speak of the presence of Jesus Christ now – in contrast to his presence at the time of his earthly life, death, and resurrection, as well as in contrast to his final presence in the future mode – they use the term 'Spirit' or 'Holy Spirit'. What they mean by this term is described, first of all, by the complex unity of which we have just spoken – that the unsubstitutably human figure, Jesus of Nazareth, and the presence and action of the God who superseded him are given together indissolubly from the climax of the Gospel story onward.[14]

At first sight, this is straightforward enough. Frei wants it to be clear that the complexity he has found appropriate to any affirmation of Christ's presence that does justice to the Gospel depiction of Christ's identity is a complexity which Christians have long acknowledged: it is a complexity to which we find witness in classical doctrines of the Holy Spirit. His conclusions about the strange presence of Jesus Christ are not, he wants to say, innovations, they are not matters about which Christians have not heard before, even if the form in which he has presented them and the kinds of arguments he has used are unfamiliar.

Nevertheless, the Spirit appears here unexpectedly; we have not been led to expect any pneumatology by what has gone before, and its inclusion here is bound to raise questions. Is Frei attempting to show how the themes and claims which Christians have traditionally dealt with under pneumatology in fact arise out of appropriate talk about Jesus' identity and relationship with the Father, such that talk about Spirit could in fact be translated back into talk about Jesus and the Father, if we so desired? Is he, that is, providing a kind of de-mythologization of Spirit language, showing how it can be converted into the acceptable currency of talk about Jesus and the Father? I don't think so; I think instead that Frei wanted to show how it was that various aspects of Christian pneumatological claims, in which the presence of Jesus is touched upon, are indirectly supported and directly shaped by the Gospel depictions of Jesus' identity. A full pneumatology would nevertheless

227

add its own specific, irreducible content to what he is saying on the basis of his exploration of Jesus' identity.

If this interpretation of Frei's arguments is correct, however, we are faced with another set of questions. On what basis should we accept that a pneumatology which has its own specific content, its own bases beyond what Frei has been investigating, will cohere unproblematically with the pneumatological comments he derives from his reading of Jesus' identity? If pneumatology is, in effect, *extraneous* to Frei's discussion (rather than derived from it), we would seem to have another source for elements of Christian talk about Christ's presence, and Frei's demonstration that such talk should be based upon the discussion of Christ's identity will only have disclosed one of several sets of constraints which such talk faces, and the question of coherence is bound to arise.

Something similar can be said concerning Frei's discussion of the Church. He introduces ecclesiology as abruptly as he did pneumatology:

> When Christians speak of the Spirit as the indirect presence now of Jesus Christ and of the God who is one with him, they refer to the church. The church is both the witness to that presence and the public and communal form the indirect presence of Christ now takes, in contrast to his direct presence in his earthly days.[15]

Once again, there is an ambiguity. Where does this affirmation come from? Is it simply that Frei wishes to make sure that *if* any claim is made for the Church as the presence of Christ, such claims will be appropriate to the complexity of Christ's identity? Or does he think that in some way this claim about the Church is appropriate to or even demonstrable from what he has said about Christ's identity?

The ambiguous logic surrounding the introduction of ecclesiology and pneumatology into Frei's argument comes far more clearly into focus when we look at David Demson's book *Hans Frei and Karl Barth: Different Ways of Reading Scripture*. Demson draws attention to a difference between Frei's account of the identity and presence of Jesus Christ in *The Identity of Jesus Christ* and Barth's similar account in the *Church Dogmatics*. He notes that

> [w]hile Barth would concur with Frei that the only presence of Christ *now* that may be properly conceived is his presence in the identity that he enacted and that is manifested in the gospel story, Barth speaks of Jesus' enacted and manifested identity as that of the One who appoints, calls, and sends the disciples. Jesus' appointment, calling, and sending of the disciples today is their inclusion in his choosing of the Twelve.[16]

Later, Demson concludes:

> It is not that Frei does not approach this account. He approaches a description of Jesus' relationship with the apostles as the constituting and definite shape of his relationship with us, but he does not cross over into a description of it. And, therefore, his procedure for biblical interpretation is governed more nearly by ... the

pattern of 'living in the Word' than by inspiration, our inclusion in the apostolate. To be governed in the procedure of biblical interpretation by inspiration, as we may describe Barth's procedure, means that we not only regard the biblical texts as held together by the threefold movement in which Jesus located and locates the apostles, but also we regard the threefold movement in which Jesus locates the apostles (as described in the text) as the definitive, concrete movement in which we, in the fullness of our lives, have been, are, and will be located by Jesus, as he joins together the apostles' mission and our mission in his mission.[17]

It seems to me that the omission that Demson identifies in Frei's argument is the ultimate source of the ambiguity surrounding Frei's introduction of ecclesiological and pneumatological themes into his argument.

The drama of the identification and re-identification of Jesus, the drama of Jesus' relation to the people of God, is not one that takes place simply between an anonymous narrator and the character whose identity is being narrated. It is, rather, a drama which involves (among others) Jesus' disciples. It is a drama which we render abstract and repeatable if we do not narrate it as, for instance, the story of Peter who identifies Jesus in his confession at Caesarea Philippi, who has his identification of Jesus broken in the immediate aftermath and on the way to the cross (until it becomes denial), and who is then re-identified by the risen Lord. Or, to take another narrative strand: Jesus' identification in terms of the people of God and subsequent re-identification of the people can be narrated in terms of his calling of twelve disciples (mirroring the twelve tribes), and his sending of those disciples as the basis of a renewed community. Had Frei paid more explicit attention to this, he would have found it easier to demonstrate that Jesus' identity is depicted as bound up with the identity of others, is bound up with a concrete, narrated calling and establishment of a renewed community. He would have found that his abstract comments about Jesus 'providing the community with an identity' were made more concrete, and he would have found that ecclesiology was always already part of his discussion of the identity of Jesus Christ.

Had Frei thematized Jesus' relationship with his disciples, he may well have found that other elements that he was forced to introduce as extraneous elements could have been tied more firmly in to the body of his argument. He might have been able to introduce Word and Sacrament by means of reference to the commissioning of the disciples and institution of the Eucharist depicted in the narratives. He might also have been helped to introduce pneumatology by means of attention to Jesus' promising and passing on of the Spirit to the disciples.

However, once we have started thinking along these lines, it requires no great leap of the imagination to realize that there are other ways in which Frei has unnecessarily narrowed his focus. Pneumatological issues would certainly arise out of consideration of Jesus' interaction with the disciples, but it would be at least as important to narrate other aspects of Jesus' complex relation to the Spirit: the descent of the Spirit at his baptism, his expulsion into the wilderness by the Spirit, and so forth. Frei's pneumatological excursions would appear considerably less extraneous if they could draw upon such elements built into the identity-description of Jesus.

It is, clearly, not enough simply to throw out hints like this, as if the identification of an element in the Gospel narratives that *sounds* relevant is all that we need to fund a robust doctrinal discussion. Nevertheless, Frei does seem in *Identity* to have narrowed his focus in his retelling of the Gospel story, and not to have noted the extent to which, alongside the mutual implication of the identities of Jesus and the Father depicted there, Jesus' identity is presented in such a way as to constitute and be constituted by the identities of *specific* others: the Spirit, the disciples, the crowd, the Jews, the Gentiles. And perhaps we might also say that the figural interpretation to which we are called needs to be set within a more specific narrative of our calling, inspiring and sending, which would itself be grounded in the identification of these specific others.

Appendix 3

Frei and Chalcedon

Jesus of Nazareth is identified in the passion and resurrection narratives as unsubstitutably the crucified and risen Saviour, whose resurrection is the climactic action of God on behalf of humanity. God acts, and Jesus appears; Jesus' manifestation in the public world in his unsubstitutable identity is the enactment of God's intention. This affirmation, as we have seen, lies at the heart of Frei's theology, and he laboured to make all his other theological affirmations sensitive to its irreducible complexity, to the unsubstitutable identity of the one who is portrayed in the Gospel narratives as our Saviour.

In his 'Remarks in Connection with a Theological Proposal', a paper in which he reflected on the claims he had worked out in the two versions of his Christological proposal, Frei claimed that the dogmatic outcome of his exegesis of the Gospels was 'what one might term a "high Christology"'.[18] He did not, however, pursue the task of redescribing his conclusions in the classical terms of that doctrine; he gave one or two hints, and referred approvingly to Niebuhr's 'moral Chalcedonianism',[19] but I suspect that he feared that to concentrate on such a redescription might involve him, or at least his readers, in turning attention from the complexity of the story towards a conceptual scheme in danger of becoming a substitute for it. He had, after all, criticized Barth for an 'all too easy explanation of enhypostasis–anhypostasis' that had distracted his attention from Jesus himself.[20]

Nevertheless, it is possible to draw on Frei's own hints to indicate how his conclusions relate to traditional categories, without necessarily falling into the traps that alarmed him. Frei was not aiming to construct an entire theology from scratch, but to show the connections and mutual modifications, the ordering and relative priorities of the things that Christians already believe. To show how his Christological affirmations relate to and shape more traditional Christological claims is, so long as it is kept appropriately modest, entirely in keeping with his aims.

Frei dropped one hint in the 'Theological Reflections' version of his proposal. In a discussion of the way in which abstract defining qualities are held together in a particular, unsubstitutable way in an individual identity, Frei noted that

> To say of an individual that the relation between his *ousia* (the 'what' of him) and his *hypostasis* (*that* he is) is accidental for the purposes of formal description,

and that the second adds nothing to the defining knowledge of the first – to say all that is not only existentially but analytically unenlightening in the context of this description.[21]

By 'analytically unenlightening', Frei meant that he could find no purchase for such a conceptual distinction in the texts which he was analysing. If 'hypostasis' is understood in this way, then it belongs to a world of distinctions removed from the Gospel texts. We have already seen that, for Frei, the difference between a set of abstract predicates and an existing person holding all those predicates together lies in the particular way in which each of those predicates is transformed as it is held together with others as a predicate of this particular person. Frei finds this structure embedded in the nature of realistic narrative and in particular in the climactic sequences of the Gospel narratives, emerging most clearly in the demythologizing nature of the resurrection narratives. He therefore finds no immediate use for 'hypostasis' terminology if it is taken in the sense of bare instantiation, such that the only thing needed to turn a collection of abstract and unrelated predicates into an actual object, a hypostasis, were the bare fact of their co-instantiation, a fact which would itself be a purely formal marker set beside each predicate. If all that 'hypostasis' does is to walk among the shelves on which the boxes of abstract predicates are held, selecting and displaying those that are needed for this particular object while remaining itself in the background, then it is a concept which stands firmly on the side of 'repeatability'.

'Hypostasis' can, however, be taken in a different sense, one rather more amenable to Frei's concerns. Frei was interested in the way in which predicates gain their intelligibility only through the unsubstitutable configuration by which they are 'demythologized' in a realistic narrative as the predicates of an unsubstitutable individual. In such a narrative predicates receive a particular and indispensable configuration as they are applied to this individual. 'Hypostasis' has been used in the tradition to speak of something very like this 'configurative individuation', and such a usage is clearly far closer to Frei's concerns, and far more directly applicable to the Gospels.

It is also clear that such configurative individuation involves in Frei's account of the Gospels enmeshment in a particular set of historical circumstances and interactions. In the Gospels, Jesus becomes who he unsubstitutably is in interaction with his setting, with the disciples, and with the one he calls Father. Jesus of Nazareth's hypostasis is therefore not simply his bare existence, nor even the particular way in which his predicates are flavoured as they are held together in his particular case, but is his inextricable involvement with others as one who became what he is in and through that involvement. Translating 'hypostasis' as 'configurative individuation in relation' therefore relates very closely to Frei's own term 'unsubstitutability'.

Yet they are not quite identical: 'hypostatic existence' is a degree or two more abstract than 'unsubstitutability', and that abstraction is important. 'Hypostasis', as I am using it, refers simply to the kind of identity in which predicates are held together in a rich and inseparable mixture, and in which they become what they are in relation to other identities. At this level of abstraction, it is a term we could use also in the doctrine of God. In his lecture notes on 'Barth on God' for the course 'Contemporary Christian Thought' (1972a), Frei writes (the emphasis in each case is his):

> No matter what may *in fact* be the case, the logic (informal) of the notion of God is *not* that one tries to imagine love (e.g.), or transcendence = freedom (e.g.) as a concept in its own right, and then ask if there is a subject (*one* who loves, is free) to whom to attribute or of whom to predicate the quality. No! God not = love or power in the absolute degree ... Rather, (1) subject and predicate not accidentally related (substance back of attribute) so that they are in principle separate, nor (2) subject and predicate not merged so that subject disappears into predicate (Feuerbach), but subject is the unique way of holding together being and governing the attribute. This *the meaning* of 'God' for Barth.

'Unsubstitutability', on the other hand, gives a particular *flavour* to 'con-figurative individuation in relation', being far more explicitly such configurative individuation *in an historical and social setting*. Unsubstitutability is the characteristic of that kind of portrayal of hypostatic existence that we find in realistic narrative.

So, Jesus' identity is, for Frei, given in and through his embroilment in historical and social circumstances, as one who became subject to 'historical forces' at a particular time and place in human history – that is the particular form which his hypostatic existence takes. I suggest that this embroilment, this historical specification of hypostatic existence, is the element of Frei's account which corresponds to at least part of what is meant by 'human nature' in traditional accounts: this is the aspect of his existence which Jesus shares most nearly *identically* with others; it is what characterizes him as a contingent and frail inhabitant of the creaturely sphere.

Talk of Jesus' 'hypostasis', then, refers us in general to the fact that the Gospels are the story of a singular identity; talk of 'human nature' refers us in general to the fact that the Gospels are predominantly a story of a particular kind, i.e., one which portrays the identity of a person embroiled in a particular time and place, a story worked out among characters and events in a worldly, historical setting, and necessarily involving the contingency and finitude of the actors.

Far more than with 'hypostasis' and 'human nature', which can fairly easily be related to Frei's conclusions, we need to tread carefully when we come to 'divine nature', so as not to overwhelm or obliterate the complexity and particularity of the Gospel narratives. It is here more than anywhere that we are in danger of oversimplifying Frei's subtly balanced conclusions. We must look carefully at the various characterizations which Frei gave of the relationship between Jesus and the one he called Father.

As we have seen, Frei regards the resurrection as an identification of Jesus as the one whose reappearance is the climactic action of God on behalf of humanity. God acts, and Jesus appears: his manifestation in the public world in his unsubstitutable identity is the enactment of God's intention. After the resurrection, Jesus appears as one hypostatically identical to the one he was before. It is repeatedly affirmed that he is the same person as the one who did and underwent all these things. Indeed it is now made clear for the first time how he could be both the one who underwent all that happened to him, and yet the rightful owner of all the promises and claims which have been made about him. The hypostatic unity of his existence in all the stages of his life is made clearer than ever before. His human nature also remains apparent (though now in mysterious ways): having become most brutally apparent on the cross, it is not eradicated in the resurrection appearances but reaffirmed by his references to his bodiliness and his wounds, by his interactions and by his absences.

Yet this hypostatic human existence, this unsubstitutable identity, is itself declared to be the enactment of God's intentions. Jesus is declared not simply to be one who enacts God's intentions, but to *be* himself that enactment in his whole hypostatic existence. The focus shifts entirely away from the Father, and on to Jesus: Jesus does not explain to the disciples on the way to Emmaus how all the law and the prophets speak of what God has done; he explains how they speak of himself, his existence and nature. It is part of the unsubstitutable identity depicted here not just that the one depicted is human, one who is embroiled in particular ways among specific people, but also that this depicted one *is* the mission of God, ingredient in the identity of God, even (to use Frei's favoured phrase) the presence of God. The hypostatic existence of Jesus of Nazareth is an act of God in which God represents Godself.

Later in his career, Frei took this one stage further. This act in which God represents Godself, an act that is identical with the hypostatic human existence of Jesus of Nazareth, is at the same time an act in which God identifies all humanity. Henceforth, all human beings are called to identify themselves in relation to Jesus of Nazareth – not because some extra has been added to their identities, but because in Jesus Christ they receive their true identities: they find their identities fulfilled. As Frei put it, the claim 'that he includes all human nature in his specificity is ... reminiscent of the *anhypostasis* and *enhypostasis* of Alexandrian Christology, the proposal that in him Godhead supplied the specificity for that generic humanity which he had assumed'.[22]

This brief sketch has, no doubt, left all sorts of dogmatic questions hanging – particularly questions surrounding my description of the act in which God represents Godself. I shall deal only with one less ambitious question here. Is it only in the resurrection that Jesus' hypostatic existence is the presence of the action of God? Does Frei's account imply a kind of adoptionism? Frei himself, albeit in a slightly different context, recognized that this question is bound to be asked. In the course of his redescription of the Gospel narrative, he asked, 'Does the writer think Jesus had become identical with the Son of Man at some climactic point (e.g., the resurrection), whereas earlier he had not been?' Frei declared that we can only answer this question speculatively, and must simply affirm that the ambiguity (which is also an ambiguity about Jesus' relation to the Father) is 'real *within the story*'.[23] If we are to reject adoptionism, it will have to be according to resources and lines of argument that stand at one remove from the narrative itself, for in the narrative itself the question is not posed – or so Frei thought.

Nevertheless, Frei's account certainly seems to me to point in a non-adoptionist direction – although in saying this I recognize that I am going beyond Frei's explicit reserve. Self–manifestation description points to the ways in which a person emerges to public view in such a way as to reformat all the descriptions which have previously been repeatably ascribed to him or her. In Jesus' case, the Gospels present constant affirmations (made at all stages of the story from nativity to passion) that Jesus is the embodiment of Israel's hopes, that he is the representative of the Kingdom, that he is the promised Saviour. In the resurrection, it is these very affirmations which are confirmed in the action of God in raising Christ, are shown to be and to have been true in ways which are decisively transformed by the whole course which his life has taken. It does not make sense, in this context, to ask *when* these descriptions become true of Jesus: to say of Jesus that he is Saviour is to redescribe the whole course which his life has taken. Yes, in the resurrection, the connection of Jesus' hypostatic existence to God's action is made clear and evident; nevertheless, that episode in the narrative plays the part of a confirmation of Jesus' identity through the whole of his life: his identity as the one who has been sent by God to enact the good of humanity on its behalf.

Appendix 4

Barth and Overbeck

In a 1974 piece on 'German Theology: Transcendence and Secularity', Frei, writing for a non-theological audience, made a claim about Barth's 'secular sensibility' in deliberately provocative fashion, while concentrating on Barth's earliest post-liberal work:

> [W]hat Barth had said in his *Romans* commentary constituted a powerful affirmation of the transcendence of God ... This consignment of man and his world to a religionless existence was in its own theological way an affirmation and acceptance of the secularization of existence, of Nietzsche's famous words in *The Joyful Wisdom* that God is dead. Only an utterly transcendent God, one who when called existent is already turned into an idol, can be true God to a secular age, a secular world, a secular man.[24]

Provocative though this is, it is firmly based on detailed work that Frei had done in his thesis on Barth's ambivalent relationship to 'skepticism'. Referring to Feuerbach and, above all, Overbeck, Frei spoke of 'the service of skepticism to Christian theology' which consists in 'the indication of the absolutely insurmountable limits of humanity or creatureliness'.[25] In Overbeck in particular,

> There is a dim apprehension of last things, of the eschatological limit (death) and the limit of origin (*Urgeschichte*). As such they are strictly limiting concepts or negative images. They serve to initiate us into the mystery of our connectedness with ultimate destiny which must remain opaque in itself. It is the temptation of humanity to transform the positive scene that lies between these two borders, the historical ebb and flow, into a more or less positive clue to what lies beyond and to our relations with it. Against that temptation with its illusory optimism, the skeptic must stand with bold and final negation.[26]

Feuerbach, on the other hand, was more flat-footed than Overbeck, and failed to push his atheism 'to the thin edge where the radical denial and the radical affirmation of revelation would finally meet'.[27]

Overbeck's was not an idealist vision, in which each particular is shown to be absolutely dependent upon a context that utterly exceeds it, such that a relation to the absolute is given in and with every particular. For Overbeck, the limit with which we are faced is far more concrete, and far more insuperable. We are faced with the concrete existence of birth and of death, beyond which limits we cannot see.[28] All that we know between those limits is the 'ebb and flow of history' with its 'indefinite connectedness of secondary instrumentalities'.[29]

Barth, Frei argues, found that his positive theological vision pushed him towards a sensibility that, paradoxically, resembled Overbeck's sceptical vision. Frei, however, argues that the relationship of theology and secular sensibility was more ambiguous in this earlier post-liberal work than it was later to become. He describes Barth's appropriation of Overbeck in those years as 'a quasi-philosophical doctrine turned quasi-theological',[30] and suggests that it was 'a mixture too heady to last': it was not clear exactly what role this non-theological philosophy played with respect to thoroughly Christian theology.

Later, Frei discussed the shift from this earlier, more ambiguous work to the later clarity that I have described in chapter 7. He speaks of Barth's negotiation of his relationship with 'the radical, *autonomous* quest for meaning and self-understanding of modern despisers and, for that matter, non-despisers of religion' who believe that that 'simply as finite, yet autonomous human beings we are finally constituted as an insoluble question to ourselves'.[31] Only 'increasingly painstakingly, and then more and more decisively' did Barth manage clearly to articulate that 'the quest for self-understanding or ultimate meaning' is not an 'autonomous quest at all', but to be referred strictly 'to the distinctive judgment and saving grace of God in Jesus Christ as the sole encompassing context within which to reflect on all such matters'.[32] His *Romans* theology of absolute crisis left open the possibility (as we saw in chapter 2) that autonomous philosophical attention to the utter questionability of human existence might be a 'negative parable' of God's judgment;[33] later, he came to assert more clearly that even our utter questionability can only be properly demonstrated theologically.

Appendix 5

Frei and Story Theology

Particularly during the 1970s, Frei allowed himself to be quite lavishly rude about 'story theology', referring to it at one point as 'slack-jawed faddism'.[34] When asked to respond to a paper by John Zuck 'Tales of Wonder: Biblical Narrative, Myth, and Fairy-Stories', he wrote:

> We have all become aware of the latest fashion (I doubt not that it will be replaced soon) in making religion – including the bible – 'meaningful' to our students with the help of appropriate intellectual devices. It is all 'story' right now: We live, indeed we *are* stories, we have to tell stories about the meaningful moments in our lives; and this elemental, irreducible situation meets its kin in the exalted stories produced by the race which 'open up' the great (universal?) truths of the race. I don't knock it when it is done with power (Stephen Crites comes to mind). For all I know it may be the Rosetta Stone religious inquiry has been waiting for. All I know is that I was doing something very different which has nothing to do with this enterprise. But I'll admit that all along I dreaded that what I was doing would be confused with or at any rate incorporated under this heading. And now it has happened![35]

His most detailed attack, however, is found in his 1976 Greenhoe Lectures (1976h), where he devoted a fair portion of his time to the story theology 'fad'. It is, he suggests, simply one more variation of the kind of modern theology against which all his work protested:

> It perpetuates a tradition with which we have been familiar in theology – especially in Protestant theology and now in Catholic theology (since the Catholics, I think, are trying to recapitulate 175 years of Protestant theology in one decade for better or worse) – but especially in Protestant theology, for 175 years ever since Schleiermacher and Kant. In this tradition we have understood theology to be in some sense an expression of, or a report about, the religious character of man. And if one wants to talk about that, there are endless ways of doing it, but one way of doing it is to suggest that man is unique because he is a symbol-creating animal.

In this tradition, when theologians talk about God

> what we are doing above all is making a statement about the relationship between God and the religious man – let us simply say God and the human being. All statements about God are statements about the religious or limit situation, if

you will – about the relationship between God and man, rather than about God himself.

Story theology gives this tradition a particular spin:

> the story is itself the *relation* (our life story is in some sense a coded form of the way we experience the ultimate), and the story is itself the *code*. The story is not only the *shape* of the experience, the story is also the *verbal expression* of the experience.

This spin does not, however, permit story theology to evade Frei's standard criticism.

> What one finally has to say about this anthropology, this doctrine of man, in which man is basically and generally related to God, is that it finally speaks about a self that lies ineffably, for any expression, behind all expressions ... [O]ne asks about that mysterious self which is related to itself, and related to the ultimate, always through symbols, and cannot get in touch with itself directly in any other way.

This is relationalism. This is 'what Barth revolted against when he revolted against liberalism'. Frei was anything but a proponent of 'story theology'.

Notes

1. Frei finds this logic symbolized in the sequence in Luke, when the women are told by the angels at the tomb, 'Why do you look for the living among the dead?' One who had remained in the grave would by definition not be the one they were looking for (*The Identity of Jesus Christ*, 1975a, p. 148).
2. *Fides Quaerens Intellectum*, p. 41.
3. *The Identity of Jesus Christ* (1975a), p. 143.
4. *Fides Quaerens Intellectum*, p. 15.
5. Ibid.
6. *The Identity of Jesus Christ* (1975a), p. 5.
7. Ibid., p. 6.
8. Ibid., p. 5.
9. *Fides Quaerens Intellectum*, p. 24.
10. Ibid., p. 44
11. Ibid., pp. 25, 33, 46.
12. *The Doctrine of Revelation* (1956a), p. 195; 'Niebuhr's Theological Background' (*1957a*), p. 50.
13. *Fides Quaerens Intellectum*, p. 64.
14. *The Identity of Jesus Christ* (1975a), p. 155.
15. Ibid., p. 157.
16. *Han Frei and Karl Barth*, p. x, Demson's emphasis.
17. Ibid., p. 110.
18. 'Remarks in Connection with a Theological Proposal' (1967b), p. 32.
19. See 'The Theology of H. Richard Niebuhr' (*1957b*), pp. 104–16 and The Humanities Council Lectures (1987c), pp. 143–46.
20. 'The Theology of H. Richard Niebuhr' (*1957b*), p. 111.
21. 'Theological Reflections' (*1966a*), p. 62, Frei's emphasis.
22. The Humanities Council Lectures (1987c), p. 137.

23. *The Identity of Jesus Christ (1975a)*, p. 135.
24. 'German Theology' (*1974b*), p. 105.
25. *The Doctrine of Revelation* (1956a), pp. 469–70.
26. Ibid., p. 470.
27. Ibid., p. 368.
28. Once again, Feuerbach proves less radical. He did not do justice to the fact that when confronted by 'actual evil and the reality of death' we find ourselves in the hands of powers beyond 'our unconverted hearts' (ibid., p. 367).
29. Ibid., p. 470.
30. 'German Theology' (*1974b*), p. 105.
31. 'The Availability of Karl Barth' (*1978g*), pp. 152–55, especially p. 153.
32. Ibid., pp. 153–54.
33. For a fuller description of the role of scepticism in Barth's earliest post-liberal work, see Frei's description of Barth's debt to biblical realism, religious socialism, and scepticism in *The Doctrine of Revelation* (1956a), pp. 150–73, 361–410, 467–504.
34. Review of Eberhard Busch's biography of Karl Barth, *Religious Education* version (*1978j*), p. 728.
35. Letter to Ray L. Hart (1976a), pp. 3–4.

Bibliography

1 Primary Sources: Annotated Bibliography

In preparing this book I have made use of Frei's published writings, of materials from the Hans W. Frei archive located at Yale Divinity School, of reviews of Frei's work (complete with his own annotations) from the collection of Geraldine Frei, and of two unpublished works that are not in the Yale archive, a copy of one of which was passed to me by Charles Campbell (?1960a), and of the other by Mark Alan Bowald (1974d).

The following bibliography includes all the writings I have used (including several that I have not, in the end, cited) but it is not complete: there are, in particular, many more materials (particularly letters and lecture notes) in the Yale archive. A full hand-list of materials in that archive can be found at www.library.yale.edu/div/div076.htm. That hand-list also contains links to online transcriptions of various materials from the archive. However, although I have not aimed at completeness, I have decided to include in the following bibliography reference to several missing papers or lectures, several of which I have tried without success to unearth, in the slight hope that someone with access to some record of one or other of them might end up reading this bibliography, perhaps after having packed this book by mistake for a long-haul flight. Such items are indicated by a date in square brackets.

Note on Letters and Titles

The list includes several of the drafts and copies of Frei's letters which can be found in the Yale archive. As it is not always possible to distinguish a copy of a letter actually sent from a draft for a letter that was altered before being sent, the details I give, and the texts I quote, will not always match the letters Frei's correspondents received.

I have given several items from the archive titles of my own invention (rather than referring to them as 'Untitled notes on various topics' or similar) and have taken the liberty of using those titles in the body of the book. The bibliography entries for those items below give the game away in all such cases.

243

Datable Material

1956a   *The Doctrine of Revelation in the Thought of Karl Barth, 1909–1922: The Nature of Barth's Break with Liberalism*, unpublished PhD, Yale University. Sections published in *1957a*, pp. 40–53, and in *Ten Year Commemoration to the Life of Hans Frei (1922–1988)*, ed. Giorgy Olegovich (New York: Semenenko Foundation, 1999), pp. 103–87.

The thesis has three chapters. The first is a general tracing of Barth's development from 1909 to the beginning of the *Church Dogmatics*. The second is a history of nineteenth-century theology from the vantage point of Barth's work, covering Hegel, Schleiermacher, Ritschl, Kähler, Herrmann, Fritz Barth and others. The third chapter asks what continuity Barth's work has with relationalism, with Overbeck's scepticism, with the Blumhardts' Biblical Realism, and with religious socialism. The conclusion poses questions about whether Barth manages to do justice to human freedom and about Christocentrism, but rather more subtly than has sometimes been the case. The extract published in the Olegovich volume is eccentrically and drastically edited. See chap. 2, and Appendix 4.

1957a   'Niebuhr's Theological Background', in *Faith and Ethics: The Theology of H. Richard Niebuhr*, ed. Paul Ramsey (New York: Harper and Row, 1957), pp. 9–64.

1957b   'The Theology of H. Richard Niebuhr', in *Faith and Ethics*, pp. 65–116.

These essays began life as a paper delivered in August 1956 in the presence of George F. Thomas. Frei describes them in the introduction to 1978k. *1957a* pp. 40–53 = 1956a pp. 174–202 with minor changes. There are sections on 'Niebuhr's Theological Concerns', 'The Academic Tradition in Nineteenth-Century Protestant Theology', 'Revelation and Theological Method in the Theology of Karl Barth' and 'The Relation of Faith and History in the Thought of Ernst Troeltsch' in *1957a*, and 'Niebuhr and the Problem of Theological Method', 'The Doctrine of God' and 'Christology' in *1957b*. See chap. 1, §2; chap. 2, §4; chap. 3, §1.

1958a   'Religion: Natural and Revealed', in *A Handbook of Christian Theology: Definition Essays on Concepts and Movements of Thought in Contemporary Protestantism*, ed. Arthur A. Cohen and Marvin Halverson (Nashville: Abingdon, 1958), pp. 310–21.

The volume also contains essays by Frei's colleague George Lindbeck. There are sections on 'Definition', 'History' and 'Contemporary Discussion', the latter divided into three sub-topics:

theology and philosophy, revelation and history, and Christian faith and human culture. It contains some concise material on Barth.

?1960a 'Analogy and the Spirit in the Theology of Karl Barth'.

An unpublished 27-page typescript, which I tentatively date to the late 1950s or early 60s: in style it resembles Frei's thesis (1956a) more than any other of his writings; Frei quotes the English translation of *Church Dogmatics* II/1 (1957) on pp. 9–10; some of the content resembles 'Religion: Natural and Revealed' (*1958a*); the introduction (p. 1) is phrased in such a way as to suggest that it was written before Barth's death in 1968; and Frei (p. 1) mis-attributes the phrase 'God-intoxicated man' to Herder (as in *The Doctrine of Revelation* [1956a], p. 555, but unlike his correct attribution to Novalis in 'Karl Barth: Theologian' [1969a], p. 171). I obtained my copy through Charles A. Campbell, who draws on it in his book *Preaching Jesus*. See chap. 2, §3.

1965a 'Feuerbach and Theology', paper delivered at the Annual Meeting of the American Academy of Religion, Vanderbilt University, in December; published in *Journal of the American Academy of Religion* 35.3 (1967), pp. 250–56.

Atheism is no one thing, and Humean atheism differs from, and is more interesting than, Feuerbachian atheism. Marx is more interesting than either. The essay contains an early stab at understanding the place of David Friedrich Strauss. Cf. Appendix 4.

1966a 'Theological Reflections on the Accounts of Jesus' Death and Resurrection', *Christian Scholar* 49.4 (winter), pp. 263–306; republished in *TN*, pp. 45–93.

The first publication in what I have been calling Frei's 'Christology project'. It was followed by a longer, slightly popularized version (*1967a*). Both versions were commented upon in 1967b. Finally, the *1967a* version was republished as *The Identity of Jesus Christ* (*1975a*) with a new Preface (1974i) and a concluding meditation (?1974f). See chap. 3 and chap. 5.

1967a 'The Mystery of the Presence of Jesus Christ', *Crossroads: An Adult Education Magazine of the Presbyterian Church* 17.2 (Jan.–Mar.), pp. 69–96; 17.3 (Apr.–Jun.), pp. 69–96.

Cf. *1966a*. The journal is defunct and obscure, and it is very difficult to get hold of this now, but the differences between it and *1975a* are nearly all cosmetic. The final chapter adds a significant pneumatological, ecclesiological and political reflection to the argument of *1966a*. See chaps. 3, 4 and 5.

1967b 'Remarks in Connection with a Theological Proposal', paper delivered at Harvard Divinity School, December; published in *TN*, pp. 26–44.

Cf annotation to *1966a* for the relationship of this paper to *1966a* and *1967a*. See chap. 5, §§2 and 4.

1968a   Review of Jürgen Moltmann, *The Theology of Hope* (New York: Harper & Row, 1967), *Union Seminary Quarterly Review* 23.3 (spring), pp. 267–72.

Frei praises Moltmann for 'recapturing the dimension of history for theological purposes' (p. 267) but then criticizes him for doing that in the sense of proclaiming that history is 'the dialectic of an all-encompassing historical process, comprehending events and cultural perspectives' (p. 271).

1969a   'Karl Barth: Theologian', in *Karl Barth and the Future of Theology: A Memorial Colloquium Held at the Yale Divinity School, January 28, 1969*, ed. David L. Dickerman, Yale Divinity School Association, pp. 1–14, 28–29, 45–64; republished in *Reflection* 66.4 (May 1969), pp. 5–9; republished in *TN*, pp. 167–76.

The earlier publication does not differ significantly from the later – except that the transcripts of the discussion following the presentation of the paper were included in the earlier version, including contributions from Frei on pp. 13–14, 28–29 and 45–64. See chap. 7, §2.

1970a   'Barth, Karl', in *Encyclopaedia Britannica* (Chicago: William Benton), vol. III, pp. 204–205.

I suspect that, as is the way with encyclopaedic publications, these articles were written some time before 1970 – and quite possibly before Barth's death in 1968. Frei concentrates on the Barth of *Romans*, and gestures towards the criticisms of Barth he had made in the conclusion to 1956a.

1970b   'Ritschl, Albrecht', in *Encyclopaedia Britannica* (Chicago: William Benton), vol. XIX, p. 352.

Describes Ritschl as one who had 'little feeling for the element of mystery in religion and no dread of a divine judgment', and who failed 'to do justice to the subtle interweaving of Christian with general human history and culture'.

1972a   'Contemporary Christian Thought', bibliography and lecture notes for course RS23a, fall (YDS 13–197).

In the bibliography, Frei's recommendations for purchase were books by Bultmann, Feuerbach, John Hick, Kierkegaard, H. Richard Niebuhr, Reinhold Niebuhr, Paul Tillich and Heinrich Zahrnt. Interestingly, in his longer list he recommends only *Against the Stream*, *CD* II/1 and *CD* III/2 of Barth's works. The lecture on Barth, dated Tuesday 24 Oct. contrasts Barth's understanding of the cognitive nature of revelation with H. Richard Niebuhr among others; that on Thursday 16 Nov. discusses Barth's understanding of the revelation of God in himself, as subject who defines all his predicates, as act, as 'nature' and 'spirit', as love, as free. See Appendix 3.

[1972b]　Lecture at Stanford University, December.
　　　　Mentioned in a letter to Wayne Meeks, 5 Jun. 1973 (YDS 3–65).

[1972c]　Lecture to Graduate Theological Union, December.
　　　　Mentioned in a letter to Wayne Meeks, 5 Jun. 1973 (YDS 3–65).

1973a　Letter to John Schutz, 16 Jan. (YDS 4–90).
　　　　Includes comments on the literary criticism of the Gospels, and some more positive comments on a focus on parable than one might expect. 'The ancient device of trying in literary fashion to parallel the parabolic mode of teaching with the biographical stretch in the latter half of the gospels, and the theme of discipleship, has always appeared to me to be a task worth pursuing, not so much in order to find a common theme for content as a possibly common structure.'

1973b　'Herder', lecture notes from an unidentified course, Feb. (YDS 18–271).
　　　　Having drawn his 21 Feb lecture from the section on Herder in *The Eclipse of Biblical Narrative* (1974a), Frei's 26 Feb. lecture deals with Herder's identification of the 'realistic spirit' in the Bible.

[1973c]　'Biblical Narrative and Literary Sensibility', Matthew Vassar Lecture, Vassar College, 23 Apr.
　　　　Mentioned in a letter to Wayne Meeks, 5 Jun. 1973 (YDS 3–65).

1973d　Abstract of *The Eclipse of Biblical Narrative* (1974a), 7 Aug. (YDS 8–140).
　　　　The abstract looks like an official one for the publishers, and emphasizes the 'broader cultural factors' which shaped the eclipse.

1973e　Letter to Larry K. Nelson, 14 Aug. (YDS 3–68).
　　　　Contains some reflections on 'ad hoc apologetics', and an attack on anthropologically based apologetics in general.

1973f　'Preface', 22 Oct., published in *The Eclipse of Biblical Narrative* (1974a), pp. vii–ix.
　　　　Frei apologizes for writing an essay in 'the almost legendary category of analysis of analyses of the Bible in which not a single text is examined, not a single exegesis undertaken'.

1973g   Letter to Wayne Meeks, 24 Oct. (YDS 3–65).

Both *Eclipse*, and the 'German Theology' article (*1974b*), had been completed. Frei gives Meeks some instructions on reading them: to read *Eclipse* first, then to read 'Theological Reflections' (*1966a*) and 'The Mystery of the Presence of Jesus Christ' (*1967a*) (although 'I have retreated some distance from the views I held at that time') and then to read 'Remarks in Connection with a Theological Proposal' (1967b) and 'German Theology' (*1974b*).

1974a   *The Eclipse of Biblical Narrative: A Study in Eighteenth and Nineteenth Century Hermeneutics* (New Haven: Yale University Press).

The book had been completed by October 1973 (see 1973f and 1973g). See chap. 6.

1974b   'German Theology: Transcendence and Secularity', in *Postwar German Culture: An Anthology*, ed. Charles E. McClelland and Steven P. Scher (New York: E.P. Dutton), pp. 98–112.

The article had been completed by October 1973 (according to 1973g). See Appendix 4.

1974c   'Religious Transformation in the Later Eighteenth Century', the Rockwell Lectures, Rice University, Texas, February (YDS 10–168, 13–198).

The three lectures were scheduled as 1974c(i) 'Lessing and the Religious Use of Irony', 1974c(ii) 'Kant and the Transcendence of Rationalism and Religion', and [1974c(iii)] 'Herder and the New Humanism'. Drafts for the first two exist: a 59-page MS in YDS 10–168 (cannibalized as the basis of 1978k). The second is, I suspect, found in a 19-page MS in YDS 13–198. The third appears not to exist, but there is the possibility that it never did: it would not be the only time that Frei had written lectures on the hoof, and had to curtail his ambitions as he ran out of time. A 7 May letter to Wayne Meeks (YDS 3–65) suggests that Frei managed to reach Herder; but deletions of references to Herder on the manuscript suggest otherwise. There are many manuscript additions to the Lessing material in YDS 10–168 which appear to intervene between it and 1978k. Frei started to prepare the lectures for publication by LSU Press, and I suspect that most if not all of these MS additions come from the next couple of years. See chap. 8, §1.

1974d   'Scripture as Realistic Narrative: Karl Barth as Critic of Historical Criticism', lecture to Karl Barth Society of North America, Toronto (spring).

Frei spoke from notes rather than from a full text, but the lecture was taped, and a transcription has been made by Mark

Alan Bowald. It contains an explanation of Frei's understanding of Barth's hermeneutical procedure and his stance towards historical claims; it also contains a fine description of Barth's Anselmian and Dantesque sensibility. A large portion of the talk is spent commenting on Barth's hermeneutical remarks prefacing his reading of Numbers 13 and 14 in *Church Dogmatics* IV/2. See chap. 7.

[1974e] Lecture at Episcopal Seminary of the Southwest (March).
On various nineteenth-century figures including Ritschl. I have been unable to discover more.

?1974f 'A Meditation for the Week of Good Friday and Easter', published in *The Identity of Jesus Christ (1975a)*, pp. 168–73.
This and 1974i were added to *1967a* when it was republished as *Identity (1975a)*.

[1974g] Lecture at the University of North Carolina at Chapel Hill (April).
Mentioned in a 7 May letter to Wayne Meeks (YDS 3–65). I have been unable to discover more.

1974h 'Author's Abstract Form', 10 May (YDS 8–140).
An abstract of *Eclipse* submitted to the *Journal of Modern History*. The reasons for the eclipse are given as '(1) the Bible's entanglement in the general preoccupation with the relation of religious beliefs to historical fact claims and (2) the lack of contact between the study of the Bible as writing and contemporary developments in literary realism, such as the novel and its study'.

1974i 'Preface', 19 Jul., published in *The Identity of Jesus Christ (1975a)* pp. vii–xviii.
The Preface shows the extent to which Frei's attitude towards some aspects of *1967a* had cooled. See chap. 8, §3.

1974j Letter to Robert Krieg, 24 Jul. (YDS 2–51).
Some comments on a proposal for a dissertation on Barth made by Fr Krieg. 'I agree that the truth issue is important to Barth, but would remind you that it is a purely technical issue and not a matter of doubt to be overcome or of explanation for a shift from non-belief to belief.' The letter also contains some interesting comments on Barth's procedure as a mixture of personal address and conceptual description – shifting gradually from the former to the latter. See chap. 8, §4.

1974k Letter to Elisabeth Hilke, 5 Aug. (YDS 2–42).
The typescript in YDS is incomplete. The letter consists of comments upon an essay by Hilke in which she compared Barth with Wittgenstein and Austin. Frei argues here against taking Barth in too purely 'grammatical' a way, and argues that he must be seen

as having some kind of 'correspondence' understanding of truth – albeit of a rather peculiar kind. See chap. 8, §7.

1974l   'Herder as Cultural Linguistic Theologian', lecture notes for unidentified course, 10 Oct. (YDS 18–271).

Frei gives as a heading, 'New lecture beginning Herder as linguistic–cultural theorist: Language as clue to him and to difference between Romantics like him and Rationalists like Lessing'.

1975a   *The Identity of Jesus Christ: The Hermeneutical Bases of Dogmatic Theology* (Philadelphia: Fortress Press).

The publication of *1967a* with minor amendments, preceded by 1974i and followed by ?1974f. See chaps. 3, 4 and 5.

?1975b   Review of James Barr's *The Bible in the Modern World* (New York: Harper & Row, 1973), several drafts (YDS 10–160).

Quite a positive review, particularly in its estimate of Barr's criticism of 'biblical theology', and the complexity and reticence of his positive suggestions. I have been unable to discover whether or where it was published, and have chosen my date on the basis of Frei's reference to David Kelsey's 1975 *The Uses of Scripture in Recent Theology*.

1975c   'The Foot Soldiers of the Enlightenment' (my title), 7 Apr., *Yale Alumni Magazine*, 38.8 (May 1975), pp. 22–23.

A short piece on the Enlightenment figures represented in the collections of Sterling Library. YDS 12–88 contains a typescript dated 7 April. See chap. 8, §2.

[1975d]   Talk on *The Identity of Jesus Christ* (*1975a*) and *The Eclipse of Biblical Narrative* (*1974a*) (April).

Frei gave a talk on his two books at Princeton in April: I have been unable to discover more about it.

1975e   Letter to Leander Keck, 22 May (YDS 3–52).

Contains comments on the relation of history-likeness to history, with reference to *Identity*. 'Since my conviction is that in the "logic" of the Christian faith the connection [between history-likeness and history] would have to be made at the crucifixion–resurrection sequence I see no way, again as a theologian, to do it except by way of the kind of "ontological" argumentation I suggest: Seeing who Christians believe Jesus is, they are bound to believe him to have been raised.' See also chap. 1, §1; cf. Appendix 1.

1975f   Letter to Gilbert Meilaender, 3 Jun. (YDS 3–62).

Describes, in relation to Meilaender's questions about *The Identity of Jesus Christ* (*1975a*), a worry that Frei may be going too far in his rejection of categories like 'estrangement' and 'alienation'.

1975g 'Notes for an Oral History', 16 Aug., Woolverton Papers, Bishop Payne Library, Virginia Theological Seminary.

 John Woolverton conducted an interview with Frei. Extracts can be found in Woolverton's article 'Hans W. Frei in Context'. I make use of it in the Introduction.

1975h 'Modernity as Temptation: Compromise in the Reaction to New Religious Ideas in the Enlightenment', proposal for a 1976 National Endowment for the Humanities Summer School (YDS 3–69).

 Frei's seminar was to cover Locke, Butler, Wesley, Rousseau, Lessing, Kant and Ezra Stiles.

1976a Letter to Ray L. Hart, 12 Jan. (YDS 2–36).

 Having seen a draft of John Zuck's article, 'Tales of Wonder: Biblical Narrative, Myth, and Fairy-Stories' (later published in *Journal of the American Academy of Religion* 44, June 1976, pp. 299–308), Frei sets out his defences against Zuck's reading of *Eclipse* on myth. See Appendix 5.

1976b Curriculum Vitae (Feb.).

 This updated CV lists, under 'Writing in Progress or Projected', 'A book on *German Religious Thought between Enlightenment and Romanticism: Aesthetics, Language and Religious Thought in Lessing, Kant and Herder* (based on the Rockwell Lectures at Rice University, delivered 1974, to be published by LSU Press)' and gives the first mention of the article on Strauss (*1985c*), at this stage called 'Strauss, Baur, and the Rise of Biblical Criticism'. The last page of this CV is a manuscript addition, and contains a brief description of Frei's teaching interests, headed, 'Modern Western Religious and Christian Thought': '(1) The history of the discussions between the critics of Christianity and its defenders, from the Enlightenment to the present, chiefly in Europe; (2) The history of the emergence of the concept "religion" to describe a distinctive phenomenon, beginning with the early nineteenth century and the discussion of claims to the meaningfulness and truth of religion; (3) Philosophical and theological hermeneutics from the Reformation to the present; (4) Analysis of modern Christian theological assumptions, concepts, systems, controversies; their setting in believing, worshipping communities and in diverse cultural contexts.'

1976c Letter to William Placher, 24 Mar. (YDS 4–78).

 Frei talks a bit about *The Identity of Jesus Christ* (*1975a*), in response to a draft of an article by Placher. He says, 'My own mind has changed on a number of issues, partially under the impact of that terribly persuasive book by David Kelsey. At the broadest level

I think I shaped too small a "world" to do justice to the scope and variety of a Christian vision.'

1976d　Notes on Maurice Wiles' Review of *The Identity of Jesus Christ*, *Journal of Theological Studies* 27, pp. 261–62 (April 1976) (GF).

Frei scribbled responses in the margins of a photocopy of this review. See chap. 8, §6 and chap. 4, §1.

1976e　Letter to Van Harvey, 22 Jun. (YDS 2–36) .

Comments on Harvey's 'A Christology for Barabbases'. See chap. 1, §1.

1976f　Letter to Denis Nineham, 1 Jul. (YDS 3–68).

A response to Nineham's review of *The Eclipse of Biblical Narrative* in *Theology*, containing a brief restatement of the argument.

1976g　Notes on Leslie Brisman's Review of *The Eclipse of Biblical Narrative* and *The Identity of Jesus Christ*, *Comparative Literature* 28.4 (fall 1976), pp. 368–72 (GF).

Another example of marginal annotation. Cf. 1976d.

1976h　'On Interpreting the Christian Story', the 10th Annual Greenhoe Lectureship, Louisville Seminary, LPTS Audio Cassette (Cass. Greenhoe, 1976).

The lectures were 1976h(i) 'Story, Fact and Mystery: A Reflection on the New Testament' and 1976h(ii) 'Interpretation and Devotion: God's Presence for us in Jesus Christ'. Frei attacks story theology, and returns to the subject matter of both *Eclipse* and *Identity*, the latter in a more explicitly Wittgensteinian vein. Frei comments on the lectures in 1976i, describing them as an attempt to push the project of *Identity* a little further. See chap. 8, §3.

1976i　Letter to the Mausers, 10 Nov. (YDS 3–61).

Frei says that he is engaged in trying to push the project of *The Identity of Jesus Christ* a little further, both by working on the exegesis of the parables, and by taking further his 'Wittgensteinian' reflections. The Greenhoe lectures (1976h, for which the Mausers were his hosts) concentrated on the latter development. See chap. 8, §3.

1976j　Review of Eberhard Busch, *Karl Barth: His Life from Letters and Autobiographical Texts* (Philadelphia: Fortress Press, 1976), *New Review of Books and Religion* 1 (December 1976), p. 6.

Frei wrote several different versions of his book review, of which this is the shortest. See also *1978g*, *1978j* and *1981j*.

?1976k　Notes on typescript of Paul W. Meyer, *The Justification of Jesus* (Shaffer Lectures, Feb. 1976), pp. 46–61 (YDS 22–303).

Some fairly extensive scribblings in the margins and on the cover of Meyer's typescript. On the cover is a long note in which Frei suggests that 'neglect of the issue of Jesus in historical and faith judgments' may simply be a putting off of an inevitable reckoning. See chap. 1, §1.

?1976l 'Theological Hermeneutics', lecture notes (YDS 13–201).

Rough notes for another undergraduate lecture course which ran in 1976 and 1978. Frei at one point writes: 'My own agenda: (a) Relative unity of canon; (b) Narrative Sense; (c) Unity of Testaments'.

1977a Letter to 'Jane', 15 Feb. (YDS 1-4).

A very favourable reader's report on 'Lewis White Beck's essays on Kant', which Frei introduces by saying of himself that, 'in the company of historians I always insist that I am a theologian but when thrown with theologians I identify myself as a historian. I deny that this is either evasive or confused because under all circumstances I am clear about one fact: I am *not* a philosopher.'

1977b Letter to Theodore Runyon, 13 May (YDS 4–81).

Frei discusses, in passing, David Tracy's *Blessed Rage for Order*, speaking of Tracy as 'clearly the most important constructive theologian in America in [his] general age range' – but of there being a 'sobering derivativeness about Tracy's scholarship and argumentation, and finally a simple-mindedness that is the heavy price of systematic coherence'.

1977c Letter to the Claytons, 12 Jun. (YDS 1–14).

Frei explains where he has got to in his work on 'Strauss and Baur' (which was to become *1985c*). It is clear from this letter that Frei was already moving in the direction of a far more social and cultural history – and that he was already beginning to form the ideas on the bureaucratization of the German universities and its impact upon German academic attempts to locate Jesus. See chap. 8, §1.

1977d Letter to Gerald Sheppard, 19 Jun. (YDS 4–86).

Gerald Sheppard had clearly discussed with Frei the possibility that he might apply for a chair in Systematic Theology in Union Seminary. Frei replies that he does not wish to, and gives as his main reason that he thinks of himself only secondarily as a systematic theologian, and primarily as a scholar and teacher of Religious Studies.

?1978a 'Modern Christian Thought, 1650–1830' and 'Modern Christian Thought, 1830–1950', lecture notes (YDS 14–211).

Frei taught this course from 1978 to 1988, and the YDS archive has many related texts (from YDS 14–211 to 16–249), including a transcript of the 1981 version of some of the lectures (1981l); some student lecture notes from 1983, and many versions of Frei's own notes, including what I take to be the 1978 version, and what is certainly the 1988 version (1988b). A rich history of modern theology could be compiled from these notes by a patient editor; I have only looked in detail at the 1978 and 1988 versions. These 1978 lectures begin with a discussion of 'sensibility'.

1978b   Letter to Richard Marius, 6 Jan. (YDS 3–61).
After an aside about having 'a pretty difficult time thinking that the suffering god has much reality to him', Frei spends a short while explaining the senses in which he is and is not a Christian. See chap. 8, §2.

[1978c]   Presentation at Union Theological Seminary, 19 Jan.
Frei discusses his presentation in a Feb. letter to Donald Shriver (YDS 4–86), mentioning only that he worries he gave 'the impression of trying to knock David Tracy'.

[1978d]   'Grace, Faith and Praxis: The Evangelical Strand in Modern Theology', Michalson Lecture, Claremont, 7 Mar.
Discussed in a 30 May letter to Gordon Michalson, Jr (YDS 3–67). The talk was apparently about evangelical theology as a language game with its own integrity, about Kierkegaard as one who betrays that integrity in his talk of 'grace', about Schubert Ogden who betrays talk of grace by reducing it to something else, and about Barth who stands between the two, and gets grace about right.

1978e   Letter to Charles M. Wood, 21 Mar. (YDS 5–108).
Frei wavers between calling himself an historian or a theologian. See chap. 8, §1.

1978f   Letter to Charles M. Wood, 2 Jun. (YDS 5–108).
Includes some comments on 'imagination', and Frei's caution with regard to it as a theological category.

1978g   'The Availability of Karl Barth', review article on Eberhard Busch, *Karl Barth: His Life from Letters and Autobiographical Texts* (Philadelphia: Fortress Press, 1976), *Virginia Seminary Journal* 30 (July), pp. 42–46; reprinted as 'An Afterword: Eberhard Busch's Biography of Karl Barth', in *Karl Barth in Re-view*, ed. H. Martin Rumscheidt (Pittsburgh: Pickwick Press, 1981), pp. 95–116; reprinted again in *TCT*, pp. 147–63 as 'Eberhard Busch's Biography of Karl Barth'.

1978h speaks of this review as recently finished. The review takes some of the ideas which Frei had canvassed in 1974c, and runs a little further with them, looking at the way in which Barth provides a 'fragmentary, piecemeal description or redescription of the temporal world of eternal grace' making clear that this is no 'as-if' fictional world, but is 'the one common world in which we all live and move and have our being'. Frei later delivered a lecture based on this article at Hendrix College, 6 or 7 Mar. 1981. There are also some rough notes for this review in YDS 9–149, in which Frei speaks of Barth as 'violently passionately other-worldly', having 'an extraordinary imagination which inhabited a world limned out by the Bible', and at the same time an 'utterly this-worldly realist', who 'believed profoundly these two were one and the same world'. This is a 'critical, post-modern orthodoxy'. See Appendix 4; chap. 7, §2.

1978h   Letter to William Placher, 21 Jul. (YDS 4–75).
         'I really don't know on what grounds I justify the claim that the narratives are true. I suppose by authority or something like it ... I am not sure what kind of truth affirmation I think theological assertions make. All I know is that theology is a second-order discipline on a distinctive language game.' See chap. 8, §7.

[1978i] Colloquium on *The Identity of Jesus Christ* (*1975a*) and *The Eclipse of Biblical Narrative* (*1974a*), Emory University (Candler School of Theology), 7–8 Nov.
         I have been unable to discover more about this.

1978j Review of Eberhard Busch, *Karl Barth: His Life from Letters and Autobiographical Texts* (Philadelphia: Fortress Press, 1976), *Religious Education* 73.6 (Nov./Dec. 1978), pp. 728–29.
         Cf. *1976j*, *1978g* and *1981j*. A typescript of this review can be found in YDS 10–162. See Appendix 5.

1978k   'Is Religious Sensibility Accessible to Study? The Case of G.E. Lessing', the first annual George F. Thomas Memorial Lecture, Princeton, 1 Dec. (YDS 10–168).
         The YDS archive contains a confusing welter of drafts reworking some of the material from the Rockwell Lectures (1974c), leading to a clean typescript of a large section of this lecture. The typescript includes introductory comments from Paul Ramsey, and a fresh introduction in which Frei discusses the discipline of Religious Studies, and spends some pages in working out what the object of study of historical research in Religious Studies might be.

1979a   Letter to John Hollar, 12 Jun. (YDS 2–38).
         Clearly someone had suggested that a translation of Ebeling's *Dogmatics* be produced, and John Hollar of Fortress Press had

asked Frei for his opinion. Frei's reply is detailed, and ambivalent, and interesting for its resurrection of the term 'relationalism'.

1979b   Letter from Terry Foreman to Brooks Holifield, 3 Sep. (YDS 2–28).

Not, strictly speaking, a writing by Frei – but a summary of points made by Frei in conversation, complete with some marginal annotations from Frei confirming Foreman's interpretation. The letter discusses a proposed American Academy of Religion (AAR) History of Modern Christianity session, set to involve Holifield, Frei, Marilyn Chapin Massey and John Stroup that coming November, for which Frei had suggested the title 'Beyond Intellectual History'. See chap. 8, §3.

1979c   Letter to Van Harvey, 24 Sep. (YDS 2–39).

'My ambition is really to write a history of modern Christology, but to do so utilizing recent reworkings of intellectual history and the history of what – for lack of a better term – I'll call "sensibility".' Cf. chap. 8, §1.

[1979d] Lecture on the Third Reich, Lay School of Religion, October.

I have been unable to discover more about this.

?1979e   'Conceptual Clarification and Sensibility Description' (my title) (YDS 11–182).

The paper is dated 1979–80, but I have been unable to confirm the occasion on which it was delivered. It may well have been at the December AAR meeting, but probably not in the seminar described in 1979b. The talk mentions an 'inexcusably pompous title', but no title is given on the typescript, and I have substituted my own. The talk is particularly illuminating on Frei's turn away from intellectual history and towards something which would include 'low culture' as well. Cf. chap. 8, §1.

1979f   Letter to William Placher, 19 Dec. (YDS 4–78).

Frei described a recent paper – ?1979e, perhaps: 'My paper was really an expression of agreement with and admiration for several attempts I am watching that try to integrate the history of doctrine with the history of sensibility and explore the latter by way of its connection with social structures and institutions rather than by assuming it to be an expression of a general, hypostatised atmosphere of an era (e.g., "secularity").' The letter also contains, a propos of a proposal that Placher should write a piece on Frei for an issue of the *Historical Magazine of the Protestant Episcopal Church* on 'recent Anglican theologians', a description of his ambivalence about calling himself a systematic theologian. Cf. chap. 8, §2.

1980a   'Hans F. Holocaust Testimony', Fortunoff Video Archive for Holocaust Testimonies, Yale University Library (HVT-170).

To quote the Archive catalogue: 'Videotape testimony of Hans F., who was born in 1922, the youngest of three children, into an assimilated family in Breslau, and moved to Berlin at the age of seven. He is now a professor of Religious Studies and much of his testimony is suffused with a psycho-historical critique of the topics he discusses. From his personal experience, Professor F. tells of his early politicization; his parents' fear for the family; his education in England, where he became a religious Christian (while his father, still in Germany, renounced his own conversion and returned to Judaism as a political protest;) and of the secularized Jews he encountered in the Washington Heights section of New York, where he and his parents lived after emigrating from Germany. He speaks of his discovery of his Jewish heritage through his Christian experiences, and the difficulty of harmonizing in oneself the secular/Christian with the cultural/religious traditions of Judaism. Professor F. pays particular attention to the insidious appeal and powerful organization of the Nazi program and asserts his belief in the necessity to bear witness.'

1980b   Letter to John Woolverton, 23 Jan. (YDS 5–109).

Frei belittles his claim to be called a 'theologian', and queries the extent to which he counts as an Anglican – something that has been ambivalent since his time in Austin. Cf. chap. 8, §2.

1980c   Letter to Van Harvey, 3 Apr. (YDS 2–39).

Frei thanks Harvey for supporting his application for a Guggenheim grant, which was to take Frei to England a little later on. 'I'm going to try and retool a little bit and learn to do a modicum of social history. I may try it out on a parish or two in England, if successful.' Cf. chap. 8, §2.

1980d   Letter to Bruce Piersault, 8 Jul. (YDS 4–75).

'No, Eclipse was not influenced by the deconstructionists; I was far too unwashed literarily to know what they or even their predecessors were up to at that point. On the contrary, I was really naively persuaded that there was such a thing as a normative meaning to a narrative text, if not to others. Since then I've become a bit more jaded under their influence, but still feel like digging in my heels rather than celebrating Nietzsche's wild relativistic rhetoric accompanied by Heidegger's pompous obbligato.' See chap. 8, §4.

?1980e   Review of Hans Dieter Betz (ed.), *The Bible as a Document of the University* (Missoula: Scholar's Press, 1980) (YDS 10–161).

YDS only has an incomplete draft, which contains brief comments on Ebeling, Barr and Ricoeur (with little critical content) and breaks off in the middle of some comments on Ricoeur. I have been unable to discover if and when it was published.

?1981a   'The Formation of German Religious Thought in the Passage from Enlightenment to Romanticism', lecture notes for course RS371b (YDS 13–199).

Lectures on Lessing, Herder, Kant and Schleiermacher. The course certainly ran until 1981, and the notes include a 1981 exam paper, but Frei may have written the lectures considerably earlier – when preparing his proposed book on *German Religious Thought between Enlightenment and Romanticism: Aesthetics, Language and Religious Thought in Lessing, Kant and Herder* after the Rockwell lectures (1974c), for instance. See chap. 1, §3.

?1981b   Notes on Erich Auerbach (YDS 13–199).

These notes are included in a pad which also contains lecture notes for ?1981a. Even if those lectures are from the early 1970s, these notes cannot be from Frei's first reading of Auerbach in 1964.

?1981c   'Historical Reference and the Gospels: A Response to a Critique of *The Identity of Jesus Christ*' (my title) (YDS 13–199).

These notes are included in the papers for ?1981a, and so may well come from the mid-1970s rather than 1981. They are a response to an unidentified article on *The Identity of Jesus Christ* (1975a), and deal at some length, and with a conversational clarity uncommon in Frei's more formal writings, with questions about the historicity of the Gospel narratives and the nature of Frei's claims about the resurrection. Cf. chap. 8, §7.

?1981d   Review of Wendelgard von Staden's *Darkness Over The Valley: Growing Up in Nazi Germany* (New York: Ticknor and Fields, 1981) (YDS 10–166).

YDS has only an incomplete manuscript draft. I have been unable to discover whether or where this was published.

[1981e]   'D.F. Strauss on Christology: An Answer to Hegel and Schleiermacher', paper delivered to 'The Biblical Theologians'.

'The Biblical Theologians' were a 'self-selected' group of about 30 theologians in the northeast of the US. I know no more about this paper, but suspect it was a version of *1985c*, which was probably complete by now.

1981f   'History, Salvation-History, and Typology' (YDS 18–278).

Described in 1981i, which places it in April. The talk is, as Frei says in the letter, 'about discerning patterns of providential government in the sequence of historical events'; Frei runs this ecclesiologically in a dialectical way: the people of God are a sign of the eschatological shape of all humanity, and human history in general foreshadows the travail and glory of God's people. As is his wont, Frei rejects any view that might 'reduce specific events to instances of either natural pattern or ideal generalization'. Such a view involves claims about agency and events; it also involves claims about typological reading and political theology. See chap. 7, §3.

1981g   Letter to Owen Chadwick, 8 May (YDS 1–10).
         See almost complete text in chap. 8, §2.

1981h   Letter to William Clebsch, 5 Jul. (YDS 1–16).
         Frei sent Clebsch, who had just delivered some talk of great historical breadth, his piece on Strauss (*1985c*), saying, 'Some day, or rather some non-day, St. Peter is going to haul us before him and ask us to account for our friendship. And he is going to smile in a mildly puzzled way and say, "Well, at least I know which one of you is the hedgehog and which the fox"' (the reference being, presumably, to Isaiah Berlin's *The Hedgehog and the Fox*). It also becomes clear that the Strauss essay is just finished (cf. [1981e]) having had 'too much Guggenheim time' spent on it, and that Frei is considering making it the linchpin of the upcoming Shaffer Lectures on Christology (1983a). See chap. 1, §1.

1981i   Letter to Julian Hartt, 19 Aug. (YDS 2–36).
         Gives a detailed synopsis and brief commentary on 1981f. See chap. 7, §3.

1981j   Review of Eberhard Busch, *Karl Barth: His Life from Letters and Autobiographical Texts* (Philadelphia: Fortress Press, 1976), *Historical Magazine of the Protestant Episcopal Church* 51 (Aug. 1981), pp. 109–21.
         Cf. *1976j*, *1978g* and *1978j*. A draft of this version of the review can be found in YDS 10–162.

1981k   Letter to Roger L. Shinn, 26 Aug. (YDS 4–86).
         'I am deeply persuaded that materially philosophy must not govern the curriculum or the spirit of modern seminary education, but that formally its thorough-minded, disciplined probing is one of our few protections against the regnant confusion of Christian depth with a soft and addle-brained mentality.' See chap. 8, §5.

1981l   'The History of Modern Theology', lecture transcripts, 2 Sep.–28 Oct. (YDS 14–212).
         Among the papers for 'Modern Christian Thought, 1650–1830' and 'Modern Christian Thought, 1830–1950' (see ?1978a), are a sheaf of transcripts. Bruce Marshall apparently taped this lecture

course, and John Wells transcribed the tapes in 1984 – although the typescript reads very much like a summary, and I suspect they are not verbatim transcripts. They get as far as Rousseau.

1981m   Letter to Mark Ellingsen, 20 Oct. (YDS 1–23).
On the existence of a 'Yale school': 'I am unable to adumbrate at any length right now, but I am personally doubtful about the persuasiveness of some of the moves I have made in the past; at the very least they need large-scale qualification. Moreover, I may not be in agreement on basic issues with some of my colleagues, and I think I am still in the process of developing a "position", and that may be true of my colleagues also, for all I know.'

1981n   Letter to Paul Ramsey, 9 Dec. (YDS 4–82).
The letter contains a rather impressionistic vision of politically engaged theology, describing 'people whose highest agenda, no matter how seriously and committedly they reflect on the problems of American and wider culture, is their single-minded devotion to the Lord of the church and of creation at large', etc. See Introduction.

?1982a   Notes on Jeffrey Stout, 'What is the Meaning of a Text?', in *New Literary History* 14 (1982), pp. 1–12 (GF).
Frei scribbled quite extensively, and critically, in the margins of his copy.

1982b   'Theology and the Interpretation of Narrative: Some Hermeneutical Considerations', paper delivered at Haverford College, revised version published in *TN*, pp. 94–116.
Frei looks at the relationship between *Wissenschaft* and Christian self-description in theology and at the impact of different forms of theology upon the *sensus literalis* of Scripture. See chap. 8.

[1982c]   Paper on Frei's project, AAR conference, New York (December).
I know no more about this.

1983a   The Shaffer Lectures, delivered at Yale Divinity School, republished in *TCT*, pp. 8–69.
YDS has 1983a(i) – a draft of most of the material on Kaufman, Tracy, Schleiermacher and Barth (YDS 17–259). The final text initially follows this draft very closely, with the addition of some brief introductory comments at the beginning and end of the section on Gordon Kaufman, and the beginning of the section on David Tracy. A short way into the Tracy material, however, the final text begins to diverge entirely from the draft, returning only for a brief spell at the start of the section on Barth. The draft also has no section on Schleiermacher. YDS also has 1983a(ii) – an anecdotal introductory section included in the typescript deleted

from the published version (YDS 10–172). The final version, 1983a(iii), was published in *Types of Christian Theology*. Much of the Shaffer material which has been collected in chapter 3 of *TCT* is reworked from 1982b. The drafts in YDS 10–171 and 10–172 show that *TCT* chapter 5, which the editors (*TCT* p. x) assign to the Cadbury lectures (1987a) but which David Ford ('On Being Theologically Hospitable to Jesus Christ: The Achievement of Hans Frei') assures us was no part of them, was originally part of the Shaffer Lectures.

1983b   Summary by Bruce Marshall of a discussion with Frei of Schleiermacher and his place in the typology, 22 Mar. (YDS 3–61).

Bruce Marshall appears to have been appointed stenographer to a reading class of Frei's. This is the first of two reports which he produced which exist in the YDS archive. Frei discussed the 'double reference' of Schleiermacher's theology: to the content of consciousness and to the reality of God, or to *Wissenschaft* and to Christian self-description.

1983c   'The "Literal Reading" of Biblical Narrative in the Christian Tradition: Does it Stretch or Will it Break?', paper delivered at a conference at the University of California (May); published in *The Bible and the Narrative Tradition*, ed. Frank McConnell (Oxford: Oxford University Press, 1986), pp. 36–77; republished in *TN*, pp. 117–52 (an edited version also reprinted in *The Return of Scripture in Judaism and Christianity*, ed. Peter Ochs [New York: Paulist Press, 1993], pp. 55–82).

This is the essay more than any other which has been taken to mark a 'break' in Frei's work, in which he crystallizes his uneasiness with the project of *Identity* and *Eclipse*. See chap. 8.

1983d   Bruce Marshall's summary of a discussion with Frei on Charles Wood, 1 Jun. (YDS 3–61).

Cf. 1983b. Frei suggested an 'appendix' to Wood's *The Formation of Christian Understanding*, which would deal not with the exercise of Christian understanding but with its content, its ascriptive focus. See chap. 8, §6.

1983e   Letter to Patrick Sherry, 5 Jul. (YDS 4–91).

Comprising 1983e(i), the letter itself, and 1983e(ii), an accompanying analysis of a dissertation, titled 'Estimate of the Work as a Whole'. In (i), Frei also discusses the essay on Strauss eventually published as *1985c*. See chap. 1, §1; chap. 8, §7.

[1983f]   Paper on Barth and Schleiermacher delivered at the AAR, December.

I know no more about this – although it may well have been an early version of 1986c.

1983g   Autobiographical Notes on Self (YDS 27–335).

Three tantalizing sheets of incredibly fragmentary and enigmatic notes. The sheets are undated, but state that Frei was married '35 years ago'.

1984a   'In Memory of Robert L. Calhoun', address given at Calhoun's memorial service, in February, published in *Reflection* 82 (1984), pp. 8–9.

Contains comments on 'generous orthodoxy' and on what it is to be an academic theologian. See extract in Introduction, §1.

1984b   '"Narrative" in Christian and Modern Reading', delivered to the Duodecim Club on 27 or 28 Apr. 1984, reprinted in Bruce D. Marshall (ed.), *Theology and Dialogue: Essays in Conversation with George Lindbeck* (Notre Dame: University of Notre Dame Press, 1990), pp. 149–63.

A piece with this title was certainly presented in 1984; whether it is identical with the piece published in *Theology and Dialogue*, I cannot say – although there is nothing inherently implausible about the content of the latter having been written this early. The essay begins with material drawn directly from the 'Literal Reading' essay (1983c), and then continues with a presentation of a typology of ways of reading realistic narrative in theology.

1984c   Letter to Gene Outka, 8 Aug. (YDS 4–74).

Discussing a criticism made of him and others by James Gustafson, Frei says, 'We make truth claims, but in view of the fact that God is not within genus and species as ordinary referential truths are, they have to be logically odd and not so much backed as illustrated by a mix of truth theories, each qualifying the other, all of them inadequate.' He goes on to illustrate his remarks with regard to the resurrection. See chap. 8, §7.

1984d   'George Lindbeck: *The Nature of Doctrine*', paper given at the launch of Lindbeck's book, 14 Sep.; published as 'Epilogue: George Lindbeck and *The Nature of Doctrine*', in *Theology and Dialogue: Essays in Conversation with George Lindbeck*, ed. Bruce D. Marshall (Notre Dame: University of Notre Dame Press, 1990), pp. 275–82.

Frei welcomes the book, giving a short but subtle interpretation in which he takes Lindbeck as a champion of 'the orthodox Christian as liberal humanist' – not a typical reading of the book. 1981n contains a similar portrait of Lindbeck. See Introduction, §1.

1984e   Letter to Gary Comstock, 5 Nov. (YDS 12–184).
          Comstock wrote two articles ('Truth or Meaning: Ricoeur versus Frei on Biblical Narrative' and 'Two Types of Narrative Theology') in which he thoroughly misunderstood Frei, but which have had more than their fair share of influence on the interpretation of Frei. Frei corresponded with Comstock while one of the articles was on the way towards publication, and argued that he was not, in Comstock's terms, a 'pure narrativist' nor really an 'antifoundationalist'. See chap. 8.

?1985a   'Proposal for a Study of Academic Education in Theological Studies' (my title) (YDS 12–185).
          A brief piece of writing which reads like an official proposal for a project (maybe written for a funding body?) but which begins by discussing the work of George Lindbeck, and so is probably later than *The Nature of Doctrine* (1984). It points firmly towards the later versions of Frei's typology, in that it speaks enthusiastically of a Weberian sociological approach, an element which was to come to far more prominence in the Princeton Lectures. See chap. 8, §2.

?1985b   Notes on proofs or photocopies of Ronald Thiemann's *Revelation and Theology* (Notre Dame: University of Notre Dame Press, 1985), pp. 130–49 (YDS 23–311).
          Notes scribbled in the margin of a proof or photocopy. They are not tremendously revealing, apart from showing that Frei had some minor doubts about details of Thiemann's presentation. There are also some clarifications of Frei's own stance: 'The narrative is explicatively and meditatively a character identification in the midst of others who are related to him as he becomes identified. The reference is a totally different matter: the narrative may refer to reality and it may refer (by way of application) to us, but that is a matter of confluence of use with narrative explicative sense, not of explicative sense alone' (this on Thiemann p. 145). See also chap. 8, §8.

1985c   'David Friedrich Strauss', in *Nineteenth Century Religious Thought in the West*, vol. 1, ed. Ninian Smart, John Clayton, Steven Katz and Patrick Sherry (Cambridge: Cambridge University Press), pp. 215–60.
          This article had been finished since early 1981 at least (see 1981h). There are various letters in the archive between Frei, the editors and CUP concerning the delay, which gave Frei some pain. This was the piece of which he was most proud: a detailed, sensitive exploration of Strauss' views and significance, with sections on Faith and Knowledge before Strauss; Strauss and his Cause Célèbre; the Centrality of Christ in Christian Theology; Christology and the

Hegelian Connection; The Life of Jesus; Strauss and Schleiermacher. See chap. 1, §3.

1985d 'Modern Christian Thought, 1650–1830', lecture notes (YDS 14–215).

One of the sets of lecture notes mentioned in 1978a. I have drawn attention to this one because the 4 Sept. lecture which begins the course discusses 'sensibility' in some detail, clarifying Frei's approach to social and intellectual history.

1985e 'Response to "Narrative Theology: An Evangelical Appraisal"', paper delivered in November, Yale; published in *Trinity Journal* 8 (spring 1987), pp. 21–24; reprinted in *TN*, pp. 207–12.

A conversational and rambling response to a fairly thorough attack on Frei's work (among others) by Carl Henry. The exchange has since been re-examined in detail by George Hunsinger, in an article 'What can Evangelicals and Postliberals Learn from Each Other? The Carl Henry/Hans Frei Exchange Reconsidered'.

1986a Proposal to the National Endowment for the Humanities (NEH), 1986 (YDS 6–123), published as 'Proposal for a Project', in *TCT*, pp. 1–7.

The briefest of outlines of the typology of Christian theology. The YDS 6–123 version has a rewritten beginning. See chap. 8, §5.

1986b 'Conflicts in Interpretation: Resolution, Armistice, or Co-existence?', the Alexander Thompson Memorial Lecture, Princeton Theological Seminary, published in *TN*, pp. 153–66.

By way of an examination of a debate on scriptural historicity between T.H. Huxley and Gladstone, Frei launches into a complex assessment of Frank Kermode's *The Genesis of Secrecy* (Cambridge: Harvard University Press, 1979), and finishes with a plea for the literal sense in terms that pick up implicitly on a Barthian/Anselmian doctrine of analogy. See chap. 8, §6.

1986c Papers for a conference on 'Love: the Foundation of Hope' honouring Jürgen Moltmann and Elisabeth Moltmann-Wendel (April) (YDS 18–268, 11–173).

Consisting of: 1986c(i), some notes Frei made in preparation for his paper; 1986c(ii), the typescript of a paper advertised as called 'To Give and to Receive: Christian Life Across the Barriers', but eventually just titled 'God's Patience and Our Work'; 1986c(iii), the typescript of a replacement paper which Frei prepared and delivered at the conference, simply titled 'Comments' (1986c[iii]); and 1986c(iv), the drafts and typescript of the section of Frei's paper which dealt with Elisabeth Moltmann-Wendel's work. At the conference, Frei apparently became distressed at the direction that was being pursued, and completely rewrote his paper. In

'Comments', Frei lambasts the conference for claiming that it can see the dialectical shape of history and the hope which awaits us, rather more clearly than he thinks the logic of Christian claims allows. Frei calls for a more tentative and broken view through a dark glass. See chap. 7, §3.

1986d   'Barth and Schleiermacher: Divergence and Convergence', paper presented at a conference at Stony Point, New York, in May; published in James O. Duke and Robert F. Streetlam (eds.), *Barth and Schleiermacher: Beyond the Impasse?* (Philadelphia: Fortress Press, 1988), pp. 65–87; republished in *TN*, pp. 177–99.

The paper clarifies the proximity of Barth and Schleiermacher, by looking at how each deals with Christian self-description and philosophy. See chap. 8, §5.

?1986e   Notes on Weber (YDS 12–187a).

The two drafts mostly deal with Max Weber, and probably come from 1986 (there is a note from a meeting in October 1986 on the back of one of the sheets). They begin with a social historical analysis of the rise of the profession in Germany, and its relation to the rise of *Wissenschaft* in German Universities, before switching to an outline of the issues surrounding the typology, and comments on the identification of Jesus. If they are drafts for the Humanities Council Lectures (1987c), they are early ones, and not much by way of actual text survived from them into the lectures.

1986f   Letter to William Placher, 3 Nov. (YDS 4–78).

Frei briefly, tentatively, and with barbaric terminology, outlines a Trinitarian view of truth. See chap. 8, §7.

1987a   The Edward Cadbury Lectures, University of Birmingham.

The various papers here are in something of a mess, and it seems best simply to list the existing drafts and transcripts, then describe the individual lectures and what exists of them.

1987a(i): 'Lecture 1: The Theological Faculty in Modern Universities: Growth of a Profession' (YDS 11–173f) – originally headed 'Lecture 2'; a discussion of the Christian identification of Jesus Christ and his cosmic scope.

1987a(ii): 'Lecture 2: The Theological Faculty in Modern Universities: Growth of a Profession' (YDS 11–173f) – a discussion which follows on from (i), treating the essence of Christianity and then the contemporary social organization of theological study.

1987a(iii): 'Lecture 2: The Theological Faculty in Modern Universities: Growth of a Profession' (YDS 11–173f) – largely about Schweitzer, although the lecture begins with a discussion of realism, including realism in the English novel.

1987a(iv): Untitled (YDS 11–173f) – deals with natural and revealed religion, theology and philosophy, medieval and modern universities, and German and American university organization.

1987a(v): 'Theology in the University: Growth of a Profession (The Case of the University of Berlin)' (YDS 11–173d) – begins with material on Weber, and on the professionalization of the German academy, then moves on to Schleiermacher, before degenerating into notes.

1987a(vi) 'IV: Kant' (YDS 11–173e) – a typescript made from a tape recording of the relevant lecture. Treats type 1 (without introducing the typology).

1987a(vii) 'The Jesus of History and the Christ of Faith: Mediating Theology as System' (YDS 11–173d and 173e) – turns from German to American material; and then turns to David Tracy for type 2.

1987a(viii) 'Ad Hoc Correlation' (editors' title) (YDS 11–173d and 173e) – material from the Cadbury Lectures dealing with types 3 and 4; published in *TCT*, pp. 70–91 (chap. 6).

1987a(ix) 'The End of Academic Theology' (YDS 11–173d and 173e) – material from the Cadbury Lectures dealing with type 5; published in TCT, pp. 92–94 (chap. 7).

According to the description provided by David Ford in 'On Being Theologically Hospitable to Jesus Christ: The Achievement of Hans Frei', the actual lectures were as follows:

Cadbury 1: 'According to the Text: The Specificity and Universality of Jesus Christ', probably 1987a(i); reworked for the Humanities Council Lectures material found in TCT pp. 133–46.

Cadbury 2: 'The Theological Faculty in Modern Universities: Growth of a Profession', reworked for Humanities Council Lecture material found in TCT, pp. 95–116 (although it also contained material, now lost, on Locke); related to 1987a(ii), (iv) and (v).

Cadbury 3: 'Teaching about Reason and History: The Rational Pursuit of Jesus'; reworked for the Humanities Council Lectures, and can also mostly be found in TCT, pp. 95–116, although there was extra material on 'Edward Farley and Van Harvey and about the contrast between England, where geology became the paradigmatic science, and Germany, where it was history;

and there was also a summary of the five types of the typology' according to David Ford; related to 1987a(ii), (iv) and (v).

Cadbury 4: 'Mediating between Church and Academy: The Turn to the Subject'; Frei was behind schedule by this time, and in fact delivered 1987a(vi), on Kant.

Cadbury 5: 'The Jesus of History and the Christ of Faith: Mediating Theology'; Frei, still behind, reached the material which he had intended for the previous lecture: Pietism, Methodism, Idealism, Romanticism, Marx and Strauss; this lecture appears to be completely missing.

Cadbury 6: 'The Jesus of History and the Christ of Faith: Mediating Theology without System' = 1987a(viii).

Cadbury 7: 'Restoring the Priority of the Text: The Hermeneutical Term'; Frei, behind, continued to deliver the material on types 3 and 4 found in 1987a(viii).

Cadbury 8: 'Knowing Jesus and Learning to Live Christianly: The End of Academic Theology?' = 1987a(ix); Frei was running behind and so this material is shorter than might be expected.

It is clearer even from the list of lectures that, far more than is apparent in the arrangement of material in *TCT*, Frei's typology project was firmly embedded (a) in his projected history of Christology, and (b) within a discussion of the Christian identification of Jesus of Nazareth. See chap. 8.

1987b   Curriculum Vitae.

     The 'Writing in Process or Projected' section now reads: 'A book on Christology in Germany and England from 1700 to 1950; A book on theological typology and sensus literalis in modern theology (based on the Shaffer Lectures at Yale Divinity School, 1983, and the Cadbury Lectures, University of Birmingham, 1987).'

1987c   The Humanities Council Lectures, delivered in Princeton.

     Comprising: 1987c(i), a short draft for a portion of the lectures (YDS 11–173); 1987c(ii), an old ending to the first lecture (YDS 11–173); and 1987c(iii), the published text of the lectures, *TCT* pp. 95–116 and 116–32: 'The Case of Berlin, 1810'; 'Types of Academic Theology'; and 'The Encounter of Jesus with the German Academy'. Cf. 1987a. See chap. 8.

1987d   'On the Going Down of Christ into Hell' (YDS 12–186).

     This and 1987e and f were prepared for a book on the Thirty-Nine articles, to be edited by John F. Woolverton and A. Katherine Grieb (Church Hymnal Corporation). 'What is important is not that there be a real location called hell, so that someone could descend into it. Rather, Jesus Christ is so real – and therefore his cross so efficacious – that he defines, undergoes, and overcomes whatever it is that is absolutely and unequivocally hellish.' See chap. 4.

1987e   'Of the Resurrection of Christ', published as 'How it All Began: On the Resurrection of Christ', in *Anglican and Episcopal History* 53.2 (June 1989), pp. 139–45; reprinted in *TN*, pp. 200–206.

The piece on the resurrection by and large presents familiar themes – and shows the extent to which the Christological heart of Frei's theology had remained stable through all the changes in his methodology. On the copy of this article in YDS 10–157, Frei appended a note 'For George [Lindbeck?] from a would-be-catechist/theologian who would like to combine second-order with (at least) first-and-a-half order statements.'

1987f   'Of the Holy Ghost' (YDS 12–186).

'In the logic of the Christian faith nothing is more naturally congruent than saying "do justice, love kindness and walk humbly with your God" and saying "The Holy Ghost, proceeding from the Father and the Son, is of one substance, majesty, and glory, with the Father and the Son, very and eternal God."' See chap. 8, §7.

?1988a   Notes on H. Richard Niebuhr (YDS 19–275).

There are three separate sets of notes, all of which may well come from the same time, and one of which (the longest) has a scribbled note about plane times in Feb. 1988 on it. There is ?1988a(i), a sixteen-page piece which begins with quotes from Niebuhr's *The Responsible Self* and then becomes a lecture, dealing with the difference between H. Richard and Reinhold Niebuhr. There is also ?1988a(ii), a shorter, seven-page manuscript, giving broken notes for a talk on Niebuhr as an interpreter of history. Then there are ?1988a(iii), some rough pages of outline notes on, among other things, Niebuhr's critical idealism. See extracts in Introduction, §1.

1988b   Lectures on Modern Christian Thought 1830–1950, 18 Jan.–27 Apr. (YDS 15–231).

This is the last of Frei's runs through his lecture course on Modern Christian Thought (see ?1978a), and there is a fairly complete set of notes for the course which were evidently written at least in part while the course was taking place.

1988c   Sermon on John 15.5 (YDS 11–175a).

The sermon is for the 'class of 1988'. It begins with a meditation on 'the strange, beautiful mosaics in early Byzantine churches: those calm, unearthly figures whose gaze is fixed on a sight not visible to us. It continues, eventually, with a discussion of the Christian community worldwide as our first community – a theme Frei runs with an ecumenical slant.

1988d   'H. Richard Niebuhr on History, Church and Nation', paper written for September conference at Harvard, published in Ronald F. Thiemann (ed.), *The Legacy of H. Richard Niebuhr* (Minneapolis: Fortress Press, 1991) pp. 1–23; republished in *TN*, pp. 213–33.

The paper was delivered in Frei's absence when he fell ill – fatally, as it turned out. In his final work, Frei carries on that strand of political thinking about history and providence which was evident in the lecture on 'History, Salvation-History, and Typology' (1981f) and in Frei's contributions to the Moltmann conference (1986c). It also picks up on Frei's engagement with Niebuhr in a way which goes beyond the already remarkable service which Frei had done Niebuhr way back in 1957 (*1957a* and *1957b*). See chap. 7, §3.

[Undatable Material]

U1   Notes on Clifford Geertz (YDS 19–279).

A rather midrashic running commentary on Geertz's 'Thick Description: Towards an Interpretation of Cultures'. It seems unlikely that these date to Frei's first encounter with Geertz: at one point he suggests to himself that he should 're-read' another of Geertz's essays.

U2   'Report on Modern Theology' (my title) (YDS 18–273).

Frei sketches some general features of modern theology, and then goes into more detail on developments between Locke and Schleiermacher. 'I shall try to give a kind of report, an overview, mixing together all sorts of things as will be evident to you ... By modern theology I chiefly refer to a vague kind of consensus that began to emerge about 1700 among a group of rather academic, middle class theologians, chiefly Protestant ...' Some time in the 1980s?

U3   'Beardslee and Hermeneutics' (YDS 12–189).

This is clearly a transcript made by someone else: there are even footnotes to bits of text which Frei had scratched out. 'There is a tenacious sense that all of us have ... that our descriptive concepts refer'; ' ... at the risk of looking utterly relativist to some and utterly reactionary to Professors Beardslee and Kermode, I want to do hermeneutics in the tradition of Christian theology as reflection on the use of Christian communal language and that as a language that has an irreducible integrity of its own, is not systematically grounded by reference to a systematic pre-understanding or pre-linguistic experience (or expression) of reality in general'. Some time in the 1980s?

U4   'Theology is a Modest Task' (my title) (YDS 18–278).
        Frei stresses against apologists and mediating theologians that 'The business of theology is to stress the logic of the Christian story, i.e., that it hangs together as a cumulative narrative.' Again, some time in the 1980s?

U5   'Reflections upon the Retirement of Julian Hartt' (YDS 11–177).
        A conversational, anecdotal and quite personal piece, which provides insights into Frei's views on providence, grace and the like.

2 Secondary Sources

As well as including all secondary works used in the body of the book, I have tried to make this as complete a bibliography as I can of secondary work on Frei – with the exception of book reviews, which I have listed only sparingly.

(various), *In Memoriam Hans Wilhelm Frei, April 29, 1922–September 12, 1988*; memorial service addresses by David Kelsey, George Lindbeck, Wayne Meeks and Gene Outka.

Abdul-Masih, Marguerite, *Edward Schillebeeckx and Hans Frei: A Conversation on Method and Christology*, Editions SR 26 (Waterloo, Ontario: Wilfred Laurier University Press/Canadian Corporation for Studies in Religion, 2001).

Auerbach, Erich, *Mimesis: The Representation of Reality in Western Literature*, trans. W. Trask (Princeton: Princeton University Press, 1953).

——, *Dante: Poet of the Secular World*, trans. R. Manheim (Chicago: University of Chicago Press, 1961).

——, 'Figura', trans. E. Manheim, in *Scenes from the Drama of European Literature*, Theory and History of Literature 9, ed. W. Godzich and J. Schulte-Sasse (Manchester: Manchester University Press; Minnesota: University of Minnesota, 1984), pp. 11–76 and 229–37.

Bahti, Timothy, 'Vico, Auerbach and Literary History', *Philological Quarterly* 61.2 (spring 1981), pp. 239–55.

——, 'Auerbach's *Mimesis*: Figural Structure and Historical Narrative', in Gregory Jay and David Miller (eds.), *After Strange Texts: The Role of Theory in the Study of Literature* (Alabama: University of Alabama Press, 1985), pp. 124–45, 181–82.

Barth, Karl, *The Epistle to the Romans*, trans. E.C. Hoskyns (Oxford: Oxford University Press, 1968).

——, *Anselm: Fides Quaerens Intellectum; Anselm's Proof of the Existence of God in the Context of his Theological Scheme*, trans. I.W. Robertson (London: SCM Press, 1960).

——, *Church Dogmatics*, trans. G. W. Bromiley *et al.*, ed. G. W. Bromiley and T. F. Torrance (Edinburgh: T&T Clark, 1956–77).

——, *Evangelical Theology: An Introduction*, trans. Grover Foley (New York: Holt, Rinehart and Winston, 1963).

Batdorf, Irvin W., 'Interpreting Jesus since Bultmann: Selected Paradigms and their Hermeneutical Matrix', *Society of Biblical Literature Seminar Papers* 23 (1984), pp. 187–215.

Berlin, Isaiah, *The Hedgehog and the Fox* (New York: Simon & Schuster, 1953).

Blandenburg, Friedrich von, *Versuch über den Roman* (Stuttgart: Metzler, 1965).

Blocher, Henri, 'Biblical Narrative and Historical Reference', in N. Cameron (ed.), *Issues in Faith and History*, Scottish Bulletin of Evangelical Theology Special Study 3 (Edinburgh: Rutherford House, 1989), pp. 102–22.

Brisman, Leslie, Review of *The Eclipse of Biblical Narrative* and *The Identity of Jesus Christ*, *Comparative Literature* 28.4 (fall 1976), pp. 368–72.

Bryant, David J., 'Christian identity and Historical Change: Postliberals and Historicity', *The Journal of Religion* 73.1 (Jan. 1993), pp. 31–41.

Buckley, James J., *Seeking the Humanity of God: Practices, Doctrines, and Catholic Particularity*, Theology and Life Series 36 (Collegeville: Michael Glazier/The Liturgical Press, 1992).

Bultmann, Rudolf, *New Testament and Mythology and Other Basic Writings*, trans. Schubert Ogden (Philadelphia: Fortress Press, 1984).

Busch, Eberhard, 'Theology as a Function of the Church: Remarks on the Problem of Theology as an Academic Discipline', in Giorgy Olegovich (ed.), *Ten Year Commemoration to the Life of Hans Frei (1922–1988)* (New York: Semenenko Foundation, 1999), pp. 10–23.

Buttrick, David G., 'Interpretation and Preaching', *Interpretation* 35 (1981), pp. 46–58; reprinted in *Ex Auditu* 1 (1985), pp. 83–91.

Callahan, James Patrick, 'The Convergence of Narrative and Christology: Hans W. Frei on the Uniqueness of Christ', *Journal of the Evangelical Theological Society* 38 (Dec. 1995), pp. 531–47.

——, 'The Bible Says: Evangelical and Postliberal Biblicism', *Theology Today* 53.4 (1997), pp. 449–63.

Campbell, Charles Lamar, *Preaching Jesus: Hans Frei's Theology and the Contours of a Postliberal Homiletic* (Grand Rapids: Eerdmans, 1997).

——, 'Hans W. Frei: 1922–1988', in Donald W. Mussner and Joseph L. Price (eds.), *A New Handbook of Christian Theologians* (Nashville: Abingdon Press, 1996).

Cartwright, Michael, Review Essay on *Types of Christian Theology*, in *Pro Ecclesia* 3:3 (summer 1994), pp. 362–72.

Charry, Ellen T., Review of Bruce Marshall (ed.), *Theology and Dialogue*, *Theology Today* 48.3 (Oct. 1991), pp. 340ff.

Childs, Brevard, 'The *Sensus Literalis* of Scripture: An Ancient and Modern Problem', in Herbert Dranner *et al.* (eds.), *Beiträge zur alttestamentlichen Theologie* (Göttingen: Vandenhoeck and Ruprecht, 1977), pp. 80–95.

Clark, David K., 'Narrative Theology and Apologetics', *Journal of the Evangelical Theological Society* 36 (Dec. 1993), pp. 499–515.

Coakley, Sarah, *Christ Without Absolutes: A Study of the Christology of Ernst Troeltsch* (Oxford: Clarendon Press, 1988).

Comstock, Gary, 'Truth or Meaning: Ricoeur versus Frei on Biblical Narrative', *The Journal of Religion* 66.2 (Apr. 1986), pp. 117–40.

——, 'Telling the Whole Story: American Narrative Theology after H. Richard Niebuhr', in *Religion and Philosophy in the United States of America: Proceedings of the German–American Conference at Paderborn, July 29–August 2, 1986*, vol. 1, ed. Peter Freese (Essen: Verlag die blaue Eule, 1987).

——, 'Two Types of Narrative Theology', *Journal of the American Academy of Religion* 55.4 (winter 1987), pp. 687–717.

——, ' "Everything depends on the type of the concepts that the interpretation is made to convey": Max Kadushin among the Narrative Theologians', *Modern Theology* 5 (Apr. 1989), pp. 215-37.

Costa-Lima, Luiz, 'Erich Auerbach: History and Metahistory', *New Literary History* 19.3 (spring 1988), pp. 467–99.

——, '*Figura* as a Kernel of Auerbach's Literary History', *Literary Research* 17.34 (fall/winter 2000), pp. 268–79.

Coughenour, James, 'Karl Barth and the Gospel Story: A Lesson in Reading the Biblical Narrative', *Andover Newton Quarterly* 20.2 (1979), pp. 97–110.

Crites, Stephen, 'The Spatial Dimensions of Narrative Truth-Telling', in Garret Green (ed.), *Scriptural Authority and Narrative Interpretation* (Philadelphia: Fortress Press, 1987), pp. 97–118.

Craigo-Snell, Shannon, 'Command Performance: Rethinking Performance Interpretation in the Context of Divine Discourse', *Modern Theology* 16.4 (2000), pp. 475-94.

Dawson, John David, *Allegorical Readers and Cultural Revision in Ancient Alexandria* (Berkeley: University of California Press, 1992).

——, 'Allegorical Reading and the Embodiment of the Soul in Origen', in Lewis Ayres and Gareth Jones (eds.), *Christian Origins: Theology, Rhetoric and Community* (London: Routledge, 1998), pp. 26–43.

——, 'Figural Reading and the Fashioning of Identity in Boyarin, Auerbach and Frei', *Modern Theology* 14.2 (Apr. 1998), pp. 181–96.

——, *Christian Figural Reading and the Fashioning of Identity* (Berkeley: University of California Press, 2002).

Demson, David, 'Response to Walter Lowe', in David Demson and John Webster (eds.), *Hans Frei and the Future of Theology = Modern Theology* 8.2 (Apr. 1992), pp. 145–48.

——, *Hans Frei and Karl Barth: Different Ways of Reading Scripture* (Grand Rapids: Eerdmans, 1997).

Dirks, J. Edward, 'Introduction' to Frei's 'Theological Reflections' (*1966a*), *Christian Scholar* 49.4 (winter 1966).

Duke, James O., 'Reading the Gospels Realistically', *Encounter* 38.3 (summer 1977), pp. 296–303.

Edwards, O., 'Historical Critical Method's Failure of Nerve and a Prescription for a Tonic: A Review of Some Recent Literature', *Anglican Theological Review* 39 (1977), pp. 115–34; reprinted in *Ex Auditu* 1 (1985), pp. 92–105.

Ellingsen, Mark, 'Luther as Narrative Exegete', *Journal of Religion* 63 (Oct. 1983), pp. 394–413.

——, *The Integrity of Biblical Narrative: Story in Theology and Proclamation* (Minneapolis: Fortress Press 1990).

Evans, Arthur R. Jr, 'Erich Auerbach as European Critic', Review Article on Erich Auerbach's *Gesammelte Aufsätze zur romanischen Philologie* (Bern & München: Francke Verlag, 1967), *Romance Philology* 25.2 (Nov. 1971), pp. 193–215.

Fodor, James, *Christian Hermeneutics: Paul Ricoeur and the Refiguring of Theology* (Oxford: Clarendon Press, 1995).

Ford, David F., *Barth and God's Story: Biblical Narrative and the Theological Method of Karl Barth in the Church Dogmatics*, Studies in the Intercultural History of Christianity 27, ed. Richard Friedl, Walter J. Hollenweger, Hans Jochen Margull (Frankfurt am Main: Verlag Peter Lang, 1981).

——, 'The Best Apologetics is Good Systematics: A Proposal about the Place of Narrative in Christian Systematic Theology', *Anglican Theological Review* 68.3 (Jul. 1985), pp. 232–54.

——, 'Hans Frei and the Future of Theology', in David Demson and John Webster (eds.), *Hans Frei and the Future of Theology = Modern Theology* 8.2 (Apr. 1992), pp. 203–14.

Ford, David F., 'Response to [Werner Jeanrond's] "The Problem of the Starting Point of Theological Thinking"', *Hermathena* 156 (summer 1994), pp. 28–39.

——, 'On Being Theologically Hospitable to Jesus Christ: Hans Frei's Achievement', *Journal of Theological Studies* 46.2 (Oct. 1995), pp. 532–46; reprinted in Giorgy Olegovich (ed.), *Ten Year Commemoration to the Life of Hans Frei (1922–1988)* (New York: Semenenko Foundation, 1999), pp. 54–65.

Geertz, Clifford, 'Thick Description: Towards an Interpretation of Cultures', in *The Interpretation of Cultures: Selected Essays* (New York: Basic Books, 1973), pp. 3–30.

Gerhart, Mary, 'The Restoration of Biblical Narrative', *Semeia* 46 (1989), pp. 13–29.

Goethe, Johann Wolfgang, *Aus meinem Leben: Dichtung und Warheit*, in E. Buetler (ed.), *Gedanksausgabe* (Zürich: Artemis–Verlag, 1948).

Goldberg, Michael, *Theology and Narrative: A Critical Introduction* (Nashville: Abingdon, 1981).

Gore, Charles (ed.), *Lux Mundi: A Series of Studies in the Religion of the Incarnation*, 15th edn (London: John Murray, 1899).

Green, Garrett, 'Editor's Introduction', in *Scriptural Authority and Narrative Interpretation* (Philadelphia: Fortress Press, 1987), pp. ix–xiii.

——, '"The Bible As ...": Fictional Narrative and Scriptural Truth', in Garrett Green (ed.), *Scriptural Authority and Narrative Interpretation* (Philadelphia: Fortress Press, 1987), pp. 79–96.

——, *Imagining God: Theology and the Religious Imagination* (San Fransisco: Harper and Row, 1989).

Gunton, Colin, Review of *Types of Christian Theology*, *Scottish Journal of Theology* 49.2 (1996), pp. 233–34.

Hartlich, C., and W. Sachs, *Der Ursprung des Mythosbegriffes in der modernen Bibelwissenschaft* (Tübingen: Mohr, 1952).

Harvey, Van A., *The Historian and the Believer: The Morality of Historical Knowledge and Christian Belief* (New York: Macmillan, 1966).

——, 'A Christology for Barabbases', *Perkins Journal* 29 (spring 1976), pp. 1–13.

Hauerwas, Stanley, 'The Church as God's New Language', in Garret Green (ed.), *Scriptural Authority and Narrative Interpretation* (Philadelphia: Fortress Press, 1987), pp. 179–98.

Hauerwas, Stanley, and L. Gregory Jones, 'Introduction: Why Narrative?', in *Why Narrative? Readings in Narrative Theology* (Grand Rapids: Eerdmans, 1989), pp. 1–18.

Hawkins, Alex, 'Beyond Narrative Theology: John Milbank and Gerard Loughlin as the Non-Identical Repetition of Hans Frei', *Koinonia* 10.1 (1998), pp. 61–87.

Hegel, Georg Wilhelm Friedrich, *Aesthetics* (Oxford: Clarendon Press, 1975).

Herder, Johann Gottfried, *Briefe, das Studium der Theologie betreffend*, in Bernhard Suphan (ed.), *Sämmtliche Werke* (Berlin: Weidmann, 1877–1913).

Henry, Carl, 'Narrative Theology: An Evangelical Appraisal', *Trinity Journal* 8 (spring 1987), pp. 3–19.

Higton, Mike A., 'Frei's Christology and Lindbeck's Cultural–Linguistic Theory', *Scottish Journal of Theology* 50.1 (1997), pp. 83–95.

——, '"A Carefully Circumscribed Progressive Politics": Hans Frei's Political Theology', *Modern Theology* 15.1 (Jan. 1999), pp. 55–83.

——, 'Hans Frei and David Tracy on the Ordinary and the Extraordinary in Religion', *The Journal of Religion* 79.4 (Oct. 1999), pp. 566–91.

——, 'An American Theologian of History: Hans W. Frei in 1956', *Anglican and Episcopal History* 71.1 (Mar. 2002), pp. 61–84.

——, 'Boldness and Reserve: A Lesson from St. Augustine', *Anglican Theological Review* 85.3 (summer 2003), pp. 447–56.

——, 'The Fulfilment of History in Barth, Frei, Auerbach and Dante', in Mike Higton and John McDowell (eds.), *Conversing with Barth* (Aldershot: Ashgate, forthcoming).

Hinze, Bradford E., and George P. Schner, 'Postliberal Theology and Roman Catholic Theology', *Religious Studies Review* 21:4 (Oct. 1995), pp. 299–304.

Holdheim, W. Wolfgang, 'Auerbach's *Mimesis*: Aesthetics as Historical Understanding', *Clio: A Journal of Literature, History and the Philosophy of History* 10.2 (winter 1981), pp. 143–54.

Hunsinger, George, 'Beyond Literalism and Expressivism: Karl Barth's Hermeneutical Realism (To Hans Frei on the occasion of his 65th birthday)', *Modern Theology* 3.3 (1987), pp. 209–23.

——, 'Hans Frei as Theologian: The Quest for a Generous Orthodoxy', in David Demson and John Webster (eds.), *Hans Frei and the Future of Theology = Modern Theology* 8.2 (Apr. 1992), pp. 103–28; reprinted in *TN*, pp. 235–70.

——, 'What can Evangelicals and Postliberals Learn from Each Other? The Carl Henry/Hans Frei Exchange Reconsidered', *Pro Ecclesia* 5.2 (spring 1996), pp. 161–82.

——, Hunsinger, George, and William C. Placher, 'Editorial Introduction', in *TCT*, pp. ix–xi.

Jeanrond, Werner, 'The Problem of the Starting Point of Theological Thinking: Presidential address to the College Theological Society, Trinity College Dublin, 24 January 1994', *Hermathena* 156 (summer 1994), pp. 1–28.

Jones, L. Gregory, Response to John Sykes, *Modern Theology* 5.4 (1989), pp. 343–48.

Kay, James F., 'Myth or Narrative? Bultmann's "New Testament and Mythology" Turns Fifty', *Theology Today* 48 (Oct. 1991), pp. 326–32.

——, *Christus Praesens: A Reconsideration of Rudolf Bultmann's Christology* (Grand Rapids: Eerdmans, 1994).

Kelber, Warner H., 'Gospel Narrative and Critical Theory', *Biblical Theology Bulletin* 18 (Oct. 1988), pp. 130–36.

Kelsey, David, *The Uses of Scripture in Recent Theology* (Philadelphia: Fortress Press, 1975).

——, 'Biblical Narrative and Theological Anthropology', in Garrett Green (ed.), *Scriptural Authority and Narrative Interpretation* (Philadelphia: Fortress Press, 1987), pp. 121–43.

Kermode, Frank, 'Deciphering the Big Book', *The New York Review of Books*, 29 June 1978.

Kerr, Fergus 'Frei's Types', *New Blackfriars*, 75.881 (Apr. 1994), pp. 184–93.

King, Robert H., 'The Concept of Personal Agency as a Theological Model', (unpublished PhD, Yale 1965).

Klaaren, Eugene M., 'A Critical Appraisal of Hans Frei's *Eclipse of Biblical Narrative*', *Union Seminary Quarterly Review* 37.4 (Oct. 1983), pp. 283–97.

Köstenberger, Andreas J., 'Aesthetic Theology – Blessing or Curse? An Assessment of Narrative Theology', *Faith and Mission* 15 (spring 1998), pp. 27–44.

Lee, David, *Luke's Stories of Jesus: Theological Reading of Gospel Narrative and the Legacy of Hans Frei* (Sheffield: Sheffield Academic Press, 1999).

Lim, Johnson Teng Kok, 'Towards a Final Form Approach to Biblical Interpretation', *Stulos* 7.1–2 (1999), pp. 1–11.

——, 'Historical Critical Paradigm: The Beginning of an End', *The Asia Journal of Theology* 14.2 (Oct. 2000), pp. 252–71.

Lincoln, Abraham, 'Second Inaugural Address March 4 1865', in Don E. Fehrenbacher (ed.), *Abraham Lincoln, Speeches and Writing 1859–1869: Speeches, Letters and Miscellaneous Writings, Presidential Messages and Proclamations* (New York: Literary Classics of the United States, 1989).

Lindbeck, George, *The Nature of Doctrine: Religion and Theology in a Postliberal Age* (London: SPCK, 1984).

Lindbeck, George, 'The Story-shaped Church: Critical Exegesis and Theological Interpretation', in Garrett Green (ed.), *Scriptural Authority and Narrative Interpretation* (Philadelphia: Fortress Press, 1987).

——, 'Scripture, Consensus, and Community', *This World* 23 (fall 1988), pp. 5–24.

——, Okholm, Dennis, and Timothy Phillips, (eds.), *The Nature of Confession: Evangelicals and Postliberals in Conversation* (Downers Grove: IVP, 1996).

Loewe, Raphael, 'The "Plain Meaning" of Scripture in Early Jewish Exegesis', *Papers of the Institute of Jewish Studies in London* 1 (1964), pp. 140–85.

Lose, David J., 'Narrative and Proclamation in a Postliberal Homiletic', *Homiletic* 23.1 (summer 1998), pp. 1–14.

Loughlin, Gerard, 'Christianity at the End of the Story or the Return of the Master-Narrative', *Modern Theology* 8.4 (Oct. 1992), pp. 365–84.

——, 'Following to the Letter: The Literal Use of Scripture', *Literature and Theology* 9 (Dec. 1995), pp. 370–82.

——, *Telling God's Story: Bible, Church and Narrative Theology* (Cambridge: Cambridge University Press, 1996).

Lowe, Walter, 'Hans Frei and Phenomenological Hermeneutics', in David Demson and John Webster (eds.), *Hans Frei and the Future of Theology* = *Modern Theology* 8.2 (Apr. 1992), pp. 133–44.

MacIntyre, Alasdair, Review of *The Eclipse of Biblical Narrative*, *The Yale Review* 65 (winter 1976), pp. 251–55.

Marshall, Bruce, *Christology in Conflict: The Identity of a Saviour in Rahner and Barth* (Oxford: Basil Blackwell, 1987).

Massey, Marilyn Chapin, 'The Literature of Young Germany and D. F. Strauss' Life of Jesus', *Journal of Religion* 59 (Jul. 1979), pp. 298–323.

Mazur, G.O., 'Hans Frei and the Continuation of the Tradition of Biblical Realism in Karl Barth and H. Richard Niebuhr', in Giorgy Olegovich (ed.), *Ten Year Commemoration to the Life of Hans Frei (1922–1988)* (New York: Semenenko Foundation, 1999), pp. 96–102.

McCaughey, J. Davis, 'Literary Criticism and the Gospels: A Rumination', *Australian Biblical Review* 29 (Oct. 1981), pp. 16–25.

McCormack, Bruce, *Karl Barth's Critically Realistic Dialectical Theology: Its Genesis and Development 1909–36* (Oxford: Clarendon Press, 1995).

Middleton, Conyers, 'An Essay on the Allegorical and Literal Interpretation of the Creation and Fall of Man', *Miscellaneous Works*, vol. 2 (London: Manby and Cox, 1752).

Milbank, John, *Theology and Social Theory: Beyond Secular Reason* (Oxford: Basil Blackwell, 1990).

Milbank, John, 'The Name of Jesus', in *The Word Made Strange: Theology, Language, Culture* (Oxford: Basil Blackwell, 1997), pp. 145–68.

Ochs, Peter (ed.), *The Return to Scripture in Judaism and Christianity* (New York: Paulist Press, 1994).

Ogden, Schubert, Review of *Types of Christian Theology, Modern Theology* 9.2 (Apr. 1993), pp. 211–14.

Olegovich, Giorgy, 'Introduction', in *Ten Year Commemoration to the Life of Hans Frei (1922–1988)* (New York: Semenenko Foundation, 1999), pp. 7–9.

Olson, Roger E., 'Back to the Bible (Almost): Why Yale's Postliberal Theologians Deserve an Evangelical Hearing', *Christianity Today* 40 (May 1996), pp. 31–34.

O'Regan, Cyril, 'De doctrina christiana and Modern Hermeneutics', in D. Arnold *et al.* (eds.), *De doctrina christiana*, Christianity and Judaism in Antiquity 9 (Notre Dame: University of Notre Dame Press, 1995), pp. 217–43.

Outka, Gene, 'Following at a Distance: Ethics and the Identity of Jesus', in Garrett Green (ed.), *Scriptural Authority and Narrative Interpretation* (Philadelphia: Fortress Press, 1987), pp. 144–60.

Niebuhr, H. Richard, *Christ and Culture* (London: Faber & Faber, 1952).

Nineham, Denis, Review of *The Eclipse of Biblical Narrative*, *Theology* 79 (Jan. 1976), pp. 46–48.

Placher, William C., 'Scripture as Realistic Narrative: Some Preliminary Questions', *Perspectives in Religious Studies* 5 (spring 1978), pp. 32–41.

——, 'Revisionist and Postliberal Theologies and the Public Character of Theology', *The Thomist* 49.3 (Jul. 1985), pp. 392–416.

——, 'Paul Ricoeur and Postliberal Theology: A Conflict of Interpretations?', *Modern Theology* 4.1 (Oct. 1987), pp. 35–52.

——, 'Hans Frei and the Meaning of Biblical Narrative', *Christian Century* 106 (1989), pp. 556–59.

——, *Unapologetic Theology: A Christian Voice in a Pluralistic Conversation* (Louisville: Westminster/John Knox Press, 1989).

——, 'A Modest Response to Paul Schwartzentruber', in David Demson and John Webster (eds.), *Hans Frei and the Future of Theology = Modern Theology* 8.2 (Apr. 1992), pp. 196–202.

——, 'Introduction', in *TN*, pp. 3–25.

——, 'Postliberal Theology', in David F. Ford (ed.), *The Modern Theologians: An Introduction to Christian Theology in the Twentieth Century* (Oxford: Basil Blackwell, 2nd edn, 1997), pp. 343–56.

Poland, Lynn, *Literary Criticism and Biblical Hermeneutics: A Critique of Formalist Approaches*, AAR Academy Series 48, ed. Carl A. Raschke (Chico: Scholars Press, 1985).

——, 'The New Criticism, Neoorthodoxy, and the New Testament', *Journal of Religion* 65.4 (Oct. 1985), pp. 459–77.

Prickett, Stephen, *Words and the Word: Language, Poetics and Biblical Interpretation* (Cambridge: Cambridge University Press, 1986).

Renquist, Tom, 'The Music of Failure', *Lutheran Partners* 16 (Feb. 2000), www.elca.org/lp/musicof.html.

Robinson, Robert B., 'Narrative Theology and Biblical Theology', in J. Reumann (ed.), *The Promise and Practice of Biblical Theology* (Minneapolis: Fortress Press, 1991), pp. 129–42.

Ryle, Gilbert, *The Concept of Mind* (London: Hutchinson, 1949).

Schner, George P., '*The Eclipse of Biblical Narrative*: Analysis and Critique', in David Demson and John Webster (eds.), *Hans Frei and the Future of Theology* = *Modern Theology* 8.2 (Apr. 1992), pp. 149–72.

Schwartzentruber, Paul, 'The Modesty of Hermeneutics: The Theological Reserves of Hans Frei', in David Demson and John Webster (eds.), *Hans Frei and the Future of Theology* = *Modern Theology* 8.2 (Apr. 1992), pp. 181–95.

Selwyn, E.G., *Essays, Catholic and Critical* (London: SPCK, 1926).

Siggins, I.D.K., Reply to Frei's 'Theological Reflections' (*1966a*), *Christian Scholar* 49.4 (winter), pp. 313–15.

Steiner, George, 'Critical Discussion (of *The Eclipse of Biblical Narrative*)', *Philosophy and Literature* 1 (spring 1977), pp. 238–43.

Stout, Jeffrey, 'Hans Frei and Anselmian Theology', in Giorgy Olegovich (ed.), *Ten Year Commemoration to the Life of Hans Frei (1922–1988)* (New York: Semenenko Foundation, 1999), pp. 24–40.

Strauss, David Friedrich, *The Christ of Faith and the Jesus of History: A Critique of Schleiermacher's Life of Jesus*, trans. Leander E. Keck (Philadelphia: Fortress Press, 1977).

Stroup, George W., 'Narrative in Calvin's Hermeneutic', in J. Leith (ed.), *Calvin Studies III* (Davidson: Davidson College, 1986), pp. 21–32.

Surin, Kenneth, '"The Weight of Weakness": Intratextuality and Discipleship', in *The Turnings of Darkness and Light: Essays in Philosophical and Systematic Theology* (Cambridge: Cambridge University Press, 1989), pp. 201–21, 293–302.

Sykes, John, 'Narrative Accounts of Biblical Authority: The Need for a Doctrine of Revelation', *Modern Theology* 5.4 (Jul. 1989), pp. 327–42.

——, 'Christian Apologetic Uses of the Grotesque in John Irving and Flannery O'Connor', *Literature and Theology* 10.1 (1996), pp. 58–67.

Tanner, Kathryn E., 'Theology and the Plain Sense', in Garrett Green (ed.), *Scriptural Authority and Narrative Interpretation* (Philadelphia: Fortress Press, 1987), pp. 59–78.

Temple, William, *Nature, Man and God* (London: Macmillan, 1953).

Thiemann, Ronald F., *Revelation and Theology: The Gospel as Narrated Promise* (Notre Dame: University of Notre Dame Press, 1985).

——, 'Radiance and Obscurity in Biblical Narrative', in Garrett Green (ed.), *Scriptural Authority and Narrative Interpretation* (Philadelphia: Fortress Press, 1987), pp. 21–41.

Thompson, Geoffrey, 'Christianity and World Religions: The Judgment of Karl Barth', *Pacifica* 7.2 (1994), pp. 185–206.

——, 'A Question of Posture: Engaging the World with Justin Martyr, George Lindbeck, and Hans Frei', *Pacifica* 13.3 (Oct. 2000), pp. 267–87.

Tilley, Terrence W., 'Incommensurability, Intratextuality, and Fideism', *Modern Theology* 5.2 (Jan. 1989), pp. 87–111.

Tindal, Matthew, *Christianity as Old as the Creation: Or, the Gospel, a Republication of the Religion of Nature* (Stuttgart: Frommann, 1967).

Tracy, David, *Blessed Rage for Order: The New Pluralism in Theology* (New York: Seabury, 1974).

——, 'Lindbeck's New Program for Theology: A Reflection', *The Thomist* 49.3 (1985), pp. 460–72.

——, 'The Uneasy Alliance Reconceived: Catholic Theological Method, Modernity and Postmodernity', *Theological Studies* 50.3 (1989), pp. 548–70.

——, *Dialogue with the Other: The Inter-Religious Dialogue* (Louvain: Peter Press/Eerdmans, 1990).

——, 'On Reading the Scriptures Theologically', in Bruce D. Marshall (ed.), *Theology and Dialogue: Essays in Conversation with George Lindbeck* (Notre Dame: University of Notre Dame Press, 1990), pp. 35–68.

——, 'On Naming the Present', in *On Naming the Present: God, Hermeneutics, Church* (London: SCM Press, 1994), pp. 60–85.

——, 'Literary Theory and the Return of the Forms for Naming and Thinking God', *The Journal of Religion* 74.3 (1994), pp. 302–19.

Valesio, Paolo, 'Foreword', in Erich Auerbach, *Scenes from the Drama of European Literature*, Theory and History of Literature 9, ed. Wlad Godzich and Jochen Schulte-Sasse (Manchester: Manchester University Press; Minnesota: University of Minnesota, 1984), pp. vii–xxviii.

Vanhoozer, Kevin J., *Biblical Narrative in the Philosophy of Paul Ricoeur: A Study in Hermeneutics and Theology* (Cambridge: Cambridge University Press, 1990).

Vanhoozer, Kevin J., 'The Spirit of Understanding: Special Revelation and General Hermeneutics', in Roger Lundin (ed.), *Disciplining Hermeneutics: Interpretation in Christian Perspective* (Grand Rapids: Eerdmans, 1997).

de Vries, Dawn, *Jesus Christ in the Preaching of Calvin and Schleiermacher* (Louisville: Westminster/John Knox Press, 1996).

Wallace, Mark I., 'The New Yale Theology', *Christian Scholar's Review* 17.2 (1987), pp. 154–70.

——, *The Second Naiveté: Barth, Ricoeur, and the New Yale Theology* (Macon: Mercer University Press, 1990).

Watson, Francis, *Text Church and World: Biblical Interpretation in Theological Perspective* (Edinburgh: T&T Clark, 1994).

——, *Text and Truth: Redefining Biblical Theology* (Edinburgh: T&T Clark, 1997).

Webster, John, 'Reply to George Hunsinger', in David Demson and John Webster (eds.), *Hans Frei and the Future of Theology* = *Modern Theology* 8.2 (Apr. 1992), pp. 129–32.

——, 'Introduction', in *The Possibilities of Theology: Studies in the Theology of Eberhard Jüngel in his Sixtieth Year* (Edinburgh: T&T Clark, 1994).

——, *Barth's Ethics of Reconciliation* (Cambridge: Cambridge University Press, 1995).

——, 'Scripture, Reading, and the Rhetoric of Theology in Hans Frei', in Giorgy Olegovich (ed.), *Ten Year Commemoration to the Life of Hans Frei (1922–1988)* (New York: Semenenko Foundation, 1999), pp. 41–53.

Werpehowski, William, 'Ad Hoc Apologetics', *The Journal of Religion* 66.3 (Jul. 1986), pp. 282–301.

West, Cornel, 'On Frei's Eclipse of Biblical Narrative', *Union Seminary Quarterly Review* 37.4 (1983), pp. 299–302.

White, Hayden, 'Auerbach's Literary History: Figural Causation and Modernist Historicism', in *Figural Realism: Studies in the Mimesis Effect* (Baltimore: The Johns Hopkins University Press, 1999), pp. 87–100.

Wilder, Amos N., Reply to Frei's 'Theological Reflections' (*1966a*), *Christian Scholar* 49.4 (winter), pp. 307–309.

Wiles, Maurice, 'Scriptural Authority and Theological Construction: The Limits of Narrative Interpretation', in Garrett Green (ed.), *Scriptural Authority and Narrative Interpretation* (Philadelphia: Fortress Press, 1987), pp. 42–58.

Williams, D.D., Reply to Frei's 'Theological Reflections' (*1966a*), *Christian Scholar* 49.4 (winter), pp. 310–12.

Woltersdorff, Nicholas, 'Evidence, Entitled Belief, and the Gospels', *Faith and Philosophy* 6.4 (Oct. 1989), pp. 429–59.

Woltersdorff, Nicholas, 'Will Narrativity Work as a Linchpin? Reflections on the Hermeneutic of Hans Frei' (with replies by P. Quinn, I. Jarvie, M. Hollis and D. Phillips), in Charles Lewis (ed.), *Relativism and Religion* (London: Macmillan, 1995), pp. 111–53.

——, *Divine Discourse: Philosophical Reflections on the Claim that God Speaks* (Cambridge: Cambridge University Press, 1995).

——, 'Inhabiting the World of the Text', in Giorgy Olegovich (ed.), *Ten Year Commemoration to the Life of Hans Frei (1922–1988)* (New York: Semenenko Foundation, 1999), pp. 61–81.

Wood, Charles M., *The Formation of Christian Understanding: An Essay in Theological Hermeneutics* (Philadelphia: Westminster Press, 1981).

——, 'Hermeneutics and the Authority of Scripture', in Garrett Green (ed.), *Scriptural Authority and Narrative Interpretation* (Philadelphia: Fortress Press, 1987), pp. 3–20.

Woolverton, John F., 'Hans W. Frei in Context: A Theological and Historical Memoir', *Anglican Theological Review* 79.3 (summer 1997), pp. 369–93.

Zuck, John, 'Tales of Wonder: Biblical Narrative, Myth, and Fairy-Stories', *Journal of the American Academy of Religion* 44.2 (1976), pp. 299–308.

Index